Palgrave Studies in Islamic Banking, Finance, and Economics

Series Editors
Mehmet Asutay
Business School
Durham University
Durham, UK

Zamir Iqbal
Islamic Development Bank
Jeddah, Saudi Arabia

Jahangir Sultan
Bentley University
Boston, MA, USA

The aim of this series is to explore the various disciplines and sub-disciplines of Islamic banking, finance and economics through the lens of theoretical, practical, and empirical research. Monographs and edited collections in this series will focus on key developments in the Islamic financial industry as well as relevant contributions made to moral economy, innovations in instruments, regulatory and supervisory issues, risk management, insurance, and asset management. The scope of these books will set this series apart from the competition by offering in-depth critical analyses of conceptual, institutional, operational, and instrumental aspects of this emerging field. This series is expected to attract focused theoretical studies, in-depth surveys of current practices, trends, and standards, and cutting-edge empirical research.

Abdul Ghafar Ismail
Rose Abdullah • Muhammad Hasbi Zaenal
Editors

Islamic Philanthropy

Exploring Zakat, Waqf, and Sadaqah in Islamic Finance and Economics

Editors
Abdul Ghafar Ismail
Putra Business School
Universiti Putra Malaysia
Seri Kembangan, Malaysia

Rose Abdullah
Universiti Islam Sultan Sharif Ali
Bandar Seri Begawan
Brunei Darussalam

Muhammad Hasbi Zaenal
Universitas Islam Negeri Syarif Hidayatullah
Jakarta, Indonesia

ISSN 2662-5121 ISSN 2662-513X (electronic)
Palgrave Studies in Islamic Banking, Finance, and Economics
ISBN 978-3-031-06889-8 ISBN 978-3-031-06890-4 (eBook)
https://doi.org/10.1007/978-3-031-06890-4

© The Editor(s) (if applicable) and The Author(s), under exclusive licence to Springer Nature Switzerland AG 2022
This work is subject to copyright. All rights are solely and exclusively licensed by the Publisher, whether the whole or part of the material is concerned, specifically the rights of translation, reprinting, reuse of illustrations, recitation, broadcasting, reproduction on microfilms or in any other physical way, and transmission or information storage and retrieval, electronic adaptation, computer software, or by similar or dissimilar methodology now known or hereafter developed.
The use of general descriptive names, registered names, trademarks, service marks, etc. in this publication does not imply, even in the absence of a specific statement, that such names are exempt from the relevant protective laws and regulations and therefore free for general use.
The publisher, the authors and the editors are safe to assume that the advice and information in this book are believed to be true and accurate at the date of publication. Neither the publisher nor the authors or the editors give a warranty, expressed or implied, with respect to the material contained herein or for any errors or omissions that may have been made. The publisher remains neutral with regard to jurisdictional claims in published maps and institutional affiliations.

This Palgrave Macmillan imprint is published by the registered company Springer Nature Switzerland AG.
The registered company address is: Gewerbestrasse 11, 6330 Cham, Switzerland

Foreword

Philanthropy literally means "love of mankind, useful to man." Over time, the definition of philanthropy evolved from personal activities to an action-oriented economic objective to encompass, for example, a group of people whose love for others compel them to donate their cherished resources to the needy. Thus, philanthropy is a wholehearted resource giving for the benefit of humankind. To champion this noble cause, individuals have established their own permanent *philanthropic* organizations in the form of foundations. Notable *philanthropic organizations such as* Yayasan Sultan Haji Hassanal Bolkiah, Kuwait Awqaf Public Foundation, and Islamic Relief Malaysia have made a tremendous impact on the human family, although many of us could be considered philanthropists in a modest way.

It is worth emphasizing that the concept of Islamic philanthropy is not new, for Islamic philanthropy emphasizes the importance of philanthropic tools and institutions. The philanthropic tools such zakat, waqf, and sadaqah are used to provide basic social safety nets for the marginalized segments of society. At this juncture, the effectiveness of intermediary philanthropic institutions such as Baitulmal, which mediates between donors and recipients, is crucial. As intermediaries, they serve as collectors and distributors (as amil) or managers (nazir) of donations. To avoid misuse of donations in addition to preventing donor fatigue, Baitulmal as an example manages the collection and generation of usufructs from donations to provide prudent services to both donors and recipients.

It is in the light of this that a book of this kind that aids in understanding Islamic philanthropy is timely for several reasons. First, Islamic philanthropy is a humanitarian aid for the needy, whether they are a group of people, a community, or a country. Islamic philanthropic outreach is encompassing because it is not limited to refugees and internally displaced people but also extends to healthy food aid, conducive sheltering, health facilities and health care, quality water aid, place of worship, education, and much more. Second, Islamic philanthropy is one of the centerpieces for the development of the ummah. Third, philanthropy was exemplified by the Prophet Muhammad (peace be upon Him) and His companions. Fourth, the ongoing Islamic economic revival is partly attributed to Islamic philanthropy.

I believe that Islamic philanthropic programs or activities provide ideal comfort for the needy, the distressed, or less fortunate people. Indeed, Islamic philanthropism hallmarks the sincere giving of the "haves to the have-nots." Therefore, Universiti Islam Sultan Sharif Ali in collaboration with our partners at Islamic Development Bank and International Islamic University College of Selangor organized a seminar on Islamic philanthropy. I would like to take this opportunity to congratulate the editors of this important book for publishing it in a timely manner regardless of the multitude of challenges they encountered. Finally, I would like to extend my deepest gratitude to those who contributed and offered their support to this publication initiative.

Universiti Islam Sultan Sharif Ali   Haji Norarfan bin Haji Zainal
Bandar Seri Begawan, Brunei Darussalam
May 2022

Preface

Humanitarian Aid

The United Nations (UN) via the Office for the Coordination of Humanitarian Affairs (OCHA) guided by the four humanitarian principles of humanity, neutrality, impartiality, and independence, has been central to mobilizing and coordinating humanitarian action as well as establishing and maintaining access to affected people, whether caught in a natural disaster or a complex emergency, such as armed conflict.

The global humanitarian system has become dangerously overstretched by the new crises in the Middle East and Africa and continuing unresolved conflicts in Afghanistan, the Democratic Republic of the Congo, Somalia, and Syria.

Crises are increasing in scale, frequency, duration, and severity (Global Humanitarian Assistance Report, 2016). As a barometer for the scale of global humanitarian need not the following: UN-coordinated appeals in 2015 called for US$28.0 billion in funding—the most extensive level of requests ever. Out of this, 77.9% (US$21.8 billion) came from government donors, and only 22.1% (US$6.2 billion) was contributed by private donors. A 45% shortfall was recorded—the largest for the current decade.

There are three country situations that the humanitarian community has highlighted as critical emergencies: Syria, Central African Republic, and South Sudan, and the neighboring countries affected.

The Statistical, Economic and Social Research and Training Centre for Islamic Countries (SESRIC), Turkey, 2014 reported that out of the 33 current active conflicts, 95% are occurring in the Muslim-dominated countries. It is combined with a steeper upward trend in the occurrence of natural disasters during the last four decades.[1] Not only are we looking at conflict-related crises with significant human rights abuses (such as slavery) as well as particularly vulnerable women and children, we also see people subjected to extreme conditions of heat or cold and starvation.

In the past, major donors have come from developed countries, with Muslim-country donors slowly emerging. Despite a record number of donor pledges in 2015 (US$28 billion) and the emergence of several 'non-traditional' donors such as the Muslim countries—Turkey and UAE alone contributed a total of US$4.3 billion and formed part of the top six government contributors of international humanitarian assistance in 2015—contributions from other Muslim-dominated countries are still lagging behind at less than 10% of total humanitarian funding. This stark reality is saddening given that a majority, four out of five significant recipients (Syria, Iraq, Palestine, and Jordan), of current humanitarian crises stemmed from Muslim-dominated countries.

Philanthropy

In Islam, philanthropy has become the centerpiece of the development of the *ummah*. Philanthropy has been exemplified by the Prophet (saw) and along with His companions. Until now, the survival of Islam also relies on philanthropic involvement. For example, in the development process al-Nabawi Mosque, Allah's Apostle saw action involving philanthropy in a long hadith that tells the Hijrah's events: "Then, he rode his mount animals, accompanied by the people. Eventually, the beast roars at the site (candidate) mosque Prophet saw at that place, on that day he also founded the prayer with the Muslims. Locations are palm groves owned by Suhail and Sahl, two orphan children under the care of As'ad bin Zurārah. The Prophet said when his mount beast roars at the site, "this place will be a place to stay (The Prophet)." Then, he called for two of the landowners, and the children bid their land for the mosque. Both of them said, "No, we even gave it over to you, O Prophet." The Prophet was reluctant to accept the grant until he bought it from both.[2] Which then until now is a place owned by the *ummah*.

---

[1] "Managing Disasters & Conflicts in OIC Countries," SESRIC, Turkey, 2014.
[2] Al-Bukhārī, Abi 'Abdillah Muhammad ibn Ismāil, al-Jāāmparedqah,.l. 3, p. 23, mi' al-Shohīh, Maktabah Salafiyah, Cairo, 1400 H (1980 M), no. 3906, vol. 3, p. 2.

A fundamental rethink of humanitarian financing required a role for philanthropy. By nature, the Islamic economic system, as far back as the Ottoman Empire, has demonstrated that it civil society leads to the seamless integration between private interests (*maslahah nafsiyyah*) and the broader public interests (*maslahah ammah*). Nevertheless, in recent times, with many Muslim countries affected by conflicts, there is a need to revitalize the Islamic Social Finance measures (faith-based giving consistent with Islamic guidelines) as a vital component of the global humanitarian system. Forms of Islamic philanthropy include almsgiving (*zakat*), endowments (*waqf*), and public charity (*sadaqah*).

There is a lack of a global platform—an integrated allocation system among Muslim donors that provides international crises. Most current Muslim aid efforts are at best ad hoc, fragmented, and situational. However, organizations such as Kuwait Awqaf Funds, Muslim Aids, and Islamic Relief are a few good examples. The allocations of *zakat*, *waqf*, and *sadaqah* among Muslim countries such as Brunei, Indonesia, Malaysia, and the Middle East are domestically focused mainly on poverty alleviation and public project-building of mosques and orphanages.

However, there is poor accounting and transparency in reporting on the sources and uses of the funds. In many cases, there are 'idle' funds that are left in excess (and often wasted), which could have been channeled to UN mechanisms as emergency aid. Hence, the standard guidelines on the best core principles of philanthropy management and establishing a standard-setting body and shariah issues related to the redefinition of *asnaf* are among the matters relevant to philanthropy. For example, the redefinition of *al-riqab* (people in bondage or slavery) could be applied to the enslaved, oppressed, or wrongly imprisoned or to the victims of trafficking.

Proposed Potential Solutions

Zakat: *Zakat* funds can be utilized beyond domestic Muslim communities. The Holy Qur'an 9:60: "The alms are only for the poor and the needy, and those who collect them, and those whose hearts are to be reconciled, and to free the captives and the debtors, and for the cause of Allah, and (for) the wayfarers; a duty imposed by Allah. Allah is knower, Wise."

Waqf: The Ottomans during the fifteenth to the eighteenth centuries have used *waqf*, especially *cash waqf*, to aid humanity all over Bursa,

Anatolia, and the European provinces of the Empire. Nevertheless, in recent years, current practices have favored 'real estate *waqf*,' resulting in more mosques being built. Hence, consensus governing *waqf* practices may greatly facilitate the growth of 'cash *waqf*' towards humanitarian aid.

Sadaqah: This is a charity that is not binding but is optional. This type includes alms given for the removal of difficulties, philanthropic (to give out of mercy to the less fortunate), the general giving of any Halal item to anyone, and so on. This type does not need to be spent on the specified categories to be rewarding, nor does it have to be spent on Muslims, although it would be more rewarding if spent on poor Muslims. It can also be bequeathed in one's will (in which case it would be only up to a third of the deceased person's entire estate).

All three elements of *zakat*, *waqf*, and *sadaqah* can be combined as distribution models to address humanitarian needs. Once this system is adopted, it can be presented to Muslim donors to use a dynamic strategic donation allocation system, possibly akin to a crowdfunding model.

Seri Kembangan, Malaysia	Abdul Ghafar Ismail
Jalan Pasar Gadong, Brunei Darussalam	Rose Abdullah
Jakarta, Indonesia	Muhammad Hasbi Zaenal

CONTENTS

Part I Introduction   1

1 Introduction   3
   Abdul Ghafar Ismail, Rose Abdullah, and
   Muhammad Hasbi Zaenal

2 Philanthropy from Islamic Tradition   23
   Muhammad Hasbi Zaenal, Abdul Ghafar Ismail, and
   Muhammad Hakimi Mohd. Shafiai

3 Mobilizing Philanthropy Instruments in Development
   Assistance   51
   Salman Ahmed Shaikh

Part II Waqf   73

4 Challenges of *Waqf* Land Development in Brunei
   Darussalam   75
   Rose Abdullah, Khairul Hidayatullah Basir, and
   Nur Haziyah Abdul Halim

5 The Ottoman Cash Waqf as Altruistic Finance Model   93
   Mehmet Bulut and Cem Korkut

xi

6 Predicting the Behavioural Intention for Cash *Waqf*:
   Evidence from Malaysia and Thailand   113
   Ruslaina Yusoff, Shariful Amran Abd Rahman, Wan Nazihah
   Wan Mohamed, Parichard Benrit, and Faizah Darus

7 *Waqf*-Based Crowdfunding: Proposed Framework for
   Entrepreneurial Development   135
   Samsinar Sulaiman, Shifa Mohd Nor, and Suhaili Alma'amun

8 Waqf Flood Evacuation Centre: New Recourse to Flood
   Victims in Malaysia   151
   Marhanum Che Mohd Salleh, Nurdianawati Irwani Abdullah,
   Nor Azizan Che Embi, and Nan Noorhidayu Megat Laksana

9 Cash Waqf for Humanitarian Aid: The Case of
   Transboundary Haze   171
   Shahida Shahimi, Siti Hanisah Fuad, and Rabiatul
   Hasanah Mahmood

Part III   Zakat   183

10 A Collection of Studies on Zakāt   185
   Hendri Tanjung and Nurman Hakim

11 The Impact of Zakat Distribution   197
   Norhaziah Nawai and Farah Shazwani Ruzaiman

12 Promoting Islamic Philanthropy in Islamic Higher
   Education of Indonesia   213
   Indah Piliyanti and Agni Alam Awirya

13 A Mobile Application for Zakat Collection in Indonesia   229
   Ajeng Pratiwi and Umma Sa'idah

14 Zakat for Disaster Relief   239
   Kamaru Salam Yusof, Abdul Ghafar Ismail, and
   Muhammad Hasbi Zaenal

Part IV Other Issues 253

15 Investment of Tabung Masjid in Malaysia toward
Fulfilling Maqasid-Al-Shariah 255
Luqman Zakariyah, Suhaimi Bin Mhd Sarif,
Azman Bin Mohd Noor, and Rahmah Bt. Ahmad Osman

16 Religious Institutions in Philanthropy-Based Activities in
Pakistan 275
Hussain Mohi-Ud-Din Qadri

17 South Africa's Muslim Philanthropists and Humanitarian
Organizations: Religious Activism, Changing
Environments 293
Muhammed Haron

18 Governance Framework for Philanthropic Organizations
Directed Towards Taqyid Al-Mutlaq 315
Roshayani Arshad, Nawal Kasim, Ruhaini Muda, and
Chakir Ahmed

Part V Concluding Remarks 333

19 Summary and Policy Recommendations 335
Abdul Ghafar Ismail, Rose Abdullah, and
Muhammad Hasbi Zaenal

Index 343

List of Contributors

Nurdianawati Irwani Abdullah Department of Finance, Kulliyyah of Economics & Management Sciences, International Islamic University Malaysia, Selangor, Malaysia

Rose Abdullah Universiti Islam Sultan Sharif Ali, Bandar Seri Begawan, Brunei Darussalam

Chakir Ahmed Ibn Zohr University, Agadir, Morocco

Suhaili Alma'amun Faculty of Economics and Management, Universiti Kebangsaan Malaysia, Bangi, Malaysia

Roshayani Arshad Faculty of Accountancy, Accounting Research Institute, Universiti Teknologi MARA, Shah Alam, Malaysia

Agni Alam Awirya Bank Indonesia, Central Jakarta, Indonesia

Khairul Hidayatullah Basir Universiti Islam Sultan Sharif Ali, Bandar Seri Begawan, Brunei Darussalam

Parichard Benrit Faculty of Humanities and Social Sciences, Prince of Songkla University Pattani Campus, Pattani, Thailand

Mehmet Bulut Department of Economics, Istanbul Sabahattin Zaim University, Istanbul, Turkey

Faizah Darus Faculty of Accountancy, Accounting Research Institute, Universiti Teknologi MARA, Shah Alam, Malaysia

Nor Azizan Che Embi Department of Finance, Kulliyyah of Economics & Management Sciences, International Islamic University Malaysia, Selangor, Malaysia

Siti Hanisah Fuad Graduate School of Business, Universiti Kebangsaan Malaysia, Bangi, Malaysia

Nurman Hakim Ibn Khaldun University, Istanbul, Turkey

Nur Haziyah Abdul Halim Universiti Islam Sultan Sharif Ali, Bandar Seri Begawan, Brunei Darussalam

Muhammed Haron Department of Theology and Religious Studies, University of Botswana, Gaborone, Botswana

Abdul Ghafar Ismail Putra Business School, Universiti Putra Malaysia, Seri Kembangan, Malaysia

Nawal Kasim Faculty of Accountancy, Accounting Research Institute, Universiti Teknologi MARA, Shah Alam, Malaysia

Cem Korkut Department of Economics, Ankara Yildirim Beyazit University, Ankara, Turkey

Nan Noorhidayu Megat Laksana Department of Usul Fiqh, Kulliyyah of Islamic Revealed Knowledge, International Islamic University Malaysia, Selangor, Malaysia

Rabiatul Hasanah Mahmood Faculty of Economics and Management, Universiti Kebangsaan Malaysia, Bangi, Malaysia

Wan Nazihah Wan Mohamed Akademi Pengajian Bahasa, Universiti Teknologi MARA Kelantan Campus, Machang, Malaysia

Ruhaini Muda Faculty of Accountancy, Accounting Research Institute, Universiti Teknologi MARA, Shah Alam, Malaysia

Norhaziah Nawai Faculty of Economics and Muamalat, Universiti Sains Islam Malaysia, Nilai, Malaysia

Azman Bin Mohd Noor International Islamic University Malaysia, Selangor, Malaysia

Shifa Mohd Nor Centre for Governance Resilience and Accountability Studies, Faculty of Economics and Managament, Universiti Kebangsaan Malaysia, Bangi, Malaysia
Institute of Islam Hadhari, Universiti Kebangsaan Malaysia, Bangi, Malaysia

Rahmah Bt. Ahmad Osman International Islamic University Malaysia, Selangor, Malaysia

Indah Piliyanti Faculty of Islamic Economics and Business, Institut Agama Islam Negeri, Surakarta, Indonesia

Ajeng Pratiwi Universitas Negeri Jakarta, Jakarta, Indonesia

Hussain Mohi-Ud-Din Qadri Minhaj University Lahore, Lahore, Pakistan

Shariful Amran Abd Rahman Faculty of Accountancy, Universiti Teknologi MARA Kelantan Campus, Machang, Malaysia

Farah Shazwani Ruzaiman Faculty of Economics and Muamalat, Universiti Sains Islam Malaysia, Nilai, Malaysia

Umma Sa'idah Universitas Negeri Jakarta, Jakarta, Indonesia

Marhanum Che Mohd Salleh Department of Finance, Kulliyyah of Economics & Management Sciences, International Islamic University Malaysia, Selangor, Malaysia

Suhaimi Bin Mhd Sarif International Islamic University Malaysia, Selangor, Malaysia

Muhammad Hakimi Mohd. Shafiai Faculty of Economics and Management, Universiti Kebangsaan Malaysia, Bangi, Malaysia

Shahida Shahimi Faculty of Economics and Management, Universiti Kebangsaan Malaysia, Bangi, Malaysia

Salman Ahmed Shaikh Department of Management Sciences, SZABIST University, Karachi, Pakistan

Samsinar Sulaiman Faculty of Economics and Management, Universiti Kebangsaan Malaysia, Bangi, Malaysia

Hendri Tanjung Ibn Khaldun University, Istanbul, Turkey

Kamaru Salam Yusof Faculty of Islamic Economics and Finance, Universiti Islam Sultan Sharif Ali, Bandar Seri Begawan, Brunei Darussalam

Ruslaina Yusoff Faculty of Accountancy, Universiti Teknologi MARA Kelantan Campus, Machang, Malaysia

Muhammad Hasbi Zaenal Universitas Islam Negeri Syarif Hidayatullah, Jakarta, Indonesia

Luqman Zakariyah International Islamic University Malaysia, Selangor, Malaysia

List of Figures

Fig. 3.1	Ijarah Sukuk structure	64
Fig. 3.2	Mudarabah Sukuk structure	65
Fig. 3.3	Musharakah Sukuk structure	66
Fig. 6.1	Research model	123
Fig. 7.1	Fundamental process of crowdfunding. Source: Scholz (2015)	142
Fig. 7.2	Fundamental process of cash *waqf*. Source: Ahmad Mukarrami (2016)	143
Fig. 7.3	*Waqf*-based crowdfunding for entrepreneurial development	145
Fig. 8.1	Model of permanent flood evacuation centre based on waqf principles	165
Fig. 12.1	The *zakat* distribution model and its impact on poverty. Source: Toro et al. (2013)	218
Fig. 12.2	The flow chart of a student application for financial aid from *Teman Sedekah*. Source: Interview with Waluyo	223
Fig. 12.3	Flow of education assistance for *dhuafa*. Source: interview with Idrus	225
Fig. 13.1	Zakat potential in Indonesia. Source: Pusat Kajian Strategis BAZNAS (2020)	230
Fig. 13.2	Home menu display	232
Fig. 13.3	Content display of zakat payment	233
Fig. 13.4	Content display of zakat map	234
Fig. 13.5	Content display of zakat reminder	235
Fig. 13.6	Graphs of potential smartphone users in Indonesia. Source: eMarketer prime data that have been edited	236
Fig. 13.7	Zakat collection diagram. Source: primary data	236
Fig. 15.1	Maqasid-based conceptual framework of Tabung Masjid investment	260

Fig. 15.2	State-wise TM donation statistics	267
Fig. 15.3	State-wise TM savings statistics	268
Fig. 15.4	Forecast of TM investment (2016–2035)	268
Fig. 18.1	Overview of social public–private partnership in Malaysia	319
Fig. 18.2	Flowchart of social public–private partnership program in Malaysia	320
Fig. 18.3	Governance information system	327

List of Tables

Table 1.1	Philanthropic institutions: Type, resources, and objectives	12
Table 1.2	Theory of philanthropy and theory of economic development	14
Table 2.1	Instruments of Islamic philanthropy	32
Table 3.1	Poverty head count ratio (PHCR) in selected OIC countries	56
Table 3.2	Overall and relative ranking of selected OIC countries on HDI	57
Table 3.3	Net migration in selected OIC countries	58
Table 3.4	Official Development Assistance (ODA) received in selected OIC countries	60
Table 3.5	Total debt service (% of exports and GNI) for selected OIC countries	61
Table 3.6	Debt service (% of GNI) and net ODA (%of GNI) for selected OIC countries	62
Table 4.1	The usage of general endowed lands 2016	81
Table 4.2	The usage of specific endowed lands 2016	82
Table 5.1	Examples of the cash waqf	102
Table 6.1	Demographic results	124
Table 6.2	Factor loading outcome	125
Table 6.3	Multiple regression analysis	126
Table 8.1	Background information for respondents	159
Table 8.2	Effect of flooding to the villages	160
Table 8.3	Experiences at flood evacuation centres	163
Table 10.1	Number of publications by year	190
Table 10.2	Research types of each publication	190
Table 10.3	Research approaches of each publication	191
Table 10.4	Subject area of articles	192
Table 10.5	Genders of Authors	193
Table 10.6	List of study locations and publications by countries involved	193

Table 11.1	Data extraction evidence	203
Table 14.1	Disaster by Most Affected Muslim People from 2013–2021	242
Table 14.2	Zakat beneficiary categories and potential links to disaster relief	246
Table 15.1	Sample characteristics	263
Table 15.2	Cross-tabulation results for state-wise TM investment strategies	264
Table 15.3	Test of homogeneity of variances	265
Table 15.4	One-way ANOVA statistics	265
Table 15.5	Tukey test results	266
Table 15.6	Variable definitions	269
Table 15.7	Testing for long-term Granger causality	270

PART I

Introduction

CHAPTER 1

Introduction

Abdul Ghafar Ismail, Rose Abdullah, and Muhammad Hasbi Zaenal

1 INTRODUCTION

In the early 2020s, the American Economic Association (https://www.aeaweb.org/jel/guide/jel.php) added "Islamic economic system" as an additional keyword under P4 categories. It shows that the term has been recognized as important in discussing economics. The Islamic economic system, however, has only been recognized recently, in the second half of the twentieth century. But the importance of this subject could also be traced back to the time of Holy Prophet (Peace be Upon Him). The Prophet was asked to deliver the messages from the Qur'an (the Holy

A. G. Ismail (✉)
Putra Business School, Universiti Putra Malaysia, Seri Kembangan, Malaysia

R. Abdullah
Universiti Islam Sultan Sharif Ali, Bandar Seri Begawan, Brunei Darussalam
e-mail: rose.abdullah@unissa.edu.bn

M. H. Zaenal
Universitas Islam Negeri Syarif Hidayatullah, Jakarta, Indonesia
e-mail: hasbi@uinjkt.ac.id

© The Author(s), under exclusive license to Springer Nature Switzerland AG 2022
A. G. Ismail et al. (eds.), *Islamic Philanthropy*, Palgrave Studies in Islamic Banking, Finance, and Economics,
https://doi.org/10.1007/978-3-031-06890-4_1

Book for Muslims) to all people, because the Qur'an contains guidance and lessons for those conscious of Allah. The life-example and sayings of the Prophet also become part of the guidance. The messages of the Qur'an brought by the Prophet and the sayings and actions of the Prophet (the Hadith) are to guide people to the right path.

One of the names of Allah is the Creator. Allah creates all things. The human beings are created by Allah and given a fixed period of life. It means that the human beings are asked to spend upon the earth.

His knowledge on all those things is perfect, comprehensive, and full. Therefore, Allah prescribes a code of procedure as the correct way to follow, but at the same time, He has given humanity the freedom of choice as to whether or not they follow the code as the basis of their life. They may choose to follow the code revealed by Allah and become a believer or refuse to follow and become a disbeliever.

The code of procedure in relation to the Islamic economic system covers many matters. One of them is the acquisition and utilization of resources. Allah is the Creator of resources and at the same time, He is the Sustainer of resources. Human, as His Creator, needs to manage the resources. The United Nations (UN) also has recognized the importance in managing resources via a sustainable agenda. Each jurisdiction also has been given guidance to adopt and adapt the agenda and recommend public policy that looks into the aspect of financing for development.

2 Financing for Development

The UN Report on Financing for Sustainable Development[1] has outlined several specific actions. The report recognizes that governments, social economies, and private entities all play a role in financial economic development. Each entity uses different methods of financing economic development. Providing financing either through grants or financing benefits the recipients because the end results would affect economic development by creating jobs and economic growth. Hence, the role of each entity will be highlighted in the following discussion.

Government entity. There are two aspects that are considered by government entity in looking at financing for development—the sources of

---

[1] United Nations, Inter-agency Task Force on Financing for Development, Financing for Sustainable Development Report 2020 (New York: United Nations, 2020), available from https://developmentfinance.un.org/fsdr2020.

revenue and the impact. Government normally relies on several sources of revenue to provide for sufficient government expenditure to meet social and economic targets and the adequacy of long-term financing to boost economies to grow and develop to their full capacity.

The sources of finance can be divided into four components: (1) revenues of government such as tax and non-tax receipts (the main sources of revenue); (2) concessional development assistance (CDA) that covers both external grants and concessional credits; (3) non-concessional loans taken out by (or guaranteed by) government from multilateral development agencies or private sources; and (4) private external finance (normally in the form of foreign direct investment and other portfolio flows). Each component may contribute to both objectives—meeting needed government expenditure and external financing for economic development.

The word "needed" can be translated into a pie chart that shows the contribution of different sources of finance. Could the components be increased simultaneously? Are there complementarities between financing sources? Could a country have a view to finance from different sources as substitutes? Better economic development generally needs more expenditure. Therefore, the components could be increased simultaneously. For example, taxes used to finance the operating expenditure are not more than half of the government revenue. Domestic financing could be used to boost a range of sectors such as infrastructure projects under public–private partnerships, halal development products, small and micro-entrepreneurs and agricultural-based products. Hence, bigger government revenue improves the government rating that then permits more access to foreign direct investment and other portfolio flows. These arguments suggest that the sources of finance become complementary. This view differs from the current narrative that often sees financing from various sources as substitutes.

The humanitarian aid, which is categorized under CDA, comes from philanthropic action. The economic development impact of aid is reduced when alternative domestic sources of finance become available. In pursuing the aid, the policymakers may consider the maximum impact of aid in the context of all other sources of finance. The provision of public services such as financing for an unbankable society could be largely driven by the aid. In the case of fiscal deficit, the aid may be used as a complement to domestic revenue.

The impact of government expenditure should be considered in the context of overall development needs, rather than the "needs" for specific sectors and the size. The development needs should be linked to measurable outcomes. If the overall outcomes matter, then it should be applied to development and climate change together. The size of government expenditure should be linked to government revenue, because government revenue may lead to higher government expenditure, unless the government wants to have a fiscal deficit.

Private entity. Basically the private entity covers financial institutions (or financial firms) and firms (or non-financial firms). Firms rely on financial institutions and financial markets for financing. Hence, financial institutions and markets can foster economic growth through several transmission channels, that is by (1) easing the exchange of goods and services through the provision of a payment system, (2) mobilizing and pooling savings from a large number of investors, (3) acquiring and processing information about firms and possible investment projects, thus allocating savings to their most productive use, (4) monitoring investment and carrying out corporate governance, and (5) diversifying, increasing liquidity and reducing intertemporal risk. Each of these channels can influence the quantity of saving and the decision to invest and hence economic growth. Many market frictions exist that are due to laws, regulations, and policies. These variables differ markedly across economies and over time. Hence, the improvements of (any of) these variables may have different implications for resource allocation and welfare depending on other frictions in the economy.

Ideally, financial institutions are expected to allocate efficiently the resources in an economy. Those who have money but do not want to invest directly in firms can park their money to be channelled to firms via financial institutions. The intermediation process would become effective if the financial institution acts smoothly as the intermediaries between those who have money and those who want money, or to be the intermediaries for those who want to share the risks. Therefore, well-functioning financial institutions do not simply act as transmission channels. They can improve economic development by making sure that those who got financing are able to create jobs and economic growth. This means that financial institutions not only provide financing, they also have expertise to assess financing applications and ensure financing for wealth creation.

Note that there are also people who are not involved with financial institutions. For example, they save their money in various ways at home, or their may save and borrow among themselves. The institutions such as Ar-rahnu, pawnbroking, *chettier*, and *duit kutu* are quite familiar to them.

These forms of financial transaction are, in fact, the norm among the unbankable society (such as poor people) who are typically not served by financial institutions. Financial inclusion is crucial for poor people's sustainability. Hence, both poor people and their financial inclusion are crucial in the wider process of economic development.

Social economy entity. Social economy entity traditionally refers to the set of associations (including charitable foundations), non-profit organizations, and cooperatives with objectives to have a positive impact not only financially but also on society as a whole. The contribution of the entity is to create inclusive and sustainable societies and economies. The entity can provide innovative solutions to improve the quality of life and well-being of individuals, communities, and places. The entity also addresses socioeconomic and environmental challenges like basic education and health, literacy, and the post-COVID-19 pandemic crisis.

The above discussion shows that the set of economic development financing tools and techniques focuses on current times of economic development. Traditional public finance techniques, the role of financial institutions, and the traditional social economy entity are given full attention. The book will emphasize the role of Islamic philanthropy that brings together different techniques and sources to create a workable financial development package. The new idea is to suggest a complement technique that stresses the financing method from people to people. The idea moves away from current approaches that focus on giving from government to people or from financial institutions to selected people or from private individuals to people. In addition, the new idea of Islamic philanthropy is also similar to what has been suggested by the UN[2] and OECD.[3]

3 From Human Resources to Donation

The resources that are provided by Allah are not only be used to benefit the owner. They will also bring benefit to other peoples. In Chapter 5 (Surah Al-Ma'idah), verse 114, Allah said, "and provide for our sustenance, for You are the best Sustainer (of our needs)." It is followed by another verse. In verse 31 of Chapter 14 (Surah Ibraheem), Allah said,

---

[2] United Nations, Inter-agency Task Force on Financing for Development, Financing for Sustainable Development Report 2020.

[3] OECD 2020, "How Islamic Finance Can Help Achieve the Sustainable Development Goals" OECD Development Co-operation Policy Papers, 30 (Paris: OECD Publishing 2020).

"and spend (in charity) out of the sustenance." The later verse shows that spending or donation (hereafter Islamic philanthropy) is an act of charity.

For the people who own the resources, there are many push factors that motivate them to donate. The main push factor is due to the fact that the charitable act affects many human dimensions. First, the human could not only preserve their faith (that is, obeying the rules of Allah and showing the gratitude of a servant to Allah and seeking to please Allah) and strengthen and purify their souls, but also invite the mercy and rewards from Allah.

Second, charitable acts also affect human behaviour. They develop good human behaviour—developing concern for others (covering humankind) and demonstrating kindness towards each other. They affect the inner self of donors in many aspects—they show the degree of scarcity of donor's resources and giving to charity, the inculcation of "better to give than to receive," and the goodness of helping others in need. It signifies acts done by people for the benefit of humankind. The act also continues to benefits others, even after the donor passes away. Overall, good behaviour could be realized—do good to fellow humans, treat humankind well, and also protect the environment.

Third, charitable acts initially involve the transfer of resources from Allah to humankind. As a good servant, humans (as Islamic economic actors) consume parts of these resources to spouses, sons, daughters, siblings, and close relatives; and partly transfer to other humans, such as the needy, the poor and the orphanage, the travellers and the debtors, and others.

The transfer of resources (hereafter Islamic philanthropy economy) can be in two different forms—compulsory or voluntary transfer. Compulsory transfer can be in the form of *zakat on mal* and *zakat fitr*; whereas voluntary transfer may involve the instruments of *waqf*, *hibah*, and *sadaqah*. These instruments differ in their purpose and in the principles on which it would appear to operate. *Zakat* (as a relief instrument) seeks to alleviate human suffering, and the principle of compassion is said to be its driving force. *Waqf* meanwhile (as an improvement instrument) seeks to maximize individual human potential and is energized by a principle that seeks to progress individuals and their society and also preserve the earth. Finally, other philanthropy instruments such as *sadaqah* (as a reform instrument) seek to solve social problems, and their stated principle is that of addressing justice issues often through legislation. Hence, *philanthropy instruments are used to build* better community structures and services and are motivated by civic responsibility.

Therefore, philanthropy instruments are meant for purity and growth. They help to establish the economy of the ummah, build societies on humanitarian grounds, reducing economic hardship for the poor and thus alleviating inequality, and creating love and brotherhood. In fact for the boundless reward the human gets, they are happy to perform the the obligation to ensure the happiness of fellow humans.

Hence, the second main push factor is an economic model, known as human economy, which can be suggested here. As discussed above, the flow of resources from spending to donation affects several human dimensions. But it also affects the human economy. The human decides whether to spend their income now or in the future. Typically, if the human wants to spend now, it is called spending on consumption. The current spending also covers the transfer of resources (or donation) for other humans, while income retained for future spending is known as saving. It can be channelled into investment in production, which will bring a return that can be used for future consumption.

Distribution relies on the resources of donors. After the transfer happens, the recipients use the transfer to buy goods from the current production. Both donors and recipients use goods from the current production. The level of current consumption increases and hence, the current production also increases. Consequently, the return on investment increases and hence, the amount of savings increases. The future spending of donors increases and subsequently the donors can also increase the amount of donation.

Therefore, the distribution of resources, either compulsory or voluntary (which may involve money or in kind), depends on the preference of donors and recipients. In the end, both affect goods from the current production that comes from industrial production.

By allowing this process, both donors and recipients exchange the resources that help the resource distribution in the Islamic philanthropy economy. Furthermore, the distribution system helps the recipients in managing their needs for life. As such, it creates a new form of support, which was formerly the responsibility of the government and its entities in a country that utilized a social security system.

The current social security system where cash benefits and social services are funded by the government budget comes from tax and non-tax receipts. The Islamic philanthropy economy provides those benefits and services that are funded from donors. The donation referred to in this economy is a compulsory obligation as well as an additional contribution referred to as a voluntary obligation. In the case of compulsory obligation, recipients are referred to a group of people known as *asnaf* (such as the needy, the poor, the traveller, the slaved person, and the debtor). It shows that the Islamic philanthropy economy (via compulsory donation) is used as a relief instrument in turning poverty reduction into a relief programme. The programme is driven to alleviate human suffering, and the principle of compassion is said to be its driving force. Voluntary obligation is used as *an improvement instrument as well as a reform instrument* to build better community structures and services.

The relief programme of compassion, improvement, and reform has been practised historically from the early days of the Holy Prophet. The Islamic philanthropy economy is classified as a secondary economic system. It supports the primary market. The transfer of goods from the primary economy to a secondary system or vice versa becomes a pillar of the Islamic philanthropy economy. The transfer also carries an economic benefit for donors, because they are the ones who initially made an investment in the primary market that brings returns to their investment. For example, the donors who invest in food production could claim a profit from produced goods, because (a) they pay less goods and services tax, and (b) food producers who make donations enhance their public image.

Therefore, the Islamic philanthropy economy also illustrates the existence of a new model of the social security system that relies on sources of revenue other than tax or non-tax receipts. The Islamic philanthropy economy provides the transfer of money and in kind, but also provides social services such as education, medical care, and housing. Thus, a mix of compulsory and voluntary donations is strongly connected to a social security system. Besides, the donations are meant for the betterment of community structures and services.

In addition, the motivation of the Islamic philanthropy economy arises due to the command from Allah and the duty of individuals to obey that command. The command creates two simultaneous engagements—human to Allah and vice versa; human to fellow human; fellow human to Allah and vice versa; and human and fellow human to planet. By doing this, the treatment of humankind and the protection of the environment are well heeded.

In summary, the objectives of the Islamic philanthropy economy are not only targeted at the welfare of humankind, but also at caring for humankind. Every religion has philanthropic components in its system, but in Islam, philanthropy has a compulsory component. Islam also lays great emphasis on supporting the disadvantage in society and preserving the earth. It shows that Islamic philanthropy makes the relationship between Allah, human, and the earth intact.

4   Institutional Set-up for Philanthropy

Multilateral development banks such as the IMF and the World Bank have emphasized the role of institutions in economic development since the last decade. The issue of institutions and economic development among others focuses on sustainability and strong institutions, and the theoretical foundation of the institution. In this case, the institutions who collect and distribute the resources can be sustained. In this sense institutions would play an important role in inclusive programmes. A strong institution is partly shown by its good governance. The statement of mission and vision (hereafter VM) to be achieved is transparent. The strategic plan is directed towards the utilization of resources that can achieve its VM.

The above introduction raises the following questions: Who is the owner or who is going to establish the philanthropic institution? What would be the type of institution? What are the type of resources (e.g., statutory body, addressing how and why a foundation will use its resources to achieve its VM)?

Institution. The institution, as presented in panel A of Table 1.1, can be established as non-profit organization or government entity. Normally, a non-profit organization is established by civilized society. It does not earn profit for its owner—for example, Islamic Relief (in Malaysia and the United Kingdom) and Aman Palestin who collect *sadaqah* for humanitarian aid in host countries and other countries. Countries like Malaysia, Brunei, and Singapore consider Islamic religious revenues (including *zakat*, *waqf*, and *sadaqah*) as government revenue. Hence, the philanthropic institution is established as a government agency or known as a Baitulmal institution.

A Baitulmal institution manages both compulsory and voluntary donations at the centre between both donors and recipients. The effectiveness of this institution is very crucial. As intermediaries who act as the collector and distributor (also known as *amil*) or manager (*nazir*), the Baitulmal manages the collection and generates the usufructs from the donation. It further provides services to both donors and recipients. For instance, the

Table 1.1 Philanthropic institutions: Type, resources, and objectives

Panel A: Type of institutions	Owner
Non-profit organization	Civilized society
Government agency	Government
Panel B: Type of resources	
Zakat	*Zakat al-maal* and *zakat al-fitri*
Waqf	*Waqf ahli*, *waqf khayri*, *waqf al-sabil*, and *waqf al-awaridh*
Sadaqah	*Sadaqah Lillah*
Panel C: Objectives to be achieved	**Objectives**
Zakat	To be channelled to targeted group (*asnaf*)—the poor, the needy, *zakat* administrators, those whose hearts are to be reconciled, Muslims and friends of the Muslim community, those in bondage (slaves and captives), the debt-ridden, in the cause of God and the wayfarer
Waqf ahli	To cater to the needs of the *waqf*'s founder's children and their descendants
Waqf khayri	To include the people belonging to the economically stricken sections of society. It is used as an investment for building mosques, shelter homes, schools, madrasas, colleges, and universities. All of this is built to help and uplift economically challenged individuals
Waqf al-sabil	Used for establishment and construction of public utility (mosques, power plants, water supplies, graveyards, schools, etc.)
Waqf al-awaridh	Used in case of emergency or any unexpected events that affect the livelihood and well-being of a particular community
Sadaqah	To be given to an individual or persons in need

staff at a Baitulmal will list out services, such as financial assistance, to *asnaf* who are applying for benefits. Thus a new relationship exists whereby the Baitulmal is expected to provide financial assistance before the other unit (for example a retailer, who delivers goods)—is established. Here, public employees should understand that the services delivered by a Baitulmal's staff act as complementary to, or even as a substitute for, existing benefits provided by the public sector.

The existence of a Baitulmal would serve as a new division of labour between the three sectors—society, philanthropy economy, and the public—whereby their respective "job descriptions" are mentioned above.

The roadmap is very clear that the Islamic philanthropy economy works towards a new paradigm that recognizes the role of society in supporting people in need.

Resources. Panel B of Table 1.1 presents the type of resources that can be collected by philanthropic institutions. In this book, the resources are limited to *zakat*, *waqf*, and *sadaqah*. *Zakat al-mal* are collected from all Muslims who are sane and possess the *nisab* (a minimum amount of wealth held for a year). Those who live during the month of Ramadhan are also obliged to pay *zakat al-fitri*.

Waqf is a special kind of philanthropic deed in perpetuity. It involves donating a fixed asset (for example, a building, land, or cash) that can produce a financial return or provide a benefit. Then the return or benefit generated serves specific categories of beneficiaries. A philanthropic institution may hold the donated assets.

In addition to *sadaqah wajibah* such as *zakat*, there are several different types of *sadaqah* such as *Lillah*. This *sadaqah* is dedicated "for the sake of Allah." It can be made to an individual or an institution such as an orphanage, hospital, or mosque. Furthermore, there is no minimum amount and no restriction on who can receive funds.

Objectives. Basically, a philanthropic institution donates the money it receives to help fund the institution's objectives and goals. Hence, the objective of the establishment of a philanthropic institution should be matched with the objective of each type of resource. The summary of objectives is presented in panel C of Table 1.1.

The objective of giving *zakat* to *asnaf* is to purify the wealth as well as to gain Allah's blessing on their wealth. Islam teaches us to sacrifice a part of our wealth, to cleanse our wealth by means of *zakat*. This is because Muslims believe that everything belongs to Allah as stated in the Quran, "To Him belongs all that is in the heavens and on earth" (2:255). When we are given wealth, there is a portion that does not belong to us, which is also stated in the Quran: "And in their wealth, there was a right for one who asks and for one who is deprived" (51:19). Therefore, *zakat* is aimed to uplift the poor, help those who are troubled, and comfort those who are in hardship. The law of *zakat* establishes the rights of the poor to support and help, and releases those who are held captive as slaves or as debtors.

The creation of *waqf* is aimed at several purposes: the maintenance and support wholly or partially of the donors' family, children, or descendants;

the provision of public infrastructure and utilities; and assistance for the livelihood and well-being of a community.

Based on the above explanation, the following discussion tries to prove the philanthropy–development nexus. There are three main elements in promoting the nexus—a philanthropic institution, type of resources that can be collected, and the utilization of resources to achieve the mandated objectives.

A philanthropic institution can bolster economic development. Its especially so because a philanthropic institution is designed to help them align their strategies, governance, operating and accountability procedures, and resource-making profile and policies with their resources and objectives. It explains why institutions appear so important to economic development. The design of philanthropic institutions could reduce the cost of collecting and distributing resources.

There are four main elements, as shown in Table 1.2, that can feed into a theory of philanthropy (Monnet and Panizza 2017). The elements represent a tool for exploring the issues philanthropic institutions face. A philanthropic institution can use the variables as the intermediate tools to investigate its effect on the objectives. From here, the elements can be used to produce a concise and clear theory of philanthropy.

The third column of Table 1.2 identifies the elements that can develop into a theory of economic development. The Theory of Economic Development's fundamental question is, Why does economic development progress cyclically rather than evenly? Islamic economists also place the labour and entrepreneur at the centre of the Islamic economic system, anticipating subsequent appeals to entrepreneurship as wealth creation. The major interest of the theory is mainly its focus on the four

Table 1.2 Theory of philanthropy and theory of economic development

	Theory of philanthropy	*Theory of economic development*
Fundamental	Resources contribute to changes	Resource analysis that creates a business cycle
Agent	Donors and institutions who aid in resource distribution	Labourer and entrepreneur at the heart of production process and wealth creation
Variables	*Zakat*, *waqf*, and *sadaqah*	Financing and capital; entrepreneurial profit; and dividend on capital
Objectives	To improve the well-being of humankind	To achieve the *maqasid shariah* by having inclusive growth

intermediate variables—namely, financing and capital, profits and dividend. It also suggests that the objectives of the theory are to achieve the *maqasid shariah* that are to preserve: religion (*al-Din*), life (*al-nafs*), intellect (*Al-'aql*), lineage (*al-nasl*), and property (*al-Mal*).

The elements in both theories basically complement each other. They can also be used to prove the spending–donating nexus and entrepreneurship–philanthropy nexus. The labourer and entrepreneur in the theory of production can also be the economic agents who donate for philanthropic purposes. The tools of *zakat* that are directly channelled to recipients may improve the well-being of humankind, which is part of achieving the *maqasid shariah*. Other tools such as *waqf* and *sadaqah* can be channelled for financing and capital that can generate profit and dividend.

Hence, given a philanthropic institution's intermediate variables and institutional variables such institutional efficiency, these two variables could be used to synthesize the relationship between philanthropy and economic development. The relationship can be hypothesized as bidirectional in that philanthropy is a catalyst for achieving *maqasid shariah*, or a better economic development progress leads towards love of humanity.

5 The Entrepreneurship–Philanthropy Nexus

The amount of savings in the Islamic economic system is channelled to enterprises who produce goods. Then, both savers or donors and entrepreneurs combine their capital to establish an enterprise. The combination of capital, labour, and entrepreneurship is crucial in producing goods in the economy. Economists always believe in the importance of the role of entrepreneur in job and wealth creation. Entrepreneurship may cover entrepreneurial initiative and creativity. At all levels, government initiates a full effort in incorporating both technological revolution and economic policy that are directed towards promoting entrepreneurship.

Culturally and socially, Muslims are endowed with good values. As a good example for all, the Holy Prophet initiated the good values. It had resulted in a major shift in the good behaviour and social action of his followers. His teaching and examples were proven during the Golden Age-era of Islamic civilization. During the early days of Islam, much of the new wealth created had been given back to society. For example, Khalifah Umar Al-khattab endowed his most valuable land in Khaybar as *waqf* for the needy and poor over fourteen hundred years ago.

His teaching, which is based on Al-Quran, creates an Islamic economic system that differs from capitalist and socialist systems. Spend beyond your needs should be considered as philanthropy (Al Quran Chapter Al Baqarah, verse 219). The people, who obey Allah, spend the provision that has been given by the Lord only up to a certain limit. A portion of His provision should revert to society.

Entrepreneurs are free to accumulate wealth. However, wealth must be reverted back into society to preserve it. This book proposes that entrepreneurs—especially those who have received provision from Allah—spend their wealth via *zakat*, *waqf*, and *sadaqah*, which, in turn, contributes to a betterment of economic development. During the Golden Age of Islamic civilization, *waqf* were used to provide public goods and services including infrastructure, education, and health. *Waqf* were also used to build mosques, schools, hospitals, and bridges. The usufruct of *waqf* was used for the benefit of the people, especially those in need. The success of *waqf*, as an example, may motivate the entrepreneurs as their duty to "give something back" to society. Therefore, entrepreneurship/philanthropy became the driving force in the long-term aims of sustainable development.

6   A New Approach to Economic Development

As discussed in Sects. 3 and 4, Islamic philanthropy tools help recipients by providing them with some relief in dealing with their present life. But, Islamic philanthropy tools are also aimed at building a better future and life in the hereafter. As reform tools, Islamic philanthropy provides recipients with the opportunity to generate an income and better prosperity on a longer-term basis. Hence, it can be mapped to the long-term development strategy of the Sustainable Development Goals (SDGs) at least up to 2030. The goals are to end poverty, protect the planet, and ensure that all people enjoy peace and prosperity. More importantly, the goals are also directed at every human being very close to his or her Creator. The development tools and policies are directed at achieving those goals. How could the Islamic philanthropy tools be transmitted to those goals? This book will seek the answer.

Most of the studies that look at the role of Islamic economic tools and economic development are only limited to: the link between Islamic finance (assets or financing) and economic development (for example Said and Ismail (2008) and Kassim (2016)) either at the Islamic banking level (for example Sukmana and Kassim (2010)) or at the microfinance level (institutions level; for example Sultan and Masih (2016)) or at the market level such as capital markets or *sukuk* on the economic development (for example Smaoui and Nechi (2017) and Abd Aziz, Idriss and Echchabi (2016)). These studies may not be enough. It depends on the their purpose.

However, Islamic economic tools are not only seen from the institutional or market perspectives—institutions such as Islamic banking, Islamic microfinance, or market perspectives such as financing for housing, firm (via *sukuk* or working capital), car, or personal. Islamic finance should go beyond those perspectives but it also covers Islamic philanthropy. Countries can also depend on Islamic philanthropy as part of Islamic finance.

This book supports development financing via a new approach that encourages Islamic philanthropy from society. It is new because the new approach will link closely both individuals that are contributors and recipients. This book will also argue the different impacts of a new approach since public revenues include main tax (taxpayer benefits—pay higher tax and receive higher benefits), but a new approach may include current payers paying for the benefits of others. As such, Islamic philanthropy is one of the central tenets of Islam that inspires humans to bond with other humans and with the larger community as a form of worship and for the greater benefit of all. This book also seeks to highlight that Islamic philanthropy tools will affect differently the development agenda.

The approach is relevant to the current economic development agenda, which tries to narrow the development gap and consider the impact of Islamic economic policy actions on disadvantaged groups in society. By narrowing the development gap and reducing poverty, a strong, sustainable, and balanced growth, and a more robust and resilient economy, can be achieved. The disadvantaged groups are, therefore, a central focus to a development agenda. However, it fails to address human matters as part of a development agenda.

In addition, philanthropy can also be used as a tool in solving the humanitarian crisis that is happening globally. The crisis is due to wars, conflicts, terrorism, climate change, food deprivation, poverty, and epidemics (e.g., COVID-19). As reported by OCHA, Global Humanitarian Overview 2020, they noted two important reasons for humanitarian aid: first, 167.7 million in 2020 needed assistance and it is expected to increase to 200 million by 2022; and second, the total humanitarian assistance was expected to reach USD28.8 billion in 2020. They identify five countries that are most affected—Syria, Yemen, Somalia, Afghanistan, and Sudan.

Therefore, Islamic philanthropy as a tool for humanitarian aid is needed to help the affected countries to find solutions for the following humanitarian crises: more people become refugees, internally displaced, need food, shelter, health facilities, water, and education. Islamic philanthropy becomes the centrepiece of development in a country or in affected countries. Philanthropy was exemplified by the Prophet Muhammad (peace be upon Him) along with His companions. Until now, the revival of Islamic economics is partly due to Islamic philanthropy.

7   The Economic Aftermath of the COVID-19 Pandemic

The COVID-19 pandemic that started in late 2019 has affected the whole world. It exposes the weaknesses in health systems and the vulnerabilities of economies. It also affects employment and productivity at levels that have not been seen since the Great Depression.

Up to this point, the prescriptions in overcoming both health and economic crises are many. The suggestion is to create a fiscal buffer—raise revenues and prudent spending—to channel more spending to public health, economic stimulus packages, and the social safety net. In facing the challenges during and after COVID-19, governments' budgets need to be revised by looking at the quantum and priority of revenue, spending, and financing. By noting these challenges, governments would face in an increase in fiscal deficits, and subsequently, surges in public debt. Governments also need additional funds and incentives for populations that need them the most, especially small and informal businesses, and the vulnerable groups that are exposed to the COVID-19 crisis. As a worst-case scenario, the longer period of the pandemic may lead to an unsustainable fiscal package. Indeed, it may affect the level of debt in an economy.

The time has come, however, for governments to embark on the Islamic philanthropy tools to support a resilient economic future by focusing on the vulnerable groups. These groups are exposed to salary deduction, reduced working, and retrenchment. In many countries, small and informal businesses have the potential to absorb workers. In Malaysia, as reported in the Department of Statistics Malaysia, SMEs employment comprises 48.4% of Malaysia's employment. However, the COVID-19 crisis has affected a lot of them as they have problems in managing their cashflows when crises occur, and hence SMEs are more prone to crisis. In

2020, the amount of *zakat* equals RM159.24 million, distributed by the *zakat* authorities in Malaysia to vulnerable groups, especially the poor and needy.

8 ORGANIZATION OF THIS BOOK

This book is divided into five parts and nineteen chapters. Chapter 2 sends an important message that philanthropy is an old concept and recently is recognized as new economics (see JEL classification code D64) and becomes part of welfare economics. However, the scholarly publications on this subject show that philanthropy is a distinct concept. The current studies are also very much influenced by Christian tradition; none has included the Islamic tradition explaining its instruments and principles. Therefore, this chapter aims to examine the comprehension of philanthropy from Islamic tradition. It will then be used to explain the current debate on the paradigm of "state or market" and the "welfare state or philanthropy."

Chapter 3 discusses how to foster sustainable and inclusive development. This chapter focuses on the solutions offered by Islamic finance through its underpinning value system and worldview and through its set of commercial and social finance institutions to intervene in development assistance through and beyond markets.

Chapter 4 presents the challenges in developing the *waqf* land in Brunei Darussalam. The chapter uses in-depth interviews with relevant stakeholders and is supported by secondary data. The interviews were done by using several sets of semi-structured interview questions with targeted, relevant officers from several government bodies such as Waqf and Baitul Mal Unit and Badan Tanmiah, MUIB, and the State Mufti's Office. Secondary data was used to support this study such as printed and published materials on the Waqf Act and data on uses of *waqf* funds.

Chapter 5 investigates cash *waqf* based on archival documents. The primary sources, *waqfiyahs*, are used for examination. The methods and purposes in these documents reveal the altruistic financial model. The basic principles of this model are determined in the light of this information.

Chapter 6 investigates the factors influencing contributors, particularly university students, to participate in cash *waqf*. The present study will provide some contributions to the various parties. First, the study provides some ideas on which conceptually independent determinants of intention are more applicable in explaining the intention to perform cash *waqf* among younger generations, specifically university students. Hence, it will contribute to the literature by investigating the factors influencing people's intention to participate in cash *waqf*. The study's findings could also be used by the respective authorities to design strategies to increase cash *waqf* participation. The findings could also help the government to diversify the present effort and find the solution to improve people's intentions, which should start from the younger generation to contribute towards cash *waqf*.

Chapter 7 proposes a mechanism for entrepreneurial financing through the integration of crowdfunding and *waqf* as a Shari'ah-compliant crowdfunding. This *waqf* crowdfunding will also provide information on utilizing cash *waqf* in crowdfunding, as a new fundraising mechanism that is proposed to solve financing issues. The mechanism features a more secure and Shari'ah-compliant approach to online fundraising for entrepreneurs that is based on the Maqasid Al-Shari'ah as guidance.

Chapter 8 investigates the effect of floods on society, and observes the experience of flood victims staying at a flood evacuation centre. It proposes a permanent flood evacuation centre base on *waqf* principles.

Chapter 9 proposes cash *waqf* as a tool for the environment and human protection from the haze crisis.

Chapter 10 highlights that there are many issues and aspects of *zakat*. Therefore, this chapter is dedicated to find the issues and aspects discussed by previous studies, particularly in the last decade. It also recommend some aspects for future research.

Chapter 11 seeks to review the literature on *zakat* distribution and its impact. This chapter will also suggest the agenda for future research on *zakat* distribution.

Chapter 12 seeks to examine the role of state Islamic higher education in optimizing both Islamic philanthropy studies and Islamic philanthropic organizations in the university. The case study was conducted at the state institute for Islamic studies of Surakarta (IAIN Surakarta) and Islamic State University (UIN) of Malang.

Chapter 13 offers the idea of an innovative mobile application, GO ZAKAT, to increase *zakat* collection to synergize several BAZ/LAZ in one application. The reality on the ground is that we are not yet able to integrate applications via auto-debit facility charity accounts and credit facilities that map *zakat*, *zakat* calculation facilities, and facilities to prepare financial statements with BAZ/LAZ transparency information. The number of smartphone users in Indonesia continues to increase each year to make this application more feasible to use. Therefore, GO ZAKAT is expected to provide solutions (for the government) to alleviate poverty and improve social welfare by making charity into national economic and financial instruments based on the amount of *zakat* potential in Indonesia. For BAZ/LAZ, it is expected to increase the collection of alms and synergize *zakat* institutions to absorb more of *zakat*'s potential in Indonesia. For the community, it is expected to facilitate the public to pay *zakat* and provide education and outreach about the effectiveness of *zakat* distribution through *zakat* institutions.

Chapter 14 focuses on the *zakat* fund model that has potential to help relief agencies save lives and money, maintain standards of humanitarianism and fairness, and maximize the use of limited resources amid post-disaster chaos. The chapter also identifies the outstanding issues related to the *zakat* fund models for disaster relief. The analysis of the solution is derived from the perspective of scholars.

Chapter 15 focuses on a unique aspect that is related to the ability of efficient investment of *tabung masjid* toward achieving Maqasid-al-Shari'ah. This chapter identifies the lack of governance mechanisms and expertise often prevents mosque management to fully utilize *tabung masjid* toward benefiting the greater community. Results provided by the study will benefit regulators and stakeholders in realizing the importance of selecting efficient investment sources for donations received from various sources by mosques.

Chapter 16 aims to examine whether the Khanqahs and Sufi Shrines of Pakistan as "faith-based organizations" are contributing to the social and economic development of society significantly or not. All the Sufi Shrines selected for inclusion in the study are somehow involved in bettering society's poor and marginalized sectors and are the most popular ones in the region. All the selected Shrines as an institution work in similar sectors and geographical areas and have with communities. The chapter assesses whether and how an explicitly religious and spiritual motivation and affiliation influences institutions' characteristics engaged in development-related activities, in part to assess whether these shrines are just a place for performing religious Sufi rituals or institutions benefiting society socially as well as economically.

Chapter 17 discusses the roles of faith-based organizations in combating and dealing with, among others, refugee crises and natural disasters. The chapter also evaluates these organizations in demonstrating to what degree they have helped to generally portray South Africans and sectors of

South Africa's Muslim community as a giving nation that illustrated their philanthropic characteristics.

Chapter 18 proposes a governance framework model incorporating antecedents and consequences of good governance. The model allows regulators, philanthropic organizations, and other relevant stakeholders to assess governance practices' types and extent.

Chapter 19 presents a summary and policy recommendations.

References

Abd. Aziz, H., Idriss, U., & Echchabi, A. (2016). Does Sukuk Financing Promote Economic Growth and Emphasis on the Major Issuing Countries. *Turkish Journal of Islamic Economics, 3*, 63. https://doi.org/10.15238/tujise.2016.3.2.63-73

Kassim, S. (2016). Islamic Finance and Economic Growth: The Malaysian Experience. *Global Finance Journal, 30*(C), 66–76. https://econpapers.repec.org/RePEc:eee:glofin:v:30:y:2016:i:c:p:66-76

Monnet, N., & U. Panizza. (2017). A Note on the Economics of Philanthropy. Graduate Institute of International and Development Studies International Economics Department Working Paper Series No. HEIDWP19-2017.

Patton, M., Foote, N., & Radner, J. (2015). A Foundation's Theory of Philanthropy: What It Is, What It Provides, How to Do It. *The Foundation Review, 7*(4) https://doi.org/10.9707/1944-5660.1263

Said, F. F., & Ismail, A. G. (2008). Monetary Policy, Capital Requirement and Lending Behavior of Islamic Banking in Malaysia. *Journal of Economic Cooperation among Islamic Countries, 29*(3), 1–22.

Smaoui, H., & Nechi, S. (2017). Does Sukuk Market Development Spur Economic Growth? *Research in International Business and Finance, 41*. https://doi.org/10.1016/j.ribaf.2017.04.018

Sukmana, R., & Kassim, S. (2010). Roles of the Islamic Banks in the Monetary Transmission Process in Malaysia. *International Journal of Islamic and Middle Eastern Finance and Management, 3*(1), 7–19. https://doi.org/10.1108/17538391011033834

Sultan, Y., & Masih, M. (2016). Does Microfinance Affect Economic Growth? Evidence from Bangladesh Based on ARDL Approach. MPRA Paper No. 72123. https://doi.org/10.13140/RG.2.1.3286.4888

CHAPTER 2

Philanthropy from Islamic Tradition

Muhammad Hasbi Zaenal, Abdul Ghafar Ismail, and Muhammad Hakimi Mohd. Shafiai

1 INTRODUCTION

The rapid accumulation of wealth and the strengthening of a few rich people's position and status have created injustice. Over the last twenty years (from 1990 to 2012), the revenue of the wealthy 1% of the world population has raised more than 60%.[1] The unjust distribution is identified as one of the significant factors of poverty for millions of people worldwide. It shows that to realize the economic life of justice and welfare

[1] Oxfam, 2021, http://www.oxfam.org/en/pressroom/pressrelease/2020-01-19/annual-income-richest-100-people-enough-end-global-poverty-four-times (July 18, 2020).

M. H. Zaenal (✉)
Universitas Islam Negeri Syarif Hidayatullah, Jakarta, Indonesia
e-mail: hasbi@uinjkt.ac.id

A. G. Ismail
Putra Business School, Universiti Putra Malaysia, Seri Kembangan, Malaysia

M. H. M. Shafiai
Faculty of Economics and Management, Universiti Kebangsaan Malaysia, Bangi, Malaysia

© The Author(s), under exclusive license to Springer Nature Switzerland AG 2022
A. G. Ismail et al. (eds.), *Islamic Philanthropy*, Palgrave Studies in Islamic Banking, Finance, and Economics,
https://doi.org/10.1007/978-3-031-06890-4_2

23

is not an easy thing to achieve. Similar views are also mentioned by Posner (1981) and Kapstein (2007).

To address economic inequalities, economists like Andreoni (1982) believe that philanthropy could be one of the tools to create economic justice and betterment. As a result, wealthy individuals like kings, rulers, celebrities, and the like donate their wealth (in immense amounts) through philanthropy. The philanthropy act also comes from the individual at large. However, others like Stiglitz (2002) say that the actual range of social programs that philanthropists do are just considered a "mask" to cover up the sense of social injustice, environmental as well as what they did.

Many factors are identified that encourage wealthy individuals to donate. For example, George Soros was inspired by his father's risk-taking during World War II, which took his family and others to escape Hungary during the Nazi occupation. By doing this, it makes him feel happy.[2] Arnold Goldstein, who built a million-dollar playground in his old neighborhood, says he wanted to provide kids he did not have when growing up. The Bill and Melinda Gates Foundation has distributed approximately USD23 billion in grants to help all people lead healthy and productive lives. Oprah, who has given scholarships in South Africa, said that she found inner peace when she started doing acts of charity: "making charity feels like a part of her life."[3] The act also comes from the people at large to donate. They donate partly because of the incentives given by government policy, such as tax exemption. However, generally, the motivations are based on their concern for others. An event also inspires it in the past. Others are inspired due to obligation orders by religion as a way of life towards the hereafter.

It shows that philanthropy also has contributed to the economy. The economic impact of philanthropy will usually benefit the people in the property, facilities, services, charities, buildings, and other either intangible or intangible objects. Therefore, the existence of philanthropy is essential in the maintenance and enhancement of social cohesion. The willingness to give and share can ease the lives of the needy, poor, weak, and oppressed economically, politically, and socially, reducing social

---

[2] Rockefeller Philanthropy Advisors, "The Giving Commitment: Knowing Your Motivation," p. 5; http://rockpa.org/document.doc?id=143 (July 15, 2020).

[3] Bill and Melinda Gates Foundation, "Building Better Lives Together," 2011 Annual Report.

jealousy and hatred among social classes. Therefore, philanthropy may lead a country towards a welfare state.

On the other hand, it may be motivated by the state of welfare in a country. It raises the debate on the "state or market" paradigm and the "welfare state or philanthropy." The market fails to produce a just and fair economic system. Alternatively, social programs should be undertaken by the government to address the state of welfare. And the state of welfare should be taken care of by the voluntary sector.

Hence, this chapter's critical message is that philanthropy is an old concept and recently is recognized as new economics (see JEL classification code D64) and becomes part of welfare economics. However, as reported in Schuyt Leat (2016), the scholarly publication in leading English-language political science journals shows that philanthropy is a distinct concept. As Schuyt summarized, the current studies are very much influenced by Christian tradition; none has included the Islamic tradition explaining the instruments and principles. The challenge, then, is to incorporate philanthropy into the welfare economic system. Therefore, this essay aims to examine the comprehension of philanthropy from Islamic tradition. It will then be used to explain the current debate on the paradigm of "state or market" and the "welfare state or philanthropy."

This chapter will be divided into four sections. Section 2 will discuss the subject of philanthropy from Islamic tradition. Our discussion will start from the *salaf* view, but this view is limited to instruments and motives and our view may be grouped as a modern (*khalaf*) view. Section 3 will touch on the principles of philanthropy, and the last section will discuss how principles of philanthropy have been applied in Islam.

2 An Insight into the Studies of Philanthropy

In Islam, philanthropy has become the centerpiece of the development of the *ummah*. Philanthropy has been exemplified by the Prophet (s.a.w) along with His companions. Until now, the survival of Islam also relies on philanthropic involvement. For example, in the development process al-Nabawi Mosque, Allah's Apostle saw action involving philanthropy in a long hadith that relates the Hijrah events. "Then, he rode his mount animals, accompanied by the people. Eventually, the beast roars at the site (candidate) mosque Prophet saw at that place, on that day he also founded the prayer with the Muslims. Locations are palm groves owned by Suhail and Sahl, two orphan children under the care of Asʿad bin Zurārah. The

Prophet said when his mount beast roars at the site, 'this place will be a place to stay (The Prophet).' Then, he called for two of the landowners, and the children bid their land for the mosque. Both of them said, 'No, we even gave it over to you, O Prophet." The Prophet was reluctant to accept the grant until he bought it from both.[4] From then until now it is a place owned by the *ummah*.

Likewise, ʿUmar ibn al-Khaṭṭāb, when he gave the land in Khaibar— narrated in a hadith of Imam al-Bukhari. From Ibn ʿUmar, the Companions ʿUmar acquired land in Khaibar, facing Rasulallah to seek the guidance. ʿUmar said, "O Rasūlallah, I get a piece of land in Khaibar, I have not been getting the best property, then what do you command me?" Rasūlallah said, "When you love, you shall hold the land, and donate outcome of it." "Then ʿUmar decide to donate the land, not sold, not inherited, and not even hibah. Ibn ʿUmar said, "ʿUmar give it to the poor, kin, thrall, *sabilillah, Ibn al Sabil*, and guests. Moreover, it does not matter/not restricted to the control of the land (for manage) eat from the outcome, either way (if appropriate) to feed other people with no means to accumulate wealth.'"[5]

Similarly, Abdurrahman ibn ʿAuf sold his land forty thousand dinars, then distributed it between the Zahara people, poor, and the Prophet (saw). He sent to ʿAisha the money, and ʿAisha said, "Who sent this money?" Said, ʿAbd al Rahmān ibn ʿAuf. She said, "The Prophet said: 'will not bow you after me, but the righteous,' and God watered Ibn ʿAuf of Salsabil paradise."[6] Said Dhahaby, ʿAbdul Rahmān ibn ʿAuf recommended fifty thousand dinars for the sake of Allah.[7] He also recommended a thousand horses for Allah's sake, giving for *Badrin* (which amounts to one hundred people), giving every one of them four hundred dinars.[8] That is life in the early development of Islam, where philanthropy was widespread among Muslims.

---

[4] al-Bukhāri, Abi ʿAbdillah Muhammad ibn Ismāil, al-Jāmiʿ al-Shohīh, Maktabah Salafiyah, Cairo, 1400 H (1980 M), no. 3906, vol. 3, p. 2.
[5] al-Nawāwy, Muqaddimah Sharh al-Nawāwī Cala Sahīh Muslim, Bāb Qawluhū Ahāba ʿUmara Ardan bi Khaibar, Dar al-Fikr, Beyrūt, vol. 11, 1981, p. 86.
[6] Abu Naīm, Ahmad Ibn ʿAbdullah, Ḥilyah al-Auliyā' wa Thobaqāt al-Aṣfiyā', Dār al-Fikr, Beyrūt, vol. 1, 1996, p. 99.
[7] Ibn Asākir, Abū al-Qasīm ʿAli, Tarīkh Madīnah Damshīq, Dār al-Fikr, Beyrūt, vol. 35, 1995, p. 299.
[8] Ibn Asākir, Tārikh Madīnah Damshīq, vol. 35, p. 300.

From the above discussion, we can identify words like "give," "donate," "palms grove," and "grant," which show the type of instruments and the motives of donation. In this section, we will explore the instruments that can be considered for philanthropy and its motives. Let us discuss the meaning of philanthropy first.

2.1 The Meaning of Philanthropy

Generally, most of us agree that philanthropy is a form of charity. Etymologically, the word philanthropy comes from the Latin *philanthropia*. In Greek, *philanthropia* is defined as "kindliness, humanity, benevolence, love to mankind" (from gods, men, or things), while the adjective of this word, that is, *philanthropos*, means "loving mankind, useful to man." It is derived from *phil-* "loving" (see *philo-*) + *anthropos* "mankind" (see *anthropo-*). Hence, the combination of these two words generates a meaning "Love or love to man."[9] Therefore, Andreoni (1982) suggests that philanthropy is defined as human behavior, usually in charitable gifts, toward others in society. The term "new philanthropy," as stated by Brown (2000), invokes together the descriptions of the hands-on, entrepreneurial style of charity practiced by many new foundations and newly wealthy benefactors. Thus, it shows that philanthropy is an honest effort for the liberation of humanity from its troubles.

The definition of philanthropy has also evolved from personal activities into one action-oriented economic objective that a group of people loves others by donating their resources. This definition is mentioned by Payton, who says that philanthropy is a form to show the collective activities undertaken by the individual through organizations or institutions. He also interprets giving, services, and association to help others in need as an expression of love. As a result, dozens of philanthropic organizations have been established.[10] Moreover, their activities and programs are many, including the fulfillment of basic needs such as food, clothing, medicine, and housing; redistribution of power; a transformation to develop values of plurality and diversity; increase in the capacity of a community (so that

---

[9] Online Dictionary, 2012, http://www.etymonline.com/index.php?term=philanthropy (July 15, 2020).

[10] Knight, "What Is the Use of Social Justice?," *Alliance Magazine*, London, vol. 8, 2003, no. 3, p. 25.

the people have the power to act); and public participation in decision-making.

As explained above, the general meaning of philanthropy is indeed different from the tradition of Islam. What we can interpret is that philanthropy is a sense oriented 'love of man' with moral motivation voluntarily, without any element of obligation from Allah (s.w.t). While in Islam, its philosophical basis is the 'obligation' of 'Allah' to achieve social justice. This understanding may create unity between the love of the human, moral motivation, and Allah's obligations (s.w.t) to achieve social justice in this world. In Islamic philanthropy, the donor and the recipient have a relationship. It is not only to perpetuate the superior–inferior relationship, but more importantly, partnership with balance and equality, and therefore the bad intentions can be avoided.[11] So, the meaning of philanthropy as we understand it today is that we give voluntarily.

2.2 Instruments

In Islam, the word philanthropy itself can be interchangeable with the word *ṣadaqah*. Therefore, in Islam, philanthropy is not limited to the source of wealth that is just voluntary donation, but may be derived from the rule that requires (obligatory) was issued, while the same legal source, their utilization, and the same way and function from the *ummah*, to *ummah* for the economic welfare of *ummah*. Hence, there are two forms of charity in Islam—obligatory and voluntary, called *ṣadaqah*. In practice, there are two kinds we can divide into the following categories, which have separate rulings: *ṣadaqah wajibah* (obligatory voluntary) and *ṣadaqah nāfilah* (voluntary). These two kinds of *ṣadaqah* have the same function of creating social justice in welfare economics. With these instruments that transfer income to poor people, demand goods and services, the poor will increase. In this context, we can see that the Islamic philanthropy allocative function of reallocating resources from the rich to the poor is an effective way of fighting poverty.

---

[11] "Is it they who allocate the mercy of your Lord? We have allocated their livelihood in worldly life. We have raised some of them over others in ranks so that some of them may put some others to work. And the mercy of your Lord is much better than what they accumulate" (Qur'an 43:32).

2.2.1 Ṣadaqah wājibah

This is a type of worship donation for all Muslims. This type is comparable with *zakāh*; it should be spent on equivalent classes as outlined by *dalīl* (reason or argument from the al-Qur'an and Hadith).

2.2.2 Zakāh

Zakāh is obligatory for every Muslim. It is part of the wealth required of a Muslim when his property was reached *nisāb*[12] to be given to people who deserve it (*mustahiq*), the group that has been assigned the right to receive in al-Qur'an. Allah s.w.t said,

> Who give not the poor-due, and who are disbelievers in the Hereafter.[13]
> The alms are only for the poor and the needy, and those who collect them, and those whose hearts are to be reconciled, and to free the captives and the debtors, and for the cause of Allah, and (for) the wayfarer; a duty imposed by Allah. Allah is Knower, Wise.[14]

Zakāh is divided into two types, and is based on the purpose of the charity function itself: one to purify the soul, and the second to purify the property.

2.2.3 Zakāh al-Fiṭrah

This type is issued in the month of Ramadan or lastly in the morning of Ied al-Fiṭr. The obligation is intended to purify the soul, as cleaner of the soul of things littering the fasting implementation in Ramadan.[15] It also serves as a donation for the poor and those eligible to receive charity on Ied al-Fiṭr. Those who are obligated include every Muslim, whether rich or poor, who is still alive and has exceeded the property from being spent on primary needs. Prophet s.a.w said,

---

[12] Gold *nisab* is 20 dinars (equivalent to 85 grams of pure gold) while *nisab* silver is 200 dirhams (equivalent to 672 grams of silver). This means that if you have 20 dinars of gold for one year, then gold should be issued *zakat* 2.5%. While *nisab* of cash, savings, stocks, bonds, and other treasures are similar in value to the amount of gold must be paid the same as *zakah* of gold and silver. *Nisab* of income is if your income has reached a value of 5 *wasaq* or 652.8 kg of grain (equivalent to 520 kg of rice), the amount must be paid is 2.5% from the income.

[13] Qur'an 41:7.

[14] Qur'an 9:60.

[15] Yūsuf al-Qardhawy, Fiqh al-Zakāh, Muassasah al-Risālah, Cairo, part 1, 1973.

The compulsory al-fiṭrah charity in Ramadan, one sha of dates, or one sha[16] of wheat, of every Muslim free and slave, male or female.[17]

2.2.4 Zakāh al-Māl

This type is *zakāh* must be paid of a Muslim from their property when it reaches a certain amount (*niṣāb*).[18] Allah s.w.t said:

> O ye who believe! Spend of the good things which ye have earned, and of that which We bring forth from the earth for you, and seek not the bad (with intent) to spend thereof (in charity) when ye would not take it for yourselves save with disdain; and know that Allah is Absolute, Owner of Praise.[19]
>
> And in whose wealth there is a right acknowledged, For the beggar and the destitute.[20]

Zakāh is not a gift or donation or favor from the rich to the poor, but right for them who prefer the poor to the rich because they bring a large reward to them. As explained in the verse above, the recipient of *zakāh* is in eight groups. They are: *first*, the *faqīr*, often equated with the poor. Since both are similar to each other, each still has the uniqueness that sets it apart. Ash-Shāfiʿiyah Madhhab and Al-Hanābilah argue that what is meant by *faqīr* is a person who has no assets and no income sufficient basic needs. Alternatively, at least their human intent suffices. Including them is that a woman does not have a husband who can provide the cost of living. Basic needs cover many forms: food for life sustenance, clothes that can cover just nakedness or protect themselves from the heat and cold, and just a place to stay for shelter from the heat and rain or unfavorable weather.

Second, the poor do not have sufficient assets to meet their basic needs; although they are still, there is little ability to get it. They got something that can produce basic needs, but in minimal quantities and far from enough to make a living and survive. We can compare that there is little difference between the *faqīr* and the poor, that the *faqīr* state was worse

---

[16] Sha, if we convert, then the amount of zakah al-Fiṭrah is worth 2.176 kg of basic foodstuffs that apply in the region, such as wheat flour, dates, wheat, and rice.

[17] Al Shaukany, Muhammad ibn ʿAli, Muntaqā al-Akhbār, Nil al-Awṭār, Dar al-Hadith, Cairo, 1993, part 4, p. 179.

[18] Husain Husain Shaḥatah, Kaifa Yuḥsab al-Ṣoydali Zakāh Māliḥi, 2005, working paper. Al-Azhar University, Cairo.

[19] Qur'an 2:267.

[20] Qur'an 70:24–25.

than the poor, because the poor still have the possibility of income, although minimal and inadequate. While *faqīr* is already not have anything and does not have any ability to get his life's primary intent.

Third, the *zakāh* administrator. They are required to know the law of *zakāh*. Also, they must be trustworthy and fair. Duties include the registrar, divider charity, saving property, and other skills closely associated with collecting and sharing *zakāh*. They work well so that the *zakāh*-making process is running correctly, on target, and not amiss. Also, they work hard to ensure that people are entitled to collect and receive it. Overall this hard work and service means they are entitled to a portion of the *zakāh* funds, even though they are rich. Indeed, *amil zakāh* was pretty tough because it was more than receiving and distributing *zakāh*. However, more than that they also had the burden of poverty and welfare distribution.

Fourth, the *mu'allaf* (one who persuaded him to Islam). This includes the fact that *mu'allaf* are not limited to those who are new to Islam, but also includes people who are still in non-Islamic religious or still unbelievers, but were persuaded to convert to Islam. *Mu'allaf*, the unbelievers, are still divided into two groups. First, they expected kindness. Second, those who avoided crime. That they expected their kindness is expected in Islam. So they are given a portion of *zakāh*, so there is a kind of encouragement to enter Islam. At the same time, those crimes are forgiven unbelievers who had been hostile to Muslims. Some *zakāh* is permitted to soften the heart and reduce or stop Muslim hostility.

Fifth, for slaves. What is meant by slaves in this case according to the Madhhab al-Hanāfiyah and ash-Shāfiʿiyyah is *Almukātibūn*, the slaves who were taking care of their release by paying/piercing their pride to their masters by way of gradual payment.

Sixth, people who owe. Understanding the *gharimin* is limited to people who have a debt to meet basic needs, and the funds of the *zakāh* are given to free him from debt. Alternatively, debt for the good is caused by an attempt to reconcile two people in a dispute, and even if the debtor is personally wealthy, he is entitled to receive *zakāh* funds to replace funds spent. This is debt resulting from a program or activity for social purposes, such as orphan foundation funds, or hospitals for treatment of the poor, or school fees for Muslims.

Seventh, fi Sabilillah. Yusuf al-Qaradawi in his book *Fiqh al-Zakāh* says that *fi Sabilillah* includes building *dakwah* centers (Al-Markāz Al-Islāmy). It supports the Islamic *dakwah* programs, publishes writings on Islam and

Table 2.1 Instruments of Islamic philanthropy

Instrument	Ownership	Motives/recipients	Governance
Zakat al-Fiṭrah	Rulers	Obligation to purify our soul	Trustee
Zakat	Rulers	Obligation to purify our wealth	Trustee
Waqf	Allah	Eternal goods for Allah	Trustee
Ṣadaqah Lillah	Allah	Expiation of sins, prevention of a bad death, diffusion of Allah's anger, avoidance of slander, cooling of one's grave, ease of livelihood, etc.	Supervise/facilitate
Nadhr	Allah	Keeping promises to Allah	Facilitate
Fidyah	Allah	Substitutes of worship	Facilitate
Kaffārah	Allah	Getting Allah's forgiveness	Facilitate
Uḍhiyyah	Allah	Pay fines to Allah	Facilitate
Aqīqah	Allah	Thanks for the birth	Facilitate

teaches Islam to the people, Islamic school tuition fees, the cost of educating a candidate *da 'i* who will fight in Allah's way with their knowledge.

Eighth, musāfir.[21] This situation is in transit, making it eligible for *zakāh*. The journey is not an immoral trip.

Row 2 in Table 2.1 shows that *zakāh* is transferred to the *zakāh* administrator, and then it will be channeled to a dedicated *asnaf* as discussed above. It shows that *zakāh* is divided into two types, is based on the purpose of the charity function itself; one to purify the soul, and the second to purify the property.

2.2.5 Nadhr

This is an action that becomes necessary due to one imposing it upon oneself. It can be done if one wishes to express gratitude, and the action can take on several forms, including *ṣādaqah*. If a person makes such an oath of giving charity, that then becomes *ṣādaqah wājibah*. If they cannot uphold the oath, they will have to give *kaffārah* and may be sinful.

> (Remember) when the wife of 'Imran said: My Lord! I have vowed unto Thee that which is in my belly as a consecrated (offering). Accept it from me. Lo! Thou, only Thou, art the Hearer, the Knower![22]

---

[21] I.e., a traveler from his country, though he was self-sufficient in the country.
[22] Qur'an 3: 35.

2.2.6 Fidyah

This is compensation for missing *salāh* (Muslim prayer) or *soum* (fasting) for a person who cannot perform them due to being in terminal illness or being deceased (in which case it is given out of a third of the wealth) or in the event of a person making a minor mistake in Hajj. The amount for each missed *salāh* or *soum* or each minor mistake in Hajj is to give 1.6 kg of wheat or its value (i.e., the same amount given for *sādaqah al-Fitr*) to the poor. *Fidyah* is *sādaqah wajibah*. *Sādaqah nafilah* may also be given either from the deceased's estate or on their behalf. Both the giver and the deceased are rewarded.

Allah said,

> (Fasting) for a fixed number of days; but if any of you is ill or on a journey, the prescribed number (should be made up) from days later. For those who can do it (with hardship) is a ransom, the feeding of one that is indigent. But he that will give more of his own free-will—it is better for him, and it is better for you that ye fast if ye only knew.[23]

2.2.7 Kaffārah

It is significant compensation, and like *Fidyah*, it is also *sādaqah wājibah*. It applies in various situations such as if a person breaks a fast intentionally, breaks an oath, or kills someone, *kaffārah* would then be binding as the form of redemption. There are five actions for which *kaffārah* will be necessary. However, they fall under two types.

The greater *kaffārah*: For redemption of this, a person may free a slave (which is no longer applicable) or fast for sixty consecutive days (if a person breaks a fast intentionally, they would need to fast for sixty consecutive days, unless they cannot fast due to poor health or old age, there are no exceptions to this). Failing that, one may feed sixty poor people for a day (i.e., two meals a day, each meal equivalent to a *fidyah*). This *kaffārah* applies to intentionally broken *saum*[24] (fast), breaking *zihar* (to consider one's wife as Haram for oneself by comparing her to a Mahram—anyone too closely related to be marriageable) and being the direct cause of someone's death (this is coupled with the set punishments).

---

[23] Qur'an 2:184.

[24] In the instance of not being able to feed sixty people in a single day then he may feed one person for sixty days, but in this case, if he were to try to quicken payment of this by giving all the money in one day to one person, *kaffārah* would not be fulfilled, and his offering would only be equal to one day of feeding.

The lesser *kaffārah* for this person's redemption may free a slave (which is no longer applicable) or feed ten poor people for two meals in one day, or give each one clothing. Failing this, he may fast for three consecutive days (the order is also different from the greater *kaffārah*). This *kaffārah* applies to breaking/violating *yamīn* (an oath) and breaking *ilā* (to take an oath on not having conjugal relationships with one's wife).

2.2.8 Uḍhiyyah

It is also known as *qurbani* or sacrifice. On the day of Idul Adha, it is an obligation order upon all mature Muslims possess nisāb. A qualified person is required to purchase a sheep or goat of more than one year in age. It slaughters that in the name of Allah after the Eid prayer, preferably on the same day. The sacrifice can also be made on the two days after Eid. If one fails to sacrifice these three days, he will still have to donate the animal's value.[25]

He may eat himself and feed his family and distribute meat amongst the poor Muslims from the meat. One is not responsible for giving *zakāh* or any necessary *ṣādaqah* for one's spouse nor one's mature children—they are responsible for themselves. One is, however, responsible for only giving *ṣādaqah al-fiṭr* for one's minor children; neither *zakāh* is given from their wealth, nor *uḍhiyyah* on their behalf.

The other type of *uḍhiyyah* is *dām*. There two types: one is like *uḍhiyyah* in the sense that it is a religious requirement for adult Muslims. The only difference is that it is specific to people who are performing Hajj. This *dām* is called *dām ash-shukr*.

The second type of *dām*, like *fidyah*, is a means of compensation for mistakes in Hajj, but the difference is the magnitude of the mistake. *Fidyah* is given instead of minor mistakes, while *dām* is instead of significant mistakes. *Dām*, like *uḍhiyyah*, is the sacrifice of a sheep or goat. It can also be made a part (i.e., 1/7) of a more massive sacrifice.

Another type of *uḍhiyyah* is *badonah*, which is like *dām*, but while *dām* is the sacrifice of a sheep or goat, *badonah* is the sacrifice of a large animal, that is, a cow or camel. It is the largest penalty in Hajj.

---

[25] One may slaughter goats or sheep, which constitute one sacrifice each, or one may slaughter a larger animal (i.e., cow or buffalo), which will be counted as seven sacrifices each. In living in a wealthy country, one should sacrifice one part locally to fulfill the *sunnah* of sacrificing oneself; and arrange for the remaining sacrifices to be performed in a more impoverished country, where the poor may also partake of it.

2.3 Ṣadaqah nāfilah

This is a charity that is not binding but is optional. This type includes alms given for the removal of difficulties, philanthropic (to give out of mercy to the less fortunate), the general giving of any Halal item to anyone, and so on. This type does not need to be spent on the specified categories to be rewarding, nor does it have to be spent on Muslims, although it would be more rewarding if spent on poor Muslims. It can also be bequeathed in one's will (in which case it would be only up to a third of the deceased person's entire estate).

There are various motives in this instrument, such as avoiding disaster for the giver and his family;[26] it will extend one's life, and prevent a bad death;[27] defuse Allah's anger;[28] close seventy-seven ugliness doors;[29] avoid slander from families, children, and neighbors;[30] remove sin as water removing fire[31] or cool one's grave.[32] Generally, ṣadaqah might be referred for all Islamic philanthropy besides the zakāh. All worshipping acts through the expenditure of money or property are broadly classified as ṣādaqah. According to al-Qur'an and al-Hadith, we can find a whole range of essential instruments in Islamic philanthropy that come from ṣādaqah.

2.3.1 Lillah (for God)

This typical Muslim act is generally called ṣādaqah, which does not have the condition of having to be passed into the possession of a person, as it can be given to institutes (e.g., Masajid, hospitals, schools, orphanages, etc.).

2.3.2 Waqf

This is to allot something as a trust for a particular cause. It can be during one's lifetime or bequeathed in one's will (up to the value of a third of

---

[26] Sees al-Tirmizy, vol. 5, Hadith 2863.
[27] See al-Thabrany, vol. 5, Hadith 422.
[28] See al-Bahauty, Mansūr ibn Yunus, Kashaf al-Qina' an Matni al-Iqna,' Dar al-Fikr, Beirut, vol. 2, 1982, p. 296.
[29] See al-Thabrany, vol. 4, Hadith 4402.
[30] See al-Asqalany, Ahmad ibn Ali ibn Hajar, Fath al-Bari Syarh Shohih al-Bukhari, Kitab Mawaqit al-Sholah, Bab al-Sholat Kafarah, Hadith 502, Dar al-Rayan li al-Turāth, Cairo, 1986.
[31] See Ibn Rajab, Jami' al-ʿUlum Wa al-Hikam, Muassasah al-Risalah, Dimashq, 2001, Hadith 29, p. 134.
[32] See Abd al-Badr, Abu ʿUmar Yūsuf, al-Istizkar al-Jami limazahib Fuqaha al-Amsar, Dar al-Wai', Cairo, 1993, p. 393.

one's estate). When executed, the donation becomes the property of Allah (and thus has specific rules regarding it), and its beneficiaries are to remain those named as the cause (e.g., the poor, orphans, students, the people of a particular locality, etc.). The difference between this and *Lillah* is that with *waqf*, ownership is not given to people or institutes, but only the benefits are ascribed. Like today's trusts, *waqf* also requires the care of trustees over it.

2.3.3 Aqīqah

This is the sacrifice of an animal or two as thanks to Allah for a newborn baby. With this too can members of the locality be fed, preference again being for the poor and close family members.

The charity is above the amount of *zakāh* and *ṣādaqah wajibah*.

This type of *ṣādaqah* is the essence of *Lillah*. It is not categorized as necessary. As long as it has pure means and pure intentions, this type of charity is always accepted by Allah. It is also this type that Allah has described as a beautiful debt, as He treats this charity as a loan that He will repay in the hereafter.

> Who is he that will loan to Allah a beautiful loan? For (Allah) will increase it manifold to his credit, and he will have (besides) a liberal reward.[33]

The summary of those instruments is presented in Table 2.1.

2.4 The Motives

The motive causes a person to act in a certain way, do a sure thing, and so on, as an incentive or the goal or object of a person's actions. From this definition, we can deduce that we operate as human beings through motivation (or *niat*). The human is God's creation who can think, and this would not be possible if it acts were without any motive, in all actions, either good motives or evil motives. Therefore, the motive will always accompany even the initial motive, with results that are sometimes incompatible; certainly, human actions are not possible without motives in a conscious condition. Including the motive is an act of giving or philanthropy.

By examining several verses in al-Qur'an, the motives are as follows: *first*, the individual gives philanthropy to help the distress (al-Qur'an:

[33] Qur'an 57:11.

2:205) directly. This act is only temporary, and it will last for only a short while. Giving *ṣādaqah* (refer to Table 2.1, under *ṣādaqah Lillah*) may fall under this act. For example, giving some money, clothes, food, providing shelter in the form of tangible assets (al-Qur'an, 2:20) or teaching, caring for the sick, helping others' own effort, giving motivation in the form of intangible assets (al-Qur'an: 3:190) are all among the types of *ṣādaqah* that could be channeled to individuals or institutions.

Second, the individual gives philanthropically because of obligatory motives as set out in Islam's teachings (al-Qur'an: 9:76). As discussed in Islamic literature, this motive can be categorized as alms that only apply to tangible property. Examples of obligatory alms are *zakāh*, *nadhr*, *Fidyah*, *kaffārah*, and *uḍhiyyah* (al-Qur'an, 8:60) for a particular individual or institution.

Third, the individual gives philanthropically for helping the public in general, but the motive (as reported in Table 2.1 under the *waqf* instruments) is an eternal treasure forever or until the instruments could not generate the benefits. This instrument may fall under the *waqf* property. The tangible properties are addressed to individuals or institutions, such as giving land, building materials, tools, money, and other objects that benefit. However, the most important reason to give is that we end up giving our money to Allah (s.w.t) as an act of love, worship, and acknowledgment that Allah s.w.t is our Lord and is everything.

2.5 The Causality Effect of Philanthropy

Philanthropy will raise two effects for the giver: social effects such as creating social justice functions and spiritual effects (to be obedient to Allah). We can describe these in terms of sociology, that there is satisfaction and dissatisfaction. Among the people, society will feel satisfaction when someone has given something useful for others. It is described as follows by a psychologist: "If someone wants to get happiness in this life, he should take part in a benefit to others. Because the pleasure one can depend on other people's pleasure and enjoyment of others depend on her pleasure." One does not need to wait for the end of the world to know how good or ill reward and punishment will come due to sin. Even now, they can be felt. Reward in the form of inner contentment, happiness, and comfort of the hearts obtained from doing some good, and so was the punishment she manifests in the form of a suffocating tangle, anxiety, inconvenience of heart, mind, soul, and even body after doing evil deeds to others.

Naturally, if something is removed, something will decrease or disappear. For example, with ten thousand minus five thousand, the remainder is five thousand. However, does this apply to the concept of giving in Islam? The Holy Qur'an calculates a multitude of numbers of goodness. Kindness will be reciprocated one 100. Logically, one gives but does not diminish, and this could be explained by a concept of Sufism, which is *tajalli*, the abundance of what Allah s.w.t gives without reducing what He has. Allah s.w.t created the creatures, giving life to them, all that does not make him lose, but by providing an abundance making it accept something else, He becomes the opening mantle of God as the creator of the universe.

3 Deriving the Principles of Philanthropy

The computer system comprises hardware and software. The same is also true of the philanthropy system, which has instruments and motives. How could we derive the principles of philanthropy that can explain: (1) descriptive comprehensive and fundamental laws, doctrines, or assumptions; (2) normative rules or codes of conduct; (3) a law or fact of nature underlying the working of philanthropy?

3.1 *Togetherness* (ukhuwwah)

Instruments and motives are aimed to create the essence of togetherness. Our needs are the needs of other people who need each other, help each other, recognize each other, understand each other, guarantee each other, synergy and alliance, and complement each other. We also cannot tackle or overpower the interests of others. This principle is also in line with the following verses:

> And when their eyes are turned toward the dwellers of the fire, they say Our Lord! Place us not with the wrong-doing folk.[34]
> And hold fast, all of you together, to the cable of Allah, and do not separate. And remember Allah's favor unto you: how ye were enemies, and He made friendship between your hearts so that ye became as brothers by His grace; and (how) ye were upon the brink of an abyss of fire, and He did save you from it. Thus Allah maketh clear His revelations unto you, that haply ye may be guided.[35]

[34] Qur'an 7:47.
[35] Qur'an 3:103.

It shows no question of superiority based on race, class, or nationality in holding this principle. This principle is conspicuously at work based on our civilization and its finer details.

3.2 Justice (ʿadālah)

As Allah said,

> O ye who believe! Be steadfast witnesses for Allah in equity, and let not hatred of any people seduce you that ye deal not justly. Deal justly that is nearer to your duty. Observe your duty to Allah. Lo! Allah is Informed of what ye do.[36]
>
> Lo! Allah commandeth you that ye restore deposits to their owners, and, if ye judge between humanity, that ye judge justly. Lo! comely is this which Allah admonisheth you. Lo! Allah is ever Hearer, Seer.[37]

Based on the above verses, the principle of justice in Islamic economic behavior is justice for all, that is, justice for all economic actors. For example, justice between consumers, producers, distributors, and other economic actors, including financial institutions and non-financial institutions. We should not favor one economic agent alone, but we shall put the advantages to others.

In Islam, all humans are the same, which has been created by the same God, Allah (s.w.t), and for this reason, they are included in one great brotherhood. All descendants of the same ancestors, Adam and Eve, they should become naturally mutual well-wishers. They are willing to come to help each other, as members of the same family. Therefore, Islam has put the most significant emphasis on the support of the community's poor and disabled members. It is the wealthy's sacred duty to give part of their wealth to meet the deprived section of society's needs. Allah said,

> But righteous is the one who, gives away wealth, out of love for Him to the near of kin and the orphans and the needy and the wayfarer and to those who ask, and to set slaves free. (2:177)
>
> So give to the near of kin his due, and to the needy and the wayfarer. This is best for those who desire Allah's pleasure.[38]

---

[36] Qur'an 5:8.
[37] Qur'an 4:58.
[38] Qur'an 30:38.

In Islam, philanthropy plays a role not only as a bridge between the rich and the poor, but the rich provide the means such as elements that can interact directly with the poor; they come to recognize, pay attention, and then they realize that it is a duty to fight against poverty, its causes, and the effects thereof. This linkage helps keep low-income groups isolated from the mainstream of social development and strengthens the social fabric.

3.3 Welfare (ri'āyah)

The essence of welfare means that each of the inputs, outputs, and outcomes should improve all parties' economic well-being. Islam practically assures its followers' welfare and security. It is the welfare of all economic actors that can sustain economic growth. Allah said,

> (And it is said unto them): Enter them in peace, secure.[39]
>
> What they spend in the life of this (material) world may be likened to a wind which brings a nipping frost: it strikes and destroys the harvest of men who have wronged their souls; it is not Allah that hath wronged them, but they wrong themselves.[40]
>
> Have you seen the one who denies the Recompense? For that is the one who drives away the orphan. And does not encourage the feeding of the poor. So woe to those who pray. [But] who are heedless of their prayer. Those who make show [of their deeds]. And withhold [simple] assistance.[41]
>
> Whatsoever Allah may restore Unto His apostle from the people of the cities is due Unto Allah and the apostle and the near of kin and the orphans and the needy and the wayfarer, so that it may not be confined to the rich among you. And whatsoever the apostle giveth you, take; and whatsoever he forbiddeth you, refrain from. And fear Allah; verily Allah is Stern in chastisement.[42]

It starts from personal life. Personal life is vital to the success and the practice of philanthropy. If we have faith, diligent prayer, care of social life, always keeping us from harmful action, we have a good personal life. All these become valuable resources for the sustainability of philanthropic practices. How could philanthropy create economic justice when our

---

[39] Qur'an 15:46.
[40] Qur'an 3:117.
[41] Qur'an 107:1–7.
[42] Qur'an 59:7.

personal life cannot be well taken care of. Therefore, our family life creates economic justice for the household.

Furthermore, the Prophet taught us to create a good life. The Prophet began educating the individual on how to behave and do good deeds and avoid the bad. Then, the Prophet taught how to communicate (for example, through marriage and transactions) within the community so that finally, the largest communities at the country level can be created, which follows the principle of equality.

3.4 Benefit (maṣlaḥah)

The benefits cover all forms of goodness and benefits and in the earthly dimension and the hereafter. It also covers material and spiritual benefits, both individual and collective. The overall benefit must meet the shari'ah elements in the form of maintenance of belief, faith, intellect, lineage, life, and property. Allah said,

> O ye who believe! Squander not your wealth among yourselves in vanity, except it be a trade by mutual consent, and kill not one another. Lo! Allah is ever Merciful unto you.[43]

3.5 Balance (tawāzun)

The principle of balance essentially covers the balance of life in this world and the hereafter. It must balance the material and the spiritual aspects, public and private aspects, the financial sector, the real sector, business, and social aspects. Also, any financial transaction is emphasizing the maximization of profits solely for the owners (shareholders). The benefits gained are focused not only on shareholders. It also benefits others. Allah said,

> Ignominy shall be their portion wheresoever they are found save (where they grasp) a rope from Allah and a rope from men. They have incurred anger from their Lord, and wretchedness is laid upon them. That is because they used to disbelieve the revelations of Allah and slew the prophets wrongfully. That is because they were rebellious and used to transgress.[44]

---

[43] Qur'an 4:29.
[44] Qur'an 3:112.

But seek the abode of the Hereafter in that which Allah hath given thee and neglect not thy portion of the world, and be thou kind even as Allah hath been kind to thee, and seek not corruption in the earth; lo! Allah loveth not corrupters.[45]

3.6 Universalism (shumūliyah)

The principle of universal essence can be performed by, with, and for all interested parties (stakeholders) without distinction as to race, religion, and class, according to the spirit of the kindness of the universe (rahmatan lil alamin). Allah said,

O mankind! Lo! We have created you from male and female, and have made you nations and tribes that ye may know one another. Lo! the noblest of you, in the sight of Allah, is the best in conduct. Lo! Allah is Knower, Aware.[46]

The Prophet Muhammad s.a.w said: "Every Muslim has to give in charity." The people then asked: "(But what) if someone has nothing to give, what should he do?" The Prophet replied: "He should work with his hands and benefit himself and also give in charity (from what he earns)." The people further asked: "If he cannot find even that?" He replied: "He should help the needy who appeal for help." Then the people asked: "If he cannot do (even) that?" The Prophet said finally: "Then he should perform good deeds and keep away from evil deeds, and that will be regarded as charitable deeds."[47]

In conclusion, we find that togetherness (ukhuwwah), justice (ʿadālah), welfare (riʿāyah), benefit (maṣlaḥah), balance (tawāzun), and universalism (shumūliyah) become the underlying principles of philanthropy. It also proves that philanthropy is not an economic activity that is purely based on materiality, but it also covers the social and justice elements. These principles also contain two elements: the principle of faith (tawhid) and the jurisprudence for every action (fiqh). The merging of these two elements is essential for the principle of philanthropy.

---

[45] Qur'an 28:77.
[46] Qur'an 49:13.
[47] Sahih Al-Bukhari, vol. 2, no. 524.

4 Applying the Principles: An Example of the Welfare Economic System

By having the principle of welfare (*ri'āyah*) and the principles of togetherness (*ukhuwwah*), justice (*'adālah*), benefits (*maṣlaḥah*), balance (*tawāzun*), and universalism (*shumūliyah*), how can a country move towards a welfare state? The question could be analyzed by the examples given by the Prophet and his companions and the following *Khalifah*.

In the early days of Islam, after completing the political and constitutional issues, the Prophet s.a.w changed the country's economic system under the provisions of the Qur'an. In realizing the economic system, the Prophet s.a.w applied the following aspects:[48]

a. Allah is the supreme ruler as well as the absolute owner of the whole universe;
b. Man is Allah's representative (*Khalifah*) on the earth, not the actual owner;
c. All that is owned is obtained by permission from Allah s.w.t. Therefore, less fortunate people have part of the property rights from others who are more fortunate;
d. Wealth must be rotated and should not be stockpiled;
e. A heritage system as a redistribution of wealth should be applied;
f. The obligation for all individuals, including the poor, should be established;
g. Economic exploitation in all its forms, including Riba, should be eliminated.

As the head of state, the Prophet introduced a new public finance concept in the seventh century. All proceeds from the accumulation of state assets must be collected and then disbursed under the state's needs, where the center's fundraiser called Bait Al-Mal is located in Nabawi Mosque. The sources of revenue for Bait al-Māl come from *kharaj*, *zakāh*, *ṣadaqah*, *jizya*, *dharibah*, and *kaffārah*. Then, Bait al-Mal expenditures are allocated to the Islamic dakwah, education, culture, scientific development, infrastructure development, national defense, and social welfare services provision.

---

[48] M.A. Sabzwari, Sistem Ekonomi dan Fiskal pada Masa Pemerintahan Nabi Muhammad, The International Institute of Islamic Thought Indonesia, p. 20, 2001, Jakarta.

The policy of Abu Bakr was to improve the welfare of Muslims. He implemented economic policies as the Prophet applied it. He was very concerned about the accuracy of the calculation of *zakāh* so that there was no excess or deficiency in payments.[49]

In distributing Bait al Māl, Abu Bakr applied the principles of equality, giving the same amount to all the companions, not differentiating between them, the servant and the free people, men and women. According to the terms of faith's primacy, Allah s.w.t will give a reward, while the necessities of life issues, the principle of equality are better than the primacy principle.[50] Thus, during the reign of Abu Bakr, the property of Bait al Māl never accumulated in a long period because it is directly distributed. All people are given an equal share of national income. Even if state revenues increase, people get the same benefits, and no one is left in poverty. The policy implications would be on the total national income and minimize the gap between the rich and poor.

This situation illustrates that Abu Bakr always keeps the *ummah* property stored in the Bait al Māl. Abu Bakr told me that I have no right to take my share of Bait al-Mal at all, which is also a testament to the Muslims after him; he is a leader who is very careful in spending money wisely with the *ummah*. The Abu Bakr governmental source of funds is from the one-fifth Ghanimah stored in Bait al Māl added to *ṣadaqah* sources; in carrying out its economic policies, he always endorses basic *maṣlaḥah* and justice.[51]

Next is the policy of ʿUmar ibn Khattāb, which lasted for ten years. He expanded Islamic territory to include the Arabian Peninsula, Palestinians, Syrians, most of Persia, and Egypt.[52] ʿUmar also sacrificed for the *ummah*, even though he and his family are no different from the poor in general. Before his death, when there was no more extended property to make ends meet, he had to borrow money from Bait al Māl, not asked. ʿUmar as personal is very fair in distributing property to the community. There is no greater but rather a lot of small parts and a bit part, all shared equally. ʿUmar policy included:[53]

---

[49] Karim, Adiwarman Azwar, *Sejarah Pemikiran Ekonomi Islam*, The International Institute of Islamic Thought Indonesia, p. 44, 2001, Jakarta.

[50] Afzalurrahman, Doktrin Ekonomi Islam, P.T. Dana Bhakti Wakaf, Yogyakarta, 1995, p. 320.

[51] al-Najjar, Abdul Wahab, Khulafa al-Rasyidun, Dar al-Turath, Cairo, p. 110.

[52] Harun Nasution, Islam Ditinjau Dari Berbagai Aspeknya, Universitas Indonesia Press, 1985, Jakarta, p. 10.

[53] Harun Nasution, Islam Ditinjau Dari Berbagai Aspeknya, p. 58.

a. ʿUmar is maintaining the *ummah* property. He does not increase the property for himself. He took on the government's economic policy to attract property from the rich to share with the poor.
b. Along with expanding the Islamic empire during the reign of ʿUmar, state revenue has increased very significantly. This case requires special attention to manage it to be appropriately utilized, effectively and efficiently. ʿUmar took the decision not to spend Bait al Māl treasure all at once but gradually as needed, including even provision as a reserve fund.
c. To distribute Bait al Māl, ʿUmar established several departments: First, the Military Services Department distributes funds to people involved in war. The Department of Justice and the Executive are responsible for payment of the salaries of judges and executive officials. The Ministry of Education and Youth of Islam distributes funds for Islamic preachers. The Department of Social Security serves to distribute funds to all poor and people who suffer.
d. ʿUmar categorizes horses, rubber, and honey as objects of charity because, in his time, all three things were commonly traded, even on a large scale, to bring benefits to the seller.

During his reign, which lasted for twelve years, ʿUthman ibn ʿAffan successfully expanded into Armenia, Tunisia, Cyprus, Rhodes, and Persia's remaining sections.[54] In the first six years of his reign, ʿUthman made new arrangements with the following ʿUmar policy. He made water drains, constructed streets, and established police organizations to secure the trade routes. ʿUthman also formed the Muslim fleet under the command of Muʿawiyah to successfully establish maritime supremacy of the Mediterranean region. Laodicea and the Syrian peninsula regions, Tripoli, and Barca in north Africa to harbor defense.

That ʿUthman has dedicated economic welfare can be seen from the story of "Raumah (name of the well)." At the time, the Muslims in Medina city lacked drinking water, and then the Prophet said, "Who will buy this Raumah, then he gave it to the Muslims without expectation of any reward?" Then, ʿUthman went out to the Jews (the owners) to buy it. However, the Jewish owners refused to sell it, unless ʿUthman was willing to pay 12,000 dirhams. The Prophet once said, "What is done today of

---

[54] Badri Yatim, *Sejarah Peradaban Islam*, P.T. Raja Grafindo Persada, 1994, Jakarta, p. 9.

'Uthman, is nothing to lose (in the Hereafter)."[55] Also, during the reign of Ali ibn Abi Talib, Bait al Māl, both at central and local levels, was going well. Cooperation between the two ran smoothly and then Bait al Māl was in surplus income. Bait al Māl was involved in the distribution of wealth, Ali ibn Abi Talib in the application of the principle of equality. He gives the same benefits to everyone regardless of social status or position.[56] These are among the examples using philanthropy for the economic welfare adopted in Islam's early days.

After passing through Islam's glory days from the Prophet Muhammad s.a.w to the Khulafa' Al-Rasyidiyah, Islamic leadership encountered much deterioration. The deterioration continued until 'Umar ibn 'Abd al Aziz came. In his reign, Islam made progress again, like the Islamic leadership in the early days.

He was a great leader throughout Islamic history. He played an outstanding role in the Umayyah Dynasty. This caliph, well-known as 'Umar II, usually made popular policies for his people. In this era, policies and governmental systems were identical to people's prosperity and the enforcement of Islamic rules. He replaced all dishonest, unjust, and incapable governors with the honest, just, and capable. 'Umar II was the trustful, just, and ascetic caliph. During his short reign (about two-and-a-half years) he had replaced all the dishonest governors, those unjust and unable to provide welfare to his people. With his revolutionary efforts to maintain harmony between man and nature, he united human involvement, religion, and nature for the final destination with the guidelines of truth and justice.[57]

The central policy of 'Umar II in managing his administration focused on two things: (1) provide guaranteed protection to the people (he did not continue the predecessor's territorial expansion); and (2) set neutral and egalitarian policies. In the early days of his reign, the Umayyah and their financial administration suffered a decline. In the face of this situation, Umar II established the tax *mawali* (for non-Arabs) and *dhimmi* regulations for payment through *kharāj* and *jizya*[58].

[55] al-Nawāwy, Yahya ibn Sharaf Abū Zakariya, Sharh al-Nawāwy 'Ala Muslim, Bāb Faḍāil al-Ṣohābah, Dar al-Salām, 1996, Cairo, p. 67.
[56] Karim, Adiwarman Azwar, Sejarah Pemikiran Ekonomi Islam, The International Institute of Islamic Thought Indonesia, Jakarta, 2001, p. 44.
[57] 'Imâd al-Dîn Khalîl, Malâmih al-Inqilâb al- Islâmi fi Khilâfah 'Umar ibn 'Abd al-'Aziz, 1971, al-Dâr al-Islamiyah, Beirut, pp. 15–16.
[58] Ahmad Syalabi, Sejarah dan Kebudayaan Islam I, Jakarta, Djembatan, 1971, pp. 391–392.

2 PHILANTHROPY FROM ISLAMIC TRADITION 47

To solve the economic condition of the country, Umar II regulated that *kharâj* was a joint property of Muslims and joint possession of the communities.[59] *Jizyah* was paid as land tax, while *kharáj* was a tax for security. As such, the policy was equally applied for both Muslims and non-Muslims. This equality attracted non-Muslims to embrace Islam. He stopped the wave of urbanization. It was related to the myriad *mawāli* in Iraq who left their home to migrate to cities. ʿUmar asked them to return and work on in their lands.[60] Arabs bought *dzimmî*'s land. This tempted *dzimmî* to migrate to cities; Arabs enjoyed crops without paying *kharáj*. As a result, many *dzimmî* adhered to Islam just to avoid *kharáj*. Such a condition deteriorated the economy. To cope with this, Umar II consulted with the ulama and made a policy: "Muslims who enjoyed the land of *kharáj* and paid the land of 'ushr' as tax, since 100 A.H. (9718–719 A.D.), must not do the land transaction." In this, it was not allowed to change *kharáj* land into the land of *ushr*. Land transaction without the government's permission was invalid. If a converted *mawāli* rented land, he did not have to pay *kharáj* tax. Instead, he was just to pay it in cash.[61]

One of the most important measures was his reform of taxation. He made adequate arrangements for the easy realization of taxes and administered it on a sound footing. He wrote a special note on *Kharaj* to ʿAbd al Hamid Ibn ʿAbdur Raḥmān which has been copied by Abu Yusuf: "Examine the land and levy the Kharāj accordingly. Do not burden a barren land with a fertile one and vice versa. Do not charge the revenue of barren land." His generous reforms and leniency led the people to deposit their taxes willingly. It is a strange paradox that despite all oppressive measures adopted by the notorious Hajjaj ibn Yūsuf for the realization of taxes in Iraq, it was less than half of the amount realized during the benevolent regime of ʿUmar II. He stressed that taxes should be collected with justice and leniency and should not be beyond the people's ability to bear. Tax collectors should not under any circumstances deprive the people of the necessities of life.[62] This view was held long before Adam Smith, famous, among other things, for his canons of taxation (equality, certainty, the convenience of payment, and economy in the collection).

---

[59] Husani, S.A.Q., Arab Administration, 1949, Soldent & Co., Madras, pp. 136–137.
[60] K. Ali, Islamic History, Dhaka, Ali Publications, 1976, p. 396.
[61] Husani, pp. 135–136.
[62] Abu Yusuf, al Kharaj, Dar al Mʿrifah, Beirut, 1933, pp. 14, 16, and 86.

In his policy, the Bait al Māl, which was one innovation of Islam and had proved a blessing for poor Muslims during the regime of pious caliphs, was freely used for private purposes by the Umayyah caliphs, and the ͨUmar II regime stopped this unholy practice and never drew a portion from the Bait al Māl. He separated the accounts for *khums*, *ṣadaqah*, and *fai* and had separate sections for each. He immediately stopped the practice of richly regarding the authors of the royal family's panegyrics from the Bait al Māl. His was proof that Umar II was careful about the poor people's prosperity. Justice was the basis of Umar II's leadership. There were no different rights and services. He forbade death and hand-cutting sentences only for unclear reasons. He said, "One must not be sentenced even only once until he has been asked (about a related case) and given defense." Up until his death, he ordered his family to give their property to the state. He even ordered to restore the rights of all the people seized by his predecessor to the state for the benefit of the people[63].

5 CONCLUSIONS

The concept of philanthropy generally means giving voluntarily. The word voluntary is not proper if we look from Islam's perspective, both in terms of its function or in terms of the history of literature. As described above, the philosophical basis of Islamic philanthropy is the "duty" of worship as a creature of God; in this case, the property is issued or recognized by the general meaning of *ṣādaqah*. From that base, there are some instruments of philanthropy, some mandatory, others voluntary. Both are in the category of Islamic philanthropy, such as *zakāh*, *waqf*, and *nadhr*. The function of philanthropy has become a principal joint economic welfare in the community. It can be seen from the function of Bait al Māl. It can be traced from the Islamic history of the reception and distribution of Bait al Māl that has functions like the National Budget nowadays when the existence of Bait al Māl at that time came from philanthropic funds. Various philanthropic motives are found in Islam. The motive is derived from Islamic law. The basis itself is better defined due to philanthropic activities. Also, Islamic philanthropic activities are influential in worship as a means to get closer to Allah, and socially, to strengthen Allah's worship, on the other side, the instruments have influenced economic and social change in a positive direction.

[63] Sayed Mahmudul Hasan, Islamic History, Delhi, 1995, Adam Publishers, pp. 338–339.

REFERENCES

Al-Qur'an. Trans. Yusuf Ali. Quran Explorer. quranexplorer.com/quran/.
Andreoni, J. (1982). Economics of Philanthropy. *The Economic Journal*, *92*(366), June.
Bill & Melinda Gates Foundation. (2011). *Building Better Lives Together*. Annual Report.
Brown, E. (2000). *Wealth, Taxes, and The New Philanthropists. Working Paper 2*. University of Southern California.
Kapstein, E. B. (2007). *Economic Justice in an Unfair World: Toward a Level Playing Field*. Princeton University Press.
Leat, D. (2016). *Philanthropic Foundations, Public Good and Public Policy*. Palgrave Macmillan.
Posner, R. A. (1981). *The Economics of Justice*. Cambridge University Press.
Rockefeller Philanthropy Advisors. The Giving Commitment: Knowing Your Motivation.
Stiglitz, J. (2002). *Globalization and Its Discontents: Unfair Fair Trade Laws and Other Mischief* (pp. 166–179). W.W. Norton.

CHAPTER 3

Mobilizing Philanthropy Instruments in Development Assistance

Salman Ahmed Shaikh

1 INTRODUCTION

According to the Global Humanitarian Assistance Report (2016), total humanitarian assistance has reached $28 billion in 2015. Out of this, 77.9% ($21.8 billion) came from government donors and only 22.1% ($6.2 billion) was contributed by private donors. The 45% shortfall was recorded—the largest for the current decade. Due to the enormity of the humanitarian crisis caused by conflicts, wars, terrorism, and climate change, there is a dire need to scale up efforts. Humanitarian aid is largely funded by governments, whereas philanthropy largely emanates from private donors, that is individuals and organizations. If private philanthropists are also engaged in mobilizing funds for humanitarian aid, then the scale of resources can be enhanced more effectively.

In comparison to the poverty gap, a lot remains to be done. Total humanitarian assistance is less than 10% of the total poverty gap funding

---

S. A. Shaikh (✉)
Islamic Economics Project, Karachi, Pakistan
e-mail: salman@siswa.ukm.edu.my

© The Author(s), under exclusive license to Springer Nature Switzerland AG 2022
A. G. Ismail et al. (eds.), *Islamic Philanthropy*, Palgrave Studies in Islamic Banking, Finance, and Economics,
https://doi.org/10.1007/978-3-031-06890-4_3

requirement. Total humanitarian assistance accounted for 4.8% of the total resource flows for the 20 countries receiving the most humanitarian assistance in 2014. Much of the resource flows that helped the recipient countries were concentrated in the form of debts, foreign direct investment, and remittances. To change matters, the policies need prioritization of values that elevate the status of human dignity in development discourse, policies, and assessment.

The concept of economic development has evolved consistently since the middle of the twentieth century. The early concept of development treated economic growth and economic development as synonymous. Economic growth was considered as both a necessary as well as sufficient condition for realizing economic development. Nonetheless, later on, it was realized that economic growth does not necessarily lead to economic development. Institutions and economic structures matter a great deal in determining the long-term effects of any growth strategy. The growth that raises income inequalities eventually becomes unsustainable and can undermine the democracy and overall well-being of the society.

Haq (1963) introduced the term 'functional inequality' in the 1960s. The term implies that income inequality has a useful economic function in patronizing a small industrial class that is allowed to grow and reap benefits of favourable policies that lead to them reaping higher profits and stimulating growth. When the benefits of that economic growth trickle down to the people who are at the bottom of the social hierarchy, then the masses also benefit. Thus, income inequality performs an important function of economic growth that is hoped to be inclusive eventually as the promised trickledown effect materializes. However, the social utility of greed could not fulfil the promise of the 'trickledown effect' in most of the economic growth stories, especially in Asia. Consequently, Haq (1995) accepted that humans are the 'means' as well as the 'ends' of any development process or policy. He reasoned that the 'ends' cannot be sacrificed for the future. If we ignore the 'ends', then it undermines the entire development process. Development process or policy shall serve human well-being as an end objective rather than treating humans as inputs to the production process and target market for conspicuous consumption.

In fostering sustainable and inclusive development, this chapter discusses the solutions offered by Islamic finance through its underpinning value system and worldview and through its set of commercial and social finance institutions to intervene in development assistance through and beyond markets. Section 2 discusses the Islamic injunctions of pure altruism that enforce the need for sharing and giving to poor people and social causes. The chapter also takes note of the ground realities of poverty and underdevelopment in Muslim-majority countries in Sect. 3. Section 4 looks at the state of development assistance and debt servicing in selected Organization of Islamic Cooperation (OIC) countries. Section 5 discusses the role of Islamic capital markets to help in mobilizing development funds for financing development infrastructure. Finally, Sect. 6 discusses the role of Islamic social and redistributive institutions to effectively mobilize, institutionalize, and utilize social savings at the micro level.

2 Islamic Worldview and Teachings on Philanthropy

The theistic concepts of Tawheed, Khilafah, and Akhirah provide the philosophical basis for the Islamic way of life. Belief in the single source of creation defies the racial, ethnic, or gender basis of discrimination. According to the Islamic worldview, all living and non-living things are created by Allah. As creatures of Allah, animals and plants are partners to humans in this world when it comes to sharing the planet and using the resources bestowed by Allah (Mian et al., 2013).

Simultaneously, the concept of Khilafah raises the stature of humans as moral beings with an inbuilt and active conscience that provides them with the ability to differentiate moral from immoral acts. Some Qur'anic passages suggest that moral conscience is inbuilt in humans (e.g. Al-Shams 8). Islamic principles inculcate the responsibility of custodianship, trusteeship, and stewardship in human beings with regards to the use and ownership of physical property and environmental resources.

The two-worldly view of life in Islam extends the decision horizon of humans. While the concept of Tawheed creates an equal basis for humans to use what is bestowed in nature, the concept of Khilafah engenders stewardship towards the responsible use of natural and environmental resources without pushing planetary boundaries, causing precious loss of biodiversity and ignoring the plight of fellow human beings who are suffering from lack of necessities in life.

The moral institutions in the Islamic framework govern all human economic activities ranging from the pursuit of earning incomes to spending these incomes. In the pursuit of earning a living, the Islamic principles emphasize productive enterprise and the avoidance of extractive and immoral means of earning. In consumption and spending activities, the Islamic moral injunctions influence preferences through moral filtering of the consumption set. The moral philosophy imbued with a socio-ethical spirit extends the decision horizon of consumers. It encourages the transformation of self-centred self-interest into self-cum-social-centric self-interest. Islamic moral injunctions explicitly extol virtuous philanthropy. Finally, by flattening all other bases of distinction except based on piety, the Islamic values garner contentment and modesty. Through this, the consumer is urged to shun envious and conspicuous consumption of luxuries.

In neoclassical economics, Andreoni (1989, 1990) explains that people engage in impure altruism when they contribute through charity or donate public goods since these charitable acts also emanate from self-interest, that is to get fame, satisfy ego, or change the living environment to improve one's own social experience and relations. On the other hand, Islamic economic principles have reformative content that lacks in neoclassical economics (Hasan, 2005). Islamic morality warms the cold economic calculus so that all human endeavours shall not just be seen in the light of pleasure–pain calculus (Naqvi, 1997). Islam does not recognize impure altruism to satisfy ego and to achieve fame and recognition (Al-Baqarah 264; Al-Maoon 6). Prophet Muhammad (pbuh) advised anonymity and secrecy in charitable giving such that the right hand does not know what the left hand is giving.[1] Allah says of the ideal believers in Qur'an: "And they give food, despite their love for it to Miskin (poor), the orphan, and the captive. (Saying): 'We feed you seeking Allah's countenance only. We wish for no reward, nor thanks from you'" (Al-Insaan 8–9). The Qur'an urges believers to spend what they love to achieve righteousness (Al-Imran: 92), spend throughout their lives (Al-Munafiqun 10), and the ideal is to spend whatever is beyond their needs (Al-Baqarah 219).

The Qur'an urges Muslims to show kindness, generosity, and benevolence to their fellow human beings. Allah says in the Qur'an, "Do good to parents, kinsfolk, orphans, Al-Masakin (the poor), the neighbour who is near to kin, the neighbour who is a stranger, the companion by your side and the wayfarer (you meet)" (Al-Nisa 36). The Qur'an says in another place, "So give to the kindred his due, and Al-Miskin (the poor) and the wayfarer" (Ar-Rum 38). Feeding orphans and the poor is regarded as a highly virtuous act (Al-Balad 12–16) in the Qur'an. The Qur'an exhorts

---

[1] Al-Muslim, Book of Zakat, vol. 3, Hadith no. 2380.

Muslim to look after orphans and treat them with kindness and generosity (Al-Fajr 17–20), work honestly in their property (Al-Baqarah 220), and avoid oppressive treatment (Al-Dhuha 9) as well as harsh behaviour (Al-Maoon 2). The Qur'an strictly prohibits usurping the endowments of orphans (Al-Nisa 2).

Prophet Muhammad (pbuh) declared that the best charity is to spend (in charity) while you are healthy, aspiring, hoping to survive, and fearing poverty, and not delaying until death comes to you.[2] Allah wants the believers to avoid miserliness (Al-Nisa 37). Instead of enjoining miserliness, Islam urges Muslims to help one another in good acts and endeavours (Al-Maida 2). Mutual cooperation and collective response are needed to tackle enormous development and humanitarian challenges.

Since Islam only accepts pure altruism, it promises numerous incentives for it in its two-worldly view of life. Several verses in the Qur'an promise due reward for pure altruism (Al-Tauba 121; Fatir 29; Al-Hadid 7). In several other verses, spending in charitable ways for the sake of Allah is compared to a good loan that Allah will repay with a manifold increase (Al-Hadid 11; Al-Hadid 18; Al-Taghabun 17; Al-Muzammil 20). In several Ahadith also, Muslims are encouraged to spend so that Allah also spends on them with His blessings.[3]

Thus, we see that the Islamic moral principles emphasize moral choices in the socio-economic sphere of life and the Islamic view of life encourages empathy, commitment, and responsibility in human behaviour.

3   State of Underdevelopment in the Muslim World

A number of Muslim-majority countries face a very high incidence of poverty. Muslim countries in the African continent in particular have a high incidence of poverty. In at least four Muslim-majority countries in Africa, the poverty headcount ratio at national poverty lines exceeds half of the total population: Guinea Bissau (69.3), Togo (58.7), Sierra Leone (56.8), and Mozambique (54.7) (see Table 3.1). Muslim countries in South Asia

---

[2] Sunan Abu Daud, Book of Wills, vol. 3, Hadith no. 2865. Also Sunan An Nisai, Book of Zakat, vol. 3, Hadith no. 2543.

[3] Al-Bukhari, Book of Commentary, vol. 6, Hadith no. 4684. Also in Al-Muslim, Book of Zakah, vol. 3, Hadith no. 2308. Also in Sunan Ibn-e-Maja, Chapters on Expiation, vol. 3, Hadith no. 2123.

Table 3.1 Poverty head count ratio (PHCR) in selected OIC countries

Country	PHCR-National (%)	Country	PHCR-National (%)
Guinea-Bissau	69.3	Egypt	32.5
Togo	58.7	Lebanon	28.6
Sierra Leone	56.8	Tajikistan	26.3
Mozambique	54.7	Bangladesh	24.3
Afghanistan	54.5	Kyrgyz Republic	22.4
Gambia	48.4	Pakistan	22.3
Senegal	46.7	Uganda	21.4
Sudan	46.5	Iraq	18.9
Guinea	43.7	Bosnia	17.9
Chad	42.3	Uzbekistan	16
Mali	42.1	Jordan	15.7
Burkina Faso	41.4	Tunisia	15.5
Niger	40.8	Turkey	14.4
Nigeria	40.1	Albania	14.3
Cameroon	39.9	Indonesia	9.8
Benin	38.5	Morocco	8.9
Syria	35.2	Malaysia	5.6
Yemen	34.8	Kazakhstan	2.5
Gabon	33.4		

Source: World Development Indicators 2019

like Afghanistan (54.5), Bangladesh (24.3), and Pakistan (22.3) also face a high incidence of poverty. Muslim countries with the lowest poverty headcount ratio include Kazakhstan (2.5) and Malaysia (5.6). Table 3.1 illustrates that at least 26 OIC countries have a poverty headcount ratio of over 20% and 14 such countries have a poverty headcount ratio of over 40%.

Poverty results in worsening other areas of development. Poor people face greater vulnerability to malnutrition and remain uneducated due to non-affordability. Their low levels of skill and lack of funds to engage in entrepreneurship make it difficult for them to achieve socio-economic mobility.

Table 3.2 presents the ranking of OIC countries on the 2019 Human Development Index within the OIC and the World group. None of the OIC countries features in the top 30 countries with the highest HDI value. The bottom 39 countries on HDI feature 24 OIC countries. This shows that a high incidence of income poverty correlates with a lower level of human development in the case of OIC countries.

Table 3.2 Overall and relative ranking of selected OIC countries on HDI

Country	HDI value	HDI rank	OIC rank	Country	HDI value	HDI rank	OIC rank
UAE	0.89	31	1	Guyana	0.682	122	29
Saudi Arabia	0.854	40	2	Iraq	0.674	123	30
Bahrain	0.852	42	3	Tajikistan	0.668	125	31
Qatar	0.848	45	4	Bangladesh	0.632	133	32
Brunei	0.838	47	5	Syria	0.567	151	33
Kazakhstan	0.825	51	6	Cameroon	0.563	153	34
Turkey	0.82	54	7	Pakistan	0.557	154	35
Oman	0.813	60	8	Comoros	0.554	156	36
Malaysia	0.81	62	9	Mauritania	0.546	157	37
Kuwait	0.806	64	10	Benin	0.545	158	38
Albania	0.795	69	11	Uganda	0.544	159	39
Iran	0.783	70	12	Nigeria	0.539	161	40
Bosnia	0.78	73	13	Ivory Coast	0.538	162	41
Azerbaijan	0.756	88	14	Djibouti	0.524	166	42
Algeria	0.748	91	15	Togo	0.515	167	43
Lebanon	0.744	92	16	Senegal	0.512	168	44
Maldives	0.74	95	17	Afghanistan	0.511	169	45
Tunisia	0.74	95	18	Sudan	0.51	170	46
Suriname	0.738	97	19	Gambia	0.496	172	47
Jordan	0.729	102	20	Guinea-Bissau	0.48	175	48
Libya	0.724	105	21	Guinea	0.477	178	49
Uzbekistan	0.72	106	22	Yemen	0.47	179	50
Indonesia	0.718	107	23	Mozambique	0.456	181	51
Turkmenistan	0.715	111	24	Burkina Faso	0.452	182	52
Egypt	0.707	116	25	Sierra Leone	0.452	182	53
Gabon	0.703	119	26	Mali	0.434	184	54
Kyrgyzstan	0.697	120	27	Chad	0.398	187	55
Morocco	0.686	121	28	Niger	0.394	189	56

Source: World Development Indicators 2019

The recent geopolitical conflicts and natural calamities have resulted in an increased number of internally displaced persons. For Yemen, Afghanistan, Nigeria, Sudan, Iraq, and Turkey, the number of internally displaced persons due to conflicts and violence stands at 3.64 million, 3 million, 2.58 million, 2.13 million 1.6 million, and 1.1 million, respectively, in 2019.

The high incidence of poverty, lower chances of socio-economic mobility, and lack of jobs to unemployed people in poor Muslim-majority countries have resulted in massive emigration. Europe and North America had been the most lucrative destinations to seek work. The remittances of the Muslim diaspora in Europe and North America constitute a major source of income for the families back home. However, with a gradual shift of economic and trade dominance from Europe and North America towards East Asia, migration within the OIC countries takes greater significance given the rising anti-globalization, protectionism, and pro-nationalism trends.

Table 3.3 shows the net migration in selected OIC countries based on five-year estimates. As per World Development Indicators, net migration is the net total of migrants during the period, that is, the total number of

Table 3.3 Net migration in selected OIC countries

Country	Net migration	Country	Net migration
Syrian Arab Republic	(2,136,954)	Tunisia	(20,000)
Bangladesh	(1,847,503)	Kyrgyz Republic	(20,000)
Pakistan	(1,166,895)	Guinea	(20,000)
Indonesia	(494,777)	Gambia	(15,436)
Afghanistan	(314,602)	Benin	(10,000)
Nigeria	(300,000)	Comoros	(10,000)
Iran	(274,998)	Togo	(9999)
Morocco	(257,096)	Libya	(9997)
Sudan	(250,001)	Guinea-Bissau	(6996)
Mali	(200,000)	Suriname	(4999)
Egypt	(190,164)	Djibouti	4501
Lebanon	(150,060)	Azerbaijan	6002
Yemen	(150,000)	Chad	10,000
Burkina Faso	(125,000)	Gabon	16,301
Bosnia and Herzegovina	(107,926)	Niger	20,001
Senegal	(100,001)	Mauritania	25,002
Tajikistan	(99,999)	Iraq	39,171
Kazakhstan	(90,000)	Jordan	51,099
Albania	(69,998)	Maldives	56,851
West Bank and Gaza	(52,816)	Kuwait	197,600
Algeria	(50,002)	Qatar	200,000
Uzbekistan	(44,314)	United Arab Emirates	200,000
Cote d'Ivoire	(40,000)	Bahrain	239,000
Guyana	(30,001)	Malaysia	249,999
Turkmenistan	(25,001)	Oman	437,000
Mozambique	(25,000)	Saudi Arabia	674,895
Cameroon	(24,000)	Uganda	843,469
Sierra Leone	(21,000)	Turkey	1,419,610

Source: World Development Indicators 2017

immigrants less the annual number of emigrants, including both citizens and non-citizens.

We can see that people from densely populated poor countries like Bangladesh, Pakistan, and Indonesia tend to migrate to other countries for searching better chances of earning incomes that can help them sustain themselves and their families back home. Countries hit by conflicts such as Syria, Sudan, and Yemen have also seen significant negative net migration. Countries with positive net migration absorb more immigrants as compared to the number of domestic emigrants they send across borders. Most of the OIC countries with positive net migration are the rich Middle Eastern countries, such as Jordan, Kuwait, Qatar, UAE, Bahrain, Oman, and Saudi Arabia. On the other hand, Turkey and Malaysia also have a significantly positive net migration.

4 Current State of Development Assistance in OIC Countries

This section looks at the current state of development assistance in selected OIC countries. Table 3.4 presents the net Official Development Assistance (ODA) received by OIC countries as a percentage of Gross National Income (GNI) and Gross Fixed Capital Formation (GFCF). It can be seen that for poor and conflict-hit areas like Afghanistan and Yemen, the net ODA received as a percentage of total GNI is greater than 20%. Nonetheless, the OIC countries with the greatest number of poor people like Bangladesh, Nigeria, Pakistan, and Indonesia only receive 1.06%, 0.87%, 0.44%, and 0.09%, respectively, net ODA as a percentage of GNI.

Table 3.5 shows the debt service burden on OIC countries in terms of how much of their exports and GNI is paid as interest and principal repayments on debt. It can be noticed that countries with a high incidence of poverty like Pakistan, Indonesia, and Bangladesh pay 35%, 39%, and 13%, respectively, of their export proceeds in debt service payments alone. Out of 42 countries for which this data are available, there are 12 OIC countries whose debt service payments alone exceed 5% of GNI. If these countries receive interest-free loans or loans at concessional terms, their debt service burden can be significantly reduced and the savings can be used for funding development projects. On the other hand, it can be noticed from Table 3.4 that there are at least 14 OIC countries that receive net ODA lower than 1% of their GNI. This suggests that in some OIC countries, the

Table 3.4 Official Development Assistance (ODA) received in selected OIC countries

Country	Net ODA (% GNI)	Net ODA (% GFCF)	Country	Net ODA (% GNI)	Net ODA (% GFCF)
Afghanistan	20.43	–	Kyrgyz Rep.	5.16	13.88
Albania	2.27	9.39	Lebanon	2.60	12.42
Algeria	0.08	0.17	Malaysia	-0.01	-0.04
Azerbaijan	0.19	0.89	Maldives	2.48	4.34
Bangladesh	1.06	3.55	Mali	9.01	42.73
Benin	4.04	15.16	Mauritania	6.38	14.15
Bosnia	1.75	8.06	Morocco	0.70	2.06
Burkina Faso	7.22	30.43	Mozambique	12.51	24.49
Cameroon	3.07	13.20	Niger	8.92	32.18
Chad	7.90	37.33	Nigeria	0.87	4.20
Comoros	7.31	49.07	Pakistan	0.44	2.50
Ivory Coast	1.71	7.75	Senegal	4.38	13.50
Djibouti	5.70	104.59	Sierra Leone	13.32	71.03
Egypt	0.85	4.96	Sudan	2.97	24.05
Gabon	0.74	3.16	Suriname	0.42	–
Gambia	14.17	66.69	Tajikistan	4.54	16.87
Guinea	5.51	28.61	Togo	5.51	21.82
Guinea-Bissau	10.46	95.88	Tunisia	2.10	9.66
Guyana	2.15	–	Turkey	0.15	0.52
Indonesia	0.09	0.26	Turkmenistan	0.05	–
Iran	0.04	0.10	Uganda	6.07	23.65
Iraq	1.03	7.97	Uzbekistan	1.07	2.93
Jordan	5.91	31.09	Gaza	11.75	48.59
Kazakhstan	0.05	0.17	Yemen	34.02	–

Source: World Development Indicators 2018

net outflow of resources in the form of interest payments would be greater than inflows received in the form of development assistance.

Table 3.6 reveals that out of 41 countries for which this data are available, 21 countries have a positive difference between Debt Servicing Payment as a percentage of GNI and Net ODA as a percentage of GNI. The remaining 20 countries have a negative difference. Countries with a positive difference have a better capacity to source development finance through capital markets by issuing Sukuk, whereas countries with

Table 3.5 Total debt service (% of exports and GNI) for selected OIC countries

Country	Debt service (% of exports)	Debt service (% of GNI)	Country	Debt service (% of exports)	Debt service (% of GNI)
Afghanistan	2.98	0.28	Kazakhstan	48.11	20.61
Albania	12.30	4.31	Kyrgyz Rep.	18.15	7.24
Algeria	0.51	0.12	Lebanon	88.21	36.32
Azerbaijan	8.58	4.70	Maldives	12.18	9.01
Bangladesh	12.82	1.82	Mali	4.83	1.35
Benin	5.85	3.61	Mauritania	14.07	5.10
Bosnia	11.01	4.73	Morocco	9.19	3.51
Burkina Faso	3.03	1.02	Mozambique	16.42	6.47
Cameroon	14.11	3.03	Niger	7.85	1.15
Chad	–	1.41	Nigeria	7.09	1.18
Comoros	3.10	0.40	Pakistan	35.35	4.03
Ivory Coast	12.35	5.27	Senegal	14.33	4.10
Djibouti	1.52	2.47	Sierra Leone	7.66	1.59
Egypt	16.10	3.01	Sudan	4.92	0.68
Gabon	–	4.24	Tajikistan	19.30	5.89
Gambia	13.41	2.65	Togo	6.84	2.13
Guinea	2.52	0.85	Tunisia	15.74	8.28
Guinea-Bissau	3.29	1.18	Turkey	34.29	11.60
Guyana	7.65	2.71	Uganda	4.85	0.88
Indonesia	39.42	7.53	Uzbekistan	13.19	4.48
Iran	0.46	–	Yemen	14.56	0.51
Jordan	19.17	7.56			

Source: World Development Indicators 2019

a negative difference would require support from Islamic social finance and non-commercial development assistance. In light of this, Sect. 5 explicates the use of Sovereign Sukuk in sourcing development finance from the capital markets. On the other hand, Sect. 6 discusses the role of Islamic social finance in regions where governments have less capacity to undertake debt commitments and where the role of third-sector institutions is vital to complement the government in meeting development needs through non-market-based non-commercial assistance.

Table 3.6 Debt service (% of GNI) and net ODA (%of GNI) for selected OIC countries

Country	Net ODA (% GNI)	Debt service % of GNI	Difference
Lebanon	2.60	36.32	33.72
Kazakhstan	0.05	20.61	20.57
Turkey	0.15	11.60	11.45
Indonesia	0.09	7.53	7.44
Maldives	2.48	9.01	6.53
Tunisia	2.10	8.28	6.19
Azerbaijan	0.19	4.70	4.52
Pakistan	0.44	4.03	3.59
Gabon	0.74	4.24	3.51
Uzbekistan	1.07	4.48	3.41
Bosnia and Herzegovina	1.75	4.73	2.98
Morocco	0.70	3.51	2.81
Egypt	0.85	3.01	2.16
Kyrgyz Republic	5.16	7.24	2.08
Albania	2.27	4.31	2.05
Jordan	5.91	7.56	1.65
Tajikistan	4.54	5.89	1.35
Bangladesh	1.06	1.82	0.76
Guyana	2.15	2.71	0.55
Nigeria	0.87	1.18	0.31
Algeria	0.08	0.12	0.03
Cameroon	3.07	3.03	-0.04
Senegal	4.38	4.10	-0.28
Benin	4.04	3.61	-0.43
Mauritania	6.38	5.10	-1.28
Sudan	2.97	0.68	-2.29
Djibouti	5.70	2.47	-3.23
Togo	5.51	2.13	-3.37
Guinea	5.51	0.85	-4.65
Uganda	6.07	0.88	-5.19
Mozambique	12.51	6.47	-6.04
Burkina Faso	7.22	1.02	-6.20
Chad	7.90	1.41	-6.50
Comoros	7.31	0.40	-6.90
Mali	9.01	1.35	-7.66
Niger	8.92	1.15	-7.77
Guinea-Bissau	10.46	1.18	-9.28
Gambia	14.17	2.65	-11.52
Sierra Leone	13.32	1.59	-11.73
Afghanistan	20.43	0.28	-20.15
Yemen	34.02	0.51	-33.51

Source: World Development Indicators 2019

5 Role of Sovereign Sukuk in Sourcing Development Funds

In what follows, the widely used Sukuk structures in practice are briefly explained and illustrated for use by the government to mobilize development funds through Islamic capital markets.

5.1 Ijarah Sukuk

A typical Ijarah Sukuk would be structured like this. For example, if the government needs to build industrial zones on industrial real estate, it will use Sukuk that can be purchased by institutional and/or retail investors. A Special Purpose Vehicle (SPV) is usually established for the issuance of Sukuk certificates. The government will sell industrial real estate to the SPV. The SPV will issue Sukuk to the investors. Sukuk represents the part ownership of the Sukuk holder in the industrial real estate. By purchasing the Sukuk certificates, the Sukuk holders would become part owners of the industrial real estate. The SPV will use the Sukuk proceeds to pay the price of industrial real estate purchased from the government. Then, the SPV would provide the industrial real estate on a lease basis to the government by using the Ijarah mode of financing. The rent received by the SPV from the lease of industrial real estate will be distributed among the Sukuk holders who own the industrial real estate. The maturity of Sukuk and the lease term would usually coincide. At the end of the lease period, the SPV will sell the industrial real estate to the government on behalf of Sukuk holders and the sale proceeds will be distributed among the Sukuk holders. The cash flows at the end would usually enable the Sukuk holders to recoup their original investments with income arising as rents during the lease period. Figure 3.1 gives the structure of Ijarah Sukuk.

5.2 Mudarabah Sukuk

This Sukuk structure is used when there is a need for obtaining financing on an equity basis rather than debt. This is suitable for countries where governments cannot meet commercial debt commitments. In this Sukuk structure, the Originator (government in this case) requiring financing does not invest capital of its own. The structure of Mudarabah Sukuk involves these steps. The SPV issues Sukuk to which the investors subscribe and pay the proceeds to the SPV. Then, the SPV and the Originator

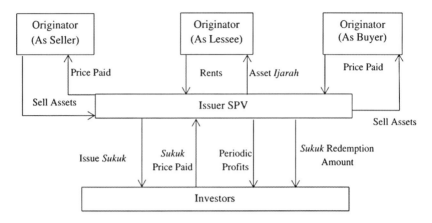

Fig. 3.1 Ijarah Sukuk structure

enter into a Mudarabah agreement with the Originator as Mudarib and SPV as Rabb-al-Mal. The Originator, as Mudarib under the Mudarabah Agreement, agrees to contribute its expertise and management skills to the Shari'ah-compliant Mudarabah enterprise with responsibility for managing the Rabb-al-Mal's capital under specified investment parameters. Profits generated by the Mudarabah enterprise are divided between the SPV (as Rabb-al-Mal) and Originator (as Mudarib) under the profit-sharing ratios set out in the Mudarabah Agreement.

When the SPV receives the Mudarabah profits, it will pass it on to the Sukuk investors. On maturity of the Mudarabah Sukuk, the Mudarabah enterprise would be dissolved under the terms of the Mudarabah agreement. The Originator will buy the Mudarabah equity capital of SPV at market value so that the proceeds can be used by the SPV to service the outstanding amounts due to the investors. The investors would be entitled to a return comprising their pro-rata share of the market value of the liquidated Mudarabah capital. Figure 3.2 gives the structure of Mudarabah Sukuk.

This Sukuk is suitable in cases where global development finance institutions like the Islamic Development Bank, Asian Development Bank, and World Bank want to provide finance in energy and transportation projects that have the potential to generate revenues from services. Such revenues can provide returns to the Sukuk holders and also achieve social impact through funding these development projects.

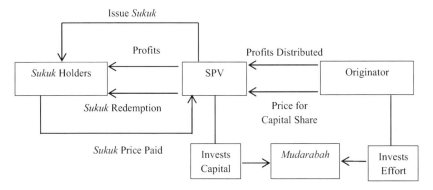

Fig. 3.2 Mudarabah Sukuk structure

5.3 Musharakah Sukuk

Like Mudarabah Sukuk, this Sukuk structure is used when there is a need for obtaining financing on an equity basis rather than debt. In this Sukuk structure, the Originator (government in this case) requiring financing also needs capital of its own to invest in Musharakah. This is suitable in financing development projects in the energy, transport, and communications sector with a public–private partnership. The structure of Musharakah Sukuk involves these steps.

The SPV issues Sukuk to which the investors subscribe and pay the price to the SPV for the purchase of Musharakah Sukuk certificates. Then, the SPV enters into a Musharakah agreement with the Originator. The SPV contributes the proceeds from the issuance of the Sukuk into the Musharakah and is allocated some units in the Musharakah in proportion to its capital contribution. On each periodic distribution date, the SPV shall receive a pre-agreed percentage share of the expected profits generated by the Musharakah assets. In the case that the Musharakah assets generate a loss, the SPV shall share that loss in proportion with its capital contribution to the Musharakah. Upon receiving its profit share, the SPV will share the profits with the Sukuk holders. At maturity, the SPV will sell the Musharakah assets at the applicable exercise price to the Originator. Upon receiving the price for the Musharakah assets sold to the Originator, the SPV will pay the Sukuk price to the investors to process redemption. Figure 3.3 gives the structure of Musharakah Sukuk.

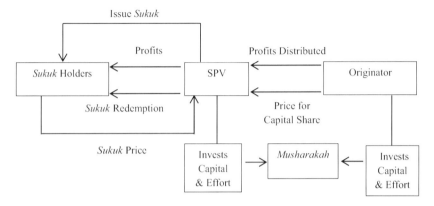

Fig. 3.3 Musharakah Sukuk structure

6 ROLE OF ISLAMIC SOCIAL FINANCE IN SUSTAINABLE DEVELOPMENT

Since the gap to fill in underdevelopment is huge in the case of most of the Muslim-majority countries, all-encompassing efforts must be undertaken involving all sorts of institutions to make the largest leap forward. Religious institutions that have a socio-economic character can also be employed in creating synergistic efforts towards achieving the development objectives, especially in Muslim-majority countries.

Governments in developing countries have much more distance to travel in achieving the development targets and yet they generally have a weak tax base to work with. Because of the transformative and sustainable nature of the new development agenda, all possible resources must be mobilized if the world is to succeed in meeting its development targets. The financial crisis of 2007–09 and subsequent contagion effects have not helped in improving the commitment to provide 0.7% of Gross National Income as Official ODA by the developed countries to the underdeveloped ones. With resources allocated to development by donor countries remaining insufficient coupled with the headwinds of financial and economic crises affecting many countries worldwide, it is important to explore alternative and complementary innovative financing mechanisms, such as Islamic social finance and redistributive institutions.

Islamic social finance package include institutions like Zakat, Waqf, and microfinance, which can cater to the financially excluded households who are missed by the commercial banks. Wilson (2007) also contends that microfinance is best provided by non-banking institutions. Sadiq and Mushtaq (2015) suggest that Zakat and Waqf-based microfinance institutions can be used to serve the social sector. Real estate-based Waqf can generate proceeds through the rental of properties, which then can be used to finance social and development needs. Cash and commodity-based Waqf can provide interest-free loans (Qard Hassan) to the needy in sectors like education, health, and agriculture. On the other hand, Takaful is an insurance concept based on the principles of shared responsibility, solidarity, and cooperation.

6.1 The Role of Zakat in Development Assistance

If we look at the institution of Zakat, we find that the payer of Zakat and the receiver of Zakat belong to two different income classes. The payer of Zakat is non-poor with surplus wealth above Nisab (wealth equal to 612 grams of silver). On the other hand, the receiver of Zakat is usually a poor person with no surplus wealth above Nisab. Thus, the threshold wealth of Nisab makes a distinction between the payer and receiver and helps to achieve targeted income and wealth transfer to the people who are usually poor.

Since this redistribution is based on wealth rather than income alone, it can achieve the redistribution objectives more effectively and consistently since wealth fluctuates much less than income over the business cycles. Metwally (1983) argues that Zakat has a wider base and it applies to both the incomes and the wealth. He emphasizes that the Zakat system has an inbuilt mechanism to reach the right targets in terms of Zakat collection and disbursement. This ensures increasing the propensity to consume more emphatically and quickly.

Furthermore, the accumulated wealth can be much more than the single-period income, especially among the high net-worth individuals of a society. That is why, in the absence of broad-based wealth taxes and loopholes in taxing off-shore wealth, the progressive income taxes alone have been unable to reduce income inequality and achieve wealth redistribution. Hartman (2002) cites the case of the US economy and argues that progressive taxes were designed to reduce income inequality. But during the last four decades, while the share of income taxes levied on the upper tenth of incomes rose 15%, the after-tax income share of the remainder of incomes declined by 13%.

Oxfam (2019) reports that 26 individual persons have as much wealth as the bottom 50% of the entire global population. As per the World Bank, there are 600 million people living below the poverty line of $1.90 per day. It means that poverty gap is $416.1 billion (1.90 × 00,000,000 × 365) per year. Comparing the wealth owned by only the richest 26 persons ($1.4 trillion and the total global poverty gap funding requirement ($416.1 billion)), one can see how redistribution of wealth can help in pooling poverty alleviation funds.

According to the Food and Agricultural Organization (FAO), there are approximately 828 million people who suffer from hunger and are food-insecure in their routine lives. The COVID-19 pandemic is estimated to have pushed as many as 100 million to extreme poverty due to the severity of the economic contraction.

Most poor countries lack basic resources to kick-start growth and to invest in health and education. Thus, the redistribution of resources is vital to enhance income as well as the capacity to earn sustainable incomes, which requires income support programmes, basic health and education, as well as microfinance to build small enterprises.

According to The Hunger Project, 2.4 billion people do not have adequate sanitation and each day, nearly 1000 children die due to preventable water and sanitation-related diarrheal diseases. It is partly because sanitation is not good business as compared to cellular services and life's other comforts and luxuries. Interestingly, according to the Food and Agricultural Organization (2015), for the world as a whole, per capita food supply rose from about 2200 kcal per day in the early 1960s to more than 2903 kcal per day by 2014. The institution of Zakat could help in providing income support to the poor people who are food-insecure due to lower and unsustainable incomes.

Nearly 50% of the people living in extreme poverty are 18 years old or younger. This goes to show that a significant portion of our global population do not have a fair start to achieve socio-economic mobility. Thus, proper nourishment, basic medicines, and vaccinations are necessary to avoid ill-health, stunting, and loss of capacities for independent productive living in adulthood. Some life-saving medicines cost less than a dollar, but they are underprovided due to commercial reasons. Unless effective redistribution happens, the purchasing power that is vital to afford even the most basic necessities of today, such as food, water, and medicine, cannot be enhanced.

Providing quality education is vital for achieving permanent poverty exit, enhancement of skills and capacities, and ensuring upward social mobility. Financial institutions can come to the rescue once the people can hold enough assets and skills for entrepreneurship. But, much before that, people require survival and human capital development in the early stages of life. There are mosque-based schools in the Muslim-majority countries that effectively channelize Zakat funds to ensure basic religious and secular education. Effective administration and management of the Zakat funds can help in scaling up the benefits in terms of strengthening institutions to create synergistic effects.

Decent work and economic growth are necessary to realize a sustainable reduction in poverty and in ensuring upward socio-economic mobility. On one hand, Zakat from endowment-surplus households (those having higher wealth than Nisab) to the endowment-deficient households can help in providing income support and affordability for skills-enhancement programmes. Zakat could also be used to provide funding for education and health institutions, thereby contributing to human capital development that can provide decent work. On the other hand, the institution of Zakat would ensure the circulation of wealth in the productive enterprise, thereby directing capital to go in the real sector of the economy rather than sitting idle in the hands of wealthy individuals.

In an empirical study, Shaikh (2016) estimates the potential Zakat collectible in 17 OIC member countries and concludes that the Zakat-to-GDP ratio exceeds the poverty gap index to GDP (PGI–GDP) ratio in all but three countries, with the poverty line defined at $1.25 a day. The study also found that the Zakat-to-GDP ratio exceeds the PGI–GDP ratio, except in four countries with the poverty line defined at $2.00 a day. The results also show that the aggregate resources pooled together from the potential Zakat collection in 17 OIC countries will be enough to fund resources for poverty alleviation in all 17 OIC countries combined.

6.2 The Role of Waqf in Mobilizing and Institutionalizing Philanthropy

Waqf is an important social institution in the Islamic framework. In the institution of Waqf, an owner donates and dedicates a movable or immovable asset for perpetual societal benefit. The beneficiaries enjoy its usufruct and/or income perpetually. Waqf can be established either by dedicating real estate, furniture, or fixtures, other movable assets and liquid forms of money and wealth like cash and shares.

The cash Waqf can pool liquid donations to build institutions, such as schools, hospitals, and orphanages (Sadeq, 2002). Cash Waqf can pool more resources and ensure wider participation of individual donors (Aziz et al., 2013). Waqf provides flexibility in fund utilisation as compared to Zakat since Zakat funds must be utilized for specific categories of recipients. The institution of Waqf can be used to provide a wide range of welfare services, such as educational institutions, health institutions, environmental preservation programmes, and financial institutions like Waqf-based microfinance (Habib, 2007) and socially driven banks (Mohammad, 2011).

Along with income support and cash transfers, poor people also require skills and productivity enhancement to get out of poverty and achieve social mobility. Haneef et al. (2014) argue that lack of finance and business training requires institutional support to unleash the potentials of micro-entrepreneurs and to establish viable micro-enterprises. Obaidullah (2008) explains that growth-oriented microfinance programmes also need to provide training, insurance, and skills-enhancement facilities. In this regard, the institution of Waqf can improve the chances of socio-economic mobility by providing a rather permanent, effective, and efficient funding source for the health and education infrastructure. The increased and improved provision of education and health infrastructure funded through Waqf can enhance the income-earning potential of beneficiaries.

7 Conclusion

This chapter highlighted the Islamic injunctions on pure altruism and philanthropy and how the Islamic worldview and institutions can help in contributing towards the effective mobilization, institutionalization, and utilization of social savings and philanthropic and humanitarian assistance. We discussed Islamic teachings of pure altruism that enforce the need for sharing and giving to poor people and social causes. We looked at the state of development assistance and debt servicing in selected OIC countries. Some countries have the capacity to source development finance by issuing Sovereign Sukuk, whereas other countries require more focus on social finance institutions. The chapter explained that Islamic finance through its commercial and social finance options has market- and non-market-based solutions to mobilize development funds for effective and impactful utilization in socio-economic development needs.

REFERENCES

Andreoni, J. (1989). Giving with Impure Altruism: Applications to Charity and Ricardian Equivalence. *Journal of Political Economy, 97*(6), 1447–1458.
Andreoni, J. (1990). Impure Altruism and Donations to Public Goods: A Theory of Warm-Glow Giving. *Economic Journal, 100*(401), 464–477.
Aziz, M. R. A., Johari, F., & Yusof, M. A. (2013). Cash Waqf Models for Financing in Education. *Proceedings of the 5th Islamic Economic System Conference* (iECONS2013).
Food and Agriculture Organization of the United Nations. (2015). World Food and Agriculture. In *FAO Statistical Pocketbook* (p. 48). Food and Agriculture Organization: Rome.
Global Humanitarian Assistance. (2016). *Global Humanitarian Assistance Report.* Development Initiatives.
Habib, A.(2007). Waqf-based Microfinance: Realizing the Social Role of Islamic Finance. Paper Presented at the International Seminar on Integrating Awqaf in the Islamic Financial Sector, Singapore, 6–7 March.
Haneef, M. A., Muhammad, A. D., Pramanik, A. H., & Mohammed, M. O. (2014). Integrated Waqf based Islamic Microfinance Model (IWIMM) for Poverty Alleviation in OIC Member Countries. *Middle-East Journal of Scientific Research, 19*(2), 286–298.
Hasan, Z. (2005). Treatment of Consumption in Islamic Economics: An Appraisal. *Journal of King Abdul-Aziz University: Islamic Economics, 18*(2), 29 – 46.
Haq, M. (1963). *The Strategy of Economic Planning: A Case Study of Pakistan.* Oxford University Press.
Haq, M. (1995). *Reflections on Human Development.* Oxford University Press.
Hartman, D. A. (2002). Does Progressive Taxation Redistribute Income. *The Road Map to Tax Reform Series, Policy Report, 162.*
Mian, H. S., Khan, J., & Rahman, A. (2013). Environmental Ethics of Islam. *Journal of Culture, Society and Development, 1,* 69–74.
Metwally, M. M. (1983). *Fiscal Policy & Resource Allocation in Islam.* Institute of Policy Studies.
Mohammad, M. T. S. H. (2011). Towards an Islamic Social (Waqf) Bank. *International Journal of Trade, Economics and Finance, 2*(5), 381–386.
Naqvi, S. N. H. (1997). The Dimensions of an Islamic Economic Model. *Islamic Economic Studies, 4*(2), 1–24.
Obaidullah, M. (2008). Role of microfinance in poverty alleviation: lessons from experiences in selected IDB member countries, Islamic Development Bank.
Oxfam. (2019). *Oxfam Briefing Paper: An Economy for the 99%.* Oxfam GB.
Sadeq, A. M. (2002). Waqf, Perpetual Charity and Poverty Alleviation. *International Journal of Social Economics, 29*(1/2), 135–151.

Sadiq, S., & Mushtaq, A. (2015). The Role of Islamic Finance in Sustainable Development. *Journal of Islamic Thought and Civilization*, 5(1), 46–65.

Shaikh, S. A. (2016). Zakat Collectible in OIC Countries for Poverty Alleviation: A Primer on Empirical Estimation. *International Journal of Zakat*, 1(1), 17–35.

Wilson, R. (2007). Making Development Assistance Sustainable Through Islamic Microfinance. *International Journal of Economics, Management and Accounting*, 15(2), 197–217.

PART II

Waqf

CHAPTER 4

Challenges of *Waqf* Land Development in Brunei Darussalam

Rose Abdullah, Khairul Hidayatullah Basir, and Nur Haziyah Abdul Halim

1 INTRODUCTION

In Brunei Darussalam, waqf is handled and administered by the Brunei Islamic Religious Council (MUIB) under Baitulmal and waqf division based on the Islamic religious Council and Kadi Courts Act Chapter 77. The *waqf* institution can play an important role in generating economic activities and at the same time mitigating socioeconomic problems of our society.

Currently, *waqf* is only dedicated to mosques, cemeteries, religious schools, books, and worship facilities such as praying mats, which continue to dominate *waqf* donation in Brunei Hubur (2019). Despite the massive support in *waqf* usage towards religious affairs, *waqf*'s function as an economic booster has been overlooked. The importance of *waqf* in

---

R. Abdullah (✉) • K. H. Basir • N. H. Abdul Halim
Universiti Islam Sultan Sharif Ali, Bandar Seri Begawan, Brunei Darussalam
e-mail: rose.abdullah@unissa.edu.bn; hidayatullah.basir@unissa.edu.bn; haziyahhalim004@gmail.com

© The Author(s), under exclusive license to Springer Nature Switzerland AG 2022
A. G. Ismail et al. (eds.), *Islamic Philanthropy*, Palgrave Studies in Islamic Banking, Finance, and Economics,
https://doi.org/10.1007/978-3-031-06890-4_4

contributing to the economy has not received much public attention. It seems that *waqf* has become a foregone income-generating Islamic philanthropic activity capable of enhancing the economy. Little is also known about *waqf* except for its name because most Muslims cannot give both a proper definition and its role.

Waqf is an Islamic endowment system that is believed to have the capability to provide income, generating benefits to the economy and thus improving the population's standard of living. However, it is known that the utilization of *waqf* in Brunei is still underdeveloped and undiversified. Thus, this chapter studies the opportunities *waqf* land provides and investigates the constraints of *waqf* land development in Brunei, and finds ways to overcome constraints to realize the potential economic value of *waqf* lands.

This chapter uses an exploratory qualitative research methodology whereby data were sourced from in-depth interviews with relevant stakeholders and supported by secondary data. The interview was done by using several sets of semi-structured interview questions with targeted, relevant officers from several government bodies such as the *Waqf* and *Baitul Mal* Unit and *Badan Tanmiah*, MUIB, and the State Mufti's Office. Secondary data were used to support this study such as printed and published materials on the Waqf Act and data on uses of *waqf* funds in Brunei obtained from the Endowment and *Badan Tanmiah* MUIB, and Strategic Planning Unit of Town and Country Planning Department to strengthen the primary sources such as land zoning in Brunei Darussalam. This study also reviews past literatures from journal articles, conference papers, seminar papers, *fatwa* papers, and articles.

2 WAQF AND SOCIOECONOMIC DEVELOPMENT

Waqf signifies any property's dedication, either in express terms or implication, for any charitable or religious object, or to refer to a human being (Omar et al., 2014). According to Omar et al., (2014), the permanent nature of *waqf* results in the accumulation of wealth for a healthy Islamic society at large, and *waqf* properties are devoted to providing a capital asset that produces an ever-increasing flow of revenues/usufructs to serve its objectives in Islamic society. Kahf (1995) also highlighted that the vast accumulation of *waqf* plays a vital role in Muslim societies and communities' social lives.

Historically, *waqf* has contributed as a fundamental economic institution used simultaneously to generate economic activities and ensure a continuous accumulation of benefits to society (Cizakca, 1998). The dynamism of *waqf* and its mechanism could together bring about contributions to economic development. *Waqf*, as an economic booster, may reduce deficit financing, eradicating poverty and encouraging the culture of entrepreneurship and other economic activities that will enhance the country's economic progress (Budiman, 2014).

Many researchers such as Budiman (2014), Dogarawa (2009), Khan (2010), and Hossein and Zamir (2015), share the opinion that *waqf* has the ability to overcome poverty by targeting the poor as the primary recipients for its benefit and provide a better quality of life. Ika Yunia and Abdul Kadir urged that equal wealth distribution can be achieved by practicing charitable activities such as *zakat*, *waqf*, and *sadaqah* (further developed micro-scale investment). It is also believed that long-term *waqf* assets could generate income flows. These activities would help in the process of production and the creation of wealth.

Efficient and productive *waqf* management may lead the institution towards better development, enabling itself to be an employment-generating tool for society. Several kinds of investment can be developed through *waqf*, which could generate a job vacancy for the unemployed. An endowment dedicated to entrepreneurial activities such as building commercial premises may create jobs directly for society.

In Indonesia, experience has shown that *waqf* has been contributed as an employment-generating tool in the rural area through *waqf* land. These *waqf* lands have been used for agricultural activities such as developing rice fields and fishery ponds. Furthermore, cash *waqf* and other productive *waqf* have also been widely practiced in Indonesia to employ the community and improve their living standards.

In Singapore, *waqf*'s establishment has contributed to Singapore's economy, as well as to social and religious affairs. The social contribution is a distribution for the poor and needy, for medicine, scholarships, burial purposes, and other general charity. According to Abdul Karim (2010), 11% of *waqf* disbursement is allocated for the poor and needy, while 6% is allocated for other charitable purposes. The *waqf*'s economic contribution in Singapore can be seen by developing *waqf* properties such as terraced houses and large-scale projects. The development of *waqf* properties has created wealth, development, employment, and other real economic activities.

Harun et al. (2012) also pointed that *waqf* properties in Singapore have been developed to the subsidiary company's maximum level under *Majlis Ugama Islam Singapura* (MUIS), known as *Wakaf* Real Estate of Singapore. The estimated 200 *waqf* properties are worth about SG$250 million and generate a yearly rental of about SG$6 to SG$7 million. These *waqf* properties have certainly contributed to Singapore's economic development.

According to Ambrose et al. (2015), several *waqf* lands were developed in various states of Malaysia into hostels for students, low-cost housing units, medical centers for hemodialysis, and business premises for Muslims entrepreneurs. Data obtained by Omar et al. (2014) revealed that less than half of thousands of acreage of *waqf* lands in Malaysia has the potential for economic development. However, some constraints restrict the smooth flow of land supply onto the market for development purposes. Omar et al. (2014) identified the constraints associated with land administration and registration of *waqf* land, human resources, and technical expertise, which hampered the initiatives to undertake the development of potential *waqf* land for development.

The problems of *waqf* institutions exist in other countries and have also been highlighted in a number of studies. For instance, Ahmad (2019) explains that *zakat* and *waqf* institutions in Northern Nigeria have not been performing to the expectation of stakeholders, even though laws have been enacted for their administration. Sulaiman et al. (2019) observed that there have been commendable efforts to develop *waqf* institutions to harness its potential for the benefit of *ummah* (Muslim nation). However, many lands and buildings are still not well managed or are abandoned. Listiana and Alhabshi (2020) observed that there are effective governing roles in Singapore provided by MUIS as the *waqf* authority. Where there have been initiatives for new *waqf* types and the redevelopment of existing *waqf* properties.

One of the main issues related to *waqf* land is *istibdal* (substitution) and investment of *waqf* land. Hisham et al. (2013) explain that the issue of land value and its location, damages to *waqf* properties, public interest, and government development are among the problems currently faced by administrators in managing *waqf* properties. Where the location of *waqf* land is not appropriate, or otherwise, and the value from the *waqf* land cannot be exploited, *istibdal* can be proposed. Hasan and Abdullah (2008) view the concept of *istibdal* as a mechanism to gain money to finance the investment project for *waqf* institution through substitution of less beneficial *waqf* land. One such case in Penang, Malaysia, where the location of a three-house shop on Jalan Bendahara off Jalan Temenggong was commercially not strategic and *istibdal* was applied where the *waqf* assets were sold to a new tenant and the revenue derived was used to acquire a more commercially viable land and building in Taman Tasik Utama, Ayer Keroh.

Few studies on *waqf* in the context of Brunei have been done. Abdullah (2011) believes that *waqf* utilization can be further expanded by providing microfinancing to the poor and needy in their income-generating activities. Kamis (2013) found that the utilization of *waqf* in Brunei is solely prioritizing religious purposes. Abdullah and Ismail (2017) emphasized that *waqf* should not be seen as limited to the cemetery, mosques, and other non-economic uses. According to Basir and Besar (2021), the commercialization or alternative utilization of *waqf* assets to promote economic activities is yet to be explored. It should be seen as a financial mechanism capable of providing necessities and facilities to Muslim society in Brunei.

As enshrined in the Islamic Religious Council and the Supreme Court of Justice Act 77, Section 43 (1), the provisions of this Act indirectly make *istibdal waqf* inapplicable in Brunei as the final opinion of the *Shafi'e* sect states that the *waqf* land cannot be sold or replaced with other lands (Abu Bakar et al., 2020). Thus, the Brunei Government Mufti has issued a *fatwa* on this issue and has not approved the *istibdal waqf* to be practiced in Brunei, which results in undeveloped *waqf* lands that are only kept by MUIB without being developed (Abu Bakar et al., 2020). However, an earlier researcher, Abdullah (2018), stated that the law of Brunei does not provide a rigid provision. References to any other school of thought, other than Shafi'e, can be practised for the sake of public interest. Therefore, *istibdal* can be allowed with certain conditions that benefit the *waqif* and society.

3 THE CURRENT STATE OF *WAQF* IN BRUNEI DARUSSALAM

The Council's responsibilities in this respect are stipulated in the Religious Council and *Kadis*' Courts Act, Chapter 77 in Section 98 and 100. Section 98 of this Act provides that any trusts, endowments, or vows that affect the terms of this Act shall be held by the Council, which is entrusted for charitable purposes to support and develop religious benefits to Muslims in Brunei Darussalam. Also, Section 100 of the Act states that MUIB is the sole trustee body that manages the *waqf*. Therefore, any individual or private sector is restricted and cannot manage any registered *waqf* property in Brunei Darussalam.

Income generated from *waqf* activities is also restricted to this Act as stated in Section 103: "(1) The income of a wakaf khas, if received by the Majlis, shall be applied by it under the lawful provisions of such wakaf khas. (2) The income of every other wakaf and every Nazar shall be paid to and form part of the General Endowment Fund."

According to Mohd. Adly Kashfullah, a religious officer at the *Waqf* and *Baitul Mal* Unit of MUIB, it is the law that the *waqf* institution in Brunei is confined to which makes it difficult for the institution to move forward and develop further. Any kind of *waqf* innovations that do not conform to written laws could not be implemented in Brunei Darussalam. This law's general characteristic would also limit *waqf* institutional activities in Brunei, particularly for economic purposes.

Several *waqf* properties were being accepted, whether directly endowed to the *Majlis* or being informed about these endowments. Amongst the properties included are cash for charitable purposes such as construction, repairing mosques and prayer halls, cemeteries, and equipment. A land which is mostly *Waqf Khas* is compared to *Waqf Am*; vehicles dedicated for conveying dead bodies to the cemetery; electrical equipment mostly is donated and delivered to mosques, *surau* and prayer halls such as air conditioners, computers, photocopy machines, lights, public announcement system, and water dispenser; others such as religious books, chairs, tables, podiums, prayer mats, slippers, and more. These kinds of *waqf* are usually dedicated to the use of the community, mosque, *surau*, and religious schools.

As the sole trustee of *waqf* assets, MUIB has the authority to make any appropriate measures on the assets endowed to develop and expand the assets to the extent permitted by the *shariah* and approval from the highest authority the *Majlis*, His Majesty the Sultan and Yang Di-Pertuan of Brunei Darussalam.

4 *WAQF* LAND IN BRUNEI DARUSSALAM

Badan Tanmiah is an organization under MUIB responsible for managing, developing, and investing the *Baitul Mal* funds. Some investments have been made to focus on rental buildings such as building flats and shops on public *waqf* land. These buildings have been providing rental income to MUIB.

Table 4.1 shows that seven lots of land had been generally endowed. Two lots of land have been developed into a 48-unit commercial building and a 24-unit residential flat, which has been rented by the Ministry of Defense. One lot of land has been developed into a residential building, and another lot of land has been developed for mosques. Another three lots of land have been developed into passages and routes.

Although few economic activities such as investment can be seen operating within this institution, MUIB has recognized that the development of *waqf* properties in Brunei Darussalam should be pursued more actively because there is still a great deal of vacant space and efforts can be made in developing the *waqf* properties.

According to statistics from MUIB, the majority of *waqf* lands have been categorized as specific *waqf* rather than general *waqf* (refer Table 4.2). Many endowed lands that fall under *Waqf Khas* are dedicated to mosque and prayer hall sites, school sites, and cemetery sites. On the other hand, lands categorized as *Waqf Am* are being utilized for developing residential and commercial buildings.

Table 4.2 shows that 32 lots of land have been endowed and categorized as Specific *waqf*. Out of these lots of land, 29 lots have been contributed to building mosques and prayer halls. Another three lots of land were

Table 4.1 The usage of general endowed lands 2016

General waqf (Waqf Am)	Commercial buildings	Residential buildings	Mosques	Passages and routes
7 Lots	2 Lots	1 Lot	1 Lot	3 Lots

Source: *Waqf* and *Baitulmal* Unit, MUIB

Table 4.2 The usage of specific endowed lands 2016

Specific waqf (Waqf Khas)	Mosques, Surau, and prayer hall sites	Religious school sites	Cemetery sites	Passages and routes
32 Lots	29 Lots	1 Lot	1 Lot	3 Lots

Source: *Waqf* and *Baitulmal* Unit, MUIB

used to build passages and routes, whereas two lots were dedicated to building religious schools and a cemetery.

The officer from *Waqf* and *Baitul Mal* Unit, MUIB, believed that the dedication of *waqf* lands for commercial and residential purposes should be more widely practised in Brunei. It is believed that this kind of *waqf* lands can significantly benefit the economy of this country. This form of contribution by *waqf* land is also encouraged by the Deputy Land Commissioner of Lands Department. However, it is noted that in the current state of the economy that potential endowers in Brunei are less inclined to endow their lands for this purpose.

There is currently no policy being imposed by the Lands Department towards *waqf* lands.[1] However, the rules and regulations of *waqf* land must be fulfilled. A *waqf* land should meet all the rules and regulations determined by the Lands Department. The following rules and regulations are determined by the Lands Department:

(i) **Conforming to the Land Code, Chapter 40**

Endowment in the form of the land shall be according to Brunei Darussalam's Land Code, chapter 40. It is strongly emphasized that lands being endowed should not contradict and violate any of the guidelines mentioned in the Land Code, chapter 40.

(ii) **Ownership**

The *waqif* shall own a private land being endowed. It should not be subjected to inheritance for the later person's ownership. Furthermore, the endowed land should not involve any kinship related to the *waqif*.

[1] Interview with the Deputy Land Commissioner, MoD, 1st April 2017.

This is to avoid disputes and conflicts upon the process of gazetting the land as an endowment.

(iii) Physical Conditions of the Endowed Land

An endowed land's physical conditions are essential to be evaluated to ensure productive and efficient use of it. The *waqf* land should be in a position to contribute its benefits to society at large. The Lands Department will revise the endowed land's physical conditions based on safety, accessibility, location, area, and development. If the endowed land falls under strategic planning, the Department of Development and Strategic Planning unit will revise the land zonings.

An endowed land should be legal, registered, and valid to be accepted as a *waqf* property.[2] Its physical condition and location should also be reviewed before making an endowment. Hence, the endowed land location must be suitable according to the strategic planning of the Town and Country Planning Department.

According to officials in the Development and Strategic Planning unit of Town and Country Planning, lands in Brunei Darussalam have been categorized and zoned according to their uses and purposes, such as residential, commercial, agriculture, and so forth.[2] This ensures that the land's condition and location are suitable to meet the desired plan for a specific development. So far, endowed lands in Brunei Darussalam have not conflicted with the land zoning because most endowed lands are dedicated to public facilities, mainly mosques.

However, the Development and Strategic Planning unit of Town and Country Planning will permit a certain percentage of land to be used for other purposes outside the predetermined zones. Land under residential zones is not necessarily restricted to residential buildings only. The land could be developed and used for commercial purposes based on the local plans of Town and County Planning. This ensures that a particular region could provide necessities and facilities for the residents around that area.

---

[2] Interview with the Development and Strategic Planning Unit of Town and Country Planning officers, 5th December 2016.

(iv) **No Financial Commitment**

Endowed lands shall have no financial commitment with either banks or third parties. They should not be involved with any financial activities and transactions that could cause a transfer of ownership. Thus, endowed lands shall not be subjected as collateral for loans or debts.

The abovementioned rules and regulations shall be fulfilled in order for a land to be accepted as a *waqf*. Once all of the requirements have been fulfilled, the Lands Department will then proceed with gazetting the *waqf* land.

5 Challenges of *Waqf* Land Development in Brunei Darussalam

What are the constraints, factors, and challenges of *waqf* land development? According to both the *Waqf* and *Baitul Mal* Unit of MUIB and Development and Strategic Planning of Town and Country Planning, there are several potential reasons behind the lower response in land *waqf*:

(i) **Availability of Land**

Lands in Brunei Darussalam are very limited to their uses. Most lands in all districts are being zoned under Government Protection or Environmental Management, such as wildlife sanctuaries, forest reserves, and nature reserves. Land zoned for commercial, residential, and agricultural purposes, which can be developed towards the economy, is mostly situated in Brunei Muara District. Also, there has been a decrease in the ownership of private land by an individual. Hence, limited lands prevent individuals from endowing lands for economic purposes.

(ii) **Increasing Value of Land**

The increased value of land in Brunei Darussalam also limits Muslim society's ability to endow a land. It is difficult for an ordinary individual to own land. Only those with wealth can possess private land and contribute for an endowment. Increased land value makes a particular individual possessive about their land as lands are seen as a popular kind of wealth. Therefore, it makes people unfavorable to endow their land for economic purposes without any reward given to them.

(iii) *Istibdal*

Among the reason for the slow development of *waqf* funds is the prohibition of *Istibdal* on idle land. On this prohibition, MUIB is restricted and has no right to sell, dispose, or transfer the *waqf* properties, except with the approval of His Majesty, as stated in Section 104 (1): "The Majlis shall not, without the approval in writing of His Majesty, sell, transfer or dispose of, or charge, mortgage or encumber, any immovable property vested in it for this Act, whether or not forming part of the General Endowment Fund."

According to Awang Haji Rosle bin Haji Jumat, a secretariat of *fatwa* in the State Mufti's Office, all religious matters are strictly based on the *Shafi'e* sect. Implementation of *Istibdal* based on *Shafiei* is limited, and it is prohibited to implement *Istibdal* on lands dedicated for mosques. It has been strengthened and supported by the State Mufti's *fatwa*. The *fatwa* states, "Waqf property cannot be sold, it is not permissible even if it is only a portion of it and even if it is deemed that there is benefit in selling it" (State Mufti, 2000). Therefore, *Istibdal* has been a challenge for MUIB to further develop the idled *waqf* lands in Brunei Darussalam.

(iv) **Accounting Practices**

According to Abu Bakar et al. (2020), all the revenue obtained by the Land Agency is consolidated together with the *Baitul Mal* properties and these accounting practices make the Land Agency difficult to plan development because they do not know how far the development of *waqf* property will benefit or not.

(v) **Allocation of Funds**

Abu Bakar et al. (2020) explain that MUIB, through the General Administration Fund, fund the development of *Baitul Mal* properties and that *waqf* at the Land Agency was also funded this way. Funding approved by MUIB is limited on an annual budget and the Land Agency is not given specific funding or capital to develop and invest in *waqf* properties. Thus, the allocation should take into account the development of *Baitul Mal* properties and the incremental rental income as this would affect the generated revenue that is to be used to pay salaries, maintenance, and annual taxes without being able to carry out other development and investment activities.

(vi) **Public Perception**

In Muslim society land *waqf* is solely for religious purposes. Therefore, the perception of *waqf* as religious welfare dominates the *waqf* endowment in Brunei Darussalam. Hence, there are few cases whereby endowed land is dedicated to boosting the economy.

From the findings, evidence was found that several factors and constraints affect the potential of *waqf* institutions to enhance the economy. These constraints are seen as the bottleneck that limits *waqfs*' contribution to religious welfare and, thus, the reason behind the unproductive and ineffective contribution to the economy. These lacking factors are human resources, expertise, top management support, working partnership, *waqf* enactment, and public awareness.

The insufficiency of human resources in handling *waqf* management is an obstacle to the development of *waqf* institutions in Brunei Darussalam. The *Waqf* and *Baitul Mal* Unit of MUIB has only two personnel involved in managing the endowments: one Senior Religious Officer and one clerk. Workload and matters relating to endowments and *Baitul Mal* have not been adequately managed and assigned to a specific employee within the unit, which leads to inefficiency within the *Waqf* and *Baitul Mal* Unit. Hence, lacking human resources becomes the constraint in promoting *waqf* awareness and limits its potential as an economic booster. However, cooperation can be developed with a higher academic institution like universities to create awareness and perform further future research in this area.

As the human resource that manages the *waqf* institution is very small, a shortage of expertise worsens its management. Experts of economic background and accountants are needed in the unit to plan future projects and investments that could contribute benefits and hence revitalize *waqf* as an institution capable of developing Brunei's economy.

The unit also has difficulties in promoting *waqf* for economic benefits. *Waqf* institution in Brunei Darussalam needs support from the top authority and management who are keen to support the effort to expand *waqf* capacity.

Waqf institutions also lack working partnerships with Islamic banks, real estate consultants, and service operators. In making this institution an economic tool, *waqf* institutions need to expose themselves to other sectors, particularly sectors that provide services.

The current *Waqf* Enactment is too general for the current situation of the economy. Due to this generality, it limits the extent to which *waqf* will contribute benefits to the economy. The latest *Waqf* Enactment has not yet been finalized. It is believed that the new enactment will expand the ability and capability of *waqf* institutions in the nearer future.

Also, the public is still unaware of the validity of investment using *waqf* funds and other Islamic instruments as a median for investing. Hence, *waqf* in Brunei Darussalam only focuses on religious matters and less on economic contributions.

6 Recommendation

MUIB should have complete human resources capable of providing expertise and services in developing the performance of the *waqf* institution. The workload should also be separated from unrelated matters outside endowments and *Baitul Mal* subjects. The human resources must be increased within *the Waqf* and *Baitul Mal* Unit with different economics, estate management, and investment portfolios. There are qualified and skilled graduates within the country who are willing to provide their expertise and service in vitalizing *waqf* institution in Brunei. Data related to *waqf* management such as accounting reports, updated data on cash *waqf*, and land *waqf* should be transparent to the endowers and public to create awareness and build trust from the public. A proper data-sharing software or database could be set up by *Waqf* and *Baitul Mal* Unit of MUIB to circulate and assimilate the information.

Gaining support from the top management may be difficult and may not always be a straightforward process. It takes a lot of effort and confidence to gain support. In the *waqf* case, this Islamic endowment system may not be the first tool thought by the government as a catalyst in enhancing Brunei's economy. Other economic tools may be more favorable than *the waqf institution*. As a result, *Waqf* and *Baitul Mal* Unit of MUIB, as a full supporter of *waqf institution*, should get the effort and word out that *waqf* is vital to the economy. It can be done by emphasizing the economic benefits of *waqf* by proposing several top management projects. Presentations should be a great start in gaining support from the top management, such as via periodically roundtable discussion to present and deliver *waqf's* current performance.

A working partnership with private and government sectors is essential in developing *waqf* institution, and more opportunities may be obtained in gaining more public endowers. *Waqf* and *Baitul Mal* Unit of MUIB could work with Bank Islam Brunei Darussalam (BIBD) to have *waqf* as part of their service provision. It can be implemented on their BIBD Mobile Banking application under the donation section. However, it is emphasized that the term '*waqf*' should be used instead of donation. It provides a clear direction that the cash given by the *waqif* is an endowment. In this way, both institutions will get the benefit. MUIB could obtain more opportunities to gain and develop cash *waqf* while BIBD could have '*waqf*' as part of their Corporate Social Responsibility (CSR) towards Muslim society in Brunei Darussalam.

As most endowed lands in Brunei fall under Special *Waqf* (*Waqf Khas*), the donor of *waqf* land should consider General *Waqf* (*Waqf* Am), so that there is a flexibility for the managers of *waqf* land to make investment decisions, especially in commercial activities, for productive returns and be able to promote the economy and socioeconomic development.

More activities and programs need to be organized to increase and improve public awareness. An Islamic crowdfunding campaign aiming for a specific *waqf* project such as developing a commercial building could be created through collecting cash *waqf* from populated areas such as universities, government offices, shopping malls, and mosques. By conducting this kind of campaign, more cash endowments could be collected and utilized for economic activities.

This exploratory and initial research should be followed by further in-depth research. Future research could look into *waqf* models involving Islamic financial contracts such as *musharakah* and *mudarabah* that could be applied to the country's endowment system, especially in productive investment. Another critical view to gather is the opinion of potential endowers and the public.

7 Conclusion

There are several findings that can be derived from this chapter. First, the current properties of *waqf* under the management of *Waqf* and *Baitul Mal* unit of MUIB are limited to cash, land, vehicles, and electrical and non-electrical equipment such as photocopy machines, water dispensers, and books. Therefore, little can be witnessed of the economic contribution generated by *waqf* in Brunei. It is believed that the economic potential of *waqf* has not been fully explored and recognized as a financial tool for economic growth, although MUIB is making a few initiatives in utilizing *waqf* towards investment activities. However, these initiatives should be pursued more actively in generating a more significant impact on the economy.

Second, land *waqf* is a common form of endowment. Apart from being legal, registered, and valid, endowing a land should also comply with the Land Department's rules and regulations. Lands are being categorized and zoned based upon their purposes, such as residential and commercial land, the zoning of Brunei Darussalam. Therefore, the status of this land should also be referred to before making an endowment. This ensures that its condition and location permits it to meet the desired intent of the endowment. Most endowed lands in Brunei Darussalam fall under Special *Waqf* (*Waqf Khas*), dedicated to mosques, school sites, and cemetery sites, while a small percentage of lands under General *Waqf* (*Waqf Am*) is dedicated to developing residential and commercial buildings. Several factors, such as a decrease in land availability, an increase in land value, impermissibility of *istibdal*, and the narrow public perceptions were identified as contributors to the unfavorable general *waqf* for economic development purposes.

It can be concluded that utilizing *waqf* as a tool in generating benefits to the economy is still underdeveloped and seen as a foreign element to be implemented among the community in Brunei Darussalam. Apart from that, several obstacles and constraints limit the potential of *waqf* towards enhancing the economy in Brunei Darussalam. These constraints include lack of human resources, lack of expertise, lack of support from top management, lack of working partnership, general *waqf* enactment, and lack of public awareness creation programs.

References

Abdul Karim, S. (2010). Contemporary Shari'a Compliance Structuring for the Development and Management of Waqf Assets in Singapore. *Kyoto Bulletin of Islamic Area Studies*, 143–164.

Abdullah, R. (2011). *Badan Tanmiah's Experiences in Managing Waqf Property* (*The Ninth Workshop in Islamic Economics and Finance 2011*). UKM, Kuala Lumpur.

Abdullah, R. (2018). Pelaksanaan Istibdal Wakaf Dari Aspek Undang-undang Brunei Darussalam, in *Istibdal Wakaf Dalam Pembangunan di Brunei*

Darussalam dan Malaysia. In Z. Bahari & K. Salam (Eds.), *Yusof and Rose Abdullah*. Universiti Islam Sultan Sharif Ali, UNISSA Press, Bandar Seri Begawan.

Abdullah, R., & Ismail, A. G. (2017). Taking Stock of the Waqf-Based Islamic Microfinance Model. *International Journal of Social Economics*, *44*(8), 1018–1031.

Abu Bakar, M., Ahmad, S., Salleh, A. D., & Md Salleh, M. F. (2020). The SWOT Analysis of Waqf Governance in Brunei Darussalam. *International Research Journal of Shariah, Muamalat and Islam*, *2*(3), 1–22.

Ahmad, M. (2019). An Empirical Study of the Challenges Facing Zakat and Waqf Institutions in Northern Nigeria. *ISRA International Journal of Islamic Finance*, *11*(2), 338–356.

Ambrose, A. H. A. A., Aslam, M., & Hanafi, H. (2015). The Possible Role of Waqf in Ensuring a Sustainable Malaysian Federal Government Debt. *Procedia Economics Finance*, *31*, 333–345.

Basir, K. H., & Besar, M. H. A. (2021). Unlocking Islamic Social Finance to Assist Micro Small Medium Enterprises in Brunei Darussalam. In M. K. Hassan, A. Muneeza, & A. M. Sarea (Eds.), *Impact of COVID-19 on Islamic Social Finance* (pp. 185–198). Routledge.

Budiman, M. A. (2014). The Significance of Waqf for Economic Development. *Equilibrium*, *1*(2), 19–34.

Cizakca, M. (1998). Awqaf in History and Its Implications for Modern Islamic Economies. *Islamic Economic Studies Journal*, 43–70.

Dogarawa, A. B. (2009). Poverty Alleviation through Zakah and Waqf Institutions: A Case for the Muslim Ummah in Ghana, MPRA Paper 23191, University Library of Munich, Germany.

Harun, R., Mohamed, Z., & Ali, N. (2012). Preliminary Findings on Waqf Management Practices among Selected Muslim Countries. In *2010 International Conference on Economics, Marketing, and Management IPEDR* (pp. 117–120).

Hasan, Z., and Abdullah, M. (2008). *The Investment of Waqd Land as an Instrument of Muslims' Economic Development in Malaysia*. http://www.kantakji.com/media/5162/z140.pdf

Hisham, S., Jaseran, H. A., & Jusoff, K. (2013). Substitution of Waqf Properties (Istibdal) in Malaysia: Statutory Provisions and Implementations. *Middle-East Journal of Scientific Research*, *13*(13), 23–27.

Hossein, A., & Zamir, I. (2015). *Introduction to Islamic Economics: Theory and Application*. John Wiley & Sons Singapore Pte. Ltd.

Hubur, A. A. (2019). "Productive Waqf Management: A Case Study of Brunei Darussalam". *International Journal of Islamic Business*, *4*(1), pp. 65–87.

Kamis, M. H. (2013). *Developing Waqf Fund through Investment Views from al-Fiqh & Law of Brunei Darussalam*.

Kahf, M. (1995). Awqaf and Its Modern Applications. In *The Oxford Encyclopedia of the Modern Islamic World*. Oxford University Press.

Khan, F. (2010). Waqf: An Islamic Instrument of Poverty Alleviation-Bangladesh Perspective. In *The Tawhidi Epistemology: Zakat and Waqf Economy* (pp. 65–96). University of Dhaka.

Listiana, L., & Alhabshi, S. M. (2020). Waqf and Legacy of Altruism in Singapore: Challenges and Development. *Journal of Ekonomi dan Bisnis Islam*, 6(1), 116–133.

Mufti, S. (2000). *Fatwa Mufti Kerajaan*. Jabatan Mufti Kerajaan.

Omar, I., Md Yusof, A., & Manaf, F. A. (2014). The Economic Transformation of Waqf Lands in Malaysia – A Structure and Agency Approach. *International Journal of Business, Economics, and Law*, 5(3), 1–11.

Sulaiman, S., Hasan, A., Mohd Noor, A., Ismail, M. I., & Noordin, N. H. (2019). Proposed Models for Unit Trust Waqf and the Parameters for Their Application. *ISRA International Journal of Islamic Finance*, 11(1), 62–81.

CHAPTER 5

The Ottoman Cash Waqf as Altruistic Finance Model

Mehmet Bulut and Cem Korkut

1 INTRODUCTION

The waqf played a significant role in fulfilling educational, religious, and infrastructure services in Ottoman society. The Ottomans integrated the waqf system, a component of Islamic tradition, to successfully integrate social, economic, cultural, and religious life. The display of this success is the waqf that extends to the most remote villages. The waqf had become widespread because they could meet the needs of society. The Ottomans institutionalized the waqf. The economic and social aspects of institutionalized and widespread waqf became more evident in the community. The fact that the waqfs were so broad has made it possible to define the Ottoman Empire as a waqf civilization.

M. Bulut (✉)
Department of Economics, Istanbul Sabahattin Zaim University, Istanbul, Turkey

C. Korkut
Department of Economics, Ankara Yildirim Beyazit University, Ankara, Turkey

© The Author(s), under exclusive license to Springer Nature Switzerland AG 2022
A. G. Ismail et al. (eds.), *Islamic Philanthropy*, Palgrave Studies in Islamic Banking, Finance, and Economics,
https://doi.org/10.1007/978-3-031-06890-4_5

Not just elites but ordinary Ottoman people established the waqf. They did not have to be very wealthy to establish a waqf. The waqf had done the services that the governments do today. So, the waqf have alleviated the burden of the state. The waqf financed waterways, sidewalks as an infrastructure service, madrasahs, schools, kulliyahs, libraries as an educational service, hospitals, clinics, patients as a health service, mosques, masjids, lodges as a religious service, and hans, caravansaries, bazaars as a commercial service. Waqf that helped the poor also had a philanthropic side. One of the waqf with a wide range of services was the cash waqf.

The main characteristic of the cash waqf was that the capital of the waqf was made up of cash. In general, the basic function of the waqf was real estate-centered until the Ottoman period. The cash was devoted to the cash waqf while the devoted goods were shops, houses, vineyards, and gardens. In this respect, the cash waqf could be considered an innovation and contribution to the Islamic civilization by Ottomans. This study will examine the cash waqf and financial mentality of Ottomans as an altruistic finance model. As the backbone of the Ottoman financial system and as the pioneer of contemporary Islamic finance practices, the role and importance of the cash waqf will be more easily grasped.

In this chapter, the cash waqf will be investigated through archival documents. The primary sources, waqfiyahs, are examined. The methods and purposes of these documents reveal the altruistic financial model. The basic principles of this system will be determined in the light of this information.

2   Cash Waqf and Discussions

A cash waqf is a type where all or part of the capital is made up of cash. Rental income in ordinary real estate waqf is used according to the purpose of the waqf. In the case of cash waqf, the cash obtained from the waqf capital is spent in the direction of the waqf's purposes. The method of operating the cash in the cash waqf forms the basis of the methods applied by today's Islamic finance institutions. For a long time, the cash waqf had been the source of financing for Ottoman entrepreneurs, traders, and artisans and had been one of the determinants of the cost of borrowing in an altruistic financial system with the profit rates they had applied. On the other hand, Pamuk regards the cash waqf as interest-bearing financial institutions because the Ottoman Empire was very flexible in practice and allowed some interest-bearing loans (2004, pp. 231–233).

There is no record about the cash waqf before the Ottomans. Hence the history of the cash waqf began with the Ottomans. There is no exact date for the first cash waqf that was established. However, it is known that the first recorded cash waqf was founded by Yagci Haji Muslihuddin in 1423. Yagci Hadji Muslihuddin endowed 10,000 aches for this cash waqf founded in Edirne (Mandaville, 1979, p. 290). The cash waqf became quite widespread after the fatwa of the Kanuni period Sheikh al-Islam, Ebussuud Efendi. The cash waqf spread in Europe and the Anatolian regions of the Ottoman Empire. It is understood that a few cash waqfs were founded even in the Arabian provinces where the society was sensitive and distant to cash waqf (Pamuk, 2012, p. 90).

2.1 Religious Pieces of Evidence of the Cash Waqf

The cash waqf are the institutions that the Ottoman Empire contributed to Islamic civilization. The Ottomans were dependent on the Hanafi jurisprudence. Hence, the views of Hanafi mujtahid imams were critical for cash waqf. Despite the opposing views of Abu Hanifa, the Hanafi school founder, his students had allowed the establishment of waqf and cash waqf. Therefore, the Ottoman ulema class considered the tendencies, traditions, and views of Abu Hanifa students about the cash waqf. At this stage, the importance of historical practices in the formation of Islamic institutions is understood.

One of the most fundamental ways of understanding the mujtahids' views and the Ottoman ulema is to examine their fatwas. An Ottoman scholar, Kemal Pasazade, mentioned the views of Hanafi mujtahids on cash waqf in his tractate. Imam Zufar, one of Abu Hanifa students, had claimed that cash, comestibles, and measurable and weighable goods could be regarded as waqf property. Moreover, Imam Muhammad, also a student of Abu Hanifa, said that the movables could be endowed if determined practices. Likewise, Imam Abu Yusuf, another famous student of Abu Hanifa, also said that some of the movables could be accepted as waqf goods. As is seen from the views of mujtahids, Imam Zufar was the one who directly permitted the establishment of the cash waqf. Imam Zufar regarded the cash waqf as a societal need. He claimed that it is appropriate to endow cash like wheat (Şimşek, 1986, p. 216).

We look at the views of the mujtahid imams related to the cash waqf. It is understood that the continuity (eternity) rule is taken at the forefront. The movable or immovable properties are endowed. The continuity of a good as a kind can be regarded as a sufficient condition for the waqf. This situation can be expressed as follows: The continuation of the same gender of good is considered the continuation of the original. The most significant obstacle related to the endowment of movables had been overcome with this view. Further evidence about the allowance of endowments of movables depends on practices during the period of the Prophet Muhammad (PBUH). It is known that during period of the wars of the Prophet (PBUH), movables such as arms and horses were endowed. The fatwa of Abu Yusuf on the endowment of movables overlapped with this practice (Okur, 2005, p. 45). As is also understood from the views of mujtahids, Ottoman ulema authorized the cash waqf in the direction of the opinions of Imam Zufar, Abu Yusuf, and Imam Muhammad.

2.2 Discussions of Ottoman Scholars on the Cash Waqf

Among Ottomans, the discussions on the legitimacy of the cash waqf started with the establishment and functioning of the cash waqf. The views of the ulema class, which had significant effects on state administration and social life, on the cash waqf had affected the role of the cash waqf in society. Ottoman society, which paid utmost attention to Islamic rules in their lives, followed the ulema class's views and those of the clergymen about the cash waqf. According to written sources, Ibn Kemal was the first scholar to express this subject from the Ottoman Empire. Ibn Kemal did not enter into the details of the legitimacy of the cash waqf. He only summarized the issue and concluded by naql. Although the date of the tractate cannot be fully determined, it can be said that Ibn Kemal is a pioneer in this issue because the debates and writings between others in the ulema class had been started after the death of Ibn Kemal. Ibn Kemal mentioned that there was a debate among the mujtahid imams about the establishment of the cash waqf. He wrote that although there were debates, the cash waqf had become widespread. Ibn Kemal explained that the discussions on the cash waqf were periodical. He also claimed that the imams who were opposed to establishing cash waqf would allow the cash waqf if they considered changing conditions. Ibn Kemal paid attention to the continuity condition. He said the real estate might be damaged or ruined, but this problem is not seen in the cash waqf (Özcan, 2000, p. 32). The tractate of Ibn Kemal also affected the following ulema.

Debates on the cash waqf had intensified in the sixteenth century. In particular, two opposite views of the two leading scholars, Ebussuud and

Çivizade, are essential for understanding the legitimacy of the cash waqf under the Islamic fiqh. While Ebussuud looked at the cash waqf positively, Çivizade was very strict in this matter. Çivizade had enabled the cash waqf to be banned for two to three years with active opposition to the cash waqf and a letter written to the Sultan. Çivizade claimed that the practices in these waqfs included interest/riba. Çivizade's views were very sharp when compared to the scholars of the time. He had been dismissed from the Shaykh al-Islam task because of his rejection of decisions that were agreed unanimously (Uzunçarşılı, 1988, p. 155). The prohibition of a community-based institution like the cash waqf caused failures in charity works and a wealth transfer mechanism. Many scholars objected to this ban.

One of the scholars who objected to the prohibition of the cash waqf was Bali Efendi. Bali Efendi witnessed troubles in society because of the cash waqf ban. The needs of mosques, masjids, madrasahs, and schools were not met during the ban. Also, the confusion of philanthropists disrupted charity works. The Bali Efendi expressed the negative influences of the ban in the letters he wrote. He wrote one of these letters to the Sultan of the time. The letters of Bali Efendi are essential. They provide an understanding of the place of the cash waqf in society and the evidence and views that provide legality for the cash waqf (Özcan, 1999, p. 217). Ottoman scholars viewed the cash waqf positively from past practices. Alongside all the positive sides, some scholars, like Birgivi, strongly opposed the establishment and practices of the cash waqf. Birgivi mentioned that the cash waqf caused interest-bearing transactions. He also claimed that the mujtahids' provisions were weak (Şimşek, 1986, p. 215). However, The general belief was that the cash waqfs were a necessity for society. Past practices also played a role in allowing the cash waqf. The ulema who supported the practices of the cash waqf avoided the term of interest. They used the word ribh (profit). Moreover, the state did not enforce anything negative about the cash waqf except for the two-to-three-year ban. Both the state and the people supported the cash waqf because they fulfilled the needs of society.

The permission given for the cash waqf is an indication of the Ottoman financial mentality. Moreover, this is evidence that Islamic law has a flexible structure, not strictly unmodified, contrary to claims. The priority of the cash waqf was charity. Thus, the Ottoman financial mentality was shaped by the charity framework. This motivation was one of the main pillars of the legitimacy of the cash waqf.

3 Samples of Cash Waqf

The cash waqfs were established like other real estate waqfs. However, the capital of the cash waqf was cash. There is also no real estate rental income in the cash waqf. The income of the cash waqf came from the cash that was operated by Islamic methods. Information about the establishment of the cash waqf can be found in waqfiyahs in archives and sharia court registers. In this study, the cash waqfs examined are read from the original form, Ottoman Turkish, in the primary sources. The resources, the waqfiyahs, to be examined in this part, facilitate understanding the living conditions of the time because the waqfiyahs draw a framework for the wage rates, profit ratio (borrowing cost), charity works, and living standards of society.

3.1 The Establishment Process of the Cash Waqf

The philanthropist who wanted to establish a cash waqf prepared the settlement deed (waqfiyah) first and registered it at the qadi's office. The founder of the cash waqf specified the name of the founder of the waqf, the name of the trustee, the amount of the donation, the conditions under which the donated money are mentioned, how the money will be handled, and the purpose of the waqf in the waqfiyah.

The establishment process of a sample waqf is divided into two stages. The founder is active in the first stage. The process is as follows:

1. The founder comes into the presence of the qadi with this document.
2. The founder repeats the conditions that he wrote in the waqfiyah in the qadi's presence.
3. The trustee also approves the statement of the founder.
4. Then, the waqf is founded.

The second stage is that of legalization. At this stage, the waqf establishment is a matter of trial, and the case is brought to court. The path followed in this stage is as follows:

1. The founder claims that establishing a cash waqf is not in line with Islamic rules.
2. The founder requests the endowed cash, the fee of the trustee back from the trustee.
3. The trustee objects to this request.

4. He also provides reasons for the objection that he has done. He says that establishing a cash waqf is appropriate for Imam Zufar. He states that he has received the fee. He has taken it as a trustee, under the conditions in the waqfiyah.
5. The qadi takes into account the views of the Imam Zufar and other mujtahids and the benefits of the waqf for society. In the end, he approves the establishment of the waqf.

As is seen, the details in the establishment process are significant for legitimacy. One of the essential things that motivate Muslim philanthropists to establish a cash waqf is that these institutions are established and operated under Islamic rules.

3.2 The Waqf of Ali Pasha b. Arslan Pasha

The Waqf of Ali Pasha b. Arslan Pasha[1] was founded at Ionnina (*Yanya*) Sanjak in 1033 H. / 1623–24 G. The founder, Ali Pasha, was the former Timişoara *Beylerbey*. Ali Pasha was undertaking the task of the Ioannina *Mutasarrif* when he founded the waqf. He appointed Mustafa Agha as a trustee. He endowed 2,000,000 akches (25,000 qurushes) as cash for the waqf. Also, he endowed a great deal of real estate: 52 shops, one coffee shop, one *bosa* shop, and one grocery store.

The operating rate for cash was set at 15% with the phrase *ten to eleven and half* in the waqfiyah. Also, the operating methods were listed as *istirbah* and *istiglal.* There are also conditions to ensure the continuity of the waqf in the waqfiyah. The debtor's characteristics are listed in detail: The merchants who are reliable, honest, having an honored direction in religion/Islam, rich, powerful can take a loan from the waqf. It is also understood from these conditions that this waqf supported the merchants. Also, it is desirable to avoid situations where there is a possibility that the loan money will not be repaid. This condition shows that the avoidance of risky loans also takes place in the waqfiyah. A strong guarantor and a worthwhile lien are also required to make sure that the money is returned.

The revenues, rental incomes, and profits of the waqf were used for many charity works. These services and additional conditions are: (1) building a public soup kitchen, storeroom, and woodshed to cook for the

---
[1] The Archives of TR Prime Ministry Directorate General of Foundations (Register: 623, p. 203, Serial: 195).

poor; (2) building of an eight-room campus for needy students from the local community; (3) the allocation of one of these rooms to the class for the lessons; (4) building stores from remaining income; (5) renting these stores and adding this rental income to the cash; (6) scholarships to students, provision of food for students; (7) paying Mevlana Süleyman Effendi b. Rehb who educate here; (8) making 150 slices of bread per day in the soup kitchen; (9) the distribution of bread to the poor and people in charge of the waqf; (10) buying and cooking a sheep every day; (11) cooking many different dishes every day; (12) making ashoura in Ashoura day of Muharram; (13) paying the wage of employees (at least eight employees) in the waqf; (14) giving food to all employees every day; (14) paying the wage of the imam and preacher at the masjid that was built by the founder of waqf before; (15) paying the wage of a teacher at the school that was located near the masjid; (16) covering the lighting and other expenses of the masjid.

Also, the waqf founder, who was also in charge of oversight, mentioned those who will carry out this duty after his death. The date of approval of the waqf is also written in the last part of the waqf.

3.3 The Waqf of Ayşe Kadın bt. Mahmud Pasha

The Waqf of Ayşe Kadın bt., a woman who founded Mahmud Pasha[2] at Murad Çelebi Quarter, Belgrade, in 6 Rajab 1090 H. / 13 August 1679 G. The founder of the waqf was Mahmud's daughter Pasha, from the ruling class. The waqf was established by way of proxy. She endowed 100,000 akches.

The operating rate for cash was 15% (*ten to eleven-and-a-half*). The operating method was not mentioned in the waqfiyah, but there is the term of *mu'âmele-i şer'iyye* that means methods appropriate to Islamic fiqh. Like the Waqf of Ali Pasha, this waqf supported the merchants. There are also conditions for people who would take a loan from the waqf, such as, he must be a reliable merchant who has an honored direction in religion/Islam. Moreover, a strong guarantor and worthwhile lien must make sure that the money is returned.

The revenue of the waqf was given generally to education services. These services are giving wages to the lecturer and a scholarship for

---

[2] The Archives of TR Prime Ministry Directorate General of Foundations (Register: 623, p. 272, Serial: 292).

students in the classroom with a ten-room complex near the Hüseyin Pasha Mosque. There was also left a fee for the task of the trustee. Verse 181 of Surat al-Baqarah, the date of acceptance of the foundation, is the last chapter. The names of witnesses are written in the part of witnesses in proportion to the waqf size.

3.4 The Waqf of Mehmed Pasha[3]

The Waqf of Mehmed Pasha (see Table 5.1) from Kaçanik was founded at Katib Şahin Quarter, Skopje (Üsküp) District in 10 Shaban 1017 H. / 19 November 1608 G. The founder, Kaçanikli Mehmed Pasha, was part of the ruling class of Ottomans. There is a long entrance section on the waqfiyah. In general, this section includes prayers for the Prophet Muhammad (PBUH), the goodness of the foster/*infak*. Mehmed Pasha endowed (1) 1,200,000 akches (10,000 gold coins); (2) a house with courtyard, kitchen, storeroom, tower, warehouse, and many rooms; (3) a barn; (4) gardens; (5) 35 silver swords; (6) a pair of copper stirrups; (7) a pair of silver stirrups; (8) a third of his property; (9) a farm in Izlukan Village with fields, tower, rooms, oven, three warehouse, storeroom, two barns, castles, and black cattle; (10) 28 mills; (11) 20 room-shops; (12) vineyards; (13) a bridge and fountain; (14) four *hans*; (15) a coffee shop; (16) eight stores; (17) an oven. Mehmed Pasha appointed his brother Ahmed Cavus as trustee.

The operating rate for cash was set at 10% with the phrase *ten to eleven* in the waqfiyah. Also, the operating methods were listed as *istirbah* and *istiglal*. There are also conditions to ensure the waqf's continuity by the return of debt in the waqfiyah. The condition that money must be given to talented merchants, not to people who could not pay the debt and state officials, is one of them. The other condition about risks is that a strong guarantor and a worthwhile lien must make sure that the money is returned.

Moreover, all other real estates are given to the rent, and the rental income is distributed for charity works. Like the previous waqf, identification people who could use debt shows that the Waqf of Mehmed Pasha also supported the merchants. For this example, not giving a loan for state officials' fixed-income staff shows that the financing of the cash waqf was not consumption-based, but production-based and trade-based.

---

[3] The Archives of TR Prime Ministry Directorate General of Foundations (Register: 633, pp. 21–24, Serial: 011).

Table 5.1 Examples of the cash waqf

	The Waqf of Ali Pasha b. Arslan Pasha	The Waqf of Ayşe Kadın bt. Mahmud Pasha	The Waqf of Mehmed Pasha
Founder	Ali Pasha b. Arslan Pasha	Ayşe Kadın bt. Mahmud Pasha	Kaçanikli Mehmed Pasha
Gender of the founder	Man	Woman	Man
Class of founder	Ruling class	Daughter of a ruler	Ruling class
Location of the waqf	Ionnina (*Yanya*) Sanjak (now in Greece)	Belgrade (now in Serbia)	Skopje (now in Macedonia)
Date of establishment	1623–1624	13 August 1679	19 November 1608
Endowed cash	2,000,000 akches	100,000 akches	1,200,000 akches
Other endowed items	52 shops, 1 coffee shop, 1 bosa shop, 1 grocery store	–	A house with courtyard, kitchen, storeroom, tower, warehouse, and many rooms, a barn, gardens, 35 silver swords, a pair of copper stirrups, a pair of silver stirrups, a third of his property, a farm in Izlukan Village with fields, tower, rooms, oven, three warehouse, storeroom, two barns, cattle and black cattle, 28 mills, 20 room-shops, vineyards, bridge and fountain, four hans, a coffee shop, eight stores, an oven
Operation rate	15%	15%	10%
Operation Methods	istirbah and istiglal	mu'âmele-i şer'iyye	istirbah and istiglal
Debtor	Merchants	Merchants	Merchants
Purposes	Various	Educational	Various

The revenues, rental incomes, and profits of waqf are distributed to many charities. The conditions and purposes of the waqf include: (1) paying various fees to people for Qur'an recitation at the mosque that was built by the founder before; (2) paying the wage of imams preachers, teachers, and other people (total 21 people) in charge of charity institutions: mosques, schools, lodges, and so on; (3) repairing constructions such as mosques, schools, mills, fountains, hans, and bridges; (4) paying *avarız* tax of the Katib Şahin Quarter in which the founder resided; (5) sending one person to the Hajj every year; (6) cooking and distributing food; (7) building a lodge near the mosque that was built in Skopje and covering the expenses of the lodge; (8) and other charity work.

After the founder had passed away, the person who would direct the waqf is written in the waqfiyah. Also, some of the income had been separated for services. It is dedicated to praying and Qur'an recitation for the soul of the founders. The founder of the waqf had also left many books for the lodge. The views of the mujtahids on the establishment of the cash waqf are located in the waqfiyah. Especially the Hanafi fiqh were emphasized. Verse 181 of Surat al-Baqarah, the date of acceptance of the foundation, is the last chapter. The names of witnesses are written in the respective section in proportion to the waqf size.

4 Cash Waqf as Altruistic Finance Institutions

There is no *state-supported capitalism* in economic terms in the Ottoman Empire, unlike Europe, in the same period. A kind of economic liberation in the Ottoman financial system had been provided from the moral point of view. For example, the cash waqfs were shaped by charity activities rather than by profit. The cash waqf covered the salaries of mosques, masjids, madrasahs, lodges, and other expenses of these institutions. Many of the services provided by today's modern states were fulfilled at the time by cash waqf.

The hadith "When a human being dies, all of his deeds are terminated except for three types: an ongoing sadaqah, a knowledge (of Islam) from which others benefit, and a righteous child who makes du'a for him," contained in the waqfiyah shows the overall purpose of the waqf. Because the waqf institutions were the best definition of ongoing sadaqah, this hadith is shown as the fundamental reason for permission from waqf institutions (Akgündüz, 1996, p. 64). Moreover, it is a sign of the Islamic religion's influence on the founding of waqf according to the founders' testaments after the founders have died.

As can be seen from the examples, women also established cash waqf. Also, there was no obligation to be wealthy or elite to establish a cash waqf. Even those who had tiny amounts of cash established cash waqf. There were also common waqfs that people came together to build.

The cash waqf had created entirely a financial model that was specific to the needs of society. In addition to basic needs, precise/detailed needs can be financed from this financial system. The basic principles of altruistic finance system are (1) Islamic and ethical, (2) microcredit mechanism, (3) regional, and (4) needs-oriented.

4.1 Islamic/Ethical Methods

The methods used in the cash waqf are prescient of the methods used in today's Islamic/participation banks. These methods had been defined within the framework of Islamic borders. The criticism of the cash waqf by the critical scholars of the period like Imam Birgivi was a risk of interest in the money transfers made in these waqfs. However, the founders added the phrase *avoidance of interest-bearing transactions* as a condition for loans in many waqfiyahs.[4] Moreover, if the ulema class did not have any approval to establish the cash waqf, they could not be so general and found even in the smallest villages.

Also, as seen from the waqfiyahs, the debtors were generally entrepreneurs like merchants, merchants, and artisans. This situation shows that the cash waqf financed not only consumption but also trade and production. The foundations made these financing operations with methods similar to modern Islamic finance instruments. The methods used by the cash waqf can be generalized with the methods (1) bida'a, (2) buying real estate for renting it, (3) istiglâl, buying the real estate of the debtor and rent it to him again, (4) mudarabah, (5) murabahah, (6) qard / beautiful loan, and (7) operations in different governmental institutions.

The borrowing cost rate for cash waqfs was generally between 10 and 15%. The fixed rate of borrowing costs can be considered an impediment to usurers' existence in the market. The fatwas of the ulema also fixed these rates. Later, the waqf law was brought legal grounds for the borrowing cost rate. Both the borrower and the lender were protected with the legitimacy of rates. The trust and respect of the waqf institution was also an essential factor in the payment of debts. It was an essential motivation for debtors to pay their debts. The waqf prevented the needy/poor from borrowing in the market with profit or interest by the qard method.

---

[4] The Waqf of Mehlika bt. Abdullah (Rodoscuk Sharia Court Register 08453.00016), v.44/b.

The income of the waqf was not given to founders but was set according to the purposes of the waqf. The founder did not have any right to the cash that he devoted before. It shows the ethical process of a cash waqf.

4.2 Operated as Microcredit Mechanism

As can be seen from the waqfiyahs, credit was generally given to professionals such as merchants and artisans. These entrepreneurs did not use a significant amount of money as a loan. Thus, these institutions worked like microcredit institutions. The cash waqf had financed the economic and trade market for an extended period.

There were also cash waqfs founded by people who had small accumulations, such as the waqfs founded by wealthy people. However, the loans given by the cash waqf were generally not large. Therefore, it can be thought that the cash waqf appeals to today's SMEs. The cash waqfs established in the most remote villages are an indication that the amount used per loan is small. The cash waqf institutionalized credit transactions in the Ottoman Empire. Thus, the credit supply increased in the market. Also, an institutional infrastructure had been created by the cash waqf for those who wanted to use credit.

4.3 Regional Institutions

The cash waqfs were influential in the region in which they were founded. The cash waqf had acted to meet the needs of a particular region. Moreover, the debtors also were from the same region where the waqf operated. The cash waqf operated in the sense of both finance and services in regional development. As seen in the examples of waqfiyahs, the cash waqfs were usually located in the area where the builder resided. The people who would work for the waqf and the masjids, mosques, madrasahs, and schools funded by the waqf were also chosen among the people of the same region. As a result, the cash waqf also affected the regional labor market.

In particular, large cash waqfs employed many people. For example, the Waqf of Mehmed Pasha employed 21 people in its region, Skopje. The cash waqf had been one of the determinants of the regional financial, labor, and trade markets for 500 years in economic terms. The Ottoman Empire, which had a strong central authority, was flexible in addressing regional needs and evaluated the regions according to their characteristics.

The cash waqf moved very fast in responding to regional needs by their rapid establishment process and operating.

4.4 Focused on the Needs of Society

The educational, religious, and infrastructural needs of society were covered by the waqf's income and the cash waqf. The waqf played an essential role in making investments for social purposes and financing charity services. As can be seen from the examples, the cash waqf that fulfilled many services had significantly reduced the state's burden.

The cash waqf financed the wages of employees and other expenses of madrasahs and schools as educational needs; lodges, masjids, mosques, zawiyahs, Qur'an courses, and recitation, caring the shrines as religious needs; caravanserais, hans, inns, guesthouses as trade/economic needs; fountains, sidewalks, waterways as infrastructural needs; almshouses, hospices, hospitals, soup houses as social needs (Bulut & Korkut, 2016, p. 28). Like all other waqfs, the cash waqf had targeted and addressed the needs of society. When the cash waqfs were forbidden, it was understood that these waqfs responded to societal needs to a significant extent. During this ban, religious services and education services funded by the cash waqf had stopped. People could not find enough resources for these services.

The aim of financing people who needed cash, which was the secondary aim of the cash waqf, is again why these waqfs are need-oriented. The cash waqf, which managed to cover two sides' needs with a single transaction, were essential contributions of the Ottomans to Islamic civilization.

5 Conclusion

The cash waqf is one of the critical institutions that the Ottomans contributed to the Islamic civilization. The cash waqf, whose primary priority was charity, provided the market's financial system to be shaped within the purposes of the waqf. The cash waqfs were used by Muslim entrepreneurs, merchants, and artisans as a solution to their financing needs. It had emerged as an institution that respond extensively to this need from the 1400s to the beginning of the twentieth century. The Ottomans' solutions to the problems the society had encountered are indicative of the flexibility in Ottoman law, finance, and religious systems. The cash waqf is the solution of Ottomans in the financial and economic system. The cash waqf that met both the basic needs of society and responded to the cash needs in the financial system was unique. The cash waqf was more flexible and faster functioning than real estate waqf.

The cash waqf that prioritized the charity works formed the basis of the Ottoman society's altruistic financial mind. The basic principles of this mind are understood in terms of the waqf's establishment and functioning. Giving a loan to people without interest is one of the fundamental prohibitions of Islam. Also, the merchant's emphasis in the waqfiyah is an indication that these waqf did not provide consumer loans but trade/production loans. The loans granted by the waqf were not high. Smaller amounts of loans show that the cash waqf can be regarded as a microcredit mechanism.

Moreover, the purposes of the foundation are more regional and need-based. As a result, the cash waqf is a reflection of the Ottoman financial mentality. This mentality aims to meet human needs and increase the prosperity of society. The fact that the cash waqf had survived for 500 years is a sign of this system's success and mentality. The examination of system and mentality is possible with the understanding of the Ottoman world view in general.

Appendix (The Waqfiyahs)

A. The Waqfiyah of the Waqf of Ali Pasha b. Arslan Pasha

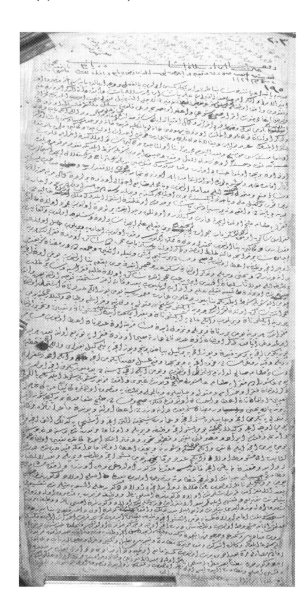

B. The Waqfiyah of Ayşe Kadın bt. Mahmud Pasha

C. The first page of the Waqfiyah of Waqf of Mehmed Pasha

REFERENCES

ARCHIVE DOCUMENTS

The Archives of TR Prime Ministry Directorate General of Foundations
Register: 623, p. 203, Serial: 195
Register: 623, p. 272, Serial: 292
Register: 633, pp. 21–24 Serial: 011

ARTICLES AND BOOKS

Akgündüz, A. (1996). *İslâm Hukukunda ve Osmanlı Tatbikatında Vakıf Müessesesi*. Osmanlı Araştırmaları Vakfı.
Bulut, M., & Korkut, C. (2016). A Comparison between Ottoman Cash Waqf (Cash waqf) and Modern Interest-Free Financial Institutions. *Vakıflar Dergisi*, 46, 23–45.
Mandaville, J. E. (1979). Usurious Piety: The Cash Waqf Controversy in the Ottoman Empire. *International Journal of Middle East Studies*, 10(3), 289–308.
Okur, K. H. (2005). Para Vakıfları Bağlamında Osmanlı Hukuk Düzeni ve Ebussuud Efendinin Hukuk Anlayışı Üzerine Bazı Değerlendirmeler. *Hitit Üniversitesi İlahiyat Fakültesi Dergisi*, 4(7–8), 33–58.
Özcan, T. (1999). Sofyalı Bâlî Efendi'nin Para Vakıflarıyla İlgili Mektupları. *İslâm Araştırmaları Dergisi*, 3, 125–155.
Özcan, T. (2000). İbn Kemal'in Para Vakıflarına Dair Risâlesi. *İslâm Araştırmaları Dergisi Sayı.*, 4, 31–41.
Pamuk, Ş. (2004). Institutional Change and the Longevity of the Ottoman Empire, 1500–1800. *Journal of Interdisciplinary History*, 35(2), 225–247.
Pamuk, Ş. (2012). *Osmanlı İmparatorluğu'nda Paranın Tarihi*. Tarih Vakfı Yurt Yayınları.
Şimşek, M. (1986). Osmanlı Cemiyetinde Para Vakıfları Üzerinde Münakaşalar. *Ankara Üniversitesi İlahiyat Fakültesi Dergisi*, 27(1), 207–220.
Uzunçarşılı, İ. H. (1988). *Osmanlı Devleti Teşkilâtından Kapıkulu Ocakları 1*. Türk Tarih Kurumu Yayınları.

CHAPTER 6

Predicting the Behavioural Intention for Cash *Waqf*: Evidence from Malaysia and Thailand

Ruslaina Yusoff, Shariful Amran Abd Rahman, Wan Nazihah Wan Mohamed, Parichard Benrit, and Faizah Darus

1 INTRODUCTION

Abu Huraira (RadhiAllahu 'anhu) narrated in a *hadith* in which the Prophet Muhammad says, 'When a man dies, his acts come to an end, but three; recurring charity or knowledge (by which people benefit), or a pious offspring who pays for him (for the deceased) (Muslim).'

By no means shall you attain Al-Birr (piety, righteousness), unless you spend (in Allah's cause), of that which you love; and whatever of good you spend, Allah knows it well. (Al-Quran 3:92)

R. Yusoff (✉) • S. A. A. Rahman
Faculty of Accountancy, Universiti Teknologi MARA Kelantan Campus, Machang, Malaysia
e-mail: ruslaina@uitm.edu.my; shariful@uitm.edu.my

© The Author(s), under exclusive license to Springer Nature Switzerland AG 2022
A. G. Ismail et al. (eds.), *Islamic Philanthropy*, Palgrave Studies in Islamic Banking, Finance, and Economics,
https://doi.org/10.1007/978-3-031-06890-4_6

By referring to the above verse and hadith, it is evident that giving charity is encouraged in Islam. Both philosophical and religious teachings have long argued that charitable giving leads to prosperity (van der Linden, 2011). There are several charitable instruments from an Islamic perspective, such as through *zakah* and *sadaqah* (donation). One of the imperative instruments of *sadaqah* is *waqf*. *Waqf* refers to a religious endowment that is a voluntary and irrevocable dedication of one's wealth or a portion of it either in cash or kind and its disbursement for *Shariah*-compliant projects (MIFC, 2015). It is an Islamic instrument of wealth distribution that can provide a perpetual benefit to society (Hashim, 2014). *Waqf* is also considered a virtuous act and is seen as the pillar of Islamic society's religious, social, cultural, scientific, economic, and political life. From an economic perspective, *waqf* can be regarded as a type of savings-investment instrument where funds are diverted from consumption and invested in productive assets that generate revenue. The profits can be used to achieve social objectives such as building hospitals, orphanages, universities, and others; thus unlocking both its economic potential and philanthropic objectives (MIFC, 2015). Meanwhile, Khan (2010) viewed *waqf* as an effective Islamic instrument of poverty alleviation if the Bangladesh government integrates *waqf* in poverty alleviation programmes and puts it into practice like the classical age of Islam.

The standard type of *waqf* is *cash waqf*. Rusydiana (2018) viewed cash *waqf* as an endowment which is different from ordinary property, while Abdel Mohsin (2008) defined *cash waqf* as the devotion of an amount of money by a founder and the dedication of its usufruct in perpetuity to the prescript purposes. According to *Yayasan Wakaf Malaysia*, cash *waqf* is

---

W. N. W. Mohamed
Akademi Pengajian Bahasa, Universiti Teknologi MARA Kelantan Campus, Kota Bharu, Malaysia
e-mail: wnazihah@uitm.edu.my

P. Benrit
Faculty of Humanities and Social Sciences, Prince of Songkla University Pattani Campus, Pattani, Thailand
e-mail: parichart.b@psu.ac.th

F. Darus
Faculty of Accountancy, Accounting Research Institute,
Universiti Teknologi MARA, Shah Alam, Malaysia

defined as a religious endowment using cash collected in a trust fund under the administrator's management to manage this endowment for the welfare benefit *ummah*. Endowment funds collected are then converted to the property to be utilized for the community's welfare and interests. What distinguishes these from the standard real estate endowments is the nature of their capital, *corpus*, which is in the form of cash. The *corpus* of the real estate *waqf*, by contrast, is in the form of real estate (Cizakca, 2004a).

There are many benefits from *waqf* contributions, including cash *waqf*. Cash *waqf* could provide some assistance to the needy in improving their life. Chowdhury et al. (2011) noted that cash *waqf* could help to restructure and improve current institutional set-up and networking performance. Budiman (2014) argued that the contributions of *waqf* for economic development can be explained in five points: (1) reducing government expenditure and participation in the economy; (2) preventing deficit financing and decreasing rate of interest; (3) restoring distribution of income and wealth; (4) eradicating poverty; and (5) enhancing economic progress. He concluded that *waqf* could fulfil the functions mentioned above without any state coercion or through the usual method, that is, redistributive taxation, but through voluntary donations made by well-to-do people in society (Budiman, 2014, p. 32). A study conducted by Saifuddin et al. (2014) proved that cash *waqf* has a strong prospect in developing the socio-economic sector, especially in poverty alleviation beyond religious purposes.

Despite the contributions of *waqf* to the society at large, there are some issues related to *waqf*, specifically from a local perspective. Osman et al. (2012) argued that the response of the Malaysians towards cash *waqf* is still lacking. Meanwhile, Alias (2011) suggested that the Malaysians' preference toward *waqf* was only for religious purposes. They only linked *waqf* with the construction of mosques and *waqf* land for cemetery use despite the more comprehensive function and roles of *waqf* itself. Alias (2011) also argued that cash *waqf* schemes of a general purpose (*waqf al am*) have not generated sufficient funds to carry out impact programmes. Even though Malaysia's cash *waqf* scheme has grown in momentum in recent years, other problems have arisen when the scheme's contributors required transparency for the use of funds. Due to a few constraints, the operations have caused the scheme to develop slowly and reached fewer individuals (Mokhtar et al., 2015). On the other hand, Haron et al. (2016) concluded that the main factors of cash *waqf* collection in Malaysia's three states are promotion, staffs, method, place of collection, and authority. Hence, it can be said that cash *waqf* development in Malaysia is still at the infancy level.

This chapter investigates the factors influencing contributors, particularly university students, to participate in cash *waqf*. The present study will provide some contributions to the various parties. First, the study provides some ideas on which conceptually independent determinants of intention are more applicable in explaining the intention to perform cash *waqf* among younger generations, specifically university students. Hence, it will contribute to the literature by investigating the factors influencing people's intention to participate in cash *waqf*. The study's findings could also be used by the respective authorities to design strategies to increase cash *waqf* participation. The findings could also help the government to diversify the present effort and find the solution to improve people's intention, which should start from the younger generation to contribute towards cash *waqf*.

2 CASH *WAQF* IN THEORY AND PRACTICE

Waqf is one of the potential mechanisms that have a significant role in generating financing for Muslim *ummah*'s needs. As an endowment, *waqf* is more in the form of fixed assets, a permanent submission by a Muslim of valuable property to Allah SWT ownership (Puad et al., 2014). *Waqf* revenues could be distributed to fulfil the poor's needs and used for society's welfare, such as mosques, schools, and higher-education institutions. However, due to a lack of awareness, society does not realize the potential of a *waqf* contribution towards the economics in which the funds obtained from *waqf* could be used for community purposes (Puad et al., 2014).

The Islamic world first introduced cash *waqf* in the eighth century (Sanusi & Shafiai, 2015), but it was only well-practised by the Ottomans and became very famous throughout the European province's sixteenth century (Cizakca, 2004b). The twenty-first century has observed *waqf* institutions' revival in many countries, including Malaysia, with the introduction of cash *waqf* (Osman et al., 2012). Societies have started to realize that people's donation in cash is a potential solution to fulfilling the necessity of public needs (Sayyed Hosseini et al., 2014). Activities include helping those in need of loans, orphans, *muallaf*, and unemployed individuals, since various parties can receive the benefits earned (Sanusi & Shafiai, 2015).

The implementation of *waqf* in Malaysia is governed under the state's jurisdiction of the 14 State Islamic Religious Councils, with each institution managing the properties of *waqf* according to its standard of management practice and enactments (Hasan & Abdullah, 2008). For instance, Johor introduced *Waqf* Prohibition Enactment 1911, Perak presented Control of *Waqf* Enactment 1951 (Puad et al., 2014), Selangor provided *waqf* legislations under the Enactment of *Waqf* (State of Selangor) 1999, while Melaka performed the Enactment of *Waqf* (State of Malacca) 2005 (Hasan & Abdullah, 2008). As such, the states in Malaysia have their legislations, and each state religious council holds an essential role in managing and distributing *waqf* properties for the common public interest.

The legality of cash *waqf* in Malaysia was confirmed by the Fatwa Committee of the National Council for the Religion of Islam on 10 to 12 April 2007 at Kuala Terengganu, which consequently dismissed the polemic concerning its implementation (Ibrahim et al., 2013; Sanusi & Shafiai, 2015). Cash *waqf* is exchanged into a fixed asset and invested before it is allocated to the beneficiaries and served to the community (Sanusi & Shafiai, 2015). On top of that, several states in Malaysia have introduced cash *waqf* schemes such as Penang with minimal shares of RM5, while Selangor, Pahang, Johor, Terengganu, and Malacca with a donation of RM10 (Ibrahim et al., 2013). It proposes the potential to develop cash *waqf* because if each Muslim adult in Malaysia donates at least RM30 a month, the collection of cash *waqf* can achieve RM4.3 billion a year (Abdullah, 2009).

The application of cash *waqf* under different regulated laws and management of different states' Islamic Religious Councils have presented some problems that might instigate the inefficiency of cash *waqf* collection in Malaysia (Osman et al., 2012). According to Alias (2011), cash *waqf* schemes have not generated a fine collection of money as the public's response towards cash *waqf* is still lacking due to misconception and lack of awareness. Most people still have the perception that *waqf* funds are solely attributed to the development of religious purposes, namely for mosques or cemeteries; thus, they are not conscious that the money donated can fulfil a diversification of purposes for the sake of the Islamic economy due to its flexible form of assets (Ibrahim et al., 2013). They are also reluctant to donate due to insufficient knowledge of cash *waqf* (Yusof & Aziz, 2013; Huda et al., 2017). Furthermore, Nurrachmi (2012) asserted that an unqualified *waqf* manager or *mutawalli* could lead to various issues like *waqf* assets being idle with no individual to manage them, corruption in distributing *waqf* money, and insufficient funds to cover the operational cost of the planned project.

In comparison to Malaysia, the management of *waqf* institutions in Thailand is still lacking since Thailand does not have any specific law governing the implementation of *waqf* and serving the purposes of *waqf* practices. The majority of the Muslims in Thailand live in four southern provinces of Yala, Pattani, Narathiwat, and Satun, but *waqf* practices could be found across the country as it contributes to improving Muslims' well-being (Duereh & Noipom, 2016). At present, the management of religious matters including *waqf* is jointly supervised by Chularajmontri (Shaykh al-Islam), Provincial Committee for Islamic Affairs (PCIA), and the Mosque Committee Member (MCM), but the position of *waqf* land is still in the scope of Thai civil law (Dorloh, 2015). The administration of Islamic religion is associated with two acts: the Administration of Islamic Organization Act 1997 and Islamic Law Enforcement in Pattani, Narathiwat, Yala, and Satun Act 1946. However, these two acts provide no explicit provision on *waqf* management in Thailand (Duereh & Noipom, 2016).

According to Dorloh (2015), the common practice of *waqf* in Thailand is that the donor offers land to the mosque, and the *imam* becomes the trustee for *waqf* property. The income generated from the land is used to manage mosques and religious schools, while the surplus of income is deposited into the *waqf* committee's account to be spent on development and poverty alleviation. However, issues may occur like undocumented *waqf*, inability to transfer properties to the mosque, and *waqf* under an individual's maintenance, since Thailand has no specific provision towards *waqf* management (Duereh & Noipom, 2016). Due to this, Duereh and Noipom (2016) suggested the amendment of the Islamic Law Enforcement in Pattani, Narathiwat, Yala, and Satun Act 1946. They proposed establishing national *waqf* organizations to ensure that Islamic experts resolve *waqf* property issues and administration.

Even though cash *waqf* practice is still considered new to some people, its procedure has gained researchers' attention to investigate its implementation, effectiveness, and interest among the Muslim public. Several studies were conducted to identify the factors that influence the collection of cash *waqf* (Faradis, 2015; Johari et al., 2015; Haron et al., 2016; Pitchay et al., 2015; Yusoff et al., 2018; Azizi et al., 2019). Others analysed its benefits towards the community and managerial aspects of cash *waqf* (Ibrahim et al., 2013; Lahsasna, 2010; Nurrachmi, 2012; Sayyed

Hosseini et al., 2014; Sanusi & Shafiai, 2015; Rusydiana, 2018; Rusydiana & Devi, 2018). Unfortunately, the amount of published research on *waqf*, especially on cash *waqf*, is still lacking in Thailand. This is probably due to the non-existence of *waqf* legislation in Thailand where none of the Thai National Land Code provision or other laws are devoted to *waqf* land (Dorloh, 2018).

An analysis on the trend of cash *waqf* collection from three states in Malaysia was performed by Haron et al. (2016), and they concluded that the south state experienced an increasing trend while the north and east coast states encountered fluctuating trends towards cash *waqf* collection. Factors that influence the public to be involved in cash *waqf* contribution include promotion, staff, method of collection, place of collection, and authority (Haron et al., 2016; Huda et al., 2017; Rusydiana, 2018; Azizi et al., 2019); religious obligation, benevolence, familiarity with *waqf* institutions, and access to cash *waqf* (Johari et al., 2015; Witjaksono et al., 2019); and *waqif* or donor's attitude, complaints, productive action, equity, product characteristic, religiosity, as well as generosity (Faradis, 2015). It is interesting to note that among the common reasons for donating cash *waqf* is religious duty, being generous (Faradis, 2015; Johari et al., 2015), and the organization responsible for collecting funds (Johari et al., 2015; Haron et al., 2016; Huda et al., 2017; Rusydiana, & Devi, 2018).

Research has also mentioned that *waqf* institutions should conduct rigorous promotion so that people would be encouraged to continuously perform cash *waqf* to gain a higher collection of funds (Johari et al., 2015; Haron et al., 2016). Also, *waqf* institutions should build a good reputation and integrity towards the public, especially the Muslims in Malaysia, since some individuals confessed that they did not trust the institutions that manage *waqf* (Johari et al., 2015; Yusof & Aziz, 2013). As stated by Faradis (2015), it relates to the equal distribution of funds and complaints regarding *waqf*. Moreover, some respondents claimed they are reluctant to donate because of insufficient knowledge of cash *waqf* (Yusof & Aziz, 2013; Huda et al., 2017). The relevant authorities must increase the community's awareness of cash *waqf* practice and rejuvenate the current *waqf* institutions to enhance efficiency and performance.

Research by Pitchay et al. (2015) ranked the developments prioritized by donors using the analytical hierarchy process. They discovered that donors have a high preference for channelling their cash *waqf* contribution towards the development and current needs of education, health, mosques, and welfare. It corresponds to the findings of a survey that the public has a strong willingness to perform cash *waqf* in accordance with educational needs due to the establishment of an Islamic *waqf* bank that would be an alternative for students to obtain a loan or finance their education (Aziz & Yusof, 2014; Aziz et al., 2013). Consequently, further studies on the awareness and intention of cash *waqf* donors, especially individuals involved in the educational domain, need to be conducted to intensify their commitment towards cash *waqf* practices.

3 HYPOTHESES TESTING

The Theory of Planned Behaviour (TPB) was presented by Ajzen (1991) by including the variable of perceived behavioural control to the original Theory of Reasoned Action (TRA) (Fishbein & Ajzen, 1975) as a result of its limitation in dealing with people's incomplete volitional control of behaviour. Since then, TPB has been extensively used in studies to predict people's behaviour with the concept that a single behaviour involves an action to achieve a specific target at a particular point of time (Ajzen & Fishbein, 2005).

The TPB model includes three variables of attitude, subjective norms, and perceived behavioural control that affect an individual's intention (Ajzen, 1991). According to Fishbein and Ajzen (1975), the intention is expressed as a subjective probability to carry out behaviour related to the willingness to try and the exertion to plan the effort to perform the behaviour (Ajzen, 1991). The variable intention has been used in many studies as a dependent variable due to its robustness in predicting behaviour (Osman, 2014). As conferred by Ajzen (1991), an individual's intention is driven by three types of belief: (1) behavioural belief, which yields a favourable or unfavourable attitude towards behaviour; (2) normative belief that is associated with other people's expectation and motivation to comply toward the expectation that resulted in perceived social pressure or subjective norms; and (3) control belief that denotes the presence of factors that may facilitate or impede the performance of behaviour that then gives rise to perceived behavioural control (van der Linden, 2011). Bringing together the three antecedents of attitude, subjective norms, and perceived behavioural control has led to the founding of intention in the Theory of Planned Behaviour.

As discussed earlier, the Theory of Planned Behaviour postulates three independent conceptual determinants of intention. Combining attitude, subjective norms, and perceived behavioural control towards behaviour would lead to behavioural intention. First, the intention to perform cash *waqf* is assumed to capture the motivational factors that influence the behaviour. It is an indication of how hard people are willing to try and how much of an effort they are planning to exert to perform the behaviour (Ajzen, 1991, p. 181). Generally, the higher the level of intention to perform in behaviour, the healthier or more likely to perform the behaviour.

Second, attitude and intention to perform cash *waqf* towards behaviour signifies the psychological tendency expressed from favourable or unfavourable evaluation or appraisal of the behaviour in question (Ajzen, 1991). In other words, it is the degree to which a person has positive or negative feelings of the behaviour of interest because the more favourable a person's attitude towards behaviour, the more likely the person will be engaged towards the behaviour (Osman, 2014; Azizi et al., 2019; Awang et al., 2017). Several studies have utilized TPB and documented a significant relationship between attitude and intention, specifically research that investigated *zakah* payment (Huda et al., 2012; Sapingi et al., 2011), corporate *waqf* (Hasbullah et al., 2016), donation to charity or giving behaviour (Awang et al., 2015; van der Linden, 2011) and cash *waqf* involvement (Osman, 2014). However, one study among Muslim donors in Malaysia found that attitude has no effect on cash *waqf* giving intention (Osman et al., 2016). Therefore, further research needs to be conducted to determine whether the attitude factor influences the Muslim's intention to contribute towards cash *waqf*. As such, the first hypothesis for this study is:

H1 There is a significant relationship between attitude and intention to perform cash *waqf*.

Third, subjective norms and intentions to perform cash *waqf* are another predictor of TPB. Subjective norms are defined by Ajzen (1991) as the perceived social pressure as to whether or not the behaviour should be performed. It also denotes the belief about whether significant others think a person will perform the behaviour since it relates to the person's perception of the social environment surrounding the behaviour (Awang et al., 2017). Subjective norms have gained much attention in behavioural intention literature, including studies on cash *waqf* performance in which Osman (2014) found a significant relationship between subjective norms and intention whereas Osman et al. (2016) concluded with an insignificant finding. Another study by Hasbullah et al. (2016) was conducted to examine the intention to contribute towards corporate *waqf* which discovered a positive relationship. However, most researchers concluded that subjective norms did not explain the variance in intention, such as the studies on *zakah* payment involving respondents in Jakarta (Huda et al., 2012) and academics in Malaysia (Sapingi et al., 2011). Subjective norms also did not affect the giving behaviour of the Malaysians (Awang et al., 2015) and European participants (van der Linden, 2011). Due to this, this study extends the analysis of subjective norms by proposing the second hypothesis of:

H2 There is a significant relationship between subjective norms and intention to perform cash *waqf*.

Fourth, the relationship between perceived behavioural control and intention to perform cash *waqf* is also examined. Perceived behavioural control refers to people's perception of the ease or difficulty of performing the behaviour of interest, which is closely linked to the self-efficacy concept (Ajzen, 1991) since it reflects the previous experience and anticipates barriers (Hasbullah et al., 2016). If attitude and subjective norms are more favourable towards the behaviour, perceived behavioural control will be better, and the individual's intention to perform such behaviour will be greater (Osman, 2014). The majority of the studies in TPB concluded that perceived behavioural control is a significant predictor towards intention, such as studies concerning *zakah* payment (Huda et al., 2012; Sapingi et al., 2011), donation to charity or giving behaviour (Awang et al., 2015; van der Linden, 2011), and cash *waqf* practice (Osman, 2014; Osman et al., 2016). Hence, the third hypothesis is:

H3 There is a significant relationship between perceived behavioural control and intention to perform cash *waqf*.

4 RESEARCH METHODS

Although the TPB has been extensively applied in various fields of study, its validity is yet to be proven, especially in the study related to the intention to perform cash *waqf*. As such, utilizing the determinants of TPB, this research examines the context of cash *waqf* to explore the influencing factors towards Muslims' intention to contribute towards cash *waqf*. Figure 6.1 depicts the model of the research.

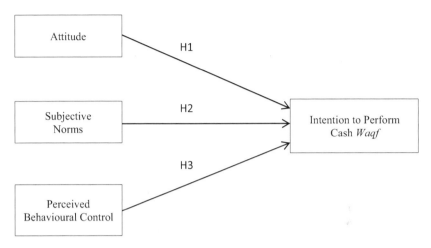

Fig. 6.1 Research model

Data for this study were collected through structured questionnaire for both Malaysia and Thailand. The questionnaire was distributed to 400 students at the Universiti Teknologi MARA Kelantan Campus, Malaysia, and 200 students at Prince of Songkla University Pattani Campus, Thailand. A total of 379 returned questionnaires were obtained from Universiti Teknologi MARA Kelantan Campus, Malaysia, and 172 questionnaires from Prince of Songkla University Pattani Campus, Thailand. Hence, a combined total of 551 were obtained from 600 questionnaires originally distributed at both universities with a return rate of 92 percent.

A questionnaire using a seven-point scale was employed to collect the data for the current study. Items from previous studies were modified for the adaptation towards cash *waqf* context. The measures of attitude, subjective norm, and perceived behavioural control towards the intention to perform cash *waqf* were adapted from various studies related to the TPB (Shih & Fang, 2004; Osman, 2014; George, 2004; Gopi & Ramayah, 2007). A Likert-type scale was used to measure the scale which ranged from "very unlikely" (1) to "very likely" (7). The items for attitude towards intention to perform cash *waqf* were adapted and adopted from Shih and Fang (2004), Osman (2014), and George (2004). Meanwhile, subjective norms were adapted and adopted from Shih and Fang (2004)

Table 6.1 Demographic results

Profile	Description	Malaysia		Thailand	
		Male	Female	Male	Female
Gender		89	290	40	132
Age group	18–24 years old	81	282	37	131
	25–35 years old	8	8	3	1
Education level					
	Diploma	4	12	0	0
	Bachelor degree	82	274	40	132
	Master	3	4	0	0
Knowledge level of cash *waqf*					
	None	40	93	11	28
	Little	33	149	19	56
	Medium	16	47	8	45
	High	0	1	2	2

and Osman (2014). Lastly, the items for perceived behavioural control were adapted from George (2004) and Gopi and Ramayah (2007).

Participants' intention to perform cash *waqf* was assessed using three items that were adopted from Osman (2014): "I plan to perform cash *waqf*," "My general intention to perform cash *waqf* is higher," and "I will choose cash *waqf* as a way for my donations." Items were anchored by a 7-point Likert-type scale ranging from 1 ("Strongly disagree") to 7 ("Strongly agree"). As with Cunningham and Kwon (2003), the mean of the three items represents the final score. The reliability estimate (Cronbach's alpha) for this measure was 0.96.

Table 6.1 shows detailed information about the respondents. The respondents comprised mainly females for both countries, which represented 76.52% from Malaysia and 76.74% from Thailand. The average age group of the respondents was 18 to 24 years for both countries. In the educational level analysis, the respondents from Malaysia were mainly bachelor degree students (93.93%), while for Thailand, all respondents were bachelor degree students. Regarding the level of knowledge towards cash *waqf* among the respondents, it shows that majority of the respondents have little knowledge about cash *waqf*, which represents 48% of respondents from Malaysia and 44% from Thailand.

Table 6.2 Factor loading outcome

	Attitude	Subjective norms	Perceived behavioural control	Intention behaviour
Variance explained	69.71%	77.34%	73.74%	88%
Eigen-value	5.6	4.42	3.87	2.64
Cronbach alpha	0.94	0.93	0.93	0.93
KMO	0.95			0.76
Bartlett's test of sphericity	Chi-square = 9493.56, p-value = 0.000			Chi-square = 1373.37, p-value = 0.000

5 Discussion

Before hypothesis testing, factor analysis was conducted to determine the reliability and validity of the items under independent and dependent instruments (attitude, subjective norms, perceived behavioural control, and intention behaviour). The Eigen-value for both independent and dependent variables was more than one, as shown in Table 6.2. Any variables with an Eigen-value of less than one have to be rejected, while the variables with an Eigen-value of more than one would be retained for further analysis (Hair et al., 2006).

The items' reliability was tested by calculating Cronbach alpha to determine the margin of free-from-random-error of the items. Cronbach alpha of 0.70 and above is considered to be reliable. Table 6.2 shows that all items under both independent and dependent variables were more than 0.70, which can be considered reliable.

To further ensure the instruments' validity, the figures for KMO and Bartlett's Test of Sphericity were also included in Table 6.2. KMO measures the sampling adequacy for each variable in the model and the complete model. KMO figures of 0.95 (attitude, subjective norms, and perceived behavioural control) and 0.76 (intention to perform cash *waqf*) indicated that the sampling was adequate, and the necessary threshold for KMO was 0.6 and above. Bartlett's Test of Sphericity relates to the study's significance and thereby shows the validity and suitability of the responses collected to the problem being addressed through the study. For factor analysis to be recommended suitable, Bartlett's Test of Sphericity must be less than 0.05. The p-values for both independent and dependent variables

Table 6.3 Multiple regression analysis

	Malaysia			Thailand		
	β	R square	p-value[a]	β	R square	p-value[a]
Attitude	2.776	1.75	0.000	2.859	0.146	0.001
Subjective norm	0.157	0.157	0.000	2.501	0.275	0.000
Perceived behavioural control	1.979	0.409	0.000	1.843	0.611	0.000

[a] Significant at 5% confidence level

were less than 0.05. It indicates that the samples were collected from the population with equal variance.

Multiple regression analysis was conducted to determine the relationship between the independent variables (attitude, subjective norms, and perceived behavioural control) and the dependent variable (intention to perform cash *waqf*). In other words, multiple regression analysis (p-value) indicates whether the independent variables affect the intention to perform cash *waqf*. Meanwhile, the r-square determines whether the independent variables explain the degree of variation in intention to perform cash *waqf*.

The results (Table 6.3) obtained from the data collection suggested that all three independent variables (attitude, subjective norms and perceived behavioural control) did influence the intention to perform cash *waqf*. With p-values of 0.000 (Malaysia) and 0.001 (Thailand), hypothesis 1 (attitude has a significant relationship with attention to perform cash *waqf*, H1) is accepted. The same results were obtained for both hypothesis 2 (H2) and hypothesis 3 (H3). The p-value for both Malaysia and Thailand's subjective norms was 0.000, while perceived behavioural control was also 0.000 for both countries. It indicates that both subjective norms and perceived behavioural control did influence the intention to perform cash *waqf*.

The current study indicates that attitude plays a significant role in determining the intention to perform cash *waqf*. It is in line with other studies that conclude attitude will affect the intention to perform such behaviour (Sapingi et al., 2011; Huda et al., 2012; Awang et al., 2015; Azizi et al., 2019; Hasbullah et al., 2016). Nevertheless, the current study contrasts with the result obtained by Osman et al. (2016). They suggested that the differences in their study environment, population, and the classification of study may influence the individual's attitude towards participating in cash *waqf*. According to Ajzen (1991), attitude is developed from the beliefs that individuals hold about the attitude's object. Hence, if the individual believes that the particular behaviour will lead to favourable circumstances, the same individual will have a positive attitude towards the behaviour and vice versa. The results of the study suggested that respondents believe in the importance and benefits of cash *waqf*. As a result, the respondents spontaneously acquire a positive attitude, which demonstrates the positive p-value toward performing cash *waqf*.

The findings also show that subjective norms have a significant relationship with the intention to perform cash *waqf* among university students. It means that social pressure did influence the intention to perform cash *waqf* among the respondents. The result is consistent with the study conducted by Hasbullah et al. (2016). They discovered a positive relationship between subjective norms and intention to engage in corporate *waqf*. Even though Osman et al. (2016) conducted the same study on cash *waqf*, they obtained a different result. Most research concluded that subjective norms did not explain the variance in intention, such as the studies conducted by Huda et al. (2012) and Sapingi et al. (2011). The current study proposed that even though cash *waqf* is voluntary, the respondents still believe that people important to them or near to them will want the respondents to be involved in cash *waqf*.

Lastly, the study also found that the relationship between perceived behavioural control and intention to perform cash *waqf* among university students is significant. It is in line with the results obtained by Osman et al. (2016), Azizi et al. (2019) and Sapingi et al. (2011). Perceived behavioural control relates to people's perception of the ease or difficulties in performing the behaviour of interest. The higher the perception of ease in performing the behaviour of interest, the higher the intention to perform the behaviour, and vice versa (Ajzen, 1991). According to Ajzen (1991), perceived behavioural control relates to experience concerning intention or second-hand information such as family and friends' experience. As students, there is a very slim chance that the respondents have any experience in performing cash *waqf*, and the setting of answering questionnaire session hinders the respondents from finding information about cash *waqf* from their family or friends. This led to the suggestion by Ajzen (1991) and Beck and Ajzen (1991) that personal feelings of moral obligation or responsibility will influence the perception of the ease or difficulties in performing the behaviour. Since cash *waqf* is religious, respondents feel that it is their moral obligation to perform cash *waqf*.

In general, the current research shows that the TPB is useable in predicting the intention to perform cash *waqf* among university students in Universiti Teknologi MARA Kelantan Campus, Malaysia, and Prince of Songkla University Pattani Campus, Thailand.

6 CONCLUSION

The results from the study strongly suggest that attitude, subjective norms, and perceived behavioural control play an important role in deciding whether or not to perform cash *waqf* among the university students in both countries. At the same time, it validates the effectiveness of TPB to predict the intention to perform such behaviour.

For the religious bodies, the results present an opportunity to expand participation in performing cash *waqf* by organizing programmes that can heighten favourable attitudes toward performing cash *waqf*. In addition, self-restructuring process such as appointing qualified and experienced people to manage cash *waqf* funds can also increase the level of confidence in religious bodies, which results in an increase in favourable attitudes towards cash *waqf*. At the same time, providing more venues such as online transfer to participate in cash *waqf* will also reinforce the public's perception of the ease of performing cash *waqf*.

Despite this study's contribution, several limitations suggest directions for future research in the area. First, this study's location is confined to Universiti Teknologi MARA Kelantan Campus, Malaysia, and Prince of Songkla University Pattani Campus, Thailand, which suggests that the findings should not be generalized to other universities in Malaysia or Thailand. Hence, it is suggested that future research cover broader geographical areas.

Second, the current study sample did not specifically focus on individuals who have experience in cash *waqf*; therefore, it could not represent individuals who have just decided to perform cash *waqf*. In the future, perhaps the sample should include those who are practically performing cash *waqf* as one method for their donating.

Third, the findings of the study largely depend on the honesty of the respondents. Similar to Gopi and Ramayah (2007, p. 357), it is known that individuals would agree more on socially desirable answers and disagree more towards socially undesirable answers rather than fully and honestly express their feelings and opinions. Since cash *waqf* is not obligatory but highly encouraged in Islam, the respondents may not be truthful in completing the questionnaire. As such, further studies should be conducted to verify the related findings.

Acknowledgement The authors would like to express their gratitude to the Accounting Research Institute (ARI), Universiti Teknologi MARA, and the Ministry of Higher Education Malaysia in facilitating this research project.

REFERENCES

Abdel Mohsin, M. I. (2008, July) Cash Waqf: A New Financial Product Model Aspects of Shariah Principles on Its Commercialization. Paper Presented at Islamic Banking, Accounting, and Finance Conference (iBAF 2008), Kuala Lumpur, Malaysia.

Abdullah, M. S. (2009, August). Eksistensi wakaf tunai di Pulau Pinang: Satu analisis mengenai potensi dan mobilisasi dana untuk pembangunan ekonomi umat Islam. Paper presented at The 4th ISDEV International Graduate Workshop (INGRAW09), Pulau Pinang, Malaysia.

Ajzen, I. (1991). The Theory of Planned Behaviour. *Organizational Behaviour and Human Decision Processes*, 50(2), 179–211.

Ajzen, I., & Fishbein, M. (2005). The Influence of Attitudes on Behaviour. In D. Albarrac, B. T. Johnson, & M. P. Zanna (Eds.), *The Handbook of Attitudes* (pp. 173–221). Erlbaum. http://web.psych.utoronto.ca/psy320/Required%20readings_files/4-1.pdf

Alias, T. A. (2011). Tax Laws Affecting Waqf in Malaysia: A Comparison with the United States and Turkey. http://www.academia.edu/1101187/Awqaf_tax_laws

Awang, S. A., Borhan, J. T., Mohamad, M. T., & Muhammad, F. (2017). The Scenario of Giving to Beggars: A Behavioural Analysis among Malaysians. *Labuan e-Journal of Muamalat and Society*, 11, 1–12.

Awang, S. A., Muhammad, F., Borhan, J. T., & Mohamad, M. T. (2015). Exploring the Patterns and Antecedents of Charitable Giving among the Muslim Community in Malaysia. *Online Journal Research in Islamic Studies*, 2(2), 46–58.

Aziz, M. R. A., & Yusof, M. A. (2014, March). An Initial Study on Student's Needs towards Islamic Waqf Bank for Education. Paper presented at International Conference on Arts, Economics and Management (ICAEM'14), Dubai, United Arab Emirates.

Aziz, M. R. A., Yusof, M. A., & Johari, F. (2013). The Inclination of Students and the Public towards the Establishment of an Islamic Waqf Bank. *World Applied Sciences Journal*, 26(1), 138–143.

Azizi, N. D., Shukor, S. A., & Sabri, H. (2019). Determinants of Repeated Endowers' Donation Intention in Cash Waqf: A Case Study in Majlis Agama Islam dan Adat Melayu Perak (MAIPk). *Jurnal Manajemen Bisnis, 10*(2), 154–163.

Beck, L., & Ajzen, I. (1991). Predicting Dishonest Actions Using the Theory of Planned Behaviour. *Journal of Research in Personality, 25,* 285–301.

Budiman, M. A. (2014). The Significance of Waqf for Economic Development. *Equilibrium Quarterly Journal of Economics and Economic Policy, 2*(1), 19–34.

Chowdhury, M. S. R., Ghazali, M. F., & Ibrahim, M. F. (2011). Economics of Cash Waqf Management in Malaysia: A Proposed Cash Waqf Model for Practitioners and Future Researchers. *African Journal of Business Management, 5*(30), 12155–12163.

Cizakca, M. (2004a, January). Incorporated Cash Waqfs and Mudaraba. Islamic Non-bank Financial Instruments from the Past to the Future? Paper presented at the International Seminar on Non-bank Financial Institutions, Kuala Lumpur, Malaysia.

Cizakca, M. (2004b). Ottoman Cash Waqfs Revisited: The Case of Bursa (1555–1823). https://muslimheritage.com/ottoman-cash-waqfs-revisited-bursa/

Cunningham, G. B., & Kwon, H. (2003). The Theory of Planned Behaviour and Intentions to Attend a Sporting Event. *Sport Management Review, 6,* 127–145.

Dorloh, S. (2015). Reviewing the Law for Muslim Affairs in Enhancing the Waqf Institution in Thailand: A Way Forward. *The Journal of Muamalat and Islamic Finance Research, 12*(2), 33–40.

Dorloh, S. (2018). The Status of Waqf Properties in the Malay-Muslim Majority Areas of Thailand: A Legal Survey. https://www.researchgate.net/publication/329829277_The_Status_of_Waqf_Properties_in_the_Malay-Muslim_1_majority_areas_of_Thailand_A_Legal_Survey

Duereh, S., & Noipom, T. (2016). An Overview of Waqf Administration: A Case Study of Thai Administrative Law. *Proceedings of International Conference on Islamic Jurisprudence (ICIJ) 2016.*

Faradis, J. (2015). The Determinants of Waqf Preference toward Money-Cash Waqf. *Global Review of Islamic Economics and Business, 2*(3), 219–229.

Fishbein, M., & Ajzen, I. (1975). *Belief, Attitude, Intention, and Behaviour: An Introduction to Theory and Research.* Addison-Wesley.

George, J. F. (2004). The Theory of Planned Behaviour and Internet Purchasing. *Internet Research, 14*(3), 198–212.

Gopi, M., & Ramayah, T. (2007). Applicability of Theory of Planned Behaviour in Predicting Intention to Trade Online: Some Evidence from a Developing Country. *International Journal of Emerging Markets, 2*(4), 348–360.

Hair, J. F., Anderson, R. E., Tatham, R. L., & Black, B. C. (2006). *Multivariate Data Analysis.* Pearson Education Inc.

Haron, M., Kamarudin, M. K., Fauzi, N. A. M., Ariff, M. M., & Zainuddin, M. Z. (2016). Cash Waqf Collection: Any Potential Factors to Influence It? *International Journal of Business, Economics and Law, 9*(2), 27–33.

Hasan, Z., & Abdullah, M. N. (2008). The Investment of Waqf Land as an Instrument of Muslims' Economic Development in Malaysia. Paper presented at Dubai International Conference on Endowments' Investment, United Arab Emirates.

Hasbullah, N. A., Khairi, K. F., & Aziz, M. R. A. (2016). Intention to Contribute to Corporate Waqf: Applying the Theory of Planned Behaviour. *International Journal of Islamic and Civilizational Studies, 3*(1), 39–48.

Hashim, M. Z. (2014). Promoting Charity via 'Waqf'. http://www.thestar.com.my/opinion/columnists/ikim-views/2014/04/15/promoting-charity-via-waqf/

Huda, N., Rini, N., Mardoni, Y., Hudori, K., & Anggraini, D. (2017). Problems, Solutions and Strategies Priority for Waqf in Indonesia. *Journal of Economic Cooperation and Development, 38*(1), 29–54.

Huda, N., Rini, N., Mardoni, Y., & Putra, P. (2012). The Analysis of Attitudes, Subjective Norms, and Behavioural Control on Muzakki's Intention to Pay Zakah. *International Journal of Business and Social Science, 3*(22), 271–279.

Ibrahim, H., Amir, A., & Masron, T. A. (2013). Cash Waqf: An Innovative Instrument for Economic Development. *International Review of Social Sciences and Humanities, 6*(1), 1–7.

Johari, F., Alias, M., Shukor, S. A., Wahab, K. A., Aziz, M. R. A., Ahmad, N., Zulkefli, Z. K., Hussin, F. A., & Ibrahim, P. (2015). Factors That Influence Repeat Contribution of Cash Waqf in Islamic Philanthropy. *Malaysian Accounting Review, 14*(2), 55–78.

Khan, F. (2010). Waqf: An Islamic Instrument of Poverty Alleviation–Bangladesh Perspective. Paper presented at the 7th International Conference—The Tawhidi Epistemology: Zakat and Waqf Economy, Bangi, Malaysia.

Lahsasna, A. (2010). The Cash Waqf Role in Financing Micro and Medium-Sized Enterprises (MMES): A New Islamic Financial Approach by Using the Cash Waqf Model—Testing the Model on Malaysian MMES Framework. Paper presented at 7th International Conference—The Tawhidi Epistemology: Zakat and Waqf Economy, Bangi, Malaysia.

MIFC. (2015). *Realizing the Social Role of Islamic Finance*. www.mifc.com

Mokhtar, F. M., Sidin, E. M., & Razak, D. A. (2015). Operation of Cash Waqf in Malaysia and Its limitations. *Journal of Islamic Economics, Banking, and Finance, 11*(4), 100–114.

Nurrachmi, R. (2012). The Implication of Cash Waqf in Society. *Al Infaq Islamic Economic Journal, 3*(2), 150–155. https://mpra.ub.uni-muenchen.de/44605/1/MPRA_paper_44605.pdf

Osman, A. F. (2014, April). An Analysis of Cash Waqf Participation among Young Intellectuals. Paper presented at 9th International Academic Conference, Istanbul, Turkey.

Osman, A. F., Htay, S. N. N., & Muhammad, M. O. (2012, April). Determinants of Cash Waqf Giving in Malaysia: Survey of Selected Works. Paper presented at Workshop Antarabangsa Pembangunan Berteraskan Islam V (WAPI-5), Indonesia.

Osman, A. F., Mohammed, M. O., & Fadzil, A. (2016). Factors Influencing Cash Waqf Giving Behaviour: A Revised Theory of Planned Behaviour. *Journal of Global Business and Social Entrepreneurship, 1*(2), 12–25.

Pitchay, A. A., Mydin Meera, A. K., & Saleem, M. Y. (2015). Factors Influencing the Behavioural Intentions of Muslim Employees to Contribute to Cash-Waqf through Salary Deductions. *JKAU: Islamic Economics, 28*(1), 57–90.

Puad, N. M. A., Rafdi, N. J., & Shahar, W. S. S. (2014). Issues and Challenges of Waqf Instrument: A Case Study in MAIS. In *E-proceedings of the Conference on Management and Muamalah (CoMM 2014)*.

Rusydiana, A. S. (2018). An Analysis of Cash Waqf Development in Indonesia Using Interpretive Structural Modeling (ISM). *Journal of Islamic Economics Lariba, 4*(1), 1–12.

Rusydiana, A. S., & Devi, A. (2018). Elaborating Cash Waqf Development in Indonesia Using Analytic Network Process. *International Journal of Islamic Business and Economics, 2*(1), 1–13.

Saifuddin, F., Kayadibi, S., Polat, R., Fidan, Y., & Kayadibi, O. (2014). The Role of Cash Waqf in Poverty Alleviation: Case of Malaysia. *International Journal of Business, Economics, and Law, 4*(1), 171–179.

Sanusi, S., & Shafiai, M. H. M. (2015). The Management of Cash Waqf: Toward Socio-economic Development of Muslims in Malaysia. *Jurnal Pengurusan, 43*, 3–12.

Sapingi, R., Ahmad, N., & Mohamad, M. (2011). A Study on Zakah of Employment Income: Factors That Influence Academics' Intention to Pay Zakah. In *Proceedings of 2nd International Conference on Business and Economic Research (2nd ICBER 2011)*.

Sayyed Hosseini, S. M., Salari, T. E., & Zaman Abadi, S. M. N. (2014). Study of Cash Waqf and Its Impact on Poverty (A Case Study of Iran). *Atlantic Review of Economics, 2*, 1–19.

Shih, Y., & Fang, K. (2004). The Use of a Decomposed Theory of Planned Behaviour to Study Internet Banking in Taiwan. *Internet Research, 14*(3), 213–223.

Van der Linden, S. (2011). Charitable Intent: A Moral or Social Construct? A Revised Theory of Planned Behaviour Model. *Current Psychology, 30*, 355–374.

Witjaksono, B., Mariyanti, T., Nasution, M. E., Huda, N., & Rini, N. (2019). Factors Which Influence the Intention of Community in Cash Waqf in Sharia Banking with Theory of Planned Behaviour (TPB) Modification Approach. *Journal of Islamic Banking and Finance, 7*(2), 50–58.

Yusof, M. A., & Aziz, M. R. A. (2013, September). The Relationship between the Level of Income and Willingness to Contribute to the Islamic Waqf Bank. Paper presented at the 5th Islamic Economic System Conference, Kuala Lumpur, Malaysia.

Yusoff, R., Rahman, S. A. A., & Mohamed, W. N. W. (2018). Factors Influencing the Intention to Perform Cash Waqf among Muslim Staff at Universiti Teknologi MARA, Kelantan Campus. Paper presented at International Conference on Islam and Global Issues, Universiti Teknologi MARA Cawangan Kelantan, Malaysia.

CHAPTER 7

Waqf-Based Crowdfunding: Proposed Framework for Entrepreneurial Development

Samsinar Sulaiman, Shifa Mohd Nor, and Suhaili Alma'amun

7.1 INTRODUCTION

Entrepreneurs are believed to be a driving force of the economy. However, lack of financial support threatens the growth spirit of the entrepreneur. One of the biggest hurdles or constraints for the potential entrepreneur is the lack of access to the funds and capital to start or grow a new business (Andersen & Nielsen, 2012; Kerr & Nanda, 2009). Generally, entrepreneurs rely on financial intermediaries or bank loans as sources of

---

S. Sulaiman • S. Alma'amun
Faculty of Economics and Management, Universiti Kebangsaan Malaysia, Bangi, Malaysia
e-mail: suhaili@ukm.edu.my

S. Mohd Nor (✉)
Centre for Governance Resilience and Accountability Studies, Faculty of Economics and Managament, Universiti Kebangsaan Malaysia, Bangi, Malaysia

Institute of Islam Hadhari, Universiti Kebangsaan Malaysia, Bangi, Malaysia
e-mail: shifa@ukm.edu.my

© The Author(s), under exclusive license to Springer Nature Switzerland AG 2022
A. G. Ismail et al. (eds.), *Islamic Philanthropy*, Palgrave Studies in Islamic Banking, Finance, and Economics,
https://doi.org/10.1007/978-3-031-06890-4_7

funds (Abdullah, 2016). However, financial intermediaries have their standard of deciding which project to fund. Banks' reluctance to support young entrepreneurs and their start-ups due to their perceived risk profile and non-existence of collateral triggered the evolution of new innovative products or mechanisms to address the funding gap for new entrepreneurs (Asutay & Marzban, 2015). Hence, the potential entrepreneur needs other sources of funding or external financing to gain capital, such as crowdfunding.

Crowdfunding has recently gained world attention as alternative financing for the entrepreneur. Crowdfunding is the subset of crowdsourcing on the Internet, which collects funds to help start-up businesses, charities, or aid for the needy such as disaster aid (Kleemann et al., 2008). Based on a report by the consultancy Massolution, funds raised via crowdfunding in Asia expanded by 167% in 2014 to reach $16.2 billion, up from $6.1 billion in 2013 (Massolution, 2015). Indeed, Asians have become the second largest market for crowdfunding after North America. Internet-based crowdfunding has seen extraordinary growth in the last few years in terms of total revenue, global spread, the number of platforms, and diversity of applications (Massolution, 2013).

Interest and non-Shari'ah compliance investment in crowdfunding have become hurdles for entrepreneurs, especially Muslim entrepreneurs, to utilize crowdfunding as their fundraising mechanism. However, along with the rapid growth of Islamic banks and Islamic financial instruments, there is an advanced Islamic mechanism for Shari'ah-compliant crowdfunding. As for Malaysia, the Guidelines on Regulation of Markets under Section 34 of the Capital Markets and Services Act 2007 were released in 2015 to introduce new requirements for the registration of equity crowdfunding (ECF) platforms and provide government arrangement for the operation of such platforms. According to Abdullah (2016), the provision of the guidelines in general is applicable for conventional equity and Islamic equity crowdfunding. According to Part E of the guidelines, what makes equity crowdfunding Shari'ah-compliant is the Shari'ah advisor (Security Commission Malaysia, 2015).[1]

On August 3, 2016, the former prime minister of Malaysia, Tun Abdullah Ahmad Badawi, launched the *Waqf* crowdfunding platform known as WaqfWorld.org. This crowdfunding platform is described as the

---

[1] Part E of the guidelines is the only provision related to the Shari'ah requirement, which stipulated a Shari'ah advisor's appointment.

"world's first" for *waqf*-based crowdfunding. This new platform was announced at the 12th World Islamic Economic Foundation Forum (WIEF) held in Jakarta, Indonesia. The unique hybrid product of crowdfunding in *waqf* represents a new financing mechanism for the entrepreneur by using Shari'ah mechanisms and regulation.

Waqf-based crowdfunding has considerable potential as a fundraising mechanism for Muslim entrepreneurs, parallel with Shari'ah-compliant equity, P2P, and reward-based crowdfunding. Therefore, this study proposed a mechanism for entrepreneurial financing through the integration of crowdfunding and *waqf* as a Shari'ah-compliant crowdfunding. This *waqf* crowdfunding will also provide information on utilizing cash *waqf* in crowdfunding, as a new fundraising mechanism that is proposed to solve financing issues. The mechanism features a more secure and Shari'ah-compliant approach in online fundraising for entrepreneurs that is based on the Maqasid Al-Shari'ah.

Section 2 discusses the overview of crowdfunding and also describing about *waqf*. Section 3 will elaborate on the mechanics of *waqf*-based crowdfunding. Section 4 will elucidate the fundamental process of crowdfunding and cash *waqf*. Section 5 summarizes the study by offering a proposal on funding entrepreneurial development.

7.2 Overview of Crowdfunding

Crowdfunding, in general, is defined as an "open call for a collective effort by people who network and pool their money together essentially through the Internet, for the provision of financial resources either in the form of a donation or in exchange for some form of reward or investment in order to support initiated by other people or organizations for specific purposes" (Lambert & Schwienbacher, 2010; Ordanini et al., 2011). Whereas crowdfunding, particularly in the area of entrepreneurship, is explained as a process in which an entrepreneur raises external financing or capital from a broad audience (the crowd) or novel investor, and in which each individual provides or is willing to invest small amounts through internet-based intermediaries (Belleflamme et al., 2013; Valanciene & Jegeleviciute, 2013).

Historically crowdfunding was initially used to gain funds in the art, music, and movie industries (Lambert & Schwienbacher, 2010). After some time, crowdfunding became more widespread; the business industry uses crowdfunding to get funds and finance the idea of their project with external financing rather than loan financing by a bank (Lambert & Schwienbacher, 2010). The development of crowdfunding was more apparent with the establishment of various platforms such as Kickstarter. com, IndieGoGo.com, RocketHub, GoFundMe, and so on (Pazowski & Czudec, 2014).

Most researchers agree that there are four types of crowdfunding: donation-based, reward-based, equity-based, and debt-based or peer-to-peer (P2P) (Asutay & Marzban, 2015; De Buysere et al., 2012; Hemer, 2011; Kuti & Madarász, 2014; Massolution, 2013). Donation-based crowdfunding is voluntary and does not expect any returns. Reward-based crowdfunding is when there is a promise of return in terms of gifts, coupons, vouchers, and so on. Debt-based crowdfunding involves credit contracts; credit is being repaid plus interest. Finally, equity-based crowdfunding is a shareholding contract, with shares, equity-like instruments, or revenue to share in the project or business (De Buysere et al., 2012). In sum, the donation and reward crowdfunding is categorized as community-based crowdfunding, while the P2P and equity crowdfunding are considered as investment-based crowdfunding.

Islamic crowdfunding has become a new demanding product for entrepreneurial development. Oukil (2013) affirmed that Islamic banks' current growth, Islamic financing, and markets worldwide enhance Islamic entrepreneurship development. Crowdfunding can be conceptualized as Islamic if the project being offered complies with Shari'ah parameters, that is the investments are socially responsible, risk sharing, interest free, not associated with gambling or zero-sum game, and free from any uncertainty. Therefore, all crowdfunding models should fit into these norms and need to be adapted to be considered as Shari'ah-compliant crowdfunding (Taha & Macias, 2014; Wahjono, 2015).

Concerning the development and smoothness of Islamic Crowdfunding practices, Wahjono (2015) highlight the uniqueness and important actor in Islamic crowdfunding other than being a project initiator, platform, and supervised under the Shari'ah Supervisory Board or Shari'ah Advisors. This research is supported by Hasan (2015), who states the role of the Shari'ah advisor is essential in order to derive solutions for any Shari'ah-related issues in Islamic crowdfunding such as Shari'ah-compliant monitoring, equity structure, repurchase price of equity, moral hazard, and other operational issues. Biancone and Secinaro (2016) also introduced the importance of a Shari'ah board to monitor the investment at every phase, providing specific Shari'ah screening and legal formalities as among some aspects that could turn equity crowdfunding in Italy into a Shari'ah compliance model. The Shari'ah screening provides extra credit to Islamic crowdfunding as it develops trust among the participants. There are many factors that contribute trust besides a third-party screening body. Therefore, the Shari'ah supervisory board needs to look into the criteria of fundraiser, project-related, and also structural crowdfunding platforms (Mohd Nor & Hashim, 2020). At the same time, Abdullah (2016) discusses Islamic crowdfunding on the Shari'ah governance aspect and the Shari'ah parameter's issuance with particular reference made to the Malaysian regulatory framework.

Marzban et al. (2014) assert that a Shari'ah-compliant crowdfunding framework addresses the current issues with an entrepreneurial, cultural, and religious factor to enhance Islamic countries' entrepreneurial sectors. In order to ensure fair distribution among capital providers in the case of liquidation and to overcome the Shari'ah concern regarding preference shares, the proposed framework uses structured contracts for start-ups based on both *Musharakah* (capital venture) and interest-free loans. As the literature on Shari'ah crowdfunding models is growing, *waqf*-based crowdfunding may have enormous potential as alternative Islamic financing for entrepreneurs. Therefore, the following section explains the concept of *waqf* and previous studies about *waqf*-based crowdfunding.

7.2.1 Waqf: *An Overview*

Waqf is a kind of charity with a particular characteristic that makes it unique from other voluntary acts. The beneficiary will benefit from *waqf* as long as *waqf*'s benefit is still running, possibly for years, a decade, or a century. The word *waqf* is derived from the Arabic root verb *waqafa*, which means 'causing a thing to stop and stand still.' It also takes the meanings of 'detention,' 'holding,' or 'keeping' (Mahamood, 2007). *Waqf* (pl. *awqaf*) is called Boniyad in Iran and *habs* (pl. *ahbs*) in North and West Africa. However, by considering its different meanings, *waqf* can be applied to non-perishable property whose benefit is extracted without consuming the property itself (Chowdury et al., 2011).

Except for Hanafis, all jurists agree that four elements that constitute a valid and effective *waqf* donation are: the declaration (*sighah*), the donor (*waqif*), the beneficiary (*mawquf alaihi*), and the subject matter (*mawquf*) (Huda, 2015; Suhadi, 2002). Besides, some basic *waqf*-fund rules should be heeded, such as *waqf* property cannot be sold, gifted, or cannot be distributed, and the usufruct of *waqf* fund must be defined and must be followed (Abdullah, 2020).

There are three main characteristics of *waqf* fund: perpetuity, the permanence of *waqf* founder's stipulation, and irrevocability (Abdullah, 2020). Perpetuity means that once a property or asset is dedicated as *waqf*, it remains *waqf* forever. The permanence of the stipulation of *waqf* founder means conditions specified by the founder must be fulfilled to their letter as long as they do not contradict or violate any of the Shari'ah rulings. If a *waqf* purpose becomes infeasible, the *waqf* revenue should be spent on the closest purpose available (Kahf, 2003). Simultaneously, irrevocability means the lack of power of the settler (*waqif*) to terminate his donation at any time. The donor's declaration or undertaking is binding, which means that the donated asset could not be taken back by its owner (Gamon & Tagoranao, 2018). This is an example of a private property becoming a public property.

In recent years, few studies emphasize *waqf* utilization, particularly on cash *waqf* for financing purposes (Abdel Mohsin, 2013). Some researchers see *waqf*'s potential as an external financing source for entrepreneurs or start-up businesses (Lahsasna, 2010; Mohd Thas Thaker et al., 2016) and also to fund the Islamic microfinance (Md. Saad & Anuar, 2009). Lahsasna (2010) recommended a financial approach using the cash *waqf* model in financing micro- and medium-sized enterprises (MSMEs). According to them, cash *waqf* is a reliable source for microcredit and microfinancing; medium-sized enterprises and entrepreneurs need to create more projects, business opportunities, and more employment. In a more advanced study, Mohd Thas Thaker et al. (2016) have developed the Integrated Cash *Waqf* Micro Enterprise Investment (ICWME-I) model as a funding source for micro-enterprises. This model is expected to provide financial services using cash *waqf* funds and participation in nonprofit organizations and micro-enterprises. Unlike the financing by the existing financial conventional institution, the proposed model does not need collateral requirement, interest rates, and stringent requirements.

Waqf-based crowdfunding is the unique hybrid product of crowdfunding in the form of *waqf* representing a new financing mechanism for the entrepreneur by using Islamic mechanisms and regulation. According to Muhammad Syaukani (2015), *waqf* is one redistributed wealth mechanism that is very useful; crowdfunding is an efficient system to collect funds. Crowdfunding is fit to act as a fundraiser of *waqf* to finance for social development purposes, such as the cost of disaster management in

Malaysia. The combination of these two mechanisms is known as *waqf*-based crowdfunding. Wan Shamilah et al. (2016) stated that *waqf*-based crowdfunding is similar to the *waqf* businesses, in which the profits from the businesses will be distributed to the beneficiaries (*Mawquf 'alaih*). The business is expected to project continuous profits that could ensure the fund's continuity to the beneficiaries.

The first *waqf*-based crowdfunding platform is known as WaqfWorld. org. It is a collaboration between three parties: namely, Legasi Tun Abdullah Ahmad Badawi as a founding patron, a research team from the Research Center for Islamic Economics and Finance (EKONIS) Universiti Kebangsaan Malaysia (UKM), and Ethis Ventures as a technology partner. However, WaqfWorld.org intends to transform the three parties into a new institution that binds all parties legally. Since it is still in its infancy, WaqfWorld is also still working on preparing a standard operating procedure (SOP), which involves the appointment of the Shari'ah advisors and other improvements to make it the best platform (AlMa'amun et al., 2016).

7.3 The Mechanics of *Waqf*-Based Crowdfunding

This section will explore the fundamental process of crowdfunding and *waqf* to provide insights on how to integrate both mechanisms and finally identify some aspects that both have in common. According to Mohd Thas Thaker et al. (2018), crowds have a positive attitude towards *waqf*-based crowdfunding as they perceived it as useful and easy to use.

The flow of Fig. 7.1:

1. Entrepreneurs present their project idea to the public through a crowdfunding platform as the intermediary or rendezvous point.
2. The platform will provide information to the public by informing the type of project, the capital amount needed, funding dateline, and current accumulated funds. An entrepreneur attempts to draw the public's attention through appealing webpages, promotional videos, and photos of the project.
3. The crowd who agrees to pledge will arrange the donations via the platform. The crowd donates money to the platform via internet banking. The fund accumulated via the platform is used by the entrepreneur to launch their project. When the project meets the funding deadline, there are two ways. First, the project only gets the money pledged if they reach their target on time. If not, funding should be returned to

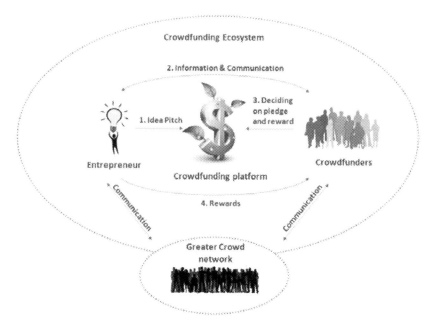

Fig. 7.1 Fundamental process of crowdfunding. Source: Scholz (2015)

the public. Second, the project owner keeps any money pledged by the crowd, even if the target amount is not reached.
4. The crowd or donators will get the reward promised from the entrepreneur if it is a reward-based crowdfunding. They also can get immaterial acknowledgment such as thank-you emails, an invitation to a movie set, or exclusive merchandise like a T-shirt. If it is an investment-based crowdfunding (P2P or equity), the crowd will receive financial return as agreed.

The flow of Figure 7.2:

1. *Waqf* gives cash to the beneficiary through various channels such as direct cash, salary deduction, *waqf* share, and so on.
2. The aggregate fund reaches *mutawalli*. *Mutawalli* plays an essential role as a trustee to distribute, monitor, and manage cash *waqf*. The existence of *mutawalli* guarantees *waqf* fund's perpetuity, making the *waqf* unique from other donations.

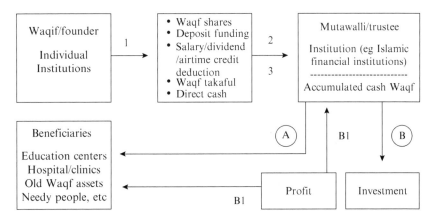

Fig. 7.2 Fundamental process of cash *waqf*. Source: Ahmad Mukarrami (2016)

3. An administration and management fee may be allocated to the *mutawalli*.

   a. Direct model: the fund is used to service the maintenance of impaired *waqf* assets to give its beneficiaries revenue.
   b. Indirect model: the *waqf* trustee invests the fund in Shari'ah-compliant investment (e.g., via *Mudharabah* or *Musharakah*) at an agreed profit-sharing ratio.

      In the event the investment generates profit, it is duly disbursed according to the profit-sharing ratio to its respective parties (e.g., beneficiaries and the trustee)

Based on the process offered, both cash *waqf* and crowdfunding shows similarity in the source of funds that is collected or donated from the public. Nonetheless, there are two differences that have been identified. First, the intention to give money contributes in crowdfunding. In crowdfunding, the objectives of the donor are according to the types of crowdfunding, whether it is donation, reward, or investment-based that seeks profit returns. In cash *waqf*, the donor gives money voluntarily with the intention to attain a non-monetary reward that is a blessing from God. Second, crowdfunding utilizes technology information or the Internet to mobilize funds. A web platform for intermediaries in crowdfunding shows the uniqueness of crowdfunding from other fundraising instruments. Cash *waqf* is usually a direct transaction from donor to receiver without any intermediary.

7.4 Framework of *Waqf*-Based Crowdfunding for Entrepreneur

Gumusay (2015) elucidates entrepreneurship from an Islamic perspective as a composition of two individually contested concepts: Islam and entrepreneurship. According to al-Qaradhawi, Islamic entrepreneurship's philosophy is driven by the economic philosophy where the business is based on *Rabbani* or is God-oriented (Mubarak et al., 2014). Therefore, this phenomenon indirectly creates the influence or relationship between spirituality in Islam and entrepreneurship. Adamu et al. (2013) found that the dimension of spirituality in Islam can positively influence entrepreneurs' attitudes and serve as a motivational drive for going into business and serve as a catalyst for positive energy, enhanced performance, and increased commitment to social responsibility.

There is a significant gap divergence between the Islamic perspective of entrepreneurship and western entrepreneurship. In the context of Islam, a Muslim business activity should strive to meet the Islamic economics objectives. There is no separation between the teachings of Islam and entrepreneurial activities. Entrepreneurship in Islam has its features and guiding principles based on al-Quran and al-Hadith. These divine sources of knowledge prescribe guidance in every walk of life. The Islamic principles are to please Allah or to achieve *mardhatillah* (the blessing of Allah). The conduct of business should be consistent with Islamic practices, including moral and ethical standards, and towards contributing to the societal welfare. A successful entrepreneur according to the Islamic ambit balances between the social, financial, and spiritual goals that seek rewards in this world and the hereafter (Hassan & Hippler III, 2014).

Figure 7.3 is the proposed framework of *waqf*-based crowdfunding for entrepreneurial development.

The flow of Figure 7.3:

1. Entrepreneurs present their project information to the public through the crowdfunding platform. The Shari'ah advisor will perform a screening process to ensure the project complies with Shari'ah principles before the project owner campaigns for or promotes the project to the crowd.

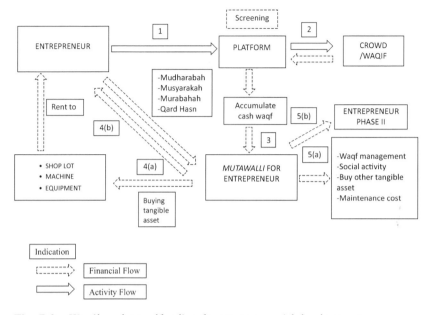

Fig. 7.3 *Waqf*-based crowdfunding for entrepreneurial development

2. Crowds who agree to perform *waqf* will transfer cash via the platform.

3. Accumulated cash *waqf* will be given to *mutawalli* responsible for managing, monitoring, and distributing cash *waqf* to the beneficiary.

4(a). *Mutawalli* buys a tangible asset needed by entrepreneurs such as shop lot, operating machine, or any equipment as fixed assets needed according to their project or business information. The tangible assets then will be rented to the entrepreneur under the *Ijarah* contract with the amount agreed by both parties.

4(b). *Mutawalli* will play a role to manage and distribute cash *waqf* to the beneficiary as stipulated by the donor. There are two possible ways of distributing *mutawalli*, namely beneficiary loans (*qard hassan*) and financing through Islamic contracts such as *Mudharabah*, *Musharakah*, and *Murabahah*.

5(a). Money from the rent of tangible assets will be reused by *mutawalli* to buy other tangible assets needed or for maintenance costs of an existing asset to increase their life expectancy, *waqf* management, and social activity.

5(b). Repayment of the loans is used to recharge the cash *waqf* pool and, in turn, become the source of funds for other needy entrepreneurs.

The framework gives two ways on how *mutawalli* can manage the fund to help entrepreneurs at 4(a) and 4(b). 4(a) shows that *mutawalli* buy the tangible asset on behalf of the entrepreneur and rent it to the entrepreneur. At the same time, 4(b) shows that *mutawalli* give funds directly to an entrepreneur through financing or partnership contracts.

In cash *waqf*, fiat money is used as the transaction instrument rather than gold and silver. The scholars argue about fiat money's permissibility as an instrument of cash *waqf* because of its features, which has no intrinsic value, managed through legal tender, and its value is defined through market value. Therefore, an alternative is needed to avoid the Shari'ah issue in cash *waqf*. The proposed framework in 4(a) is in line with Razali (2015), who stated that one alternative to avoid the Shari'ah issue in cash *waqf* is by converting cash *waqf* funds into the form of tangible assets. The framework is also more or less the same as the *Baitul Maal Wa Tamwil* (BMT) practice in Indonesia. According to Razali (2015), cash *waqf* offers four benefits when transforming the cash into a tangible assets. First, there is no argument among scholars regarding the permissibly of tangible assets. Second, the tangible assets have are real and physical. Third, the ownership of the tangible asset is difficult to transfer to the possession of another person compared to cash. Finally, the element of *riba* can be evaded.

With 4(b), the *waqf*-based microfinance idea is used as a foundation of the framework. As suggested by Md. Saad & Anuar (2009), an Islamic microfinance institution (IMFI) or *mutawalli*, in this case, acts as the trustee of the accumulated cash fund. The IMFI will distribute cash *waqf* to needy entrepreneurs. The loan is given to entrepreneurs based on profit sharing (*mudharabah*), cost plus (*murabahah*) capital venture (*musharakah*). Through this contract, when the entrepreneur repays their loans, the money can be used to recharge the cash *waqf* pool and become the source of funds for other needy entrepreneurs. IMFI will disburse the entrepreneur's loan and monitor the entrepreneur's performance periodically to avoid any default in the future.

7.5 Conclusion

This chapter aims to propose an Islamic mechanism for entrepreneurial development fundraising by utilizing crowdfunding and *waqf* as Shari'ah compliant crowdfunding. This study successfully proposed a framework based on crowdfunding and *waqf* as financing sources and development for the entrepreneur. A *waqf*-based crowdfunding framework gives both *waqf* and entrepreneurial institutions an idea to manage and gain fundraising efficiently. The framework mechanism makes the fundraising activity faster and efficient by using technology and encourages people to contribute to *waqf* funds easily, which aligns with the *waqf* institution's role in nurturing social development and a sustainable economy. Since the study is based on library research, the information acquired is limited, and the researcher tends to consider and rely on earlier research as the primary source of data. As the complement for a shortcoming in this study, the following recommendation can be made for further study to fill the gap left blank. Since the framework only gives an idea of crowdfunding and *waqf* to help entrepreneurs, the study about regulation and act should be discussed to enable the framework to be implemented. Besides, governance issues that could arise in the framework should be discussed further. To conclude, cash *waqf* and crowdfunding are believed to be efficient mechanisms in collecting funds from the crowd to meet social needs in this world and get rewards in the hereafter.

References

Abdullah, A. (2016). Crowdfunding as an Emerging Fundraising Tool: With Special Reference to the Malaysian Regulatory Framework. *Islam and Civilisational Renewal, 7*(1), 1.

Abdullah, M. (2020). Classical Waqf, Juristic Analogy and Framework of Awqaf Doctrines. *ISRA International Journal of Islamic Finance, 12*(2), 281–296.

Abdel Mohsin, M. I. (2013). Financing through Cash-*Waqf*: A Revitalization to Finance Different Needs. *International Journal of Islamic and Middle Eastern Finance and Management, 6*(4), 304–321.

Adamu, I. M., Kedah, Z., & Osman-Gani, A. M. (2013). Entrepreneurial Motivation, Performance, and Commitment to Social Responsibility: Toward Future Research. *International Journal of Entrepreneurship and Small Business, 18*(2), 194–210.

Ahmad Mukarrami, A. M. (2016). Waqf as a Tool to Fulfill Social Responsibility: Cash Waqf. *Islamic Finance News, 13*(43), 1.

AlMa'amun, S., Shafiai M. H. M., Adnan M. S. A. & Munshi U. (2016, September). Waqfworld: When *Waqf* Meets Crowdfunding. *Islamic Finance Today Magazine*.

Andersen, S., & Nielsen, K. M. (2012). Ability or Finances as Constraints on Entrepreneurship? Evidence from Survival Rates in a Natural Experiment. *Review of Financial Studies, 25*(12), 3684–3710.

Asutay, M., & Marzban, S. (2015). Alternative Ways of Developing GCC Islamic Funds Industry: Entrepreneurial Development. In M. Asutay & A. Turkistani (Eds.), *Islamic Finance: Political Economy Perspectives* (pp. 1–15). Gerlach.
Belleflamme, P., Lambert, T., & Schwienbacher, A. (2013). Individual Crowdfunding Practices. *Venture Capital*, 15(4), 313–333.
Biancone, P. P., & Secinaro, S. (2016). The Equity Crowdfunding Italy: Model Sharia-Compliant. *European Journal of Islamic Finance*, 5, 1–10.
Chowdury, M. S. R., Ghazali, M. F., & Ibrahim, M. F. (2011). Economics of Cash Waqf Management in Malaysia: A Proposed Cash Waqf Model for Practitioners and Future Researchers. *African Journal of Business Management*, 5(30), 12155–12163.
De Buysere, K., Gajda, O., Kleverlaan, R., Marom, D., & Klaes, M. (2012). A Framework for European Crowdfunding. *European Crowdfunding Network*.
Gamon, A. D., & Tagoranao, S. (2018). The Role of Waqf Properties in the Development of the Islāmic Institutions in the Philippines: Issues and Challenges. *Intellectual Discourse, Special Issue, 2018*, 1191–1212.
Gumusay, A. A. (2015). Entrepreneurship from an Islamic Perspective. *Journal of Business Ethics*, 130(1), 199–208.
Hassan, M. K., & Hippler, W. J., III. (2014). Entrepreneurship and Islam: An Overview. *Econ. Journal Watch*, 11(2), 170–179.
Hemer, J. (2011). *A Snapshot on Crowdfunding*. Arbeitspapiere Unternehmen und Region No. R2/2011. Karlsruhe: Fraunhofer ISI.
Huda, M. (2015). *Mengalirkan Manfaat Wakaf 'Potret Perkembangan Hukum dan Tata Kelola Wakaf Di Indonesia*. Granata Publishing.
Kahf, M. (2003, January 6–7). The Role of Waqf in Improving Ummah Welfare. Paper presented at An International Seminar on Waqf as a Private Legal Body.
Kerr, W., & Nanda, R. (2009). *Financing Constraints and Entrepreneurship*. National Bureau of Economic Research. *Inc., 15498*.
Kleemann, F., Voß, G. G., & Rieder, K. (2008). Un(der) Paid Innovators: The Commercial Utilization of Consumer Work through Crowdsourcing. *Science, Technology & Innovation Studies*, 4(1), 5.
Kuti, M., & Madarász, G. (2014). Crowdfunding. *Public Finance Quarterly*, 59(3), 355–366.
Lahsasna, A. (2010). The Role of Cash Waqf in Financing Micro and Medium-Sized Enterprises (MMES). *Proceeding of Seventh International Conference—The Tawhidi Epistemology: Zakat and Waqf Economy*, 97–118.
Lambert, T., & Schwienbacher, A. (2010). *An Empirical Analysis of Crowdfunding*. Social Science Research Network, 1578175.
Mahamood, S. M. (2007). Pembentukan Dana Wakaf Menurut Perspektif Syariah Dan Undang-Undang Serta Aplikasinya Di Malaysia. *Jurnal Syariah*, 15(2), 61–83.

Marzban, S., Asutay, M., & Boseli A. (2014, April 26–27). Shariah-Compliant Crowdfunding: An Efficient Framework for Entrepreneurship Development in Islamic Countries. Paper presented to Harvard Islamic Finance Forum 2014, Boston, USA.

Massolution. (2013). *Crowdfunding Industry Report*.

Massolution. (2015). *Crowdfunding industry Report*.

Md. Saad, N., & Anuar, A. (2009). Cash Waqf and Islamic Microfinance: Untapped Economic Opportunities. *Islam and Civilisational Renewal, 1*(2), 337–354.

Mohd Nor, S., & Hashim, N. A. (2020). Trust Motivates Funders in Shariah Crowdfunding. *Geografia: Malaysian Journal of Society and Space, 16*(2), 228–238.

Mohd Thas Thaker, M. A., Mustafa, O. M., Duasa, J., & Abdullah, M. A. (2016). Developing a Cash *Waqf* Model as an Alternative Source of Financing for Micro-Enterprises in Malaysia. *Journal of Islamic Accounting and Business Research, 7*(4), 254–267.

Mohd Thas Thaker, M. A., Mohd Thas Thaker, H., & Pitchay, A. A. (2018). Modelling Crowdfunder' Behavioral Intention to Adopt the Crowdfunding-Waqf Model in Malaysia: The Theory of the Technology Acceptance Model. *International Journal of Islamic and Middle Eastern Finance and Management, 11*(2), 231–249.

Mubarak, M. Z., Abd. Rahman, A., & Yaacob, M. R. (2014). Spirituality in Islamic Entrepreneurship: Motivation and Achievement of Successful Entreprenuers in Kelantan. *Journal of Techno Social, 6*(2), 27–36.

Muhammad Syaukani, A. A. (2015, July 29). *Crowdfunding Berasaskan Waqaf Sebagai Instrumen Pendanaan Tabung Bantuan Bencana*. Paper presented to Conference on Malaysian Islamic Economics and Finance (CMIEF 2015), Selangor, Malaysia.

Ordanini, A., Miceli, L., Pizzetti, M., & Parasuraman, A. (2011). Crowdfunding: Transforming Customers into Investors through Innovative Service Platforms. *Journal of Service Management, 22*(4), 443–470.

Oukil, M. S. (2013). Entrepreneurship and Entrepreneurs in an Islamic Context. *Journal of Islamic and Human Advanced Research, 3*(3), 111–131.

Pazowski, P., & Czudec, W. (2014). Economic Prospects and Conditions of Crowdfunding. In *Proceedings of the Management, Knowledge and Learning International Conference 2014*, 1079–1088.

Razali, O. (2015). *Institusi Wakaf, Sejarah Dan Amalan Masa Kini*. Dewan Bahasa dan Pustaka.

Scholz, N. (2015). *The Relevance of Crowdfunding: The Impact on the Innovation Process of Small Entrepreneurial Firms*. Springer Gabler.

Securities Commission Malaysia. (2015). *Guidelines on Regulation of Markets under Section 34 of CMSA*.

Suhadi, I. (2002). *Wakaf: Untuk Kesejahteraan Umat*. Dana Bhakti Prima Yasa.

Taha, T., & Macias, I. (2014). Crowdfunding and Islamic Finance: A Good Match? In F. M. Atbani & C. Trullols (Eds.), *Social Impact Finance* (pp. 113–125). IE Business Publishing. Palgrave Macmillan.

Valanciene, L., & Jegeleviciute, S. (2013). Valuation of Crowdfunding: Benefits and Drawbacks. *Economics and Management, 18*(1), 39–48.

Wahjono, S. I. (2015, December 1–2). *Islamic Crowdfunding: Alternative Funding Solution.* Paper presented to 1st World Islamic Social Science Congress (WISSC 2015), Putrajaya, Malaysia.

Wan Shamilah, W. M., Hakimi, M. S., & Mohd Fairuz, M. S. (2016). The Role of Muslim Millionaires in Enhancing Waqf-Based Crowdfunding: A Proposed Framework. In *Proceeding of the 3rd Conference on Malaysian Islamic Economics and Finance (CMIEF) 2016* (pp. 129–141).

CHAPTER 8

Waqf Flood Evacuation Centre: New Recourse to Flood Victims in Malaysia

*Marhanum Che Mohd Salleh,
Nurdianawati Irwani Abdullah, Nor Azizan Che Embi,
and Nan Noorhidayu Megat Laksana*

1   Background

Floods that are considered a yearly incident in certain countries including Malaysia are becoming more severe nowadays. In Malaysia, heavy rains for over a few days during the monsoon season usually happen at the end of year from October to January in east coast states (Terengganu and Kelantan) as well as Johor, and these have caused massive floods and

---

M. Che Mohd Salleh (✉) • N. I. Abdullah • N. A. Che Embi
Department of Finance, Kulliyyah of Economics & Management Sciences,
International Islamic University Malaysia, Selangor, Malaysia
e-mail: marhanum@iium.edu.my; irwani@iium.edu.my; izanebbm@iium.edu.my

N. N. Megat Laksana
Department of Usul Fiqh, Kulliyyah of Islamic Revealed Knowledge,
International Islamic University Malaysia, Kuala Lumpur, Selangor, Malaysia
e-mail: nanhidayu@iium.edu.my

© The Author(s), under exclusive license to Springer Nature
Switzerland AG 2022
A. G. Ismail et al. (eds.), *Islamic Philanthropy*, Palgrave Studies in
Islamic Banking, Finance, and Economics,
https://doi.org/10.1007/978-3-031-06890-4_8

caused thousands of people to move to evacuation centres, forced schools to close, and have destroyed crops. Floods have brought negative effects not only to the society but also to the government. The government would generally have to spend money for flood expenses, which include during (preparing evacuation centres, foods, needs of the victims, medicine, and others) and after floods (building new houses, repairing house damage, and providing for other needs). As reported by one online newspaper, newsonline.com, in January 2017, more than 15,000 people, mainly from smaller towns and villages in rural areas, had to leave their homes to the relief centres. Meanwhile as reported by the International Federation of Red Cross and Red Crescent Societies (IFRCS), seven states in Peninsular Malaysia, namely, Johor, Kelantan, Pahang, Perak, Terengganu, Malacca, and Selangor, and Sabah in East Malaysia, have been flooding in January 2017.

Accordingly, in Terengganu, more than 3,500 people were evacuated by the authorities to 63 relief centres when overflowing rivers burst their house areas due to the continuous rains. Meanwhile in Kelantan, over 5,200 people were placed in 55 relief centres with the same factor of flooding as happened to Terengganu. The worst case was in Johor where more than 8,000 victims were moved to the evacuation centres. Overall, the floods have also caused more than 9,000 children in the state to miss school, as some 29 primary and secondary schools were forced to close due to the rising waters (www.todayonline.com). Based on observation, the victims will need to stay at the evacuation centres from two to four weeks while waiting for the water to recede and the conditions to return to normal. They were normally transferred to evacuation centres, which included existing relief centres, schools, halls, mosques, abandoned buildings, and makeshift shelters on higher grounds. Based on comprehensive research done by the Malaysian Institute of Architects (PAM) on major floods that hit the east coast of Malaysia in 2014, among the weaknesses of the evacuation centres were that they were not equipped to handle disasters, with no electricity, water, food, or proper sleeping areas, most probably facilities needed by the victims.

The research also suggest that there is a need to develop well-equipped existing and new evacuation centres at suitable locations. In this regard, the objectives of this research are: to investigate the effect of the floods on society, with Kelantan as a case study; to observe the experience of the flood victims staying at the flood evacuation centres; and to propose a permanent flood evacuation centre base on waqf principles.

This essay is structured as follows: after research background, it provides findings from existing literature related to flood and the evacuation centres. Next is research methodology, followed by discussion on research findings and also suggestions for a permanent flood evacuation centre based on waqf principles. This essay concludes with suggestions for future research.

2 Review of Existing Literature

Flooding delivers a continuous threat to environment, infrastructure, and lives throughout the world (Azimah et al., 2019). It creates hardship on families to manage basic needs (e.g., food and shelter) and leads to a momentous emotional and social effect that remains for a long period (Mat et al., 2017; Rahim & Seman, 2019). Surprisingly, there is scarce literature on flood evacuation centres and lack of social resources for flood victims is acknowledged among both local and international researchers. Flooding frequently affects Malaysia, especially the east coast (Kelantan, Terengganu, and Pahang) every year (Padlee et al., 2018). Subsequently, it brings untold suffering and massive losses while government aid is not sufficient for flood victims in Malaysia (Lai et al., 2015). In general, the government is responsible for providing substantial resources to the victims promptly (Khalid & Shafiai, 2015). Hence, government aid is thin when there are large flood events and they are unable to recover the flood victims (Aldrich et al., 2015; Norkhadijah et al., 2018). Hence, Lai et al. (2015) highlight several issues of disaster management in Malaysia such as fragmented decision-making, limited financial resources, exclusion of citizens from planning, and poor public response to hazards. Further, it is necessary to implement and introduce an effective and reliable source, with management to reduce losses as well as provide an effective evacuation centre for the future (Hussin, 2015). Efficient management of evacuation centres is a priority during severe floods (ChePa et al., 2016).

2.1 Flood Evacuation Centre

An evacuation centre is an assembly place where the disaster victims gather (Somasundaram & Davies, 2014), which is prepared with financial, social, emotional, and technical support (Rahim & Seman, 2019). Moreover, an evacuation centre provides basic needs comprising of food, health and safety services, logistics, volunteers, telecommunication, and additional services for special needs (Padlee & Nik Razali, 2015). However, the task of handling the post-flood situation is down to management and operation. Where flood evacuation centres are implemented in temporary locations to assist flood victims who might be affected by flood, then the problems are addressed (ChePa et al., 2016). Accordingly, Subri et al. (2016) depicted several problems, such as: obligatory prayers, shortage of religious and spiritual guidance, lack of clean water, and stealing in flood evacuation centres. Prior study also reported that flood evacuation centres had inadequate food supply, lack of understanding among victims, and insufficient infrastructure and equipment (Said et al., 2013). Contrarily, evacuees perceived good services from evacuation centres and were satisfied with services in three states of the east coast (Padlee et al., 2018). However, resilient social support from people, organizations, and groups/cohorts is well-established and such groups are willing to provide helping hands in terms of donations, religious aid, finances, properties, infrastructural supports, and skills in the management of resource of income to recover and establish solutions for flood victims (Aldrich, 2012; Begg et al., 2017; Chan et al., 2018; Folland & Rocco, 2014; Lai & Chan, 2015). Thus, post-flood recovery management should consider and include the facilities and assistance from stakeholders besides those of the government (Chan et al., 2018).

Several studies have proposed evacuation centre models for flood victims. For instance, preceding a Chinese study by Li et al. (2019), Mat et al. (2017) anticipated crowd simulation that can run manifold simulations in a number of situations, enable to assist in planning, and aid in development and testing of new training modules by saving time and cost. Interestingly, the simulation may incorporate the psychological effect of victims. On the other hand, ChePa et al. (2016) proposed a web-based and mobile app evacuation centre by using a firefly algorithm that forms an optimal plan. This optimal plan is created for a rearrangement of resources and victims. Later, Shafie et al. (2019) proposed optimized solar photovoltaic (PV) panels at tilted angles and software and portable solar generators for a Malaysian flood evacuation centre. The main purpose is to supply power in flood evacuation centres (also anticipated by Jamil et al., 2019). Meanwhile, Azimah et al. (2019) developed the Hydraulic Model (HEC-RAS), which is integrated with GIS (geographical information system). This model is developed to identify the flood-prone area, then propose the suitability of existing evacuation centres and suggest appropriate places to set up new evacuation centres. Hence, a similar approach was proposed earlier by Mustaffa et al. (2016).

In relation to assistance, social capital from private sector, NGOs, religious institutions, and aid and individuals all play an important and effective role (Chan et al., 2018). Similarly, social factors (social capital and networks) drive community resilience through enhancing disaster resilience by strengthening social infrastructure (Aldrich & Meyer, 2014). Social capital can be segmented into three categories: bonding, bridging, and linking (Grootaert et al., 2004). Bonding considers the internal capital within a community group, for instance: ties between family members, reliable friends, neighbours or people from the same race/religion (Putnam, 2000). Bridging considers the external capital gathered from different ethnic groups, various geographical backgrounds, or occupational backgrounds (Szreter & Woolcock, 2003). Finally, linking refers to the connecting between community and people in formal organizations, for example local government (Grootaert et al., 2004). Thus, social capital directly or indirectly assists in reconstructing houses, providing food and monetary aid, sharing knowledge and other forms of assistance that benefit victims both physically and mentally (Kien, 2011).

Further, more stakeholders may provide opportunities to create new resources of income, and wider mobilizing of public and private funds for flood victims (Chan et al., 2018). Meijerink and Dicke (2008) stated that collective and visible arrangements within state, market, and civil society enhance the stakeholders' engagement in regards to providing resilient flood management. However, it is not possible to break or untie social and cultural practices unless the government promises to provide employment opportunities in better alternative ways with adequate resources, including agricultural opportunities, public amenities, and so on (Salleh et al., 2017). As a result, society has to play an important role in the arrangements of post-flood recovery rather than depending on government to restructure affected communities (Chan, 2015). In fact, community engagement in flood recovery management mentally enhances the community's resilience along with infrastructural development (Bhandari, 2014).

2.2 Issues with Regards to Flood Evacuation Centres

Very limited literatures have discussed the social model of flood evacuation centres both in local and international contexts. There are few studies conducted on the issues or problems that occurred in flood evacuation centres. The most recent study was conducted by a group of researchers from University Science Islam Malaysia (USIM) led by Irwan et al. (2016) on the Shariah issues at flood evacuation centres. Even though their research was only focused on five centres in Pahang, the results can be relevant to other centres. In this case, based on non-structured interviews with 60 respondents, it is found that there were 10 themes relating to Shariah issues raised by the victims, most frequent being the covering of aurah (intimate parts) and ikhtilat (intermingling between men and women). Furthermore, Irwan et al. (2016) also found that there were also issues related to obligatory prayers, lack of religious and spiritual guidance, clean water, and theft. The other issues were related to Friday prayer, cleanliness, and also attitude problems. On a similar note, past study conducted by Mohd Zulhafiz et al. (2013), a group of researchers from University Science Malaysia, investigated various conflicts/problems that happened in flood evacuation centres in Kedah. Based on mixed-methodology approach (surveying 683 respondents and focus group discussion with 30 local leaders), the authors concluded that various problems have existed at the flood evacuation centre mainly because of inadequate food supply, absence of understanding among the victims, limited spaces for overloaded victims, and insufficient infrastructure and equipment in the centres. In this context, some recommendations are made, such as upgrading the equipment and infrastructures in the centres such as provision of a comfortable space for the victims to stay in the long term, ensuring sufficient stock of food, and also conducting counselling sessions for the flood victims.

A recent study that has examined the aspect related to the management of flood evacuation centres was carried out by Noraziah et al. (2016) where the authors have proposed a decision aid model, namely an Adaptive Emergency Evacuation Centre Management (AEECM) system using the firefly algorithm. Hence, AEECM was proven able to provide a decision for relocation of victims and resources to other evacuation centres when these centres are flooded. In addition, it provides information on the quantity of victims and resources required to be transported to the new evacuation centres. It is believed that the proposed decision aid model and the adaptive system is useful to support the National Security Council's respond instruments for handling disaster management level II (state level), particularly in enhancing the existing flood management system. In 1995, Chan studied the effectiveness of the government resettlement schemes for flood victims. Overall, the author claimed that relocation is expensive and further complicated by political and ethnic sensitivities in Malaysia. It is not easy to convince Malaysians to break from their cultural and social ties. Unless the Malaysian government can promise job opportunities and residential land, then they will not feel compelled to move. It is suggested to the government to offer alternative places that are at least of the same quality (in terms of land prices), with, for example, agricultural potential, accessibility, and public amenities.

From another perspective, comprehensive research has been undertaken by the Malaysian Institute of Architects (PAM) in 2015 as a result of a major flood that hit the east coast area of Malaysia in 2014. The focus of their research was on developing a Malaysian Disaster Preparedness Centre (MDPC) as a one-stop agency for disaster coordination in collaboration with the National Security Council, government agencies, fellow professionals, and NGOs. This research also aimed to develop standards and guidelines for flood prevention and mitigation at both macro- and micro levels. Kuala Krai has been selected as a case study as it was affected by the flood in that year with entire homes and villages being completely submerged in floodwater. Overall, Strength Weaknesses Opportunity and Threats (SWOT) analysis was chosen as a basis to detect both the strengths and deficiencies in the present disaster management system, mainly in terms of location, infrastructures (water supply, sanitary and sewerage system, electricity, transport system, drainage system), buildings, evacuation, relief efforts, assessment, rehabilitation, and relocation.

With regard to research conducted in other countries, Somasundaram and Davies (2014) have conducted a case study of the Australian Red Cross and Environmental Health Australia working in evacuation centres in Queensland. They found that the relationship between these two organizations has led to various benefits for the management of evacuation centres such as involvement in each other's events and training. The relationship has become injected in each organization's day-to-day business ensuring the relationship's sustainability beyond individual staff movements. In Japan, there were limited researches on issues or problems encountered in the evacuation centres, and the Japanese were more concerned about preparing a community-based disaster management (CBDM). In the Philippines, Ramos et al. (2015) have evaluated a health assessment survey of evacuation centres severely affected by Haiyan. Of the 20 evacuation centres assessed, none had a designated manager. Most were located in schools (70%) with the estimated number of evacuees ranging from 15 to 5,000 per centre. Only four (20%) met the World

Health Organization standard for number of toilets per evacuee; none of the large evacuation centres had even half the recommended number of toilets. All of the evacuation centres had available drinking water. None of the evacuation centres had garbage collection, vector control activities, or standby medical teams. Fourteen (70%) evacuation centres had onsite vaccination activities for measles, tetanus, and polio virus. Many evacuation centres were overcrowded. The authors opined that in disaster-prone areas such as the Philippines, schools and community centres should not be chosen as evacuation centres unless they are equipped with adequate sanitation services.

3 METHODOLOGY

This research is conducted qualitatively where the objectives are achieved via two means: case study and review of literature. Prior to proposing a permanent flood evacuation centre based on waqf concept, this research observes the experience and needs of the flood victims in relation to the future possibility of its existence. Two places of flood located in Kelantan have been chosen to conduct the case study: Pasir Putih and Tumpat. Overall, a total of 26 families have participated in this research. They were basically asked about the effect of flooding on their finances, properties, and health. Other than that, the victims also shared their experience of residing at the flood evacuation centres.

4 FINDINGS

4.1 Background of Respondents

As presented in Table 8.1 below, most of the families under study consist of members between 4 to 10 persons. It is observed that the majority of them were self-employed and their income basically below RM1000.

4.2 Effect of Flood to Finances, Life/Health, Sources of Income, and Property

This study first asked the families whether they have been affected by the flood in terms of finances, life/health, source of income/job, and property. Table 8.2 basically details the responses of the families. In the aspect of finances, most of them shared that they have to withdraw their savings

Table 8.1 Background information for respondents

Family Background

1	Widow, monthly income is below than 1000, take care of 7–9 family members, own house.
2	Married, take care of 4–6 family members, monthly income is below than 1,000
3	Married, labourer, monthly income is around 1,000 roughly, take care of more than 10 family members, own house
4	Married, diploma holder, civil servant, take care of 7–9 family members, monthly income 4,000 or above, own house, bungalow
5	Married, self-employed, monthly income below 1,000, take care of 4–5 family members, own house
6	Married, self-employed, monthly income 1,000–2,000, take care of more than 10 family members, own house
7	Widow, unemployed, no source of income, take care of 4–6 family members, own house
8	Married, unemployed, monthly income below 1,000, take care of 7–9 family members, own house
10	Married, unemployed, monthly income around 1,000–2,000, take care of 4–6 family members, rent house
11	Married, self-employed, take care of 7–9 family members, monthly income below 1,000, own house
12	Married, self-employed, monthly income below 1,000, take care of 4–6 family members, own house
13	Widow, unemployed, no income, take care of 4–6 family members, own house
14	Widow, self-employed, monthly income below 1,000, take care of 4–6 family members, own house
15	Widow, unemployed, no income, take care of more than 10 family members, own house
16	Married, self-employed, monthly income below 1,000, take care of 7–9 family members, own house
17	Married, self-employed, monthly income below 1,000, take care of 4–6 family members, own house
18	Unemployed, monthly income below 1,000, take care of 4–6 family members, rental house
19	Married, self-employed, monthly income from 1,000–2,000, take care of 1–3 family members, own house
20	Married, self-employed, monthly income below 1,000, take care of 7–9 family members, own house
21	Widow, take care of grandchildren, rubber tapper, 2 children, stay at own house and land
22	Married with 4 children, housewife, husband is a carpenter, income 300–400 a month, own house (family land)
23	Widow, tailor, monthly income RM500–RM700
24	Widow, no income
25	Married with 5 children, housewife
26	Married with 4 children, house builder, diploma holder

Table 8.2 Effect of flooding to the villages

Family	Finances	Life/health	Sources of income	Property
1.	Yes, have to withdraw from savings account to fix all the damage but still insufficient, financial assistance from the government is not enough, have to borrow from others	Yes	Yes, difficult to go out for work and no other job is available when flood happens	Yes
2.	Yes, used the savings to fix the damages but still insufficient, financial assistance from the government is not enough, have to borrow money from others	Yes	Yes, difficult to go out for work and lost their permanent job and no other job is available when flood happens, therefore always shortage of money to pay all expenses during and after flood	Yes
3.	Yes, but still insufficient to accommodate the loss	No	No	No
4.	Yes, used savings to fix the damages, any financial assistance is insufficient to bear the cost, have to borrow money from others	Yes	Yes, difficult to go out to work, lost permanent job, no other job available during and after the flood	Yes
5.	Yes	Yes	Yes, difficult to go out to work, lost permanent job, no other job available during and after the flood	Yes
6.	Yes, used savings to bear the cost, financial assistance from government is insufficient, have to borrow from others	No	Yes, difficult to go out to work, lost permanent job, no other source of income	Yes
7.	Yes	Yes	Yes, unable to find any jobs	Yes
8.	Yes, have to borrow from others to accommodate the cost	Yes	Yes	Yes

(*continued*)

8 WAQF FLOOD EVACUATION CENTRE: NEW RECOURSE TO FLOOD... 161

Table 8.2 (continued)

Family	Finances	Life/health	Sources of income	Property
9.	Yes, not enough savings, must borrow money from others	Yes	Yes, cannot go to work	Yes,
10.	Yes,	Yes	Yes, difficult to go to work, lost permanent job	Yes
11.	Yes	Yes	Yes, difficult to go to work, lost permanent job	Yes, furniture and transport
12.	Yes, used savings to bear the damages cost, not enough saving, financial assistance from the government is insufficient, have to borrow from others	Yes	Yes difficult to go to work, lost permanent job	No
13.	Yes, used savings to bear the cost of damages, not enough savings, financial assistance from the government is insufficient, have to borrow form others (siblings)	Yes	Yes, difficult to go to work, lost the permanent job, no job is available	Yes, electrical appliances and transport
14.	Yes, used savings to bear the damages cost, not enough savings, financial assistance from the government is insufficient	No	Yes, difficult to go to work, lost the permanent job	Yes, furniture and transport
15.	Yes, no savings	Yes	Yes, lost the permanent job	Yes, house and agricultural products
16.	Yes, used savings to bear the damages cost, not enough savings, financial assistance from the government is insufficient	No	Yes, difficult to go to work, lost permanent job, nothing can be done during flood	Yes, electrical appliances and furniture
17.	Yes, used savings to bear the damages cost, not enough savings, financial assistance from the government is insufficient	Yes	No	No
18.	No	No	No	No

(continued)

Table 8.2 (continued)

	Family Finances	Life/health	Sources of income	Property
19.	Yes, used savings to bear the damages cost, not enough savings, financial assistance from the government is insufficient, have to borrow form others	Yes	Yes, difficult to go to work, lost permanent job, nothing can be done during flood	Yes, electrical appliances, transport, and agricultural products
20.	Yes, no savings to withdraw to pay all expenses during flood	No	Yes, difficult to go out for work and no other job is available when flood happens	Yes
21.	Yes, not enough money to pay vehicle loan, have to borrow money from relatives, no savings	No	Yes, for husband, difficult for him to go out for work and no other job available when flood happens, therefore always shortage of money to pay all expenses during and after flood	Yes, no electrical appliances, but small furniture affected
22.	No	No	Yes	Yes, sewing machine
23.	No	Fever before and after flood	Yes	Yes
24.	Yes, I have no savings	Fever	Yes	Yes, house/door/roof
25.	Yes, not enough savings	No	Yes	Yes, house and car
26.	I have no savings	No	Yes	No

to fix the damage to their houses and most of the time it is not enough to cover all the losses. In this instance, sometimes they have to borrow money from their relatives and friends. Asking them whether they have received financial assistance from the authority or any non-government organization, some of the respondents stated that the funds that they received are not enough to fix, rebuild their houses, or replace their income during the flood season. In addition, floods have also affected the respondents' life/health even though they have not caused serious illnesses. Meanwhile, the other aspects that were affected by flood as reported by the respondents include their sources of income/job and also property, including houses, vehicles, furniture, and house appliances.

4.3 Experiences Staying at Flood Evacuation Centres

This research further investigates the respondents' experiences during their stay at flood evacuation centres. In this case, they were asked to list good and bad things at the centres. As seen in Table 8.3, the respondents generally were satisfied with the food prepared for them and all necessities

Table 8.3 Experiences at flood evacuation centres

Family	Experiences staying at flood relocation centre	Agreement on proposal to establish permanent waqf flood relocation centre
1.	Good	Agreed
	Bad—No activity for children	
2.	Good	Agreed
	Bad—No activity for children	
3.	No experience	Agreed
4.	Good—Food	Agreed
	Bad—Toilet far/no water supply, have to hike to level 4 to find water, difficult for elderly	
5.	Good	Agreed
	Bad—Food is not properly cooked	
6.	Good—Everything including food, sleeping area	Agreed
	Bad—Cleanliness of the place, nobody took care of it compared to 2014	
7.	Bad—More spaces and toilet needed	Agreed
8.	Good—Food	Agreed
	Bad—Improper toilet	
9.	No	Agreed
10.	Bad—Inadequate infrastructures	Agreed
	Good—Food	
11.	Nil	Agreed
12.	Nil	Agreed
13.	Nil	Agreed
14.	Good—Food (same menu)	Agreed
	• Bonding with each other	

(continued)

Table 8.3 (continued)

Family	Experiences staying at flood relocation centre	Agreement on proposal to establish permanent waqf flood relocation centre
15.	Good—Bonding with each other Bad—Improper toilet • No appetite • The food finished early	Agreed
16.	Bad—Sleepless • Improper toilet	Agreed
17.	Good—Bonding with each other • Food • Shower	Agreed
18.	Yes (twice a year) Bad—Uncomfortable • Toilet far • Children very stressed because they were scolded by their parent to not touch the school's equipment	Agreed
19.	Yes (twice a year) Bad—Uncomfortable	Agreed
20.	Yes (twice a year)	Agreed
21.	Good—Food Bad—Toilet far/no water supply	Agreed
22.	Good—Food and treatment Bad—Toilet far/no water supply	Agreed
23.	Good—Food, sleeping area Bad—Toilet far/no water supply	Agreed
24.	Bad—No proper place for solat	Agreed
25.	Bad—No proper place for solat • No blanket • No proper washroom	Agreed
26.	Bad—No proper place for solat • Toilet not proper Good—Food	Agreed

were enough during their stay. Unfortunately, the list of bad experiences was longer than the list of good ones. Hence, the respondents were not satisfied with the cleanliness, water supply, facilities, lack of activities prepared for their children. They also informed that the spaces provided for their families were very limited and not comfortable for women to change clothes and sleep in an open area. Further than that, they also shared with researchers that there were few activities conducted by the Social Welfare

Department (KEMAS), and they hoped for more activities and that those activities should improve their skills and generate some income. This is because most of them are self-employed. In this context, the researchers further enquired about the respondents' willingness to participate in case there were activities (modules) prepared for them where they can generate money from them, such as making frozen food, sewing, or other activities. There will be activities for women, men, and also for their children. Religious activities like Tazkirah, Qur'an classes, or any activities that bring benefits to the society were also suggested to the respondents. Overall, the researchers received positive feedback from the respondents under study regarding the suggestion to have well-equipped permanent evacuation centres for flood victims. The next section discusses this research proposal based on the model of a permanent flood evacuation centre based on waqf principles.

5   Suggestions for Permanent Flood Evacuation Centre Based on Waqf Principles

Figure 8.1 presents the proposed model in this research. There are differences of this model compare to other models of flood evacuation centres. First, the establishment of the centre would be based on waqf assets (tangible and intangible). Second, the aims of the centre are not only to prepare a relief centre for the flood victims, but more importantly, it will become a social and religious centre where all social and religious activities will be conducted for the victims during their stay. In this context, the

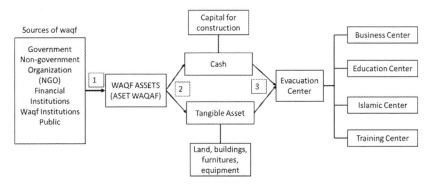

Fig. 8.1 Model of permanent flood evacuation centre based on waqf principles

advantages of this centre are more for the long-term period. Via a business centre, there will be appropriate business activities prepared for the victims to start new businesses and later on to generate income for them during the flood—for example, frozen food for women or haircuts for men, artworks for anybody interested. The business centre would be a starting point for the victims (villages) to learn new things/businesses that can enhance their standard of living even after the flood season. The centre might be useful for them to continue their businesses/activities after the flood to generate income. Thus, they can eliminate the issue of vacant buildings with a permanent flood evacuation centre.

In addition, the permanent flood evacuation centre could also offer an education centre for learning purposes. While providing a venue for the children to do their learning activities (drawing, colouring, reading, artworks, etc.), it also may cater for the adults to have learning sessions. The other important part of this permanent flood evacuation centre is the religious (Islamic) centre that is Musollah (big prayer space) for the Muslims to perform prayer together. As based on recent research by Irwan et al. (2016) and previous research by Mohd Zulhafiz et al. (2013), there were Shariah and non-Shariah issues identified in the flood evacuation centres, caused by external and internal factors. External factors might be related to infrastructures or management of the centre whereas the internal factors would basically reflect the strength of the individual victims to face the flood as misfortune (the flood victims may experience trauma or nightmares) regarding what has happened to their life or property. In this context, the Islamic centre would be the best place for the victims to get their strength to continue life. Religious activities can be arranged and performed in this Islamic centre.

As a permanent evacuation centre, its function could continue even after the monsoon season. Given that there are enough facilities and well-kept condition, this centre may provide space to conduct training for outsiders. However, a proper structure for a management team needs to be established to sustain its function and ability to generate more income in the future. In a nutshell, the proposed permanent flood evacuation centre based on waqf principles would be meaningful if it received support from the relevant authority and also society for the sake of maqasid Shariah.

6 Conclusion

In conclusion, there are two important values that typify this research: worldly and hereafter values. In other words, it includes aspects of physical and spiritual values that should be maintained and enhanced when facing calamity (disaster) among flood victims. Society needs to have a spirit of cooperation and mutual help when others have been tested with disasters or difficulties. Thus, the existence of a permanent flood evacuation centre based on waqf principles would provide an avenue for general society to give assistance to the needy (flood victims), regardless of monetary or non-monetary help. Furthermore, the centre would offer both physical (complete facilities, food, necessities, business opportunities to generate income) and also the spiritual needs (comfortable space to perform religious obligations, module for reflection (tazkirah), qur'anic classes, etc.). It is hoped that once the spiritual aspects are given priority in managing the flood evacuation centres, any Shariah issues that arise at the centre as reported by previous research can be minimized. All in all, support from the government and cooperation from the victims are very important to realize the proposal of this research.[1]

References

Aldrich, D. P. (2012). *Building Resilience: Social Capital in Post-disaster Recovery*. University of Chicago Press.

Aldrich, D. P., & Meyer, M. (2014). Social Capital and Community Resilience. *American Behavioral Scientist*, 59(2), 1–16. https://doi.org/10.1177/0002764214550299

Aldrich, D. P., Oum, S., & Sawada, Y. (2015). *Resilience and Recovery in Asian Disasters: Risks, Governance and Society* (1st ed.). Springer Japan.

Azimah, M. N., Adib, M. R. M., & Mustaffa, A. A. (2019). Integration of Hydraulic Model (HEC-RAS) with Geographical Information System (GIS) in Developing Flood Evacuation Center Along Sembrong River. *IOP Conference Series: Earth and Environmental Science*, 220, 1–11. https://doi.org/10.1088/1755-1315/220/1/012057

Begg, C., Kuhlicke, C., Masson, T., & Ueberham, M. (2017). Interactions Between Citizen Responsibilization, Flood Experience and Household Resilience: Insights

---

[1] The authors would like to express heartfelt thanks to the Ministry of Higher Education, Malaysia, and the International Islamic University Malaysia under the Fundamental Research Grant Scheme (FRGS15-222-0463) for providing financial support.

from the 2013 Flood in Germany. *International Journal of Water Resources Development, 33*(4), 591–608.

Bhandari, R. B. (2014). Social Capital in Disaster Risk Management: A Case Study of Social Capital Mobilization Following the 1934 Kathmandu Valley Earthquake in Nepal. *Disaster Prevention and Management, 23*(4), 314–328. https://doi.org/10.1108/DPM-06-2013-0105

Chan, N. W. (2015). The Role of Social Capital and Commuity Resilience in Facing Flood Disaster in Malaysia. In *Proceedings of International Symposium of International Academic Consortium of Sustainable Cities* (pp. 1–13). Yokohama City University.

Chan, N. W., Roy, R., Lai, C. H., & Tan, M. L. (2018). Social Capital as a Vital Resource in Flood Disaster Recovery in Malaysia. *International Journal of Water Resources Development, 1*, 1–19. https://doi.org/10.1080/0790062 7.2018.1467312

ChePa, N., Hashim, N. L., Yusof, Y., & Hussain, A. (2016). Adaptive Emergency Evacuation Centre Management for Dynamic Relocation of Flood Victims Using Firefly Algorithm. *Journal of Telecommunication, Electronic and Computer Engineering, 8*(8), 115–119.

Folland, S., & Rocco, L. (2014). *The Economics of Social Capital and Health: A Conceptual and Empirical Roadmap. World Scientific Series in Global Healthcare Economics and Public Policy.* World Scientific.

Grootaert, C., Narayan, D., Woolcock, M., & Nyhan-Jones, V. (2004). Measuring Social Capital: An Integrated Questionnaire. Washington, DC. Retrieved from http://documents.worldbank.org/curated/en/515261468740392133/Measuring-social-capital-an-integrated-questionnaire

Hussin, W. N. T. B. W. (2015). *Knowledge Sharing Via Social Media in Flood Disaster Event.*

Irwan, M. S., Wan Mohd Fazrul Azdi, W. R., Walid, M. S., Nisar Mohammad, A., Amir, S., Mohd Aizuddin, A. A., Mohd Azhar Ibrahim, R., Mohd Nur Adzam, R., Syadiyah, A. S., & Bilal, J. (2016). Fiqh Issues at Flood Relief Centers: An Exploratory Study in Temerloh District, Pahang. *Jurnal Pengurusan dan Penyelidikan Fatwa, 8,* 10–20.

Jamil, S. J. T., Ahmad, N. A., & Jamian, J. J. (2019). Connecting Solar Generated Electricity During Flood Disaster in the FELDA Communities of Malaysia: The Public Perception. *IOP Conference Series: Earth and Environmental Science, 291,* 1–5. https://doi.org/10.1088/1755-1315/291/1/012035

Khalid, M. S. B., & Shafiai, S. B. (2015). Flood Disaster Management in Malaysia: An Evaluation of the Effectiveness. *International Journal of Social Science and Humanity, 5*(4), 398–402. https://doi.org/10.7763/IJSSH.2015.V5.488

Lai, C. H., & Chan, N. W. (2015). A Preliminary Study of the Role of Social Capital in Flood Recovery in Kelantan State. In *Proceedings of Geografi & Alam Sekitar Kali Ke-5, Universiti Pendidikan Sultan Idris.* Tanjong Malim, 568–573.

Lai, C. H., Chan, N. W., & Seow, T. W. (2015). A study on the contributions of social capital in flood disaster recovery after the December 2014 major flood in Kelantan State, Malaysia. In *Proseedings Transformasi Sosial; Fakulti Kemanusiaan, Seni & Warisan Universiti Malaysia Sabah*, 9–17.

Li, Y., Hu, B., Zhang, D., Gong, J., Song, Y., & Sun, J. (2019). Flood Evacuation Simulations Using Cellular Automata and Multiagent Systems—A Human–environment Relationship Perspective. *International Journal of Geographical Information Science, 33*(11), 2241–2258. https://doi.org/10.1080/13658816.2019.1622015

Mat, R. C., Abubakar, J. A., Aziz, A. A., Yusoff, M. F., & Noorjasri, N. A. (2017). 3D Simulation for Flood Evacuation. *Advanced Science Letters, 23*(5), 3883–3887.

Meijerink, S. V., & Dicke, W. (2008). Shifts in the Public–private Divide in Flood Management. *International Journal of Water Resources Development* (December). https://doi.org/10.1080/07900620801921363

Mohd Zulhafiz, S., Salfarina, A. G., Mohd Nazri, S., & Abd Malik, A. A. (2013). Conflict in Flood Relief Shelter: Case Study of Padang Terap District, Kedah, Malaysia. *Journal of Society and Space, 9*(1), 69–78.

Mustaffa, A. A., Rosli, M. F., Abustan, M. S., Adib, R., Rosli, M. I., Masiri, K., & Saifullizan, B. (2016). A study of flood evacuation center using GIS and remote sensing technique. *IOP Conference Series: Materials Science and Engineering, 136*, 1–9. https://doi.org/10.1088/1757-899X/136/1/012078

Noraziah, C. P., Nor Laily, H., Yuhanis, Y., & Azham, H. (2016). Adaptive Emergency Evacuation Centre Management for Dynamic Relocation of Flood Victims Using Firefly Algorithm. *Journal of Telecommunication, Electronic and Computer Engineering, 8*(8), 115–119.

Norkhadijah, S., Ismail, S., Abidin, E. Z., Hashim, Z., Rasdi, I., How, V., ... Mohamad, S. (2018). Disaster Debris Management During the 2014–2015 Malaysia Flood Incident. *Journal of Medicine and Health Sciences, 14*(5), 112–119.

Padlee, S. F., & Nik Razali, N. N. (2015). The Perceived Quality and Satisfaction with Services at Evacuation Centres: The Case of Kemaman Evacuation Centre. *South East Asia Journal of Contemporary Business, Economics and Law, 8*(2), 21–29.

Padlee, S. F., Razali, N. N. H. N., Zulkiffli, S. N. A., & Hussin, N. Z. I. (2018). An Assessment of the Perception and Satisfaction with Flood Evacuation Centre Service Quality in East Coast States of Peninsular Malaysia. *Journal of Sustainability Science and Management, 4*, 65–77.

Putnam, R. D. (2000). *Bowling Alone: The Collapse and Revival of American Community* (1st ed.). Touchstone by Simon & Schuster.

Rahim, A. A., & Seman, W. M. A. W. (2019). Concept of Privacy from Islamic Perspective in Flood Evacuation Centre. *Planning Malaysia: Journal of the*

Malaysian Institute of Planners, 17(2), 259–266. https://doi.org/10.21837/pmjournal.v17.i10.646

Ramos, R. A., Reyes, V. C., Sucalditob, M. N., & Tayagbet, E. (2015). Rapid Health Assessments of Evacuation Centres in Areas Affected by Typhoon Haiyan. *Western Pacific Surveillance and Response Journal, 6*(1), 39–43. https://doi.org/10.5365/wpsar.2015.6.2.HYN_003

Said, M. Z., Gapor, S. A., Samian, M. N., & Aziz, M. (2013). Conflicts in Flood Relief Shelter: A Case Study of Padang Terap District, Kedah. *Geografia: Malaysian Journal of Society & Space, 9*(1), 69–78.

Salleh, M. C. M., Abdullah, N. I., Embi, N. A. C., & Laksana, N. N. M. (2017). New Recourse to Flood Victims in Malaysia: A Proposal on Permanent Waqf Flood Evacuation Centre. In *Conference on philanthropy for humanitarian aid* (pp. 106–117). Conference on Philanthropy for Humanitarian Aid.

Shafie, S., Kadir, M. Z. A. A., Azis, N., Radzi, M. A. M., Zuha, W. H. W., & Mustafa, M. A. (2019). High Efficiency Portable Solar Generator Utilizing Optimum Solar Panel Orientation. In *2018 IEEE 5th International Conference on Smart Instrumentation, Measurement and Application, ICSIMA 2018* (pp. 28–30). IEEE. https://doi.org/10.1109/ICSIMA.2018.8688811

Somasundaram, T., & Davies, B. J. (2014). Collaboration to Improve Evacuation Centre Operations in Queensland. *International Journal of Disaster Resilience in the Built Environment, 5*(3), 305–317. https://doi.org/10.1108/IJDRBE-01-2014-0012

Subri, I. M., Razali, W. M. F. A. W., Said, W. M., Ahmad, N. M., Shaharuddin, A., Aziz, M. A. A., ... Jailani, B. (2016). Fiqh Issues at Flood Relief Centers: An Exploratory Study in Temerloh District, Pahang. *Jurnal Pengurusan Dan Penyelidikan Fatwa, 8*, 10–20.

Szreter, S., & Woolcock, M. (2003). Health by Association? Social Capital, Social Theory and the Political Economy of Public Health. *International Journal of Epidemiology, 33*, 1–18. https://doi.org/10.1093/ije/dyh013

CHAPTER 9

Cash Waqf for Humanitarian Aid: The Case of Transboundary Haze

Shahida Shahimi, Siti Hanisah Fuad, and Rabiatul Hasanah Mahmood

1 INTRODUCTION

From 1994, Malaysia was plagued for two decades by periodic cross-border haze pollution (Hayasaka et al., 2014). This kind of humanitarian crisis refers to a series of forest fires events in terms of human-made disasters in Indonesia that threaten the health and safety of local and neighboring countries' communities. Haze not only comprises dust, smoke, and dry particles, but it also consists of toxic gases and harmful excess air like carbon monoxide, nitrogen dioxide, and ozone (Mastura & Nuur 2009). ASEAN considered transboundary haze a severe issue and came out with the ASEAN Agreement on Transboundary Haze Pollution (AATHP) in

---

S. Shahimi (✉) • R. H. Mahmood
Faculty of Economics and Management, Universiti Kebangsaan Malaysia, Bangi, Malaysia
e-mail: shahida@ukm.edu.my

S. H. Fuad
Graduate School of Business, Universiti Kebangsaan Malaysia, Bangi, Malaysia

© The Author(s), under exclusive license to Springer Nature Switzerland AG 2022
A. G. Ismail et al. (eds.), *Islamic Philanthropy*, Palgrave Studies in Islamic Banking, Finance, and Economics,
https://doi.org/10.1007/978-3-031-06890-4_9

2002 and this was signed by Brunei, Malaysia, Myanmar, Singapore, Thailand, and Vietnam in November 2003, while Indonesia became the 10th AATHP member in July 2015. This agreement was enforced to control cross-border haze pollution by preventing, monitoring, and mitigating the lands and forest fires. However, this agreement seems unable to solve this crisis as Malaysia was blanketed with smoke haze in October 2016.

Deforestation and open burning are the crucial factors of this event, especially in the palm oil industry. The high demands of palm oil worldwide increase the pace of opening new palm oil cultivation areas since it is used widely in cooking, hygiene, and skincare products because of its low cholesterol and rich vitamin content. The palm oil growers and producers' passion for maximizing their profits caused environmental hazards and these were ignored. Besides, more land has been cleared year by year for expanding palm oil cultivation areas. The method of slash and burn (S&B) by palm oil companies and local farmers was widely used in Indonesia to dispose of the waste of deforestation due to low cost and adequate time (Varma, 2003). The draining of peatlands, especially in Sumatra and Kalimantan for pulp and paper plantation purposes, caused heavy smoke and became unable to control. The scenario becomes worse when Asian countries were hit by lasting global warming—the El Nino phenomenon—as part of a natural factor delaying the eastern monsoon in 2015.

As the haze spread across to other countries like Singapore, South Thailand, and the Philippines, it caused a significant air quality decline. Air pollution levels in Malaysia are measured by using the Air Pollutants Index (API), where a reading below 50 is considered healthy, 100–300 indexes are unhealthy, and anything above 300 is considered critical. Severe transboundary haze in Malaysia occurred in November 1997 in Sarawak and August 2005 in Selangor, where a Haze Emergency was declared, referring to the API reaching above the 500 level. The chronology of critical situations by this crisis continued in 2010. About 170 schools in Johor were closed due to the deterioration of air quality at an index level of 432. Malaysia had experienced the Haze Emergency once again in 2013 due to most parts of peninsular Malaysia being affected by unhealthy air when the API reading was above 500.

As a result, significant medical costs were incurred since haze is harmful to human health, with skin irritations, eczema, asthma attacks, and heart attacks because it consists of dust and toxic gases. The economy possibly suffers (Chilsom et al., 2016) due to the suspension of economic activities like construction, tourism, and the airline industry. In 2001, Malaysia

Airlines (MAS) was making losses when it had to cancel 70 of its domestic flights due to critical vision. Malaysian daily activities were also affected when 4,478 schools needed to be closed in and slow their outdoor activities (Utusan, 2016). Based on the chronology above, this kind of anthropogenic hazard should be settled by providing appropriate solutions to prevent continuous calamities towards society regarding safety and health.

Furthermore, this prevention is supported with Goal No. 15 of the Sustainable Development Goals (SDGs), which is "Life on Land" that promotes the protection, restores and promotes sustainable use of terrestrial ecosystems, sustainably manage forests, combat desertification, and halt and reverse land degradation and halt biodiversity loss. However, the primary concern to solve this crisis is the high cost incurred. President Joko Widodo stated the 2015 haze crisis cost accounts for USD 33.5 billion compared to USD 9 billion in the 1997 haze crisis. Surprisingly, cash waqf as a humanitarian aid due to the haze crisis has not been formally discussed in previous studies. Thus, this chapter proposes cash waqf as a tool for the environment and human protection from the haze crisis.

2 LITERATURE REVIEW

Environmental degradation is closely related to the haze crisis. According to Holdren et al. (1995), the environment is fully sustained when people's ordinary life had been maintained and improved by balancing the biological diversity and conservation of air, water, and land resources. It is in line with the objective of Sustainable Development Goal No. 15 of the UN that promotes protection and restoration of sustainable terrestrial ecosystems, sustainably managed forests, combatting desertification, and halting and reversing land degradation and biodiversity loss. As haze is a human-made disaster, firms should take initiatives by transforming from only focusing on clean-up and control methods to the full coverage of environmental harm through the entire product life cycle (Handfield et al., 2005). Hence, Matos and Hall (2007) suggest that green activities should be performed by extending and attacking the source of contamination inclusively, then environmental sustainability is achieved.

Jones and Jackson (2016) find a lack of consistent behavior and awareness among construction staff about environmental attitudes and beliefs. The staff will consider a sustainable method once it benefits them rather than the industry, and this was supported by Tudor et al. (2007). Nikoloyuk et al. (2010) also found such a scenario is happening with the palm oil industry players when they damage the environment by replacing the forest with agricultural land palm oil. Also, Ayat Rahman et al. (2008) opine that this problem occurred when the smallholders, mostly local farmers, were not efficient in managing the planting materials, unsystematic fertilizer application, and harvesting unripe fruit bunches. As a result, smallholders' incomes have been affected since the authority parties will penalize them. Hence, SDGs promote all the key players in the plantation industry with efficient forest management to prevent severe haze.

As the cost of haze recovery is high, a substantial fund is needed. Waqf plays a role in social empowerment in many aspects. Waqf's root means to prevent, stop, restrain, or abstain. Its word comes from the Arabic verb "waqafa" (Ahmed & Khan, 1997; Bearman, 2003; Ibrahim et al., 2013). In the Arabic language, waqf means a prohibition, hold, or confinement (Kahf, 1992). It is strongly supported by the statement that Awqaf plays a role in sustaining funds through investment in helping the needy, for instance, poor people when the crises and famines hit and those in extreme poverty (Ahmad Bello, 2009). It works as an institution and to manage help for the needy (Çizakça, 2002). The waqf characteristic as a perpetual charity shows that waqf is a significant contributor to societal development.

Waqf is compatible as a primary vehicle in supplementing the fulfillment of the obligation to social amenities. However, investment in the cash waqf mechanism can expand waqf funds to accomplish goals for the needy.

The cash waqf can be an alternative to develop waqf assets or to support and build institutions like schools, health centers, or orphanage houses (Sadeq, 2002). Cash waqf is a movable asset, liquid, and can move from one place to another (Mohammad Hussin & Mohammad Hussin, 2011). It is one of the platforms for a particular person who does not have immovable assets, such as land, to make assets waqf property. Moreover, cash waqf is an alternative method for Muslims to achieve modern economic development. It is in line with the statement that waqf is easy to manage and distribution to beneficiaries becomes more comprehensive (Abdullah Nadwi & Kroessin, 2013).

As mentioned before, cash waqf as a fund for humanitarian aid had not yet been discussed. Many researchers opine that cash waqf can mitigate poverty and Muslim social life using this fund as microfinance. Çizakça (2004) proposes cash waqf as a medium of microfinance financing for the poor. The same idea is proposed by El-Gari (2004), where he suggests cash waqf from wealthy Muslims as a qard Hassan bank—a non-profit financial intermediary—to finance loans for the poor. Also, Kahf (2003) suggests investing the waqf fund, and the returns are considered as microenterprise financing. According to Armendariz and Morduch (2010), microfinance funds are essential to reduce poverty and promote positive social change. Thus, cash waqf roles can be varied by considering the needs of funds for humanitarian crises worldwide.

The characteristic waqf as a movable asset makes it a convenient alternative as humanitarian aid. The cash waqf system is an essential service at zero cost (Cizacka, 2000). As we know, the impact of humanitarian crises makes the cost higher. The unique characteristic of cash waqf has the potential to accumulate a considerable amount of funds. Therefore, this essay proposes using cash waqf as an appropriate mechanism to accommodate the haze crisis's impact by providing the materials needed for haze management.

3 METHODOLOGY

The study uses a qualitative approach by applying the case study and library analysis methods. A case study is conducted to analyze the effect of a company involved in the palm oil industry that committed forest fires and determined palm oil industry players' roles for environmental protection. A case study is a popular methodology in social science studies, especially regarding community-based issues such as poverty, unemployment, and family matters (Johnson, 2006). Yin (1984) defined a case study as "an empirical inquiry that investigates a contemporary phenomenon within its real-life context; when the boundaries between phenomenon and context are not evident; in which multiple sources of evidence are used." Here a single case study is constructed of *shariah*-compliant companies in Malaysia. The subject matter of the case study is the IOI Group Bhd. from 2013 to 2016. The second method is the purposive library research method. This research refers to the dissertations and theses from many sources. Otherwise, this research uses journal articles due to their narrow focus and specific information.

4 CASE STUDY

IOI Corp. Bhd. is a *shariah*-compliant Malaysian company and member of RSPO.[1] It is active in palm oil cultivation in Indonesia. In April 2016, RSPO-certification for IOI Corp. Bhd. had been suspended due to legal and policy non-compliance matters. As a leader in Malaysian palm oil production, IOI Corp. Bhd complained about its subsidiaries PT Sukses Karya Sawit, PT Berkat Nabati Sawit, and PT Bumi Sawit Sejahtera due to a large open burning scale. These subsidiaries breached the RSPO principle 2, compliance with applicable laws and regulations; and principle 7, responsible development of new planting.

On March 24, 2016 the RSPO Board of Governors endorsed the decision of the complaints panel. The certificate was suspended by RSPO officially in April, and as a consequence, big customers such as Unilever, Nestle, and Kellog decided to drop IOI as their supplier. Next, on May 10, Moody's downgraded the rating of IOI Group to Baa2 rate. In response to this, IOI asked for an appellation with the RSPO complaints panel by filing the case with Zurich District Court in Switzerland. Finally, IOI dropped the case in June 2016 and decided to cooperate with RSPO regarding that issue.

The three subsidiaries that were bound by breach of RSPO principles are categorized as palm oil growers. The NGOs' complaints raised the point of no New Planting Procedure (NPP) being published and no timebound plan. Besides, they cleared the land without the approval of Ijin Usaha Perkebunan (IUP) and ran deep peat clearance. As a result, these three companies must be excluded from future RSPO-certification and the trademark usage on palm oil production.

Once the RSPO announced the suspension of the IOI Group, some of its customers, such as Cargill Inc. and Unilever Global, took this suspension seriously and switched to other palm oil suppliers. It is because these companies are strictly producing products from certified palm oil and sustainable sources. The IOI group admitted that the suspension significantly troubled business operations, 25,000 shareholders, the supply chain, and especially the small farmers. Customers' withdrawal had shrunk IOI's share price by 9% (*The* Star, 2016) and IOI is expected to be unable to achieve the 7% estimated profits for 2017 (The Edge Financial, 2016). The worst impact of the suspension is that IOI's reputation was damaged

---

[1] RSPO is a multi-stakeholder non-profit group for the promotion of sustainable palm oil.

as a sustainable palm oil producer. Even if the company regains the certificate, it will take a long time for the suspension to be lifted.

The RSPO trademark is used by production companies that earned the certification, indicating zero environmental and social damages. In conjunction with reputation risk, IOI no longer can use the RSPO trademark on their palm oil. As mentioned above, the IOI Group can regain its certificate from RSPO but it is not easy. The IOI Group must purchase the certificate from the Malaysian-based CIMB Group as third parties on behalf of RSPO. CIMB provides commodity trade financing claims that the bank was not interested in dealing with IOI since it lost too many customers and additional costs.

Many NGOs have observed and critiqued the operation of the IOI Group, especially in plantation activities. International NGOs such as Greenpeace, Friends of Earth, and Rainforest Rescue have repeatedly complained about the violation of RSPO standards. IOI allows its subsidiaries to deforest and illegally plant palm oil over the limited area set by RSPO. NGOs are not permissive of damages to forests and the habitat of endangered species. Besides, open burning activities contribute to high carbon and air pollution. In 2014, RSPO sent a warning to the IOI Group and its subsidiaries, Loders Croklaan, for not complying with RSPO principles. The NGO critics kept increasing when in 2015, Rainforest Action Network and the Environmental Investigation Agency accused IOI Group of being unable to improve its sustainable practices and warned that RSPO should suspend its certification.

5 FINDINGS AND DISCUSSION

In the context of the palm oil industry in Malaysia, *shariah*-compliant[2] palm oil companies are expected to adhere to *maqasid al-shariah*, especially in environmental protection. Thus, industrial pollution, environmental harm, forest exploitation, and the mismanagement of nature are vehemently opposed to *shariah*'s objectives. Based on the IOI Group's case study above, IOI suffers significant losses due to the suspension of RSPO certification. The result is consistent with the previous studies that suggest that a sustainable standard positively affects firms' financial performance. According to Lappeenranta (2009), MSPO-certification is part of

---

[2] *Shariah*-compliant refers to companies or institutions that comply with *shariah* screening determined by the Shariah Advisory Council, Security Commission Malaysia.

CSPO by the Malaysian government and guarantees the production of sustainable palm oil by strengthening the existing laws towards the protection of ecology, habitats, and species. Hence, air pollution can be reduced when the palm oil cultivators are restricted to slash and burn disposal of trees. Joshua et al. (2012) also suggest that RSPO certification is significant to reduce sales expenses and boost revenues. Besides, environmental certification provides easy excess to European markets, especially in the agriculture industry (Humphries & Kainer, 2006). In short, efficient forestry management is not only for haze crisis prevention; it is also to sustain the company's profits.

As a *shariah*-compliant company, preservation of the environment should be in its consideration in investment decision making. The company seems to use the title of *shariah*-compliant for reputation and capital financing purposes. However, the status of the *shariah*-compliant company by IOI Group does not reflect its effort to fulfill the protection of life and environment in *maqasid shariah*. Ahmed (2013) finds that the current practices did not undertake the screening process regarding companies' commitment toward socially responsible practices to support ESG goals. This study is consistent with Wilson (2004) and Forte and Miglietta (2007), where the issues of employee rights, human rights, and the environmentally friendly are not taken into account in the current Islamic investment decision-making processes. In this respect, innovation in Islamic finance and all endeavors to test the legality of a new product must readily comply with the intent or purpose (*maqasid*) of the *shariah*, such as to protect the environment with a proper preserving and conserving management over business activity (Saiful, 2010).

Cash waqf is indeed helpful in spurring on the humanitarian aid solution affected by the transboundary haze crisis. The cash waqf mechanism is a savior to the danger of haze, but it also encourages other people to feel good and to donate and help others in need. Moreover, the impact of the haze crises is an ongoing problem because problems are not solved effectively. Because of that, this study proposes to establish a cash waqf mechanism in order to provide a lifeline for vulnerable communities harmed by disaster and poverty, especially in Muslim countries.

Regarding the IOI case above, it is significant that it is a cash waqf for the canal's construction. As we know, many Malaysian palm oil companies are operating in Indonesia. When deforestation occurs, there are no problems due to burning on a large scale involving thousands of land hectares. A canal donated by the cash waqf method can clean the burning by digging canals to flow water to the peat forest. The annual haze also impacts society, resulting in school closings to avoid being hit by the haze among students. The haze crisis does not affect a small group, but it harms all the communities, especially the Malaysians, who have affected diffusion of a choking haze from Indonesia. So, health care by cash waqf is appropriate due to the high cost needed. Providing free effective masks is one of the solutions. Many people wear an ineffective mask that does not filter the dangerous compounds, and some people have no mask at all. So, the free effective mask can protect society from the haze. We believe implementation of the cash waqf method can help protect society facing a high risk from haze crises.

6 Conclusion

The cash waqf is a potential instrument to develop and expand funds for humanitarian aid. The availability of funds is significant to prepare and face the high cost of transboundary haze. Thus, it is relevant to the implementation of cash waqf to have more comprehensive funding sources in line with the primary objective of social empowerment in any aspect, particularly the health aspect. It shows that the strong relation between cash waqf as a financial tool and societal needs also shows Islam's nature. It is also shown that social development is a boost to economic development and growth. The role of palm oil industry players is essential in preventing the haze crisis becoming worse, where they should adhere to the guidelines and regulations regarding forestry management, as stated by the regulator.

References

Abdullah Nadwi, M., & Kroessin, M. (2013). Cash Waqf: Exploring Concepts, Jurisprudential Boundaries, and Applicability to Contemporary Islamic Microfinance.
Ahmed, H. (2013). Financial Inclusion and Islamic Finance: Organizational Formats, Products, Outreach and Sustainability. In Z. Iqbal & A. Mirakhor (Eds.), *Economic Development and Islamic Finance* (pp. 203–229). World Bank Publications.
Ahmad Bello, D. (2009). Poverty Alleviation through Zakah and Waqf Institutions: A Case for the Muslim Ummah in Ghana.

Rahman, A., Abdullah, R., Shariff, F. M., & Simeh, M. A. (2008). The Malaysian Palm Oil Supply Chain: The Role of the Independent Smallholder. *Palm Oil Industry Economic Journal, 8*(2), 17–27.
Bearman, P. J. (Ed.). (2003). *Wakf.* Brill.
Edge Financial Daily. (2016, April 8). IOI Corp Suffers Another Blow, Lowa Big Customers. Kuala Lumpur, Malaysia.
El-Gari, Mohamed A. (2004). The Qard Hassan Bank. International Seminar on Nonbank Financial Institutions. Islamic Alternatives.
Handfield, R. B., Sroufe, R., & Walton, S. V. (2005). Integrating Environmental Management and Supply Chain Strategies. *Business Strategy and the Environment, 14*(1), 1–19.
Hayasaka, H., Noguchi, I., Putra, E. I., Yulianti, N., & Vadrevu, K. (2014). Peat-Fire-Related Air Pollution in Central Kalimantan, Indonesia. *Environ. Pollut, 195,* 257–266.
Holdren, J. P., Daily, G. C., & Ehrlich, P. R. (1995). The Meaning of Sustainability: Biogeophysical Aspects. In M. Munasinghe & W. Shearer (Eds.), *Defining and Measuring Sustainability: The Biogeophysical Foundations.* World Bank.
Humphries, S., & Kainer, K. (2006). Local Perceptions of Forest Certification for Community-Based Enterprises. *For Ecol Manag, 235*(1–3), 30–43.
Ibrahim, H., Amir, A., & Masron, T. A. (2013). Cash Waqf: An Innovative Instrument for Economic Development. *International Review of Social Sciences and Humanities, 6*(1), 1–7.
Kahf, M. (1992). *Waqf and Its Sociopolitical Aspects.* IRTI, Jeddah, Saudi Arabia.
Kahf, M. (2003). The Role of Waqf in Improving the Ummah Welfare. International Seminar on Waqf as a Private Legal Body organized by the Islamic University of North Sumatra, Medan, Indonesia.
Johnson, M. P. (2006). Decision Models for the Location of Community Corrections Centers. *Environment and Planning B-Planning & Design, 33*(3), 393–412.
Joshua, L., Ginny, N., Desmond, F., Sarah, G., Samantha, L., & Donald, G. (2012). *Profitability and Sustainability in Palm Oil Production.* WWF.
Lappeenranta. (2009). *Sustainability of Palm Oil Production and Opportunities for Finnish Technology and Know-How-Transfer.* The University of Technology.
Matos, S., & Hall, J. (2007). Integrating Sustainable Development in the Supply Chain: The Case of Life Cycle Assessment in Oil and Gas and Agricultural Biotechnology. *Journal of Operations Management, 25*(6), 1083–1102.
Mohammad Hussin, M. H. S., & Mohammad Hussin, M. H. (2011). In A. Elias (Ed.), *Understanding Shari'ah and Its Application in Islamic Finance.* IBFIM.
Nikoloyuk, J., Burns, T. R., & de Man, R. (2010). The Promise and Limitations of Partnered Governance: The Case of Sustainable Palm Oil. *Corporate Governance: The International Journal of Business in Society, 10*(1), 59–72.

Sadeq, A. M. (2002). Waqf, Perpetual Charity, and Poverty Alleviation. *International Journal of Social Economics, 29*(1/2), 135–151.

Star, T. (2016, May 9). FGV Sets Precedent with Withdrawal from RSO Cert. Kuala Lumpur, Malaysia.

Utusan. (2016). *Haze Return Mei-September 2016.* Utusan.

Varma, A. (2003). The Economics of Slash and Burn: A Case Study of the 1997–1998 Indonesian Forest Fires. *Ecological Economics, 46,* 159–171.

PART III

Zakat

CHAPTER 10

A Collection of Studies on Zakāt

Hendri Tanjung and Nurman Hakim

1   INTRODUCTION

Zakāt is obligatory for Muslims in the form of paying a portion of their wealth or property for the recipients. In Qur'an Surat Taubah verse 60, the list of recipients is indicated, as Allah said: "Alms are for the poor and the needy, and those employed to administer the (fund); for those whose hearts have been recently reconciled (to Truth); for those in bondage and debt; in the cause of Allah; and for the wayfarer, (Thus) it is ordained by Allah. And Allah is full of knowledge and wisdom." The verse states eight categories of Zakāt recipients: the poor, the needy, those employed to administer the (fund), those whose hearts have been recently reconciled (to Truth), those in bondage, those in debt, those in the cause of Allah, and the wayfarer. The rate, as stated in the tradition of the Prophet PBUH, is fixed at 2.5%.

Zakāt is considered one of Islam's five pillars after confessing God's oneness (Tawheed) and offering prayers (Shalat). There are 27 verses of

H. Tanjung (✉) • N. Hakim
Ibn Khaldun University, Istanbul, Turkey
e-mail: hendri.tanjung@ppsuika.ac.id

© The Author(s), under exclusive license to Springer Nature Switzerland AG 2022
A. G. Ismail et al. (eds.), *Islamic Philanthropy*, Palgrave Studies in Islamic Banking, Finance, and Economics,
https://doi.org/10.1007/978-3-031-06890-4_10

the Qur'an explaining the obligation of Zakāt.[1] Zakāt is *ibaadat maaliyah ijtimaiyyah*, which has an important role in Islamic teaching as well as economic development.[2] From an Islamic teaching point of view, Zakāt is proof of the Muslim faith.

Due to its importance, since then Zakāt has been institutionalized. In Indonesia, the National Zakāt Board was established to manage Zakāt for combating poverty. Other Muslim countries also prioritized an increase in Zakāt funds for poverty alleviation. In addressing this function, Zakāt should be collected and distributed correctly.

Zakāt means to grow. Growth means that a person who pays Zakāt will be growing internally or spiritually as well as materially. When one institutes Zakāt, then at the macro level, that Zakāt fund will come entirely to the economy. The economy of people and culture will grow. As a result, the welfare of social economy will grow too.

Zakāt also means to purify. When someone pays Zakāt, he/she purifies his/her heart from greediness. By paying Zakāt in which people give their own money, it will decrease their love for wealth.

Another issue regarding Zakāt is that which is Zakāt-based. Currently, Zakāt is collected only on cash balances, but some scholars are saying that Zakāt is compatible with all other assets, such as gold, camels, mining, and also inventories of factories. Zakāt should be levied on factory assets. Another idea is that the private sector should pay Zakāt, but the government sector must pay Zakāt. The public sector should also pay Zakāt. Islamic universities must pay Zakāt if they have funds. If we interpret Zakāt's extent, we cannot imagine how many Zakāt funds would be collected. If Zakāt funds were collected successfully in this sense, poverty would be easily eliminated.

Another idea is that Zakāt should not encourage the beggar. The way of collecting Zakāt should also be efficient because one category of the recipient Zakāt is amil (the Zakāt administrator).

Based on the above, there are many issues and aspects of Zakāt. Therefore, we want to know the issues and aspects discussed by previous studies, particularly in the last decade. The purpose of this chapter is to explore issues regarding Zakāt and recommend some aspects for future research.

---

[1] Yusuf Qardhawi, Fiqh uz Zakāt, p. 42.
[2] Yusuf Qardhawi, Al-Ibaadah fil Islam, p. 235.

2 LITERATURE REVIEW

A review of the literature of Zakāt between 2003 and 2013 was conducted by Johari, Abd Aziz, and Mohd Ali (2014). They found that at least 24 out of 108 publications on Zakāt related Zakāt to poverty. This means that discussion about poverty has been consistently discussed for the last two decades.

From 2014 onwards, some researchers had conducted studies about the topic "Zakāt and poverty alleviation." Aisyah (2014) concludes that Zakāt in Islamic teaching could only play a significant role in poverty reduction if Zakāt integrates with the overall development strategy and programs of individual countries and uses a larger percentage of Zakāt proceeds for productivity that will enable the enhancement of Zakāt in poverty reduction.

Shirazi (2014) finds that if Zakāt is implemented to the letter and spirit, enough resources can be generated, enough for poverty alleviation from all the Islamic Development Bank (IDB) member countries. However, by individual country efforts, countries in group 1 and some in group 2 can quickly fill the resource gap for poverty alleviation, while all countries in group 3 cannot alleviate poverty by their efforts. Hence, overall, Zakāt could be utilized to alleviate poverty.

Although Zakāt is still not significantly effective in reducing poverty in Kwara State (one of the Muslim-dominated states) in Nigeria, as stated by Abdusalam, Johari, and Alias (2015). They believe that the Zakāt institution needs to be standardized in order to be effective in poverty alleviation.

The role of Zakāt in a poverty alleviation strategy and as a sustainable development tool has been highlighted by Olanipekun, Brimah, and Sanusi (2015). They found some verses in the Qur'an and some hadith that discussed Zakāt and its relation to poverty alleviation.

Suheera, Nashri, and Jamaldeen (2015) have been investigating the role of Zakāt in alleviating poverty in Srilanka. They found that Zakāt has played an essential role in lifting Muslims out the poverty trap in the research location, Nintavur.

Kasri (2016) provides evidence regarding the positive impacts and effectiveness of Zakāt targeting reducing poverty in Greater Jakarta, Indonesia. The main result of her study suggests that the incidence, depth, and severity of poverty amongst the Zakāt recipients have decreased due to contributions from Zakāt organizations. Additionally, there are indications that Zakāt targeting policies seem to be relatively significant during the period. Most disadvantaged groups of society, such as the households led by someone who is relatively uneducated, unemployed, and single parents, are amongst the beneficiaries prioritized by the organizations.

Uddin (2016) proposes a new model for the role of Zakāt in Bangladesh poverty alleviation. He offers an IBZH (Islamic Bank Zakāt House) model. Since IBZH is a proposed model, it will function under the present eight Islamic banks and the conventional banks in equivalent relationship with Islamic banking windows to have a form of its own. Its structure can be classified into three, and the board of trustees can be categorized as the following: (i) Shari'ah board, (ii) management committee, and (iii) audit committee. He believes that if successful in establishing this model on real grounds, then the governmental budget will also affect Zakāt payment.

Abdullah and Haqqi (2017) investigated who is entitled to al-Gharimun as stated in Al-Qur'an At- Taubah verse 60. They saw the category of al-Gharimun as the recipient of Zakāt. This research is very interesting because only a few studies have addressed this issue.

Abd Samad et al. (2018) examined the relationship between corporate Zakāt debt and the performance of Islamic bank companies in Malaysia. They want to know whether there is a relationship between company Zakāt and company performance.

Abdullahi (2019) studied Zakāt as marketing tools. He shows how *Zakah*, *Halal* consumption, and corporate social responsibility are connected and highlights the role of *Zakah* as a social marketing tool. It shows how *Zakah* affects consumption through marginal propensity of *Zakah* recipients who spend *Zakah* money on basic needs.

Ben Jedidia and K. Guerbouj (2020) examined the impact of Zakāt on economic growth among a sample of Muslim countries. They find evidence that Zakāt stimulates the country's growth. The findings have substantial implications for the economic policy in Muslim countries. Authorities may further rely on Zakāt to boost economic growth.

From the above literature review, we can conclude that some researchers tried to related Zakāt management with macro policy (Aisyah, 2014, and Ben Jeddida & Gurbouj, 2020) and micro policy (Uddin, 2016; Abd Samad et al., 2018; Abdullahi 2019). Some of them provided the Qur'an dan hadith argument for Zakāt and poverty (Olanipekun, 2015). Some of them explained the recipients of Zakāt (Abdullahi & Haqqi, 2017). The interesting question is, which previous researchers had studied subjects of Zakāt?

The role of Zakāt in poverty alleviation has been successful in Nintavur Srilanka (Seheera et al., 2015) and Greater Jakarta Indonesia (Kasri, 2016), but not in Kwara State, Nigeria (Abdussalam et al., 2015). This means that the role of Zakāt has varied among countries, as supported by Shirazi (2014). The interesting question is, which location has been studied by researchers?

3 DATA AND METHODOLOGY

This study will be conducted using a qualitative approach. This chapter will focus on several aspects: research type, research approach, research subjects, the gender of the author, country of author, studied location, and publication area.

This chapter adopts a descriptive analysis based on literature for 10 years between 2011 and 2020, inclusive. Three hundred thirteen articles had been gathered based on an online Google Scholar search on seminar papers, journals, and articles. The review focuses specifically on the articles written in the areas of Zakāt. It follows that the articles would be classified into seven categories: poverty alleviation, fiqh of Zakāt, development, and measurement of Zakāt, managing Zakāt, paying Zakāt, tax and Zakāt, and performance of Zakāt institution.

The classifications are made based on either the content or the abstract of the articles. It is noted that some areas might overlap due to the different nature and research interests of the specified journals.

4 EMPIRICAL RESULTS

4.1 Number of Publications by Year

There were 313 articles published that were related to Zakāt from the observed ten-year period. Table 10.1 presents the distribution of articles by year. It shows that the average number of articles published per year is 28.6, and most articles were published in 2016.

4.2 Research Types of Each Publication

Table 10.2 shows the types of research used for every article published. According to Uma Sekaran (2013), four commonly used research types are analytical, descriptive, empirical, and exploratory. Analytical research

Table 10.1 Number of publications by year

Year of publication	Number of articles	Percentage
2011	21	6.7
2012	17	5.4
2013	28	8.9
2014	27	8.6
2015	36	11.5
2016	67	21.4
2017	18	5.8
2018	26	8.3
2019	33	10.5
2020	40	12.8
Total	313	100.0

Source: Data analyzing, 2020

Table 10.2 Research types of each publication

Year of publication	Research types				Total
	Descriptive	Analytical	Empirical	Exploratory	
2011	2	8	4	7	21
2012	3	4	6	4	17
2013	5	12	5	6	28
2014	6	9	11	1	27
2015	11	10	7	8	36
2016	12	10	25	20	67
2017	1	8	3	6	18
2018	3	9	11	3	26
2019	0	14	15	4	33
2020	3	14	20	3	40
Total	46	98	107	62	313

Source: Data analyzing, 2020

attempts to establish why it is that way or how it came to be. Analytical research usually concerns itself with cause–effect relationships. Descriptive research attempts to determine, describe, or identify what is. Descriptive research uses description, classification, measurement, and comparison to describe what phenomena are. Empirical research methods are a class in which empirical observations or data are collected to answer particular research questions. Exploratory research is done if few or no previous studies exist, and predictive research speculates on future possibilities after further analysis of available proof of cause and effect.

Most publications contained all four of the above research types. Findings show that most articles (107) are empirical, followed by analytical (98), exploratory (62), and descriptive (46). If we group those articles into only two groups, then the first group is 'empirical-exploratory' with 169 articles, and the other group is 'analytical-descriptive' with 144 articles.

4.3 Research Approaches of Each Publication

According to Punch (2013), there are three different research approaches: qualitative (subjective approach), quantitative (numerical analysis), and mixed-method (combining both approaches). In this study, only two approaches are used: qualitative and quantitative. Table 10.3 shows the methods of research used for every article published within ten years.

Most of the articles are qualitative by nature, in which we could see that 174 of 313 published articles used quantitative methods almost every year. One hundred thirty-nine articles use qualitative methods.

4.4 Quantitative List by Subject Area of Articles

Table 10.4 shows the growth of each subject according to the year of publication and subject involved. It shows that articles related to 'Development

Table 10.3 Research approaches of each publication

Year of publication	Research approach		Total
	Quantitative	Qualitative	
2011	14	7	21
2012	10	7	17
2013	17	11	28
2014	16	11	27
2015	26	10	36
2016	36	31	67
2017	6	12	18
2018	10	16	26
2019	17	16	33
2020	22	18	40
Total	174	139	313

Source: Data analyzing, 2020

Table 10.4 Subject area of articles

Subject of article	Year of Publication										Total
	2011	2012	2013	2014	2015	2016	2017	2018	2019	2020	
Poverty alleviation	3	5	2	4	9	10	9	3	5	9	**59**
Fiqh of Zakāt	3	1	3	4	6	7	0	0	2	2	**28**
Development and measurement of Zakāt	4	3	5	3	5	8	2	7	8	6	**51**
Zakāt management	1	2	5	6	5	14	1	4	2	4	**44**
Paying Zakāt	6	4	8	3	6	15	0	6	5	9	**62**
Tax and Zakāt	2	0	1	1	0	3	0	1	5	3	**16**
Zakāt institution performance	2	2	4	6	5	10	6	5	6	7	**53**

Source: Data analyzing, 2020

and Measurement of Zakāt' have been written and published every year (59 articles from the observed period). The most publications (62 out of 313 articles) are about paying Zakāt, followed by Zakāt and poverty alleviation, with 59 published articles.

4.5 Genders of Authors and Authorship

Table 10.5 shows that there are 242 male and 71 female authors who published articles about Zakāt from 2011 to 2020. We conclude that out of every four authors of Zakāt articles, three of them are males.

4.6 Study Location and Publications by Geographical Affiliation

Table 10.6 shows the ranked list of publications based on geographical affiliation. The table is divided into three parts: the authors' country, the conducted study, and published papers. For the first part, the highest ranked is Indonesia (158 authors) followed by Malaysia (103 authors). For the second part, Indonesia is the most studied country, with 153 articles found to perform the study in Indonesia, followed by Malaysia (100 articles) and Nigeria (17 articles). For the third part, Indonesia and

Table 10.5 Genders of Authors

Gender of the author	Male	Female
2011	12	8
2012	12	5
2013	24	4
2014	24	4
2015	29	7
2016	53	14
2017	12	6
2018	19	7
2019	28	5
2020	29	11
Total	242	71

Source: Data analyzing, 2020

Table 10.6 List of study locations and publications by countries involved

Country	Number of authors	Studied location	Publication area
Indonesia	155	150	139
Malaysia	103	100	76
Brunei Darussalam	3	2	–
Pakistan	5	3	4
Qatar	2	–	–
Bahrain	1	1	–
Turkey	2	1	5
USA	2	2	20
UK	4	3	32
Nigeria	12	17	–
India	1	1	1
Egypt	10	2	–
Saudi Arabia	12	11	4
Bangladesh	3	4	–
Japan	1	–	2
Australia	1	–	–
Brazil	1	–	–
Maroko	1	1	–
Oman	1	–	–
Philippines	1	1	–
Sweden	1	–	–
Thailand	1	1	–
Tunisia	2	2	–
Algeria	1	–	–
Palestine	1	–	–
Other	1	11	4

Source: Data analyzing, 2020

Malaysia have become the preferred country for publishing articles, with 139 articles 76 articles, respectively.

Analysis of the articles published related to Zakāt study for the year 2011 to 2020 has provided the following findings:

a. There are vast numbers of articles based on Zakāt in relation to a wide range of issues that have been published. The peak of publications was in 2016, with 67 articles.
b. Most authors prefer to use empirical research to answer particular issues on Zakāt in countries or areas of study that arise. Analytical and descriptive methods did not gain popularity in most articles within this area.
c. Most papers use the qualitative method since the topics involve figures and analyzing thought from previous Islamic scholars.
d. The highest number of articles covers management subjects. Since this is the pillar for Zakāt collection and distribution, it is followed by poverty alleviation.
e. Indonesia was the most studied location for Zakāt issues, and also Indonesian journals had become the most preferred publication forum for authors to publish their studies on Zakāt.

5 Conclusion

From the above analysis, it can be concluded that scholars have intensively discussed the issue of Zakāt. The number of published articles discussing Zakāt increased from 2011 to 2020. Further, the issue prompted most scholars to use empirical and qualitative approaches to solve it. The most discussed issues are related to the management of Zakāt and poverty alleviation. This chapter recommends Muslim countries to manage Zakāt properly because the impact is significant to alleviate poverty. However, the approach needs to be strengthened and analyzed from time to time, so it will help the poor to have a better life. However, since there are quite a few articles published in this field, more research needs to be done in linking Zakāt with poverty alleviation. The journals should also focus on the articles related to these fields, and at the same time, universities should provide enough research grants to support those fields. Furthermore, more articles should be made available online, hence the studies on Zakāt may become more visible and impactful.

REFERENCES

Abd, S. K., Said, R., Mohd Nasir, I. N., Mahshar, M., & Kamarulzaman, M. H. (2018). Analysis of the Role of Zakat on Islamic Banking Performance. In R. Said, S. N. Mohd, Z. Azhar, & K. Anuar Kamarudin (Eds.), *State-of-the-Art Theories and Empirical Evidence*. Springer.

Abdullah, R., & Haqqi, A. R. A. (2017). Zakah for Asnaf Al-Gharimun in Brunei Darussalam: Concepts and Practices. *Al-Iqtishad: Jurnal Ilmu Ekonomi Syariah*, 9(2), 243–258.

Abdullahi, S. I. (2019). Zakah as tool for social cause marketing and corporate charity: a conceptual study. *Journal of Islamic Marketing*, 10(1), 191–207.

Abdussalam, O. I., Johari, F., & Alias, M. (2015). Is Zakah Effective to Alleviate Poverty in a Muslim Society: A Case of Kwara State, Nigeria. *GJAT*, 5(1), 33–41.

Aisyah, M. (2014). The Role of Zakah and Binary Economics in Poverty Reduction. *Esensi: Jurnal Bisnis dan Manajemen*, 4(2), 178–197.

Ben Jedidia, K., & Guerbouj, K. (2020). Effects of zakat on the economic growth in selected Islamic countries: Empirical evidence, International Journal of Development Issues.

Johari, Fuadah Abd Aziz, Muhammad Ridhwan, Mohd Ali, & Ahmad Fahme. (2014). A Review on Literatures of Zakat between 2003-2013.Library Philosophy and Practice (e-journal) paper 1175.Libraries at the University of Nebraska-Lincoln. December 2014.http://digitalcommons.unl.edu/libphilprac/1175

Olanipekun, B. S. (2015). The Role Of Zakat As A Poverty Alleviation Strategy And A Tool For Sustainable Development: Insights From The Perspectives Of The Holy Prophet (PBUH). *Arabian Journal of Business and Management Review*, 5(3), 1.

Shirazi, N. S. (2014). Integrating Zakāt and Waqf into the Poverty Reduction Strategy of the IDB Member Countries. *Islamic Economic Studies*, 22(1), 79–108.

Suheera, Nashri Jamaldeen (2015). The Role of Zakat on Poverty Alleviation: An Empirical Study at Nintavur, Sri Lanka. Paper presented at the Second International Symposium.

Uddin, A. E. (2016). Through Islamic Banks' Zakat House (IBZH): Investment of Zakah Funds in Microfinance to Remove Poverty in Bangladesh: A New Model. *International Journal of Islamic Economics and Finance Studies*, 2(1), 1–26.

CHAPTER 11

The Impact of Zakat Distribution

Norhaziah Nawai and Farah Shazwani Ruzaiman

1　Introduction

Zakat is one of the five pillars of Islam, and has a direct impact not only on the relationship between man and Allah S.W.T but also between man and society. This is due to the fact that payment of zakat can be used as an indicator of the obedience of the person to Allah S.W.T. The payment of zakat also can be used to share wealth from the rich to the poor and promote Muslims' economic activities, and it assures the minimum living standard of Muslims. Zakat can be defined as growth and purification. According to Farishta (2003), the exact meaning of zakat is growth, where it is the growth in purity of the soul through honest action and dealings. Furthermore, Kahf (1999) explained that in giving out zakat, the savings will be purified from something illegal.

In Islamic law, the zakat needs to be distributed among the categories of those who are entitled (Ahmad Bello, 2009). Muslims have the obligation to give specific amounts of their wealth to the specified beneficiaries

N. Nawai (✉) • F. S. Ruzaiman
Faculty of Economics and Muamalat, Universiti Sains Islam Malaysia, Nilai, Malaysia
e-mail: norhaziahn@usim.edu.my

© The Author(s), under exclusive license to Springer Nature Switzerland AG 2022
A. G. Ismail et al. (eds.), *Islamic Philanthropy*, Palgrave Studies in Islamic Banking, Finance, and Economics,
https://doi.org/10.1007/978-3-031-06890-4_11

with certain conditions and requirements. The main objective of zakat is to achieve socio-economic justice. Yusoff (2011) stated that zakat distribution has the ability to increase consumption since the marginal propensity to consume of the zakat payer is lower than the zakat recipient.

Zakat management is the most critical aspect in determining the direction of zakat institutions to ensure the optimization of zakat funds (Sari et al., 2013). Normally, management of zakat involves two activities: collection and distribution (Oran, 2009). The effectiveness of zakat management is important to enable zakat funds to help improve the lives of the poor and needy (Mahyuddin & Abdullah, 2011).

There have been various studies done on zakat management collection and distribution. These studies not only explore in depth, but also allow other researchers to suggest and produce new knowledge on zakat. Thus, this essay seeks to review the literature on zakat distribution and its impact. This chapter will also suggest the agenda for future research on zakat distribution. This chapter is divided into six sections, starting with the introduction in Sect. 1, and followed by zakat distribution in Sect. 2. Section 3 discusses the impact of zakat distribution while Sect. 4 elaborates the material and methods. Sect. 5 is a discussion and we end with the conclusion in Sect. 6.

2 Zakat Distribution

Zakat is an important source of revenue to improve the economic condition of the poor. Zakat collection as well as distribution need to be effective to help develop the community. Jasni and Anwar (2012) suggest that the strict enforcement of law, complemented by organized institutions, will have an impact on zakat collection and distribution as well as the confidence of a community towards the institutions.

Zakat can only be distributed to eight groups. The fair distribution of zakat should be implemented as far as possible to the eight groups of recipients. Among the evidence of incompetence in zakat distribution is a study by Norma and Naziruddin (2014). They have analyzed the practice of zakat distribution in several states in Malaysia. However, the result shows that there is a persistent gap between collection and distribution in a few states. Additionally, the management involved in zakat distribution need to reevaluate to achieve maximum zakat distribution performance (Eza Ellani et al., 2014). Furthermore, Rusni and Nur Iffah (2016) have limited their study to Selangor and the Federal Territory of Malaysia. The study used annual data retrieved from both institutions and found that in terms of zakat management, both institutions have similar practice but different in distribution to the *riqab* group of recipients.

One of the recipient groups has been discussed in several studies. For instance, Johari et al. (2014) have identified the dispersal of a *muallaf* group in terms of urban-rural poverty that was involved in zakat distribution. The finding suggests that the amount of zakat funds has been allocated to *muallaf* in urban areas in the state of Selangor. Zakat distribution to *muallaf* is very important to be implemented and managed properly for the welfare of *muallaf* (Anuar et al., 2016).

Norazlina and Abdul Rahim (2011) seek to analyze the efficiency of zakat institutions. They proposed to used Data Envelopment Analysis (DEA) and identify the appropriate methods to evaluate the efficiency of zakat institutions. For instance, Ahmad and Ma'in (2014) have used the proposed model to analyze the efficiency of zakat management of Lembaga Zakat Selangor. Unfortunately, the result shows that in terms of distribution, the efficiency is lower than collection. However, Abdullah et al. (2012) have proposed another model, the Zakat Effectiveness Index (ZEIN), in order to address the effectiveness and efficiency issues. The analysis showed that ZEIN is a potentially useful tool to measure the performance and efficiency of zakat management.

A study by Lubis et al. (2011) has investigated another appropriate system to develop the effectiveness and efficiency of zakat management process. They have suggested the use of the Geographic Information System (GIS). GIS has the advantage of maintaining and managing the cost and avoiding wasting money. Plus, GIS can enhance the capabilities of statistical distribution analysis.

Zakaria, M (2014), has investigated the influence of human needs in the perspective of Maqasid as-Shariah, namely religion, physical self, knowledge, family, and wealth on zakat distribution effectiveness. The result shows that all variables positively influence zakat distribution effectiveness. In order to enhance zakat management, Wahid and Ahmad (2014), suggest several factors for management in Lembaga Zakat Selangor. The study shows that the level of confidence of zakat distribution depends on three main factors: the corporate image of Lembaga Zakat Selangor, zakat collection, and zakat distribution.

Zakat funds can be distributed to needy recipients in the form of business capital. Most zakat institutions are currently organizing the program for business start-ups using zakat funds. However, if no monitoring takes place for capital assistance, the program will end in failure (Abd Rahman et al., 2008). Plus, the recipients will be demotivated to continue their businesses. In order to address the issue, another study by Rahman and Ahmad (2011) examined the factors that influence the success or failure of businesses. The study found that there are a few factors that are significant in influencing the success of the business, such as the business period, monitoring, the characteristics of the business, efficiency of zakat management, and social skills. In addition to that, Abdul Manan et al. (2011) have done a study to evaluate the role of zakat institutions, focusing on Lembaga Zakat Selangor, in ensuring businesses are successful. The result shows that by providing capital, training, and knowledge, zakat recipients can enjoy success in their business and achieve a better standard of living.

Another study suggests that trust became one of the factors for effective zakat distribution. Zulkurnain et al. (2016) proposed a conceptual framework for examining the trust towards zakat institutions among business owners. They found that shared values, communication, non-opportunistic behavior, and the perception of distribution are potential factors that will influence the trust towards zakat institutions.

3 The Impact of Zakat Distribution

The precise practice of zakat distribution is necessary to ensure the zakat funds are fully utilized and have the maximum impact on recipients, especially in countries that do not enforce zakat payment. A number of researches have attempted to measure the impact of zakat. For instance, Irawan et al. (2011) attempted to explore the impact of zakat programs in Bandung, Indonesia towards poverty alleviation. The research used primary and secondary data and found out that the zakat program has a positive impact on poverty alleviation. Besides that, Beik and Arsyianti (2016) have examined the role of productive zakat programs in reducing poverty levels of households. By using the CIBEST model that comprises four indices, they found that zakat programs are able to increase the welfare index and reduce the material poverty and absolute poverty index.

Furthermore, Abdelbaki (2014) has analyzed the impact of zakat on poverty and income inequality in Bahrain. He estimates the amount of zakat due in Bahrain but states that zakat's role in eliminating poverty and income inequality is limited. Atia (2011) concluded in her study that zakat is an important mechanism in Egypt for social stability and ensures that the poor have their needs met. Unfortunately, another study on the impact of zakat on poverty alleviation in Egypt has negative results. The study found out that zakat collection in Egypt couldn't eradicate poverty from the Egyptian economy alone (Abdelbaki, 2014). However, according to Rusni and Nur Iffah (2016), if zakat funds were collected and distributed according to Shariah, poverty will be reduced and Muslim society would be better.

Senadjki et al. (2015) have analyzed the impact of zakat on income inequality and poverty in Malaysia by using panel data from 2001–2012. The result shows that zakat has no significant effect on income inequality but is significant in reducing both poverty and hardcore poverty. Another study that used panel data to analyze the impact of zakat distribution on aggregate consumption in Malaysia has found that zakat distribution has a positive impact on aggregate consumption even though the impact is small and short-lived (Suprayitno et al., 2013).

Jehle (1994) attempted to examine the impact of zakat on income inequality in Pakistan. By employing the AKS (Atkinson Kolm & Sen) index, the result showed that zakat did reduce income inequality in Pakistan. Different authors have measured in different ways. Shirazi (1996) has used the FGT (Foster, Greer, and Thorbecke) index and found that the poverty gap had fallen from 11.2 to 8% with the help of zakat funds. The impact of zakat on poverty alleviation is further seen in Shirazi and Bin Amin (2009) who estimate resource shortfall and potential zakat collection for poverty elimination in 38 OIC member countries. The result shows that Malaysia only requires 0.02% of GDP to eliminate poverty and make it the lowest among the other countries.

Furthermore, Patmawati (2006) studied the impact of zakat on reducing poverty in the state of Selangor, Malaysia. Her analysis revealed that zakat distribution was able to reduce poverty incidence and narrow the severity of poverty in the state. In the state of Kelantan, Malaysia, Ahmad Fahme et al. (2013) have examined the effectiveness of monthly zakat distribution in reducing poverty, and the result shows that monthly distribution has a positive effect towards income improvement and the zakat will reduce poverty. This is supported by Zaki (2015), who in his research zakat distribution has a positive impact in improving monthly income, even though the income is lower than the poverty line. The role of zakat and knowledge on reducing poverty has been proved by Abdelmawla (2014), where zakat and education have a significant impact at reducing poverty in Sudan by 1%.

Zakat funds can be used with other methods of financing. For example, Irawan and Arimbi (2012) investigate the impact of zakat funds using *qardhul hasan* financing for economic empowerment. The research uses a case study and the result shows that *qardhul hasan* financing relatively helps the zakat recipients with assistance and saving deposits. There is also a linear relationship between *qardhul hasan* financing and recipients economic empowerment.

Those studies have shown the fact that the presence of zakat distribution programs was able to reduce and slowly eliminate poverty. The results provided proved the importance of the role of zakat institutions in managing zakat funds.

4 MATERIAL AND METHODS

An extensive number of relevant articles published in journals, theses, and online books were obtained using different databases such as Scopus, Science Direct, Google Scholar, Emerald, and Proquest. In order to find related articles, search terms were used: namely, zakat distribution, impact of zakat, zakat management, zakat issues, and poverty alleviation. The search generated several articles published on zakat distribution. A summary of all articles is provided in Table 11.1.

5 DISCUSSION

Analysis of the articles published related to zakat distribution has provided as follows:

- There are various articles that have been published that discuss a range of issues relating to zakat distribution.
- In terms of the study of the efficiency of zakat distribution, most authors prefer to use the empirical research method. However, there are a few studies that apply the descriptive or exploratory methods.
- Most researchers use a mixed method, since the topic of zakat distribution involves data and analysis of thought from Islamic scholars.
- Malaysia has the most published articles in the area of zakat management, specifically zakat distribution.

The review of articles has shown that some of the positive and negative issues of zakat distribution practice are being widely discussed among

Table 11.1 Data extraction evidence

Authors	Topic	Design	Result
Suprayitno (2020)	The Impact of Zakat on Economic Growth in Five States in Indonesia	Employs the Error Correction Model (ECM) to analyze the impact of zakat in long-term economic growth in five states in Indonesia	The findings show that zakat has a significant and positive relationship with economic growth. The results of the ECM analysis show that the distribution of zakat positively influences economic growth. The long-term elasticity of zakat variables is positive and significant
Anggadini et al. (2020)	Economic Growth: The Impact of Zakat Funds and Tax on Business Capital	Secondary data—zakat fund distribution data, tax on business capital data and the Gross Regional Domestic Product (PDRB) data of West Java Province from 2010 to 2017	The results of the study show that the zakat fund distribution and tax on business capital data have a significant effect on economic growth. It shows the distribution of zakat funds and local taxes simultaneously providing an influence on economic growth variables of 76%
Dian Fitriarni Sari et al. (2019)	Investigating the Impact of Zakat on Poverty Alleviation: A Case from West Sumatra, Indonesia	Primary data through 200 questionnaires distributed in West Sumatra. The study uses the Poverty Indicator and Average Time Taken to Exit Poverty calculation method	The results indicate that zakat promotes poverty reduction. The research also proves concisely the poor can exit the poverty line with zakat

(*continued*)

Table 11.1 (continued)

Authors	Topic	Design	Result
El Ayyubi and Eka Saputri (2018)	Analysis of the Impact of Zakat, Infak, and Sadaqah Distribution on Poverty Alleviation Based on the CIBEST Model (Case Study: Jogokariyan Baitul Maal Mosque, Yogyakarta)	Primary data through 100 questionnaires distributed at Jogokariyan, Baitul Maal, mosque, Yogyakarta. The study uses the Islamic poverty index of the CIBEST model to analyze the data	The results indicate that there is an increase in welfare and a decrease in material poverty, spiritual poverty, and absolute poverty, as seen from changes in the Islamic CIBEST's poverty indexes for *Mustahik* households
Oran (2009)	Zakat Funds and Wealth Creation	Proposed a stage-implementation plan, a long-term strategy for fighting poverty. In the short run, target one subgroup or poor in particular	This proposal does not conflict with the created 'IDB Poverty Alleviation Fund' but instead complements it
Mahyuddin and Abdullah (2011)	Towards Achieving the Quality of Life in the Management of Zakat Distribution to the Rightful Recipients (the Poor and Needy)	Conceptual article. The study reviews the management of zakat distribution in terms of quality of life of the zakat recipients	A more proactive mechanism for zakat distribution is a must to ensure the quality of life of the *asnaf* is guaranteed. The form of mechanism could come in the form of monetary capital and equipment to help recipients improve their standard of living
Jasni and Anwar (2012)	A Comparative Study of the Administration of Zakat Laws in the Province of Aceh and the State of Kedah	Using qualitative methods and interviews with a number of respondents in order to examine the administrative aspects of Islamic law on zakat	Strict enforcement of law, accompanied by institutions organized with manpower and focused objectives, will have an impact on the zakat collections as well as the confidence of community towards the institutions

(*continued*)

Table 11.1 (continued)

Authors	Topic	Design	Result
Norma and Naziruddin (2014)	Is Zakat Capable of Alleviating Poverty? An Analysis on the Distribution of Zakat Funds in Malaysia	Analyze the current practice of zakat distribution in several states in Malaysia	Provides several recommendations for zakat distribution improvement
Eza Ellani et al. (2014)	Financial and Non-Financial Distribution Efficiency Performance among Zakat Institutions in Malaysia	Uses secondary data that are annual reports of zakat institutions from 2005 to 2010 and primary data through questionnaire surveys that have been sent to managerial-level executives in 14 zakat institutions in Malaysia	There is an improvement in distribution performance of zakat institutions, although the efficiency scores obtained are not consistent. Majlis Agama Islam Negeri Sembilan (MAINS) achieved the best score for financial distribution efficiency. While Majlis Agama Islam dan Adat Istiadat Melayu Kelantan (MAIK) achieved the best score for non-financial distribution efficiency. Majlis Agama Islam Wilayah Persekutuan (MAIWP) is a zakat institution that has the lowest score for both distribution and efficiency
Rusni and Nur Iffah (2016)	Prioritization of Zakat Distribution in Selangor and the Federal Territory of Malaysia: Are They Following the Right Distribution Principles according to Shariah?	Conceptual article. The study reviews and analyzes the current practice of zakat distribution in Selangor and the Federal Territory of Malaysia	The study observes that zakat distribution in Selangor and the Federal Territory in Malaysia gives more to fi sabilillah recipients compared to other recipient groups

(*continued*)

Table 11.1 (continued)

Authors	Topic	Design	Result
Fuadah et al. (2014)	The Importance of Zakat Distribution and Urban-Rural Poverty Incidence among *Muallaf* (New Converts)	Descriptive analysis and interviews with two officers from Selangor State Islamic Religious Council (SIRC)	The finding suggests that a huge of amount of zakat has been allocated to the development of *asnaf Muallaf* in the state of Selangor, especially in urban areas
Anuar et al. (2016)	The Zakat Distribution Management of Majlis Agama Islam Negeri Johor for the *Muallaf Asnaf*	Document analysis and questionnaires gathered from 30 *muallaf* in Johor. Two constructs were used, namely perception of *muallaf* on the management of zakat distribution and the effects of the distribution of zakat on the new converts	The respondents are quite satisfied with the system of zakat distribution in Johor. The study concludes that zakat distribution to new converts is very important and is to be implemented and managed properly for the welfare of the *muallaf*
Wahid and Ahmad (2014)	Factors Influencing the Confidence Levels of Zakat Distribution: Study on the Muslim Community in Selangor	Primary data through interviews with 643 respondents. The respondents were chosen based on the 9 districts in Selangor. The study uses factor analysis to analyze the data	The study shows that the level of confidence towards zakat institutions is dependent on three main factors, namely the corporate image of Lembaga zakat Selangor (zakat institution), zakat collection, and zakat distribution
Irawan et al. (2011)	An Analysis of the Impact of Zakah Programs in Poverty Alleviation: Case Study in Bandung, Indonesia	Primary data: interviews with selected informants. Secondary data: literature survey and data of Rumah Zakat Indonesia and Dompet Dhuafa	Zakat programs have positive impact on poverty alleviation.

(*continued*)

Table 11.1 (continued)

Authors	Topic	Design	Result
Beik and Arsyianti (2016)	Measuring Zakat Impact on Poverty and Welfare Using CIBEST Model	Interview through questionnaires in DKI Jakarta and Bogor Regency with 221 respondents from February to May 2015. CIBEST model comprises 4 indices: welfare index, material poverty index, spiritual poverty index, and absolute poverty index	Zakat utilization program able to increase welfare index by 96.8%. The material poverty index and absolute poverty index to be reduced by 30.15% and 91.30%, respectively. An increase of two households living under spiritual poverty means suffering due to weakening of spiritual values despite being materially better off due to zakat programs
Patmawati (2006)	Economic Role of Zakat in Reducing Income Inequality and Poverty in Selangor	Examine by using Lorenz curve, Gini coefficient, and Atkinson index. Using 5 indices of poverty: the household count ratio, average poverty gap, income gap, Sen index, and FGT index	Empirical findings of the positive measures of the Lorenz curve and Gini coefficient indicate the positive contributions of zakat distribution in reducing income inequality. However, results related to the Atkinson index show that the current practice of zakat distribution increases income inequality, increases income loss, and reduces social welfare. Zakat distribution reduces poverty
Ahmad Fahme et al. (2013)	Impact of Zakat Distribution on Poor and Needy Recipients: An Analysis in Kelantan, Malaysia	Primary data through questionnaire to 481 respondents in Kelantan. The study applies regression analysis to analyze the data	The results indicate that zakat elasticity is about 0.46. If zakat distribution increases by 1%, the monthly income will increase by 0.46%. Zakat distribution is significant in determining positive income distribution among the group

(*continued*)

Table 11.1 (continued)

Authors	Topic	Design	Result
Irawan and Arimbi (2012)	The Impact of Qardhul Hasan Financing Using Zakah Funds on Economic Empowerment (Case Study of Dompet Dhuafa, West Java, Indonesia)	Quantitative, case study analysis and explanatory research	The result shows that *Qardhul Hasan* is able to improve economic empowerment
Abdelmawla (2014)	The Impacts of Zakat and Knowledge on Poverty Alleviation in Sudan: An Empirical Investigation (1990–2009)	Data collected from the Central Bureau of Statistics (CBS) Sudan. Two variables were used, namely the percentage spent on the poor out of total zakat funds and educational attainment (proxy for knowledge)	The result reveals that zakat and educational attainment impact significantly at the 1% level on reducing poverty in Sudan

Source: Authors' compilation

researchers. The most-discussed issues are related to the management of zakat. It is crucial to determine the effectiveness of zakat collection and distribution to alleviate poverty among its recipients. The proposed model and framework of zakat efficiency can be discussed extensively using real data. However, the there is a limited amount of research devoted to whether zakat distribution can eliminate poverty or increase the recipient's income. Thus, future research could examine the impact of zakat distribution through programs implemented by institutions or by groups of recipients. Therefore, more conclusive empirical evidence could be provided.

6 Conclusion

Zakat can positively affect economic variables such as poverty alleviation and economic growth. This essay presents a review of literature on the importance of zakat management, especially zakat distribution. It is very important for Muslims to really understand the benefits of zakat funds.

Zakat as a charity tool can be used for poverty alleviation for the eight groups of recipients. The effectiveness of zakat distribution in terms of creating economic programs or similar can help recipients in their daily lives. Since there are quite a few studies related to the impact of zakat funds, it is important for researchers to continue their studies in this field. It is also suggested that journal articles related to this field should be available online to help researchers to locate them.

References

Abd Rahman, R., Ahmad, S., & Wahid, H. (2008). Perlaksanaan Bantuan Modal Zakat: Analisis Perbandingan. *Seminar Kebangsaan Ekonomi Malaysia, 2008*, 450–459.

Abdelbaki, H. H. (2014). Assessment the Impact of Zakat on Aggregate Consumption and Poverty: Evidence from Egypt. *British Journal of Economics, Management & Trade, 4*(8), 1306–1322.

Abdelmawla, M. A. (2014). The Impacts of Zakat and Knowledge on Poverty Alleviation in Sudan: An Empirical Investigation (1990–2009). *Journal of Economic Cooperation and Development, 35*(4), 61–84.

Abdul Manan, H., Muhamat, A. A., & Rosly, H. E. (2011). An Appraisal by Its Entrepreneurial Asnaf (Usahawan Asnaf) on Lembaga Zakat Selangor's Role in Ensuring Business Success: An Empirical Study on the Lembaga Zakat Selangor. In *2011 IEEE Colloquium on Humanities, Science and Engineering, CHUSER 2011*, Chuser, 580–585. https://doi.org/10.1109/CHUSER.2011.6163800

Abdullah, N., Mahyudi, M., Yusop, M., & Omar, C. (2012). A Technical Note on the Derivation of Zakat Effectiveness Index (Zein). *International Journal of Economics, Management and Accounting, 1*(1), 75–86.

Ahmad Bello, D. (2009). *Poverty Alleviation through Zakah and Waqf Institutions: A Case for the Muslim Ummah in Ghana*. MPRA Paper No. 23191. Retrieved May 16, 2013, from www.mpra.ub.unimuenchen.de/23191/1/MPRA_paper_23191.pdf

Ahmad Fahme, M. A., Zaleha, M. N., Muhammad Ridhwan, A. A., Mohd Faisol, I., & Fuadah, J. (2013). Impact of Zakat Distribution on Poor and Needy Recipients: An Analysis in Kelantan, Malaysia. *Australian Journal of Basic and Applied Sciences, 7*(13), 177–182.

Ahmad, I. H. J., & Ma'in, M. (2014). The Efficiency of Zakat Collection and Distribution: Evidence from Two Stage Analysis. *Journal of Economic Cooperation and Development, 35*(3), 133–170.

Anggadini, S. D., Surtikanti, S., & Hassan, F. M. (2020). Economic Growth: The Impact of Zakat Funds and Tax on Business Capital. *Jurnal Ekonomi dan Bisnis Islam, 5*(2), 141–156. https://doi.org/10.24042/febi.v5i2.7112

Anuar, P., Rashidi, A., Abd Ghafar, D., Zilal, S., & Muhammad Shafiee, E. (2016). The Zakat Distribution Management of Majlis Agama Islam Negeri Johor for the Mua'alaf Asnaf. *ISLAMIYYAT, 38*(1), 25–34.

Atia, M. (2011). Islamic Approaches to Development: A Case Study of Zakat, Sadaqa and Qurd al Hassan in Contemporary Egypt. In *International Conference on Islamic Economics and Finance*, pp. 1–14. http://www.iefpedia.com/english/wp-content/uploads/2011/12/Mona-Atia.pdf

Beik, I. S., & Arsyianti, L. D. (2016). Measuring Zakat Impact on Poverty and Welfare Using the CIBEST Model. *Journal of Islamic Monetary Economics and Finance, 1*(2), 141–160. http://www.journalbankindonesia.org/index.php/JIMF/article/view/524/508

El Ayyubi, S., & Eka Saputri, H. (2018). Analysis of the Impact of Zakat, Infak, and Sadaqah Distribution on Poverty Alleviation Based on the CIBEST Model (Case Study: Jogokariyan Baitul Maal Mosque, Yogyakarta). *International Journal of Zakat, 3*(2), 85–97.

Eza Ellani, A. L., Mohd Rizal, P., & Mohamat Sabri, H. (2014). Prestasi Kecekapan Agihan Kewangan dan Bukan Kewangan di Kalangan Institusi Zakat di Malaysia. *Jurnal Ekonomi Malaysia, 48*(2), 51–60.

Farishta, G. Z. (2003). *The Law and Institution of Zakat*. The Other Press.

Fuadah, J., Ahmad Fahme, M. A., Muhammad Ridhwan, A. A., & Nursilah, A. (2014). The Importance of Zakat Distribution and Urban-Rural Poverty Incidence among Muallaf (New Convert). *Asian Social Science, 10*(21), 42–53.

Irawan, F., & Arimbi, A. (2012). The Impact of Qardhul Hasan Financing Using Zakah Funds on Economic Empowerment (Case Study of Dompet Dhuafa, West Java, Indonesia). *Asian Business Review, 1*(1), 15–20. http://journals.abc.us.org/index.php/abr/article/view/Febianto

Irawan, F., Arimbi, A., & Asrul, K. (2011). An Analysis on the Impact of Zakah Programs in Poverty Alleviation: Case Study in Bandung, Indonesia. *SSRN Electronic Journal*. https://doi.org/10.2139/ssrn.1895109

Jasni, S., & Anwar, M. A. (2012). A Comparative Study of the Administration of Zakat Laws in the Province of Aceh and the State of Kedah. *Kajian Malaysia, 30*(1), 107–138.

Jehle, G. A. (1994). Zakat and Inequality: Some Evidence from Pakistan. *Review of Income and Wealth, 40*(2), 205–216. https://doi.org/10.1111/j.1475-4991.1994.tb00059.x

Johari, F., Mohd Ali, A. F., Ab Aziz, M. R., & Ahmad, N. (2014). The Importance of Zakat Distribution and Urban-Rural Poverty Incidence among Muallaf (New Converts). *Asian Social Science, 10*(21), 42–53. https://doi.org/10.5539/ass.v10n21p42

Kahf, M. (1999). The Performance of Institution of Zakah in Theory and Practice. In *International Conference on Islamic Economics towards the 21st Century*, Kuala Lumpur, April 26–30.

Lubis, M., Bilal, M., Lumpur, K., Yaacob, N. I., Omar, Y., Dahlan, A., et al. (2011). Enhancement of Zakat Distribution Management System: Case Study in Malaysia. In *International Management Conference 2011 Proceedings*, pp. 1–10. http://irep.iium.edu.my/4261/1/IMAC2011_EnhancementZakat Distribution.pdf

Mahyuddin, A. B., & Abdullah, A. G. (2011). Towards Achieving the Quality of Life in the Management of Zakat Distribution to the Rightful Recipients (the Poor and Needy). *International Journal of Business and Social Science*, 4(2), 237–245.

Norazlina, A. W., & Abdul Rahim, A. R. (2011). *Efficiency of Zakat Institutions and Its Determinants*. 8th International Conference on Islamic Economics and Finance, Center for Islamic Economics and Finance, Faculty of Islamic Studies, Qatar Foundation, Qatar.

Norma, S., & Naziruddin, A. (2014). Is Zakat Capable of Alleviating Poverty? An Analysis of the Distribution of Zakat Fund in Malaysia. *Journal of Islamic Economics, Banking*, 10(1), 69–95.

Oran, A. F. (2009). Zakat Funds and Wealth Creation. *International Association for Islamic Economics*, 13(1), 143–153.

Patmawati, I. (2006). *Economic Role of Zakat in Reducing Income Inequality and Poverty in Selangor*. Unpublished thesis, Universiti Putra Malaysia.

Rahman, R. A., & Ahmad, S. (2011). Strategi Pembangunan Keusahawanan Asnaf Fakir dan Miskin Melalui Agihan Bantuan Modal Zakat. *Jurnal Pengurusan*, 33, 37–44.

Rusni, H., & Nur Iffah, M. N. (2016). Prioritization of Zakat Distribution in Selangor and the Federal Territory of Malaysia: Are They Following the Right Distribution Principles according to Shariah? *Intellectual Discourse*, 2016, 435–457.

Sari, D. F., Beik, I. S., & Rindayati, W. (2019). Investigating the Impact of Zakat on Poverty Alleviation: A Case from West Sumatra, Indonesia. *International Journal of Zakat*, 4(2), 1–12.

Sari, M. D., Bahari, Z., & Hamat, Z. (2013). Review on Indonesian Zakah Management and Obstacles. *Social Sciences*, 2(2), 76–89. https://doi.org/10.11648/j.ss.20130202.18

Senadjki, A., Nachef, T., & Nursyazana, R. (2015). The Impact of Zakat on Income Inequality and Poverty in Malaysia: A Panel Data Analysis. *Market Forces*, 10(1), 1–11.

Shirazi, N. S. (1996). Targeting, Coverage, and Contribution of Zakat to Household's Income. *Journal of Economic Cooperation among Islamic Countries*, 17, 3–4.

Shirazi, N. S., & Bin Amin, M. F. (2009). Poverty Elimination through Potential Zakat Collection in the OIC-Member Countries: Revisited. *Pakistan Development Review*, 48(4), 739–753.

Suprayitno, E. (2020). The Impact of Zakat on Economic Growth in 5 States in Indonesia. *International Journal of Islamic Banking and Finance Research*, 4(1), 1–7.

Suprayitno, E., Kader, R. A., & Harun, A. (2013). The Impact of Zakat on Aggregate Consumption in Malaysia. *Journal of Islamic Economics, Banking and Finance*, 9(1), 1–24.

Wahid, H., & Ahmad, S. (2014). Faktor mempengaruhi tahap keyakinan agihan Zakat: Kajian terhadap masyarakat Islam di Selangor. *Jurnal Ekonomi Malaysia*, 48(2), 41–50.

Yusoff, M. (2011). Zakat Expenditure, School Enrollment, and Economic Growth in Malaysia. *International Journal of Business and Social Science*, 2(6), 175–181.

Zakaria, M. (2014). The Influence of Human Needs in the Perspective of Maqasid al-Syari'ah on Zakat Distribution Effectiveness. *Asian Social Science*, 10(3), 165–173. https://doi.org/10.5539/ass.v10n3p165

Zaki, M. Z. (2015). *An Analysis of the Management of Zakat Allocation and Distribution in Brunei Darussalam*. Unpublished Ph.D. thesis. University of Exeter, UK.

Zulkurnain, M. G., Saad, R. A. J., & Syahir, M. A. W. (2016). A Conceptual Framework for Examining Trust towards Zakat Institutions. *International Journal of Economics and Financial Issues*, 6(7), 98–102.

CHAPTER 12

Promoting Islamic Philanthropy in Islamic Higher Education of Indonesia

Indah Piliyanti and Agni Alam Awirya

1 INTRODUCTION

Poverty is one of the most common social problems in Indonesia. Statistics Indonesia (BPS) reported that the poverty rate in 2020 rose to 9.78% of the total Indonesian population (BPS, 2020). Under the coordination of the National Team for the Acceleration of Poverty Reduction, the government currently runs various integrated poverty reduction programs executed by central and local government (tnp2k.go.id). Poverty has many dimensions and does not merely entail low levels of income or expenditure (Sen, 1992, 2001). Inadequate education is also a dimension of poverty. Hence, education holds an immense power to alleviate poverty. Higher

---

I. Piliyanti (✉)
Faculty of Islamic Economics and Business, Institut Agama Islam Negeri, Surakarta, Indonesia

A. A. Awirya
Bank Indonesia, Central Jakarta, Indonesia
e-mail: agni_aa@bi.go.id

© The Author(s), under exclusive license to Springer Nature Switzerland AG 2022
A. G. Ismail et al. (eds.), *Islamic Philanthropy*, Palgrave Studies in Islamic Banking, Finance, and Economics,
https://doi.org/10.1007/978-3-031-06890-4_12

education can be a solution to poverty; the more knowledgeable are human beings, the greater they are able to contribute to the community.

Contribution to the community is part of the concept of philanthropy. Philanthropy that is simply defined as "the love of humankind" is aimed to enhance the quality of human life. Philanthropic action of individuals among others includes building universities and giving scholarships to higher education students (Cascione, 2003). In Islamic history, Islamic philanthropy funds have been used for developing higher education, such as Al Azhar University in Egypt, which is one of the best practices of *waqf*-based higher education (Hasan et al., 2019).

Based on higher education Law Number 12 of 2012, the functions of higher education in Indonesia are education and teaching, research, and community service. Higher education is under the coordination of the Directorate of Higher Education of the Ministry of Education and Culture and the Directorate of Islamic Higher Education of the Ministry of Religious Affairs. In 58 states Islamic higher education is under the Ministry of Religious Affairs, and 30 institutions offer *zakat* and *waqf* management studies and some of them also manage Muslim philanthropy funds in their institutions (diktis.kemenag.go.id). It is assumed that a great deal of the potential of *zakat* in Indonesia and the need for human resources to fulfill the aims of Islamic philanthropy should come from state Islamic higher education to provide *zakat* and *waqf* studies as well as to realize *zakat* management practice in their institutions. The development of *zakat* and *waqf* at higher levels of education plays a significant role in preparing and training skillful human resources. This chapter aims to examine *zakat* and *waqf* management studies as well as *zakat* management practice in selected state Islamic higher education institutions in Indonesia.

The motivation for giving and serving is generally primarily based on the religious drive (Cascione, 2003; Baqutayan et al., 2018). In line with this, *zakat* dan *waqf* management studies seek to improve student religiosity. The role of Muslims in the distribution of wealth and income is the core of Islamic charity, as stated in the holy Qur'an: "in order that it may not (merely) make a circuit between the wealthy among you" (Al Hashr. 59:7). The effort to encourage student religiosity is in line with the findings of Opoku (2013) that religiosity is one of the important factors that encourages the Islamic philanthropy of higher education students.

This chapter seeks to examine the role of state Islamic higher education in optimizing both Islamic philanthropy studies and Islamic philanthropic organizations in the university. The case study was conducted at the state institute for Islamic studies of Surakarta (IAIN Surakarta) and Islamic State University (UIN) of Malang. The results of this chapter are expected to provide an overview of the development of *zakat* and *waqf* management studies and the practice of collection and distribution of *zakat* and *sadaqah* in state Islamic higher education.

2 Islamic Philanthropy and Education

The concept of giving in Islam is rooted in Islamic teaching about *zakat*, *sadaqah*, and *waqf*. *Zakat* means purifying wealth and is a form of prayer, financial worship to God (Benthall, 1999). On the other hand, *zakat* also proves the commitment to helping the poor and is a mechanism of wealth distribution (Osili & Ökten, 2015). Meanwhile, *sadaqah* and *waqf* constitute other charity forms in the voluntary model of Muslim generosity. *Sadaqah* is the manifestation of the process that transforms the 'ancient morality of the gift' into the 'principle of justice' (Singer, 2008). *Sadaqah and waqf* are more flexible than *zakat* viewed from time, beneficiaries, and the amount of money given (Qardhawi, 2011).

As a religious obligation, *zakat* beneficiaries have been specified in the Qur'an (At Tauba 9:60), in which one of them is giving *zakat* to "*fi sabilillah.*" The translation of *fi sabilillah* among *ulama'* is general. Thus, giving *zakat* in the form of a scholarship is legal. The reinterpretation of *zakat* beneficiaries in terms of *fi sabillillah*/fighting ignorance is stated in fatwa Majlis Ulama Indonesia Number 120 of 1996: "*zakat* is enabled to give [a] scholarship based on several requirements: having a good academic record, prioritized for those who are less fortunate, and the field of science student's choice is beneficial to the development of Indonesia."

Sadaqah and *waqf* have been widely accepted in developing an education program due to their flexibility. *Waqf* is the protection or prevention from acquisition by a third person. Islam has encouraged both mandatory and voluntary forms of charity. *Waqf* has been defined from the *Shariah* perspective as holding a *maal* (an asset) and preventing its consumption to utilize it in a righteous or philanthropic act that benefits the Ummah. *Waqf* was used for the development of civilization in early Islam (Chakra, 2008).

Higher education institutions in America have been using endowment funds to manage their institutions. In 2019, Harvard University had the largest endowment among universities in America with $39.4 billion (Kennedy, 2020). Not only Harvard, but most of the top universities in

America get donations from philanthropists (Cascione, 2003). Conversely, in the history of Islamic endowment, *waqf* has been used to develop higher education institutions in some countries such as the Al Azhar University of Egypt, the University of Al Qarawiyyin of Morocco, the University of Al Muntasiriyyah of Iraq, the University of Cordova of Spain, the King Abdulaziz University of Saudi Arabia, and Universitas Islam Indonesia (Hasan et al., 2019). Some of the institutions for Islamic study in the West, such as the Oxford Centre for Islamic Studies, were supported by Bin Ladens. Stanford University in America opened a center for Islamic studies (The Sohaib and Sara Abbasi Program in Islamic Studies) with the support of the Abbasi Family, a Pakistani-American Muslim business family. Latief (2013) stated that the center for Islamic studies in Cambridge has full financial support from the Saudi royal family (Alwaleed bin Talal Foundation). Some of the universities in Malaysia also have used *waqf* as funding for higher education (Munadi, 2017).

3 ISLAMIC PHILANTHROPY ORGANIZATION IN INDONESIA

Islamic philanthropy in Indonesia can be traced back to the practice of *Pusat Kesehatan Umum* (public health center) in delivering health services to the needy in the colonial era (Fauzia, 2013; Fauzia, 2017a). It had grown to be a modern and professional institution in the 2000s under law Number 38 of 1999, enhanced by Law Number 23 of 2011 on *zakat* institution management (Fauzia, 2017b). The objective of *zakat* management is to create prosperity and reduce poverty in Indonesia.

In the latest law governing *zakat* management administration, as stated in Chapter III Article 6 and 7, is that the *zakat* institution is divided into two: the government board of *zakat* (locally known and BAZNAS) and private *zakat* institutions (known as LAZ). On the other hand, government regulation number 14 of 2014 on *zakat* implementation states that BAZNAS is to be assisted by the *zakat* collector unit (locally called UPZ). The form of the *zakat* collector unit consists of state agencies from central to local government in the villages. Higher education is included in the *zakat* collector unit (BAZNAS, 2020). The number of higher education institutions deemed as UPZ is 15, consisting of state universities and private universities throughout Indonesia (Piliyanti & Sayekti, 2020).

The wide variety of *zakat* management organizations in Indonesia consists of 548 BAZNAS and 87 LAZ (BAZNAS, 2020). Studies concerning *zakat* management at the university level remain limited since *zakat* management can be found in BAZNAS and LAZ. On the other hand, universities have potential *muzzaki* from *zakat* within their stakeholders and they could therefore be *zakat* collector units (Agustian, 2016). *Zakat* as a profession is one of the contemporary reinterpretations of *ulama'* regarding their own profession (Qardhawi, 2011). The preference of paying *zakat* via a university agency can have different outcomes. Salbi (2012) noted that the preference of *muzzaki* to pay *zakat* through agencies was 78% while Lessy (2016) only showed 40% choosing to pay *zakat* through modern methods of *zakat* management institutions. Mahanani stated that the factors, which significantly affect the employees in paying *zakat* through *zakat* management in universities, included service and occupational status in the office (Mahanani, 2014). From these findings, it is inferred that higher education institutions are promising to collect *zakat* and *sadaqah* amongst lecturers, staff, alumni, and students.

4 ZAKAT DISTRIBUTION MODEL

The forms of innovations of *zakat* distribution are categorized into four (Mufraini, 2012): (1) traditional consumption, that is *zakat* distributed *to mustahiq* to be used directly such as *zakat fitr* given to the poor to meet their daily needs or *zakat mal*; (2) creative consumption, that is *zakat* embodied in other forms of consumption such as in the form of school supplies and scholarships; (3) traditional productive, that is *zakat* given in a number of productive forms such as goats, cows, and so forth. By so doing, this empowers the *mustahiq* to be able to create a business that later produces jobs for the poor; and (4) creative productive, that is *zakat* is in the form of a source of capital to build a social project or to add capital for small businesses.

Figure 12.1 shows that the traditional paradigm of *zakat* distribution is only for the consumptive purpose. The impact of this distribution model is to meet the needs of the poor, simply to reduce poverty. Furthermore, the new paradigm model suggests that the innovation of *zakat* utilization by BAZNAS and LAZ in Indonesia as guided in the manual by the Ministry of Religious Affairs can be categorized into four models as described, each of which has the goal of reducing poverty. However, when the management of *zakat* is still emphasized in the first model, the impact is only to reduce the depth of poverty—not to reduce poverty itself. Conversely, if the allocation of the *zakat* utilization has been developed by

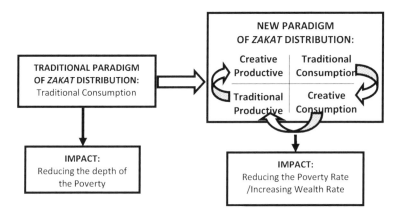

Fig. 12.1 The *zakat* distribution model and its impact on poverty. Source: Toro et al. (2013)

BAZNAS or LAZ in a productive creative model, it should be able to decrease the number of poor people.

Before the existence of modern and professional *zakat* institutions, the development of Islamic education was funded by *kyai* in Pesantren (traditional Islamic boarding schools) and *waqf* for developing some Islamic universities in Indonesia. LAZ with national networks has developed *zakat* and *waqf* for education programs such as Dompet Dhuafa, which build "SMART ekselensia Indonesia" for a marginal family in Indonesia.

SMART Ekselensia Indonesia organizes Junior High Schools (SMP) and Senior High Schools (SMA) for five years: specifically, three years for junior high school level and two years for high school level. The students come from various provinces in Indonesia, from Sumatra to Papua. SMART Ekselensia Indonesia stands as a form of concern and presents concrete steps for eradicating ignorance and in the end, it can break the chain of poverty. The vision of SMART Ekselensia Indonesia is to become a model school that produces graduates with Islamic personalities, leadership, independence, and high achievement. However, unfortunately, the education programs managed by Dompet Dhuafa have not yet targeted higher education.

5 Data Collection

The primary data of this study were collected through in-depth interviews at *zakat* management organizers in selected state Islamic higher education institutions. In addition, secondary data are used to determine the number of state Islamic higher education institutions offering *zakat* and *waqf* management studies and managing Islamic philanthropic organizations in universities. Interviews were conducted with the head of the *zakat* and *waqf* management studies as well as the head of the Laboratorium *Zakat*, Infak dan Sedekah (LAZIS) of the faculty of Sharia. Interviews were also conducted with the head of the *Teman Sedekah* organization of Islamic Economics and Business and the founder of the Fataba Foundation under the Tarbiah Faculty of IAIN Surakarta. An interview, for example, was conducted with the manager of the "El Zawa" *zakat* management organization owned by the State Islamic University of Malang.

6 Data Analysis

This essay used a qualitative exploratory approach. It was aimed at describing a phenomenon. This study examined the role of Islamic philanthropy in Islamic Higher Education, which is still limited. For that reason, exploratory research is deemed very suitable to explore deeper the role of Islamic philanthropy in Islamic higher education, including the practice of fundraising and distribution (Stebbins, 2001).

Islamic philanthropy in state Islamic higher education is contemporary in practice compared to the conceptual framework of Islamic philanthropy. The analysis focused on the role of state Islamic higher education in developing Islamic philanthropy studies and managing Muslim philanthropy funds for education.

7 Result and Discussion

The empirical results focus on why *zakat* and *waqf* management studies turn out to be a specific study program and how Islamic philanthropy funds are organized in state Islamic higher education. These aspects are expected to provide a picture of the development of *zakat* management in state Islamic higher education and student involvement in it.

State Islamic higher education relies on the state budget (APBN) to manage the institution. However, in the long term, relying on APBN funds alone will not be sufficient. Hence, raising philanthropic funds to help those in need in the Islamic higher education environment is the first step to building the independence of institutions such as higher education institutions in America that rely on endowment funds (Kennedy, 2020).

IAIN Surakarta is one of the state Islamic higher education institutions in Indonesia that has a *zakat* and *waqf* management study program and has a variety of philanthropy practices, including managing *zakat*, *sadaqah*, and *waqf* in every faculty. It has not become a Zakat Collecting Unit (UPZ) from BAZNAS.

Zakat and *waqf* management studies have been under Shariah faculty since 2015. The vision of *zakat* and *waqf* management studies is to organize theory and practice education and teaching in the field of *zakat* and *waqf* management. The huge potential of Muslim philanthropy funds in Indonesia as well as the need for Islamic philanthropy practices have led the Islamic faculty to open a study program for *zakat* and *waqf* management. In addition, the faculty has adequate resources: lecturers who have relations with various *zakat* and *waqf* institutions as well as supporting infrastructure to open new study programs. The lecturers are not only from the internal Shariah faculty, but also involve lecturers of the Shariah management study program, and practitioners of *zakat* institutions to provide an overview of the practice of *zakat* institutions to students. In addition, students are given the opportunity to take part in fieldwork lectures by volunteering to become interns at Islamic philanthropic institutions.

In line with the vision of the institution, a laboratory has been developed to practice how *zakat*, *sadaqah*, and *waqf* as public funds are professionally managed. *Zakat* management organization development is carried out in line with the developed curriculum in *zakat* and *waqf* management studies. In turn, the learning process becomes easier because it is supported by direct implementation in *zakat* management practice. The "Laboratorium Zakat Infak Sedekah" (LAZIS) was established in 2017. It functions as a laboratory for students of *zakat* and *waqf* management studies. The LAZIS collects *sadaqah* rather than *zakat* among lecturers and staff in Shariah faculties. This is deducted from their monthly salary. *Sadaqah* is more flexible than *zakat* in collection and distribution. For *maslahah* (benefit) reasons, the amount of *sadaqah* is determined with a minimum number. This mechanism is in line with the results of a study by Salbi (2012), which shows that professional *zakat* deduction is often considered to be simplified and then it is equalized in determining a portion of 2.5%. Due to its limited operations, LAZIS has not managed *waqf*. This finding also supports Mahanani (2014), that higher educational institutions have the potential to support *zakat* fundraising and funding.

> The establishment of LAZIS at the Sharia Faculty aims to provide learning for students as well as to build a religious and conscious environment for the payment of *zakat*, *sadaqah*, and *waqf* in the IAIN, especially the *zakat*, and *waqf* management studies student. (Hayatuddin, Head of *Zakat* and *Waqf* Management studies, IAIN Surakarta)

Since the objective of LAZIS is dedicated to the student laboratory, the student portion in the *zakat* management organizer is quite dominant. There are 20 students who serve as administrators of LAZIS. There are only three lecturers who are involved in the board of the LAZIS committee and one lecturer on the Shariah supervisory board.

Islamic philanthropy practices in the IAIN Surakarta have been carried out since 2008, led by several lecturers at the Tarbiyah (Islamic Education) Faculty by collecting alms to help students who need assistance with tuition fees. In 2014, *zakat*, *sadaqah*, and *waqf* distribution were supported by the establishment of the Fataba Foundation as a legal formal practice of generosity under the Tarbiah faculty. This institution is independent and managed by lecturers, outside the faculty organizational structure. The Islamic boarding school for students of Syifaul Qur'an is a pioneer in managing more professional *zakat*, *sadaqah*, and *waqf* funds. This boarding school accommodates Tarbiah faculty students who memorize the Qur'an (*Hafiz/Hafiza*) to volunteer to teach the Qur'an to new students. The construction of the boarding school begins with receiving *waqf* land from one of the retired lecturers at the Tarbiah faculty and the construction and maintenance of the boarding school using *sadaqah* and *waqf* from lecturers at the Tarbiah faculty.

> The Islamic philanthropy practices in the IAIN environment were initiated by several lecturers at the Tarbiah faculty in 2008 to help students who cannot afford tuition fees. In its development, this movement has grown from 2014 by opening *sadaqah* and *waqf* for the construction of *Tahfiz* boarding schools for students. (Munadi, Nur Alwiyah, founder of the Fataba Foundation)

Furthermore, the practice of Islamic philanthropy in another faculty of IAIN Surakarta started with the collection of *sadaqah* among Islamic economics and business faculty lecturers, who helped students in need by pay tuition fees since 2017. Since 2019, the philanthropic action has transformed to be an official organization under Islamic economics and business faculty named *Teman Sedekah* or *sadaqa* buddy. The establishment of *Teman Sedekah* as an official Islamic philanthropy organization is the best path to the broader network of donations, not only from lecturers, but also staff, students, and alumni of Islamic economics and business. The charity campaign is in line with the aim of the Islamic economics and business department of IAIN Surakarta, which emphasizes student religiosity. The objective of *Teman Sedekah* as described by the head of *Teman Sedekah* is as follows:

> *Teman Sedekah* is a semi-independent pilot platform at Islamic economics and business of IAIN Surakarta which aims to be a philanthropy forum from lecturers to help students in need to pay tuition fees. It is referred to as semi-independent because this initiation came from several lecturers to raise funds for underprivileged students. This institution was legalized by the dean of Islamic economics and business as an institution under the faculty but did not receive funding from the faculty. (Waluyo, head of *Teman Sedekah* of Islamic economics and business faculty at IAIN Surakarta)

Because it is still a pilot, the volunteers come from lecturers assisted by students. With the consideration that *zakat* funds have been officially managed by BAZNAS and LAZ, the fundraising of *Teman Sedekah* is limited to the lecturer and student to raise *sadaqah* and distribute it to the student in need. The amount of alms is set at a minimum to ease deductions from salaries as well as for togetherness among lecturers. If you increase the number of donations, however, it will be directly given to volunteers. The fundraising campaign will be held when the student needs additional tuition. The number of student applicants has increased. The flow chart, as presented in Fig. 12.2, shows the requirements of student applications to get financial aid from *Teman Sedekah*.

Student involvement in the management of *Teman Sedekah* is, among other things, for fundraising activity and also helps provide information on student profiles to identify those who deserve assistance in paying tuition fees. After that, students who are assisted by *Teman Sedekah* will become *Teman Sedekah* volunteers on their mission to become liaisons between those who will give alms and students who need educational funding assistance. The campaign carried out by students is to circulate a charity box in each class periodically. This is coordinated by the student association.

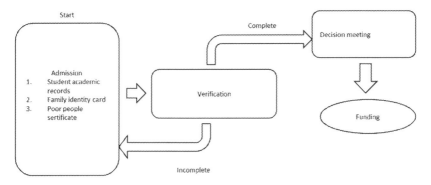

Fig. 12.2 The flow chart of a student application for financial aid from *Teman Sedekah*. Source: Interview with Waluyo

As a comparison, in other Islamic higher education institutions such as the State Islamic University (UIN) Malang, the establishment of el-Zawa is not under *zakat* and *waqf* management studies. El-Zawa is an independent organization unit under UIN Malang and was established as a study center for *zakat* and *waqf*. El-Zawa stands for *al-Zakat wa al-Waqf* and signifies the combination of *zakat* and *waqf*. The word Zawa means to remove and to distance. Thus, this unit is expected to be able to keep the Muslim community away from unclean assets through the culture of *zakat* and *waqf*. El-Zawa was founded to develop science, research, and community services in the field of *zakat* and *waqf*. In addition, it was developed to create a campus-based pilot center for *zakat* and *waqf* management in Indonesia.

El-Zawa was established on November 22, 2006, based on the idea that there is a need for a *zakat* institution as a service to help students who are unable to pay tuition fees, with funds from *zakat* from lecturers and staffs of UIN Malang. (Idrus, UIN Malang)

The management of el-Zawa consists of 4 lecturers and 46 students. The student involvement in el-Zawa has the same mission as IAIN Surakarta, which is to give an opportunity to the student in managing *zakat* and *waqf* professionally. Since the Islamic philanthropy source is a public fund, trustworthiness is key in managing these Islamic voluntary activities.

8 Fundraising of an Islamic Philanthropy Organization

LAZIS of the Faculty of Shariah and *Teman Sedekah* of Islamic economics and business IAIN Surakarta tends to maximize the *sadaqah* rather than *zakat* for stakeholders due to its flexibility. Furthermore, the student is also encouraged to practice *sadaqah* from their own money, time, and thought to help each other. The fundraising uses an internal source (Kalida, 2004). The efforts of LAZIS and *Teman Sedekah* are to increase student religiosity. The role of the Muslim community in providing benefits all over the world (*rahmatan lil alamin*) is one of the points emphasized by Islamic institutions. The efforts to encourage student religiosity is in line with the findings of Opoku (2013), which show that religiosity is one of the important factors that encourage Islamic philanthropy in higher education students.

LAZIS and *Teman Sedekah* emphasize fundraising from *sadaqah*. The source of funding for el-Zawa at UIN Malang is 95% from *zakat* of lecturers and employees of UIN Malang, which is deducted directly from their salaries. Apart from that, the source of *sadaqah* and *waqf* is internal from students and 5% from external campus.

In contrast to other LAZ outside of higher education institutions, fundraising is relatively constrained by the LAZ branding. For example, LAZ IAIN Surakarta has certainly been identified as the academic environment of IAIN Surakarta. Although the fundraising was extended to areas outside the IAIN academic community, public perception was certainly different. On the other hand, this phenomenon can actually encouraged the birth of creativity in fundraising. Efforts to remove this image are a challenge that LAZ managers must face. Online fundraising is one of the steps to expand higher education fundraising.

An interesting finding was revealed from this research: *waqf* funds are produced mostly by Islamic higher education in Indonesia. In contrast, history shows that at the beginning of Islam, *waqf* became one of the endowments to support the higher education sector in various countries. Even universities in America generally use endowment funds to manage their institutions. Several Islamic universities in Indonesia have also used *waqf* funds to establish and manage universities.

9 Distribution Mechanism

The Tarbiah Faculty has started to be more focused on distributing Muslim philanthropic funds to establish and manage *Tahfid* boarding schools and scholarships. The fund is 100% for the education sector. LAZIS of the Shariah faculty IAIN Surakarta gives scholarships to students in need because the funds obtained from donors are still limited to internal campus and only rely on *sadaqah*, not *zakat* or *waqf* funds. Likewise, *Teman Sedekah* maximizes the potential of charity in the internal environment of the Faculty of Islamic Economics and Business of IAIN Surakarta and is distributed to help the students. UIN Maliki has two forms of distribution of funds, the consumptive and the productive model. The productive fund distribution is called utilization. The forms of distribution activities carried out by el-Zawa include: (1) traditional consumptive: condolence money, charity for the elderly, honoraria for employees, honoraria for assisted schools, and expenses for *Ibn Sabil* (travelers who are away from their hometown and cannot afford travel expenses); and (2) creative consumptive: health assistance, superior orphan scholarships, strong root scholarships, el-Zawa cadre education scholarships, and dhuafa scholarships. The distribution activities carried out monthly by el-Zawa (Fig. 12.3) are charities for the elderly, employee honoraria, and honoraria for assisted schools, as well as various kinds of scholarships, while incidental ones are condolence money, medical assistance, and expenses for *Ibn Sabil*. From the distribution of *zakat* and *sadaqah* funds, the majority is

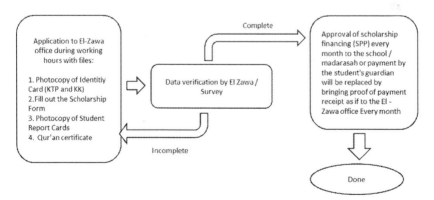

Fig. 12.3 Flow of education assistance for *dhuafa*. Source: interview with Idrus

given in the form of creative consumptive by providing superior orphan scholarships given to orphans around the UIN Malang. Figure 12.3 shows the flow of educational assistance for *dhuafa* students to el Zawa of UIN Malang.

10 Conclusion

Muslim philanthropic funds have contributed to the development of education in various countries all over the world. *Waqf* is a source of funding for the development of education in higher education. In Indonesia, the development of Islamic philanthropic institutions and Muslim philanthropic funds that are managed in a modern and professional manner requires people who have knowledge, skills, and personality to prepare the labor market in the Islamic voluntary sector. In addition, the large potential of *zakat*, *sadaqah*, and *waqf* requires modern, trustworthy, and professional management. The management of Muslim philanthropic funds at state Islamic universities in Indonesia shows diversity even though they are under one institution.

At IAIN Surakarta, each faculty manages its own Islamic philanthropy funds and maximizes *sadaqah* funds more than *zakat* funds for thier flexibility and ease of management. Meanwhile, at UIN Malang, the Islamic philanthropic funds were raised from *zakat* from lecturers and staff. In terms of the distribution of funds, the Tarbiah faculty is a pioneer in allocating *zakat*, *sadaqah*, and *waqf* funds for education by building an Islamic boarding school for *Tahfiz* for students under the Fataba Foundation. LAZIS and *Teman Sedekah* are new pilots in the Faculty of Sharia and the Faculty of Islamic Economics and Business. They maximize the distribution of funds for providing scholarship to students from a low economic class to pay tuition fees from *sadaqah* due to its flexibility. Meanwhile, el-Zawa UIN Malang shows more variety of consumptive distribution for the productive sector to help micro-, small, and medium enterprises around the UIN Malang campus buildings. Although Islamic philanthropy funds at IAIN Surakarta and UIN Malang have not been said to be significant enough, they show the contribution of the institution to the development of knowledge in the field of *zakat* and *waqf* to students through *zakat* and *waqf* management studies. They also provide *zakat* and *sadaqah* management practices for students as well as a commitment to increase awareness to share and distribute wealth through *zakat* and *waqf*. The involvement of students at the Fataba foundation, LAZIS, *Teman Sedekah*, and el-Zawa foundations shows that institutions provide opportunities for students to improve their knowledge, skills, and attitudes through social institutions at the university.

References

Agustian, D. (2016, Juni 3). *BAZNAS Jabar Bentuk UPZ kampus UNPAD*. Retrieved from BAZNASJabar: http://baznasjabar.org/baznas-jabar-bentuk-upz-di-kampus-unpad/

Baqutayan, S., Ariffin, A., Mohsin, M., & Mahdzir, A. (2018). Waqf between the Past and Present. *Mediterranean Journal of Social Sciences, 9*, 149–155. https://doi.org/10.2478/mjss-2018-0124

BAZNAS. (2020). *Struktur Organisasi*. Retrieved from Baznas: http://pusat.baznas.go.id/upz/

Benthall, J. (1999). Financial Worship: The Quranic Injunction to Almsgiving. *The Journal of the Royal Anthropological Institute, 5*(1), 27. https://doi.org/10.2307/2660961

BPS. (2020). *Tingkat Kemiskinan 2019*. Diakses 5 Desember 2020. https://www.bps.go.id/brs/view/id/i229

Cascione, G. L. (2003). *Philanthropists in Higher Education: Institutional, Biographical and Religious Motivation for Giving*. Routledge Falmer.

Chakra, M. Umer. (2008). Reformasi Ekonomi Sebuah Solusi Perspektif Islam. Jakarta: PT Buki Aksara.

Fauzia, A. (2013). *Faith and the State: A History of Islamic Philanthropy in Indonesia*. Brill. https://doi.org/10.1163/97890042492

Fauzia, A. (2017a). Penolong Kesengsaraan Umum: The Charitable Activism of Muhammadiyah during the Colonial Period. *South East Asia Research, 20*(10), 1–16.

Fauzia, A. (2017b). Islamic Philanthropy in Indonesia: Modernization, Islamization, and Social Justice. *Austrian Journal of South-East Asian Studies, 10*(2), 223–237. https://doi.org/10.14764/10.ASEAS-2017.2-6

Hasan, R., Hassan, M. K., & Rashide, M. (2019). The Role of Waqf in Educational Development—Evidence from Malaysia. *Journal of Islamic Finance, 8*(1), 001–007. IIUM Institute of Islamic Banking and Finance ISSN 2289-2117 (O)/2289-2109.

Kalida, M. (2004). Fundraising dalam Studi Pengembangan Lembaga Kemasyarakatan. *Aplikasia, Jurnal Aplikasi Ilmu-Ilmu Agama, 2*, Desember 2004: 148–160.

Kennedy, M. (2020). Higher Education Institutions with Largest Endowments, Fiscal 2019. American School and University. Retrieved September 11, 2020, from https://www.asumag.com/research/top-10s/article/21129877/higher-education-institutions-with-largest-endowments-fiscal-2019

Latief, H. (2013). Filantropi dan Pendidikan Islam di Indonesia. *Jurnal Pendidikan Islam*, 28(1), 50–71.
Lessy, Z. (2016). Trend Civitas Akademika UIN Sunan Kalijaga DalamMembayar. *Zakat dalam Al-Maslahah*, 12(2), 367–383.
Mahanani, Y. (2014). *Faktor-faktor yang Mempengaruhi Preferensi Pegawai berzakat di UPZ LAZ IPB*. Retrieved from ipb: www.ipb.ac.id
Mufraini, M. A. (2012). *Akuntansi dan Manajemen Zakat*. Kencana Prenada Media Group.
Munadi, M. (2017). Pengelolaan Endowment Fund di Perguruan Tinggi Malaysia: Studi Kasus di Universitas Teknologi Malaysia. *Al-Ulum*, 17, 306–331. https://doi.org/10.30603/au.v17i2.199
Opoku, R. A. (2013). Examining the Motivational Factors behind Charitable Giving among Young People in a Prominent Islamic Country. *International Journal of Nonprofit and Voluntary Sector Marketing*, 18(3), 249–261. https://doi.org/10.1002/nvsm.1457
Osili, U., & Ökten, Ç. (2015). Giving in Indonesia: A Culture of Philanthropy Rooted in Islamic Tradition. In I. P. Wiepking & F. Handy (Eds.), *The Palgrave Handbook of Global Philanthropy* (pp. 388–403). Palgrave Macmillan. Retrieved September 13, 2020, from http://repository.bilkent.edu.tr/bitstream/handle/11693/37810/Giving%20in%20indonesia%20A%20culture%20of
Piliyanti, I., & Sayekti, E. (2020). Benchmarking Lembaga Zakat Berbasis Kampus: Kajian Atas Efisiensi Lembaga Menggunakan Data Envelopment Analysis (DEA). *Jurnal Perspektif Ekonomi Darussalam*, 6(1). ISSN. 2502–6976. %20philanthropy%20rooted%20in%20islamic%20tradition.pdf;jsessionid=4DA15296C0ABE58B02A3C0F35E5949FC?sequence=1. https://doi.org/10.24815/jped.v6i1.14460
Qardhawi, Y. (2011). *Fiqh Zakat*. Pustaka Litera Antarnusa.
Salbi, A. (2012). Studi Deskriptif Perilaku Dosen UMS dalam membayar Zakat. Retrieved from ums: http://eprints.ums.ac.id/20140/14/Naskah_Publikasi_Ilmiah.pdf
Sen, A. (1992). *Inequality Reexamined*. Oxford University Press.
Sen, A. (2001). *Development as Freedom*. Oxford University Press.
Singer, A. (2008). *Charity in Islamic Societies*. Cambridge University Press.
Stebbins, R. (2001). Exploratory Research in the Social Sciences: What Is Exploration? In *Exploratory Research in the Social Sciences* (pp. 2–18). Sage.
Toro, M. J., Suam, H. H., Amien Gunadi, M., & Piliyanti, I. (2013). Zakat Untuk Sektor Produktif: Studi Pada Organisasi Pengelola Zakat Di Surakarta. *Jurnal Penelitian Sosial Keagamaan*, 7(2). https://doi.org/10.18326/infsl3.v7i2.431-450

CHAPTER 13

A Mobile Application for Zakat Collection in Indonesia

Ajeng Pratiwi and Umma Sa'idah

1 INTRODUCTION

Nowadays, Indonesia is facing fierce global competition, and because of that, our society, especially the younger generation, is required to continue to develop the ability to master science and technology, granting high competitiveness on the world stage through education, research, and the process of growing national innovation. Based on the World Economic Forum in its Global Competitiveness Report 2020, Indonesia's competitiveness index has decreased this year, 40th out of 140 countries that have been assessed. The Human Development Index (HDI) is one of the indicators that led to decreased competitiveness in Indonesia. Indeed, the HDI of Indonesia is still low. Based on Statistics Indonesia, Indonesian's HDI in 2019 reached 71.92, which is ranked 111th out of 189 countries.

HDI can be improved by increasing the state income to better allocation of funds to improve well-being. Indonesia still relies on income taxes as the state's largest source of income. However, the distribution of the tax

A. Pratiwi • U. Sa'idah (✉)
Universitas Negeri Jakarta, Jakarta, Indonesia

© The Author(s), under exclusive license to Springer Nature Switzerland AG 2022
A. G. Ismail et al. (eds.), *Islamic Philanthropy*, Palgrave Studies in Islamic Banking, Finance, and Economics,
https://doi.org/10.1007/978-3-031-06890-4_13

has not been aimed directly at poverty alleviation. Taxes cannot be the sole instrument of state revenue because Indonesia has experienced a decline in tax revenues from year to year. Based on data from the Ministry of Finance's Tax Report, the realization of tax revenue in 2020 decreased 5% from the previous year.

Indonesia has an excellent opportunity to increase revenue by utilizing the third sector's state, namely the modern state's public order. As a predominantly Muslim country, Indonesia has other revenue sources that have been neglected, namely zakat. On the other hand, zakat is an instrument that has a positive effect on the economy. Therefore, if the potential zakat is optimized and used as state income, Indonesia will come out of the budget deficit problem.

Zakat, from a humanitarian perspective, has a significant role in the improvement of human welfare and thorough strengthening of social solidarity. Therefore, to realize zakat's function in improving welfare, the institutional strengthening amil becomes an integral part of strengthening the national zakat system. Law No. 23 the Year 2011 on the Management of Zakat outlined that zakat management aims, first, to improve the effectiveness and efficiency of service delivery in zakat management, second, to increase the benefits of charity for public welfare and poverty reduction.

Indonesia has enormous potential zakat. The research results of Badan Amil Zakat Nasional (BAZNAS) in 2019 (Fig. 13.1) stated that the

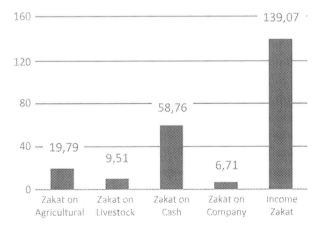

Fig. 13.1 Zakat potential in Indonesia. Source: Pusat Kajian Strategis BAZNAS (2020)

potential of zakat in Indonesia reached Rp 233.84. But in fact, the zakat that is absorbed and managed by zakat management institution until 2018 reaches only Rp 8.1 trillion. This shows that Muslims currently have less interest to pay on zakat in zakat management institutions.

The collection of zakat is not optimal due to several factors, namely (1) the rules for zakat, (2) unsystematic zakat collection, and (3) the harmonization of the tax system in Indonesia. The law on zakat management No. 23 of 2011 states that in order to improve effectiveness and efficiency, zakat must be institutionalized according to shariah in Islam. Zakat management is the planning, implementation, and coordination of the management of zakat. Accordingly, zakat institutions have the task of assisting the collection, distribution, and utilization of zakat.

Unsystematic zakat collection comes from a preference to pay zakat directly to the people who are deserving (mustahik). It is caused by a lack of awareness about the importance of zakat and its impact on the national economy. The other cause is public trust in zakat management institutions still being low. The trust of zakat payer (muzakki) is very influential to zakat collection targets. With regard to zakat institution confidence issues, there are several factors that play a part in muzakki trust. The first factor is accountability. The management of zakat, infaq, and shadaqah are considered to have weaknesses in aspects of public accountability, transparency, and institutional arrangement (Shabri, 2014).

Therefore, this study offers the idea of an innovative mobile application, GO ZAKAT, to increase zakat collection to synergize several BAZ/LAZ in one application. Indeed, the reality on the ground is not yet able to integrate applications via auto-debit facility charity accounts and credit facilities that map zakat, zakat calculation facilities, and facilities to prepare transparent financial statements of BAZ/LAZ information. The number of smartphone users in Indonesia continues to increase each year, making this application more feasible to use.

GO ZAKAT is expected to provide solutions (for the government) to alleviate poverty and improve social welfare by relating charity to national economic and financial instruments based on the amount of zakat potential in Indonesia. For BAZ/LAZ, it is expected to increase the collection of alms and synergize zakat institutions to absorb more of zakat's potential in Indonesia. For the community, it is expected to facilitate the public to pay zakat and provide education and outreach about the effectiveness of zakat distribution through zakat institutions.

2 Description of GO ZAKAT Mobile Application

The GO ZAKAT mobile application (Fig. 13.2) aims to increase the collection of zakat in BAZ/LAZ with a digital zakat system. Based on the author's field surveys, most BAZ/LAZ only creates applications in PlayStore zakat calculation and educational applications of the charity's fundamental knowledge. In this case, BAZ/LAZ does not have a mobile banking application to transfer outstanding zakat or to find BAZ/LAZ nearby. From multiple applications for zakat in PlayStore, many provide not a specific application for payment, but a zakat tithe is used as additional content.

The advantage of the application GO ZAKAT is that it provides ease of use for the five-content tithe. Besides providing five such contents, people do not pay dearly because they only pay the initial cost for this application in PlayStore. Furthermore, this application can be accessed in online or offline settings. This application is beneficial for the public to pay zakat

Fig. 13.2 Home menu display

13 A MOBILE APPLICATION FOR ZAKAT COLLECTION IN INDONESIA   233

only using a mobile phone and is also able to educate people about the importance of tithing. This application is also beneficial to synergize BAZNAS as a national charity regulator with other amil zakat institutions to raise funds for charity.

GO ZAKAT as a digital zakat mobile application has many advantages in the features provided, namely:

1. **Zakat payment.** This content (Fig. 13.3) is intended to pay zakat via transfer and auto-debit pulses through the LAZ provider. Muzakki election will be given facilities for BAZ/LAZ along with the account number. Then muzakki zakat can transfer funds under the BAZ/LAZ destination. Also, this application provides the facility of payment of infaq with auto-debit pulses through the LAZ provider.

Technical instructions of zakat payment:

a. Click the payment of zakat content on the display menu GO ZAKAT
b. Select what BAZ/LAZ would you go to tithe
c. After getting out to see the location, choose location of BAZ/LAZ to which you want it to go
d. After getting the BAZ/LAZ destination, select the transfer to the bank you choose
e. Enter the account number to make the transfer.

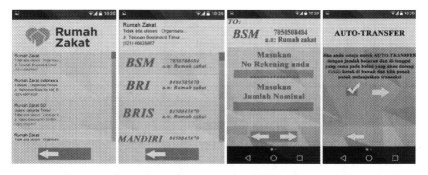

Fig. 13.3   Content display of zakat payment

2. **Zakat map.** This content (as shown in Fig. 13.4) aims to make it easier for muzaki to find the nearest BAZ/LAZ. Muzaki will be given an integrated map facility with BAZ/LAZ locations in Indonesia.
3. **Zakat news.** This content aims to provide the latest information and developments in zakat institutions. The advantage is this content also provides transparency for the financial statements of BAZ/LAZ, so that it can convince users to pay zakat via zakat institutions.

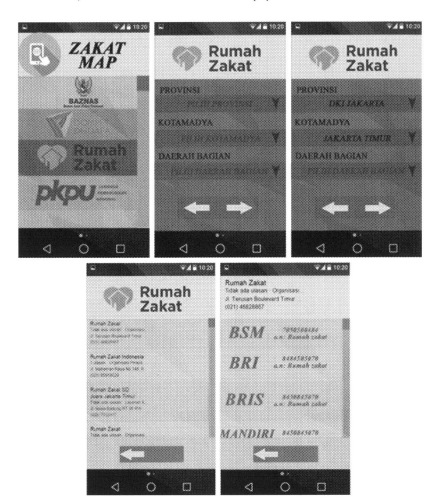

Fig. 13.4 Content display of zakat map

Fig. 13.5 Content display of zakat reminder

4. **Zakat counting.** This content is aimed to calculate the treasure that will be issued for zakat. Calculations in counting zakat can be adjusted with the category you choose.
5. **Zakat reminder.** This content (Fig. 13.5) aims to provide education about the importance of tithing and a reminder alarm for the conduct of other muamalah. In this context, we can customize the sound of the alarm and its time.

3 Discussion

Indonesia became has become third in the ranking of number of smartphone users in Asia after China and India (Fig. 13.6). Smartphone user growth from year to year is always increasing. It is estimated that growth will continue to increase until 2017. This provided a significant opportunity for innovation in zakat collection with the mobile application GO ZAKAT.

Based on the research results, 35 respondents from the general public who are domiciled in Jakarta showed that the largest percentage of zakat collection came from the mosque (UPZ), 54% from a domestic setting, followed by 29% of muzakki who pay zakat directly. The study also proved that there is very little awareness among the public regarding how to pay zakat at BAZ/LAZ.

Fig. 13.6 Graphs of potential smartphone users in Indonesia. Source: eMarketer prime data that have been edited

Fig. 13.7 Zakat collection diagram. Source: primary data

The Indirect Zakat System (IZS) has a more significant impact than the zakat direct system (Fig. 13.7). IZS is a system where muzaki pay their zakat through BAZNAS/LAZ and mosques, while Direct Zakat System (DZS) is a system where muzakki pay their zakat directly to mustahik without intermediaries amil. DZS and IZS legitimate fiqh, but when viewed from the fight against poverty, IZS will have a much more significant impact.

Zakat collection through BAZ/LAZ has the potential to utilize zakat, which is greater than the DZS system and zakat payment to the mosque. IZS makes the zakat distribution system more effective and able to absorb potential zakat, because when zakat is collected by IZS, amil BAZ/LAZ will create economic empowerment programs that are more productive. So mustahik has the opportunity to increase their income and well-being on a more permanent basis.

Although paying zakat at the mosque is said to be the IZS, zakat collection in the mosque is the only output to consumer distribution activities given directly to mustahik. There is almost no difference from DZS in this respect. Therefore, it is better that muzaki pay their zakat through BAZ/LAZ.

4 CONCLUSION

The results show that zakat collection through BAZ/LAZ has a low take-up. Thus, the mobile application GO ZAKAT can be innovative in optimizing zakat collection to provide ease of transaction services and education of the public. Indeed, optimizing zakat collection in amil zakat institutions will improve productivity and prove their zakat opportunities as part of the budget revenue. The GO ZAKAT mobile application reinforces the drive to provide convenience in public facilities tithing. The application also offers solutions to governments and agencies to synergize zakat BAZ/LAZ in optimizing zakat collection so that the potential of zakat can be absorbed. Optimal zakat collection will be able to make zakat an instrument of state revenues.

REFERENCES

Indonesian's Human Development Index in 2019. [online]. https://www.bps.go.id/pressrelease/2020/02/17/1670/indeks-pembangunan-manusia%2D%2Dipm%2D%2Dindonesia-pada-tahun-2019-mencapai-71-92.html

Ministry of Finance Indonesia. *Financial Report 2020.*

Pusat Kajian Strategis BAZNAS. (2020). *Outlook Zakat Indonesia 2020.* Badan Amil Zakat Nasional (BAZNAS).

Shabri, H. (2014). Performance Comparison Amil Zakat Institutions Managed by the Government and Private Organization in West Sumatra Province, 103–117.

Undang-Undang No. 23. (2011). *Tentang Pengelolaan Zakat.*

CHAPTER 14

Zakat for Disaster Relief

Kamaru Salam Yusof, Abdul Ghafar Ismail, and Muhammad Hasbi Zaenal

1 INTRODUCTION

Disaster is something that no one wants. But in human life, it is impossible to avoid. It happens with the will and wisdom of Allah Subhanahu wa ta'ala. Allah says that "And We will surely test you with something of fear and hunger and a loss of wealth and lives and fruits, but give good tidings to the patient" (2:155), and "Who, when disaster strikes them, says 'Indeed we belong to Allah, and indeed to Him we will return'?" (2:156).

On the hand, through disaster relief, we serve the communities that we love. It can serve both conditions of the human being—the affected and

---

K. S. Yusof (✉)
Faculty of Islamic Economics and Finance, Universiti Islam Sultan Sharif Ali, Bandar Seri Begawan, Brunei Darussalam

A. G. Ismail
Putra Business School, Universiti Putra Malaysia, Sri Kembangan, Malaysia

M. H. Zaenal
Universitas Islam Negeri Syarif Hidayatullah, Jakarta, Indonesia
e-mail: hasbi@uinjkt.ac.id

© The Author(s), under exclusive license to Springer Nature Switzerland AG 2022
A. G. Ismail et al. (eds.), *Islamic Philanthropy*, Palgrave Studies in Islamic Banking, Finance, and Economics,
https://doi.org/10.1007/978-3-031-06890-4_14

the helper. Disaster relief requires efforts on many fronts: providing rescue, health and medical assistance, water, food, shelter, and long-term recovery efforts. Much of successful and rapid relief relies on available funds. In Islam, we have Islamic religious funds.

Zakat (as one of the Islamic religious funds) is considered by Muslims to be an act of piety through which one expresses concern for the well-being of fellow Muslims, as well as preserving social harmony between the wealthy and the poor. Zakat also promotes a more equitable redistribution of wealth and fosters a sense of solidarity amongst members of the community.

Zakat fund models related to humanitarian aid have a long history. In 615H zakat was revealed together with salaah. As one of the pillars in Islam, zakat is considered as a religious obligation for all Muslims who meet the necessary criteria of wealth. It is a mandatory charitable contribution, the right of the poor to find relief from the rich, and is considered to be obligatory alms.

However, the distribution of zakat for disaster relief has only came into the picture recently. Wahid et al. (2017) reported that zakah acts as a social security mechanism that plays a significant role in rebuilding the lives of victims.[1] They took the examples of the Zakah Unit of Universiti Kebangsaan Malaysia, Lembaga Zakat Selangor and Kedah, and Zakat Foundation in Pakistan who contributed to flood victims. In the Kingdom of Saudi Arabia, charity organizations such as IIRO and al Haramain got funding that came from zakat.[2]

In this chapter, we focus on the zakat funds model that has potential to help relief agencies save lives and money, maintain standards of humanitarianism and fairness, and maximize the use of limited resources amid post-disaster chaos.

We focus on identifying the outstanding issues related to zakat fund models for disaster relief. This chapter provides an analysis of the solutions from such models according to various scholars.

---

[1] Habibah Abdul Wahid, Mohd Anuar Ramli, Muhd Imran Abd Razak, and Muhammad Izzul (2017).
[2] https://odihpn.org/magazine/saudi-arabia%C2%92s-humanitarian-aid-a-political-takeover/.

2 Information of Disaster Relief

Generally, disaster relief is defined as the intervention aimed at meeting the immediate needs of the victims of a disastrous event. The relief work seeks primarily to prevent loss of life and reduce suffering as much as possible for affected children, as well as their families and communities. It is also aimed at strengthening the local community to prepare for, respond to, and recover from disasters.

So far, the disaster relief has affected many jurisdictions. Table 14.1 shows, based on the few examples that affected the Muslim community, the past five years has seen many large disasters, including the COVID-19 pandemic, the 2018 Kerala flood, the refugee crisis in Syria, and the civil war in Yemen. The destruction from disasters can leave populations without shelter, food, and water, and in need of urgent medical care. In these situations, it can be necessary to supplement local capacity with regional or international aid. For example, within the first 30 days of the 2015 Malaysia flood, the charity organization arranged delivery of food aid (such as food kits), non-food items (such as hygiene kits, cleaning kits, cooking kits, face masks, and mosquito nets), and education (back-to-school kits and uniforms).

Disaster relief requires efforts on many fronts: providing rescue, health and medical assistance, water, food, shelter, and long-term recovery. Much of successful and rapid relief relies on funding from the public.

In this chapter, we will suggest zakat funds as a model that has potential to help relief agencies save lives and money, maintain standards of humanitarianism and fairness, and maximize the use of limited resources amid post-disaster chaos.

3 Zakat as Solution for Disaster Relief

Disasters that occur either due to natural incidents or hydrometeorology or caused by human acts through war, murder, expulsion, or otherwise all result in particular phenomena. Among these are refugees, homelessness, disability, and other matters. It all creates a new form in the local community or neighbours or perhaps in a society far from where the crisis takes place.

The birth of this new form of human being raises issues that need to be addressed and solutions that need to be discovered. This is especially so in relation to the zakat institution that serves to channel the accumulation of

Table 14.1 Disaster by Most Affected Muslim People from 2013–2021

Jurisdiction	Year	Type of disaster	Type of relief	No. of people affected
Sulawesi, Indonesia	January 2021	Earthquake	Medical services, power-supply equipment, repair for broken houses	87,373
COVID-19 Pandemic	December 2019		Governments provided fiscal and monetary aid for coronavirus-hit economies	Total cases: 99.8 million; total deaths: 2.14 million, as of mid-January 2021
Sulawesi, Indonesia	September 2018	Earthquake and tsunami	Providing food and non-food items as well as water and sanitation, child protection, health and nutrition, and livelihood interventions	82,000
Kerala, India	August 2018	Flood	Providing food, non-food items (displaced from their homes), hygiene kits, child-friendly spaces, and educational support	32 million
Lombok, Indonesia	July and August 2018	Earthquake	Emergency relief on the ground, including sanitation and child protection	419,424
South Sudan	Since 2013	Refugee crisis due to civil war	Food and shelter	900,000 people have been driven from their homes
Syria	Since 2014	Refugee crisis due to civil war	Water and sanitation, food, health, child protection and educational needs of Syrians in Syria, Lebanon, Iraq, and Jordan	4.2 million by the end of 2015

(*continued*)

Table 14.1 (continued)

Jurisdiction	Year	Type of disaster	Type of relief	No. of people affected
Malaysia	December 2014	The worst floods in 30 years have affected several states, especially the northern and eastern regions	Economic livelihood recovery, disaster risk reduction, and WASH (water, sanitation, and hygiene), and health and nutrition	Displacing over 200,000 people
Bangladesh–Myanmar border	August 2017	Slavery	Food and clean drinking water, safe sanitation, shelter, healthcare, nutrition, clothing, and personal safety	500,000 people, up to 60% of whom are children, have crossed the border into Bangladesh
Yemen	2015	Civil war	The economy and health services	7 million

property that has been quoted either by the body itself or by other bodies of the zakat collector.[3]

The pertinent issues related to this matter are: (a) Are zakat institutions able to work with non-Muslim organizations to help those affected by the disaster?; (b) Which types of asnaf fall under the category of disaster relief? (c) Can non-Muslim disaster victims be given allocation from zakat? (d) Can zakah be given to disaster victims or refugees who are far from zakat collector jurisdictions? and (e) What type zakah can be used to finance zakat settlement? And if possible, what are the rates they can take?

We will answer each issue in the following discussion:

3.1 Issue # 1: *Are zakat institutions able to work with non-Muslim organizations to help those affected by the disaster?*

The current organization of disaster relief is partly undertaken by non-Muslim organizations such as the British Red Cross, CARE International,

---

[3] There are two types of bodies that manage zakat: either a zakat collector or a zakat distributor/divisor. Sometimes it is in the form of isolation but there is also a body that manages these two tasks at once. Which of these bodies is more qualified to be called 'amil zakat? It is discussed by ulama'-ulama' and can be referred to in another discussion.

Oxfam, Save the Children, Tearfund (United Kingdom), The International Islamic Charitable Organization (Kuwait), Qatar Charity (Qatar), the IIRO and al Haramain (Saudi Arabia),[4] World Vision Malaysia, Aman Palestin, MyCare (Malaysia), WeCare (Brunei), and Dompet Dhuafa (Indonesia). The question of cooperation between Muslims and non-Muslims is a discussion had by previous Islamic scholars. It covers various aspects and each aspect has a legal dimension. The possibility of such cooperation lies in a battle to face the common enemy. It is also possible to implement joint projects in the country. It is likely to be in work like travel, business, and so on. Each has its own law that will not be discussed here.

The focus of the discussion is the involvement of cooperation between the Islamic body and non-Muslim organizations in humanitarian deeds to assist victims of disasters or war or refugees, and so on, fairly.

The basis for cooperation in this good thing is the word of Allah *Subḥānahu wa ta'alā*:

> O you who have believed, do not violate the rites of Allah or [the sanctity of] the sacred month or [neglect the marking of] the sacrificial animals and garland [them] or [violate the safety of] those coming to the Sacred House seeking bounty from their Lord and [His] approval. But when you come out of ihram, then [you may] hunt. And do not harbour hatred of a people for having obstructed you from al-Masjid al-Haram or led you to transgress. And cooperate in righteousness and piety, but do not cooperate in sin and aggression. And fear Allah, Allah is severe in penalty. (5:2)

In interpreting this verse, Sheikh Sayyid Al-Tantawi[5] has brought to bear a saying of the Prophet sallā Allāhu ʿalayhi wa-sallam that supports and gives a more detailed meaning to this verse as an example of how to help in this matter of goodness. The Prophet sallā Allāhu ʿalayhi wa-sallam said that anyone who shows others to something good then gets the reward just like the reward he gives.[6]

---

[4] The funding comes from zakat.
[5] Syeikh Sayyid Al-Tantawi (1986), 41.
[6] The hadith was narrated by Hadis narrated by Muslim, in his Sahih. Kitab al-Imarah (1980), vol. 6, p. 41.

However, scholars have different opinions if there are some issues related to this collaboration.[7] Among them is whether this cooperation brings mafsadah to Muslims or to the bodies or organizations that manage the humanitarian work. Or it may be that if it involves the mobilization of the property acquired from the source of zakat, it must be channelled to a recipient that is not allowed by the Shariah. At that moment, the permissibility of cooperation will change the prevailing circumstances. Therefore, as long as there is no issue in promoting good cooperation and it works within the objectives of the partnering organization, and further, the latter has a decisive role, then the cooperation can proceed as it is.

3.2 Issue # 2: *Types of asnaf that fall under the category of disaster relief*

Allah *Subḥānahu wa ta'alā* has explained the types of human beings entitled to obtain property from the collection of zakat. He clearly mentioned that "Zakat expenditures are only for the poor (fakir) and for the needy (masakin) and for those employed for it and for bringing hearts together [for Islam] and for freeing captives [or slaves] and for those in debt and for the cause of Allah and for the [stranded] traveller—an obligation [imposed] by Allah. And Allah is Knowing and Wise" (9:60).

The verse is clear and scholars have agreed on the types of asnaf (or zakat recipients) that belong to these groups. It is considered as qat'iyy (or definitive) in terms of groups. Namely the zonniyy (speculative) in the verse is what is meant for each of the groups. What does poor (or fuqara') mean? What is needy (or masakin)? What does "those employed for it" mean? And also the meaning of other types. Discussions on this issue are very long and a well-known Islamic scholar, Yusof Al-Qaradawi, has discussed this at length in his writings (Fiqh Zakat).[8] We attempt to closely link these groups with the victims of the disaster being discussed. Can they

---

[7] Mentioned by Imam Al-Qurtubi in his tafsir entitled Al-Jami' li Ahkam al-Quran, vol. 6, p. 47 (1938). Among the scholars mentioned in this tafsir are Imam al-Qurtubi ialah Al-Akhfasy, Ibnu 'Atiyyah, Imam Al-Mawardiyy, Ibnu Khuwaizimandad.

[8] The Fiqh al-Zakat book is part of a lengthy discussion on Fiqh al-Zakat, Dirasah Muqaranah li Ahkamiha wa Falsafatiha fi Dau 'al-Qur'an wa al-Sunnah (or Fiqh Zakat, Comparative Study of Its Laws and Philosophy Based on the Qur'an and Al -Sunnah). This book was originally based on a PhD thesis of al-Qaradawi that was completed at al-Azhar University in 1973. The title of his thesis was *al-Zakat wa Atharuha fi Hill al-Masyakil al-Ijtima'iyyah* (Zakah and Its Effects in Solving Social Issues).

be included in one of these groups? Or maybe they can be included in the various (more than one) asnaf. All this is actually revived based on the interpretation given by scholars beforehand to the definition of the group entitled to receive zakat as mentioned by Allah in the above verse. The near potential for disaster victims is that of the four groups of asnaf—fuqara', masakin, Ibn Sabil, and riqab. This is further laid out in Table 14.2.

Fuqara' and masakin—The word fuqara' in the verse has been defined by scholars variously. It has been discussed extensively in the classical and contemporary literature.[9] There is a likeness between the two, but the strong opinion among scholars is that both are actually different—some differentiate both of them based on whether they ask or not from others (opinion Imam Al-Tabari); some see one of them as worse than the others (Imam Syafie sees faqir as much more difficult than the poor), and some see the inability of the group to have a certain limitation of property. But some who look from the margins do not have the ability to obtain property. The conclusions from the discussion on this matter are the poor and the needy are people who have no property and are in great need.

Table 14.2 Zakat beneficiary categories and potential links to disaster relief

Category	Link to disaster relief
Al-Fuqara' *The poor*	Poverty and vulnerability closely linked in humanitarian crises; a majority of people living in the top recipient countries of humanitarian need are chronically poor. Al-Fuqara is therefore directly applicable to a large proportion of people in need of humanitarian assistance
Al-Masakin *The needy*	Could apply to anyone in need of assistance in the aftermath of a crisis or disaster
Al-Riqab *People in bondage or slavery*	Could apply to people who are enslaved, oppressed, or wrongly imprisoned; or to victims of trafficking
Ibnas-Sabil *The wayfarer, or stranded traveller*	Refugees and internally displaced people

[9] Like Abu Yusof of the Hanafi School and Ibn Qasim of the Maliki School. See Hasyiah Al-Dasuki, vol. 1, p. 492, and also see the discussion on this in the classical works such as Nihayah al-Muhtaj by Sheikh Ramli, Al-Mughni by Sheikh Ibn Qudamah, Al-Dur Al-Mukhtar, Bada'I al-Sona'I by Al-Kasani, Majmu 'Sharh al-Muhazzab by Imam An-Nawawi.

When this problem is matched with the condition of disaster victims today, most of the victims fulfilled the features set by most scholars in their writing and explanations, despite the differences. But this does not cover all the victims. There are victims who may not be able to occupy this category if they have other possessions elsewhere and beyond their needs.

Ibn Sabil—The translation of this term is very interesting. It means street kid. From these words the understood meaning has differed among scholars. They almost agree on the meaning of walking or sailing travellers. But there are some related issues: (i) Are they given property and money or given other materials in kind (such as tickets and expenses) only? (ii) Are they assisted during times of incomplete travel or assistance from the start of their journey (before commencing journey)? And (iii) does the purpose of their trip need to be viewed or not? In the sense that if the purpose of the journey is not because of something required by Islamic law, will he also be helped? There are also other questions discussed by scholars at length. The conclusions of this discussion have provided the opportunity for the zakat distribution body to provide some of the victims of disaster or financial assistance from the contribution of zakat to this group.

Riqab—Riqab was originally a group categorized as a servant who wanted to be released or promised by his master to be released if he could afford to find some property for his release. This situation occurred in the days when the system of slavery was still practised in the world at one time. The situation changed over time and changed the meaning of this riqab. There are some countries that have cancelled this group from the list of zakat recipients. For example, Brunei Darussalam has abolished this group or category of riqab from the list of recipients of zakat as there is no such group in the world today.

The difference in opinion on the meaning of this riqab indeed occurred among earlier scholars. Some provide the meaning of this riqab is 'mukatabah' and there is a definition of the use of zakat property to be used in the purchase of the servant in order to be released. This distinction is famous and discussed by them in their books since time immemorial. It is not necessary to extend it here.

There is little in the sense of a disaster victim as a victim of warfare or murder committed by human beings. The question arises is whether zakat money can be used to pay ransom or payment to redeem the prisoners of Islam captured by the enemy. Opinions that can be considered frankly from amongst the Islamic scholars (especially the Muslim scholar of the

Hambali sect) allow this situation because an enemy-captured Muslim is considered to fulfil the characteristics of the riqab mentioned by the verse.[10]

There is also a contemporary view of the contemporary clerics when interpreting the meaning of this riqab and enabling all the work that helps Muslims who are in a state of suppression in terms of thinking, economics, and so on; all regarded as releasing riqabs. Yusof Al-Qaradawi does not quite agree with this view because the over-loathing and widespread view of these fears will lead to irregularities in religion and make it too easy.[11]

3.3 Issue # 3: *Can non-Muslim disaster victims be given allocation from zakat?*

Scholars have differences of opinion as well on this issue. These differences are based on the sources of zakat or sadaqah obtained. One who concurs (ijma') among the fuqaha' which discusses this is that the property of the Muslims is not halal given to non-Muslims from the category of 'muharib' or 'kafir harbi'. The apostates are also included in this category.[12] But if not Muslim they are from those of the ahl zimmah, then the rule is different. Scholars distinguish the rules of giving to the zimmah members according to the categories of property: (i) common charity property (sodaqah tatowwu') is to be given to zimmah members in order to maintain the relationship and benefit of Muslims and humanity. This is the view of most of the scholars; (ii) if the property is of zakat fitrah, the fuqaha' Hanafi allows it to be given to non-Muslims as long as they are not harbiyy. However, they still say that giving the zakat to Muslims is more appropriate;[13] (iii) zakah of property other than Zakat Fitrah is not allowed to be given to non-Muslims. Al-Munziri believes that this is ijma'. But Dr Yusof Qaradawi dismissed Al-Munziri's allegations as many of the earlier scholars allowed such gifts as Zufar, Ibn Sirin, and Al-Zuhri.[14] Although the opinions of these three scholars have been rejected by most other scholars, automatically it shows that this is in fact unacceptable (not ijma').

---

[10] See Al-Raud al-Mari, vol. 1 case. 402 and also Ahkam al-Qur'an by Imam Al-Qurtubi, vol. 2, p. 956.

[11] Such opinion is the view given by Sheikh Mahmood Syaltot. Dr Yusof Al-Qaradawi mentions his views in his Book Fiqh Al-Zakah, vol. 2, p. 621.

[12] See Al-Bahr Al-Zikhar, vol. 2 p. 185.

[13] Abu 'Ubaid in his famous book *al-Amwal* mentions that many on tabi'in give their zakat fitrah to the rahban (rabbi). See Al-Amwal, p. 613.

[14] And it is said that Sayyidina Omar r.a has given zakat money to the People of the Book.

The majority of scholars who did not make this matter were based on the hadith of Muaz bin Jabal who was famous when he was sent by the Prophet Sallallahu 'Alayhi Wa sallam to Yemen; (iii) Yusof Al-Qaradawi, when discussing this matter, is more inclined to the view of allowing the granting of this zakat property to non-Muslims (on the basis of poverty and need, and not on the basis of 'muallaf qulub') under certain conditions. Among the key requirements are:[15] there is an excess of zakat property, and the allocation does not harm the maslahah of poor Muslims.

3.4 Issue # 4: *Can zakah be given to disaster victims or refugees who are far from zakat collectors' jurisdictions?*

This issue relates to the transfer of zakat property from where it was collected or obtained. Scholars have discussed this as well because most of the disasters that occur are usually not where the zakat is collected or obtained. In fact, it may involve the cross-border of a country or continents.

According to the original views of most scholars, they do not approve of the transfer of zakat property from the place where it is collected, regardless of the zakat of animals, cereals, or zakat fitrah. It originally had to be divided into the society where it was collected. This is what Muaz did when he was commissioned by the Prophet sallā Allāhu ʿalayhi wa-sallam to be the operator of zakat in Yemen. It is supported by the scholars because the purpose of zakat is to ease the burden of the poor in the area with the acquisition of the wealth of rich people.

However, scholars have also agreed to allow the transfer of zakat in case of any of the following: locals who do not require zakat property; there is no asnaf in the area; lack of people who need it for the property (less asnaf); and too much zakat property from the area.

Whenever the situation occurs, then it is required that the head of state transfer the zakat property according to the maslahah and be given to the nearest country. This situation is narrated by Abu Ubaiyd in his book *al-Amwal* that Sayyidina Omar Radhi Allahu'anhu has dismissed the property of zakat which was sent to Medina by Muaz at first. But in the end he received for the reason given by Muaz because of the delivery of zakat property.[16]

But if there is still a need in the state, there is a difference among the opinion of scholars whether it should not be (the opinion of Shafie

---

[15] See Fiqh Zakah by Yusof Al-Qaradawi, vol. 2, p. 708.
[16] *Al-Amwal*, p. 596.

Mazhab), or makruh (views of the Hanafi School), or seen in the distance (according to the Maliki School).

However, the views that fit the present condition that have become the main reasons are based on maslahah and requirements. In this case, the trustees of zakat organizations and zakat collectors control it according to best practice and provide maslahah to the Muslim community.

3.5   Issue # 5: *Can zakah be used to finance zakat settlement?*

This issue is actually based on the definition given by scholars on the remarks of 'al-amilin alayha' as mentioned by Allah on the verse of asnaf zakat (Surah Al-Tawbah: 60). Allah has placed this category in the third place after being mentioned faqir and poor. This shows that it is a necessity and needs to be given special attention. Granting this category is important.

Indirectly he gave a lecture (through *'isyarah al-nass'*) that the head of state should appoint those who will perform this work according to current needs. At the time of the Prophet sallā Allāhu ʿalayhi wa-sallam, the *'su'ah'* were appointed to take zakat from the countries and villages. Their work reminds him, calculates, quotes, and then passes zakat to asnaf after it is identified who is entitled. This work is quite complicated and complex. Therefore they deserve their special part. This execution was continued after the Prophet sallā Allāhu ʿalayhi wa-sallam. But in order to qualify for a job and to be categorized in this 'al-amilin', scholars have placed some conditions: Muslim; Mukallaf (Aqil and Baligh); understand the zakat law; have knowledge of the work of managing zakat; and some other conditions (among them are they must be men, but many scholars refuse to accept this rule).

Upon meeting these requirements, these amil are entitled to their rights. The difference among scholars is that they have the right to acquire more than their needs if the asnaf rights are many and beyond their needs. According to Shafie's views, it is their right and they are entitled to such rights even beyond their needs. But if this is not enough then they need to be given from baitulmal.

4   CONCLUSIONS

In conclusion, it can be said that zakat, if properly discussed in more detail by examining all the views given by scholars of various sects, will provide much breadth and can be practised in solving many issues arising today.

Indeed, the determination of the type and asnaf of zakat are enshrined in the Qur'an, but the explanation and interpretation of each one of the asnafs has actually given the Muslim today opportunity to channel it for human need. Directly, the practice from this concept allows the distribution of zakat property to victims of tragedy, accident, illness, and all forms of victims who need help. These victims sometimes need more help and support from other Muslims. The extent given by some scholars to enable the granting of this zakat, even if not all to non-Muslims, will have a good impact on the human condition to the glorification of the universal humanity of Islam.

References

Al-Qurtubi, I. (1938). *Al-Jami' li Ahkam al-Quran. Volume 6* (p. 47). Dar al-Kutub Al-Misriyyah.
Muslim, S. (1980). *Kitab al-Imarah.* Matbaah Mustafa Al-Halabi.
Syeikh Sayyid Al-Tantawi. (1986). *Kitab: Al-Tafsir Al-Waseet li al-Quran al-Karim.* Dar Al-Saadah.
Wahid, H. A., Ramli, M. A., Razak, M. I. A., & Zulkepli, M. I. S. (2017). Determination of Zakat Recipient to Flood Victims. *International Journal of Academic Research in Business and Social Sciences, 7*(12), 1289–1304. https://doi.org/10.6007/IJARBSS/v7-i12/3767

PART IV

Other Issues

CHAPTER 15

Investment of Tabung Masjid in Malaysia toward Fulfilling Maqasid-Al-Shariah

Luqman Zakariyah, Suhaimi Bin Mhd Sarif, Azman Bin Mohd Noor, and Rahmah Bt. Ahmad Osman

1 INTRODUCTION

The word masjid or mosque has evolved from the world of sajada, which means devoted, loyal and with bowed heads with full respect and reverence (Wahab, 2008). Mosques are institutions for Muslims to perform congregational prayers and reflect the submission of the Oneness of God. It is one of the most important institutions for Muslims due to its role as a centre for various religious activities. It is also a place for communal gathering, holding various religious ceremonies and rituals, religious

---

This paper is one of the outputs of the Fundamental Research Grant Scheme (FRGS) funded by the Malaysian Ministry of Higher Education

---

L. Zakariyah • S. B. M. Sarif (✉) • A. B. M. Noor • R. B. A. Osman
International Islamic University Malaysia, Selangor, Malaysia
e-mail: luqzak@iium.edu.my; suhaimims@iium.edu.my; azman@iium.edu.my; rahmahao@iium.edu.my

© The Author(s), under exclusive license to Springer Nature Switzerland AG 2022
A. G. Ismail et al. (eds.), *Islamic Philanthropy*, Palgrave Studies in Islamic Banking, Finance, and Economics,
https://doi.org/10.1007/978-3-031-06890-4_15

education and training (Ismail, 2003). During the time of the Prophet Muhammad (PBUH), mosques played a larger role and covered the aspects of administration, economy, social, security education and expansion of religion (Mokhtar, 2003).

Mosques require a fund (hereafter, mosque fund or Tabung Masjid (TM)) to perform such activities, and individual donations are one of the major funding sources. The fund is needed from the establishment of the mosque itself to cover various expenses for some routine activities including utility expenses, maintenance expenses and so on. There are other ways mosques manage a fund that include voluntary charity, that is *zakat*, *infaq*, *sadaqah* and *waqf*. According to the information announced, the average collected fund for mosques in Indonesia is around Rp 12 million per month, which is equivalent to USD 16,000 (Adnan, 2013). Cash savings in the banks for mosques in Perak amounted to RM 3,783,680 from 2009 to 2011 (Razak et al., 2014). With more than 10,000 mosques nationwide, mosques are used merely for matters relating to the wellbeing of the nearby community in Malaysia.

Public entities including mosques that utilize public funds as their financial resources should have sound disclosure mechanisms to prove their accountability to the public. Mosques should become more concerned with the transparency and presentation of financial statements due to their dependence on public donations. In recent years, mosque fund management has attracted researchers' attention (Adil et al., 2013; Hamdan et al., 2013; Mohamed et al., n.d.; Zain et al., n.d.; Zakariyah, 2016). The majority of these studies are in the context of Malaysia, focusing on accounting, accountability and fund management issues. Sulaiman et al. (2008) found that the embezzlement of funds from mosques is more common due to lack of accountability and lack of commitment to accounting. Lack of internal control systems have already been identified for mosques in different parts of Malaysia (Adil et al., 2013; Sulaiman et al., 2008; Wahab, 2008).

This study has focused on a unique aspect that related to the ability of efficient investment of TM toward achieving Maqasid-al-Shari'ah. The lack of governance mechanisms and expertise often prevents mosque management to fully utilize TM toward benefiting the greater community. Results provided by the study will benefit regulators and stakeholders in realizing the importance of selecting efficient investment sources for donations received from various sources by mosques. This study is divided into four segments. First, the brief literature on mosque accounting and investment practices in the context of Malaysia is discussed. Then, a Maqasid-based conceptual framework is established followed by hypothesis development. In the third segment, methodological issues are discussed along with results derived from various statistical tests. Finally, the study concludes with a discussion of the results and directions toward future research that would enrich mosque literature.

2 Literature Review

Mosques symbolize the balance of actions in the worldly world through charitable actions for the social welfare of the Islamic community and hereafter reflected through congregational prayers. Mosques deal with public funds received from the government, corporate and public donations, and control over the financial activities in handling funds received and expended have become an interesting research area.

Zain et al. (n.d.) have contributed to the mosque literature by discussing several issues and challenges faced by mosques in the Federal Territory of Malaysia. They have observed that accounting is loosely practised in the selected mosques but is regarded as pivotal to exhibit accountability of the mosques in pursuing their missionary activities. The difference of accounting practices among mosques to record income and expenditure are due to the absence of monitoring devices and lack of supervision by the authorized personnel. Such findings may not be generalizable to mosques in other parts of Malaysia due to the case study approach taken by Zain et al. (n.d.).

The importance of accounting and accountability practices indicated by Zain et al. (n.d.) was further explored by Ludigdo et al. (2014). The transcendental phenomenological study on a single mosque reveals that accountability is a spiritual calling defined as the mandate on the dimension of the relationship between human beings and Allah, as well as trust among human beings.

The importance of internal financial control systems in ensuring sound accounting practices have led to the review of a relevant study conducted by Masrek et al. (2014) on 13 district mosques in the central region of Malaysia. The study adopted a qualitative research approach with an unstructured interview and found that internal control practices by district mosques on both receipts of income and fund disbursement required significant attention regarding the segregation of duties and thus reflected on the findings provided by Zain et al. (n.d.) on mosques in the Federal Territory.

Fund management practices of mosques have recently received much-required attention based on the studies of Said et al. (2013) and Zakariyah (2016). Said et al. (2013) adopted a cross-sectional data analysis to examine factors contributing to mosque financial performance. Using a structured questionnaire, the study conducted a survey of 203 mosque treasurers all over Malaysia and reported that good internal control and active involvement of mosque committees in fundraising activities enhance mosque financial performance. These results provide more significance toward having an internal control indicated by Masrek et al. (2014). However, the low adjusted R^2 value triggers toward the exploration of a framework that could better explain the financial performance of mosques.

As such, we have focused on a similar study conducted by Adil et al. (2013) focusing on the financial management practices of mosques in Malaysia. The study utilized an approach similar to Said et al. (2013) and conducted a survey on 193 chairman and treasures of mosques in Malaysia with a response rate of 42.2%. Using a questionnaire based on a seven-point Likert scale, the study focused on six variables including financial management practices, budget preparation, fund usage, accountability, internal control and activity planning. One-way ANOVA results suggest that Malaysian mosques can enhance internal control systems and performance to achieve the missions and goals of these crucial institutions of societal development. Lack of correlation and regression analysis in the study limits the ability to understand the interrelationships among variables, which was present in the study of Masrek et al. (2014).

Mohamed et al. (n.d.) found that there were no standard guidelines to be followed in managing funds collected by mosques. Regarding disclosure of funds collected and expanded, there were mosques that disclosed every detailed item to the public as opposed to mosques that kept all the records only for the knowledge of the management. Other elements of internal control such as physical custody, recording of transactions and authorization were at the acceptable level of Jameq (district) Mosques in the central region of Malaysia. In a similar study, Mohamed et al. (2014) suggested that the internal control system practised by Jameq mosques on both receipts of income and funds disbursement requires significant attention.

3 MAQASID-BASED FRAMEWORK

Maqasid-Al-Shariah is translated literally as the direction of the 'Shari'ah' (Dusuki & Bouheraoua, 2011), or as the guidance principle, higher objectives and intent of Islamic law and the welfare and advantage to be derived from the implementation of Islamic laws and principles (M. H. Kamali, 2003). The aims and objectives of Shari'ah set by Allah are everlasting and unchangeable. There are both good and bad things in life and Shari'ah has set priorities for human beings to follow.

Maqasid-Al-Shariah provides the knowledge, understanding and justification of the principles of Shari'ah with an intrinsic aim of benefiting the Ummah. Shari'ah covers the entire spectrum of Islamic life that includes belief, moralities, virtues and principles of guidance, an economic, political, cultural and civilizational matter that concerns not only the Muslim community but the entire humanity (Abdullah, 2015). Shari'ah is the entire worldview of Islam that consists of the body of divine guidance, its structures, format and construct.

Objectives of Shari'ah can be classified into three categories: that is, daruriyyah (necessities), hajiyyah (requirements) and tahsiniyyah (beautification). Daruriyyah covers five fundamental elements in human life including ad-din (religion), an-nafs (life), al-'aql (intellect), al-nasl (ancestry) and al-mal (wealth). Compliance with principles of Islam is one way to protect ad-din. An-nafs can be preserved by conducting lawful actions that are permissible under Islam. Al-'aql refers to the protection of mind and human intellect from any element that could diminish mental and intellectual ability. The fourth element, an-nasl, is preserved through marriage. Finally, the protection of al-mal is possible through lawful earnings.

Hajiyyah can be seen as benefits that seek to remove severity and hardship that do not pose serious threats to the survival of human life, while tahsiniyyah can be regarded as things that seek to attain refinement and protection in the conduct of people at all levels of achievement (Kamali, 2008). Regarding the practical dimension, Mustafa (2009) has listed three specific objectives of Shari'ah-based Abu Zahara's classification known as educating the individual, establishing justice and public interest. These classifications are not far from the original classifications of Imam Shathibi. Al-Ghazali's Theory of Maslahah is incorporated in the classification provided by Abu Zahara to develop interrelationships among the objectives and establish a conceptual model for TMs.

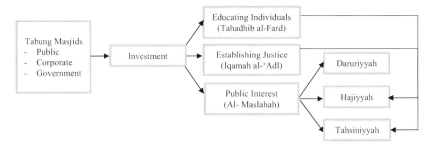

Fig. 15.1 Maqasid-based conceptual framework of Tabung Masjid investment

Figure 15.1 provides the conceptual framework for the current study that aims to empirically test the ability of TM investment toward achieving Maqasid-al-Shari'ah. Currently, mosques in Malaysia are receiving donations from the public, corporations and government sources. After using these donations for utilities, maintenance and various other expenditures, mosques have the freedom to invest any surplus donations in any Shari'ah-compliant investment. A general investment strategy found from the survey of the current study is savings in Islamic banks.

The conceptual framework has tried to establish a relationship between efficient investment of TMs and fulfilling Maqasid-al-Shariah based on the practical and theoretical classifications provided by Abu Zaharh and Imam Shathibi. It is theorized that through the above model investment of surplus TM will lead toward educating an individual, establishing social justice and ensuring public interest. The public interest or Maslahah classification is then expanded to Shathibi's classification of Maqasid-al-Sharia'h that included daruriyyah, hajiyyah and tahsiniyyah. Discussions on various classifications have led to the understanding that hajiyyah can be preserved by establishing social justice while tahsiniyyah can be related to educating individuals. Thus, interrelationships among various objectives of Shari'ah are achieved that can be satisfied from the efficient investment of TM.

4 Hypothesis Development

The study conducted by Razak et al. (2014) on the economic significance of mosque institutions in Malaysia provides good insights about the importance and difference in investment activities of mosques in a single state. Results indicate that society moderately agrees with the use of the mosque funds for the purpose of farming, education, real estate and business but feedback from 260 mosques reveal that the total amount of cash deposited in a bank or other financial institutions amounted to RM 3,783,680. Regarding banking-in-money collected from the collection boxes, Masrek et al. (2014) found that the majority of the mosques have adequate controls in place, such as depositing at least on the next working day and not using the money to pay any expenses before banking it first. The difference in methodologies applied by both studies does not provide generalized findings for mosques. Thus, the following hypotheses are formulated:

H1 Statistically significant differences exist in the investment of TM.

H1a Amount saved in banks is significantly different among Masjid.

H1b Investment in TMs is significantly different among Masjid.

H1c Use of TMs in maintenance is significantly different among Masjid.

H1d Capital investment with TMs is significantly different among Masjids.

Undoubtedly, poverty is becoming a common issue around the world. As a result, the majority of the world's population lives in abject poverty of less than $2.50 per day (Poverty, 2010). Hence, they lack the basic necessities for living such as shelter, food, healthcare and education and so on. Research has shown that poverty is responsible for poor health, low levels of energy and mental impairment. Also, the study of Olasupo (2013) reveals that hunger could lead to even greater poverty by reducing people's ability to work and learn, decline in knowledge, as well as experience even greater hunger. The phenomenon of poverty is not limited to Muslim communities. This could be as a result of several challenges confronting the countries of the globe, including global financial meltdown (Chossudovsky, 2008).

The ability of Islamic charitable institutions to reduce poverty in Muslim countries has been explored in various studies. Pramanik et al. (2015) have investigated the potential of waqf resources in human resource development and poverty alleviation in the context of Bangladesh. Waqf funds can uplift human resources among the productive poor through various training and entrepreneurial development programs. Hasan and

Abdullah (2008) opt for the concept of using waqf resources for enhancing human resources. Hasan (2010) in his integrated model of zakah and waqf institutions suggests that sufficient educational facilities and human capital development can help in poverty alleviation.

In Southeast Asia, Madrasa plays a vital role in providing education mostly to orphans and children from needy families. Waqf estates have been used to build schools, colleges and universities. Sadeq (2002) expressed that in Bangladesh 8000 educational institutions and more than 123,000 mosques are based on waqf, namely cash waqf facilities provided by Social Islamic Bank Bangladesh that can provide support to Islamic religious schools and institutions for education that are experiencing liquidity problems (Ibrahim et al., 2013). Mosques have the responsibility to play a greater role in the educational development of Muslim Ummah. Thus, following hypotheses are formulated:

H2 Investment of TM has a positive influence on poverty alleviation.

H2a Investment of TM has a positive influence on human capital development.

H2b Investment of TM has a positive influence on economic development.

5 METHODOLOGY

The study has aimed at determining the difference in investment strategies among masjids in Malaysia and the significance of such investment in economic development. Information regarding donations and the investment of such donations is gathered through a self-administered questionnaire. A total number of 287 respondents are conveniently chosen from nine states in Malaysia covering all four regions of the country. Research assistants were appointed to administer the questionnaire and collect responses. Participants in the study were responsible for managing mosque funds generated through individual donations on various occasions. This population is chosen since they have relevant knowledge regarding donations and fund management practices among Mosques in different states of Malaysia. A brief description of the sample on state and type of TM is provided in Table 15.1.

Table 15.1 Sample characteristics

State	Frequency	Cumulative percentage	Tabung Masjid type	Frequency	Cumulative percentage
Selangor	50	17.4	District	49	17.1
Terengganu	40	31.4	Qariah	147	68.3
Kelantan	37	44.3	State	16	73.9
Melaka	60	65.2	Upgraded	9	77.0
Negeri Sembilan	59	85.7	Federal	15	82.2
Sabah	20	92.7	Private	25	90.9
Pahang	1	93.0	Surau	7	93.4
Perak	12	97.2	Others	19	100.0
Kuala Lumpur	8	100.0			

6 Results and Discussion

6.1 Cross-Tabulation Statistics

Cross-tabulation is an effective method to summarize the relationship between two categorical variables. A cross-tabulation is a table that depicts the number of times each of a possible category combination occurs in the sample data. Table 15.2 provides cross-tabulation results indicating the difference in TM investment strategies among various states in Malaysia.

It can be observed from Table 15.2 that Selangor has the highest number of mosques with savings exceeding RM 100,000, while Melaka, Negeri Sembilan and Pahang did not have a single mosque with such a large amount of savings in their bank accounts in 2015. On average, the majority of mosques in Malaysia had a balance ranging from RM 10,000 to 50,000 at the end of 2015. It is interesting to note that the majority of respondents (80%) from TM management indicated that they are not interested in investing the surplus money from donations. They are not interested in capital investment either (82%) but agreed (48%) that they want to spend the donation on mosque maintenance.

6.2 One-Way ANOVA Results

One-way analysis of variance involves one independent variable that had some different levels. In our study, we have transformed the nine states into four regions (central, east, north and north) to test the difference in

Table 15.2 Cross-tabulation results for state-wise TM investment strategies

State	Selangor	Terengganu	Kelantan	Melaka	Negeri Sembilan	Sabah	Pahang	Perak	KL
Surplus_2015									
<10,000	9	1	16	30	25	5	0	2	4
10,000–50,000	14	25	17	30	29	9	0	3	2
50,001–100,000	13	11	2	0	5	5	1	5	1
100,001–150,000	2	1	2	0	0	0	0	1	0
150,001–200,000	11	1	0	0	0	1	0	1	1
200,000>	1	1	0	0	0	0	0	0	0
Inv_TM									
No	46	34	33	43	34	19	1	12	8
Yes	4	6	4	17	25	1	0	0	0
Donation_Maintenance									
Strongly disagree	1	6	1	0	0	1	0	0	5
Disagree	1	7	14	1	0	8	0	5	3
Indifferent	4	10	15	14	11	6	0	0	0
Agree	24	14	7	40	44	3	1	7	0
Strongly agree	20	3	0	5	4	2	0	0	0
Cap_Inv									
No	45	36	29	39	48	19	1	12	8
Yes	5	4	8	21	11	1	0	0	0

Table 15.3 Test of homogeneity of variances

	Levene statistic	p-value
Surplus_2015_1	7.267	0.000
Inv_TM_1	22.379	0.000
Donation_Maintenance_1	6.514	0.000
Cap_Inv_1	20.790	0.000

Table 15.4 One-way ANOVA statistics

ANOVA

	Sum of squares	Mean square	F	Sig.
Surplus_2015	25.917	8.639	8.190	0.000
Inv_TM	1.871	0.624	4.080	0.007
Donation_Maintenance	57.569	19.190	22.242	0.000
Cap_Inv	2.552	0.851	6.214	0.000

variance of investment strategies among mosques in those regions. Levene's test statistics in Table 15.3 provide a significant p-value for all investment variables indicating toward a violation of homogeneity of variance assumptions. This suggests that the variance of variables across the group is not equal and thus a stringent significant value ($p < 0.01$) is used in this study following the recommendation of Pallant (2011). Table 15.4 provides the main effect of each investment indicator. Each indicator passes the significance score of less than 1% and thus indicates that there is a difference in the surplus savings in 2015, intention to invest in TM, and use TM for maintenance and capital investment among mosques in four regions of Malaysia.

The post-hoc comparison was made using the Tukey HSD test. Results provided in Table 15.5 indicate that surplus savings in banks for mosques in the southern region is significantly different from mosques in other regions. Such difference does not exist among mosques in central, eastern and northern regions. Mosques in all four regions are found to be indifferent in their intention to invest in TM. A significant difference exists in the intention between mosques in central, eastern and southern regions in Malaysia. Tukey test results indicate that mosques in the central and southern regions have a greater intention to utilize TM on mosque maintenance than mosques in the eastern region. Finally, mosques in the southern region have a lower intention towards capital investment than the central and eastern regions.

Table 15.5 Tukey test results

		Mean difference (I-J)	Std. error	Sig.
Surplus_2015				
Central	East	0.081	0.141	0.939
	North	-0.411	0.311	0.550
	South	0.713	0.163	0.000
South	Central	-.7136	0.163	0.000
	East	-0.632	0.168	0.001
	North	-1.125	0.325	0.003
Inv_TM				
Central	East	0.131	0.054	0.070
	North	0.244	0.119	0.170
	South	-0.040	0.062	0.919
South	Central	0.040	0.062	0.919
	East	0.171	0.064	0.040
	North	0.283	0.124	0.102
Donation_Maintenance				
Central	East	0.956	0.127	0.000
	North	0.688	0.282	0.071
	South	0.038	0.147	0.994
South	Central	-0.038	0.147	0.994
	East	0.918	0.152	0.000
	North	0.650	0.294	0.122
Cap_Inv				
Central	East	0.004	0.051	1.000
	North	0.137	0.112	0.615
	South	-0.213	0.059	0.002
South	Central	0.213	0.059	0.002
	East	0.217	0.061	0.002
	North	0.350	0.117	0.016

6.3 Forecasting Tabung Masjids

Figures 15.2 and 15.3 provide an indication of the investment strategy of masjids in Malaysia. It can be observed from these figures that states with a higher number of donations have a higher number of savings in their bank account. The survey results have indicated that 96% of the participating mosques save the surplus donation in banks and they prefer Islamic banks (92%). This has provided an opportunity to forecast the savings amounts for TM using the profit-sharing rate of 4.29% for Waheed-term

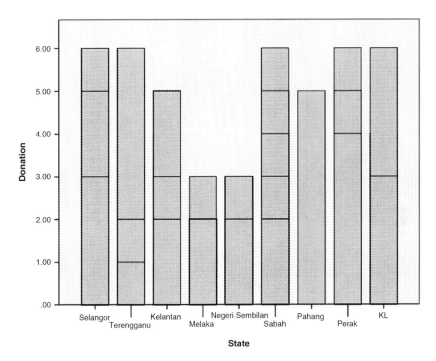

Fig. 15.2 State-wise TM donation statistics

investment accounts provided by Bank Islam. At present, the majority of the mosques (72.2%) are using a current account and this forecast would provide helpful evidence to the mosque management about the potential of the donation in making a significant economic contribution.

We have used the "Excel Forecast" tool with the surplus donation saved by mosques and the profit-sharing rate provided by Bank Islam. We have forecasted (Fig. 15.4) that the current savings can reach to a maximum value of RM 60,000,000 and to a minimum value of RM 30,000,000 in 20 years. It should be mentioned that these calculations are made with a range provided by the mosque representative and do not include actual figures. Still, the amount forecasted provides an indication that TM managers should focus on selecting appropriate investment strategies for surplus donations as this can serve the well-being of a greater Muslim community.

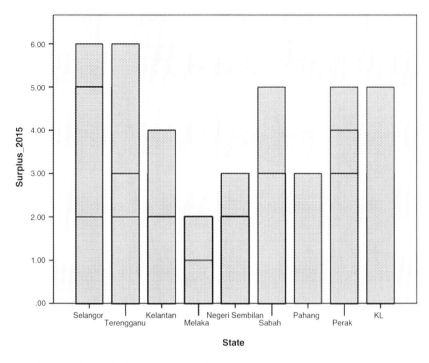

Fig. 15.3 State-wise TM savings statistics

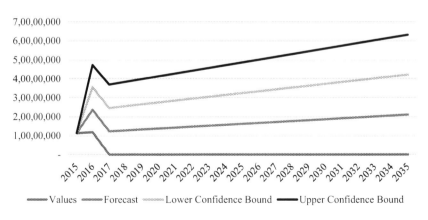

Fig. 15.4 Forecast of TM investment (2016–2035)

6.4 Granger Causality Statistics

We have claimed in the earlier section that TM, if invested properly, would contribute to the well-being of Muslim Ummah. The Granger causality test is performed with the forecasted values to provide statistical validity to the claim. The Granger causality test for the case of two stationary variables y_t and x_t, involves as a first step the estimation of the following VAR model, where it is assumed that both ε_{yt} and ε_{xt} are uncorrelated white noise error terms (Aesteriou & Hall, 2007).

$$y_t = \alpha_1 + \sum_n^{i=1} \beta_i x_{t-i} + \sum_m^{j=1} \gamma_j y_{t-j} + e_{1t} \qquad (15.1)$$

$$x_t = \alpha_2 + \sum_n^{i=1} \theta_i x_{t-i} + \sum_m^{j=1} \delta_j y_{t-j} + e_{2t} \qquad (15.2)$$

Two sets of variables are tested for Granger causality. Forecasted savings of TM are used as an independent variable. To generate the time series, forecasted GDP, HCD and GINI values for Malaysia are derived from the International Futures Forecasting Systems (IFS) website. A brief description of variables used for causality analysis is provided in Table 15.6. The

Table 15.6 Variable definitions

Variables	Abbreviations	Definitions
Investment Surplus of TM in 2015	Surplus_2015	The surplus of TM represents the balance saved in the bank account in 2015 having a value less than RM 10,000 to a value more than RM 200,000
Development indicators		
Economic development	L_GDP	The log converted gross domestic product (GDP) measures the national income and output for Malaysia
Poverty alleviation	L_GINI	The Gini index measures the extent to which the distribution of income (or, in some cases, consumption expenditure) among individuals or households within an economy deviates from a perfectly equal distribution
Human capital development	HCD	A composite index measures average achievement in three basic dimensions of human development—a long and healthy life, knowledge and a decent standard of living

Table 15.7 Testing for long-term Granger causality

Model: $\Delta y_t = \alpha_0 + \alpha_{1i} \sum_m^i \Delta x_{t-i} + u_t$

Where, y = (GDP per capital, human capital development, Gini index); x = investment of surplus TM

	F-statistics	p-value	Lags	Causality relationships
x-variable				
L_F_INV	4.084	0.042	2	L_F_INV → GINI
	7.008	0.000	2	L_F_INV → HCD
	5.545	0.019	2	L_F_INV → L_GDP
y-variable				
GINI	20.802	0.000	2	GINI → L_F_INV
HCD	7.509	0.007	2	HCD → L_F_INV
L_GDP	22.447	0.000	2	L_GDP → L_F_INV

time series consists of a total of 20 observations covering a period from 2016 to 2035.

Table 15.7 provides the model used to test long-term causality along with the results. Causality, in the long run, exists only when the coefficient of the cointegrating vector is statistically significant and different from zero (Granger & Lin, 1995). The results reported in Table 15.7 show that there is strong evidence in favour of the hypothesis that investment of TM has a positive impact on economic development, human capital development and poverty alleviation. In all three cases, the causality direction runs from the investment proxy variable to the dependent variable, while the opposite directional causality is also found to be statistically significant. Also, we observe that in all cases the coefficients of the cointegrating vectors are statistically significant and the F-type test rejects the hypothesis that those coefficients are equal to zero, suggesting that in all cases there is a long unidimensional causality relationship.

7 Conclusion

This study aimed at providing insights on TM investment and its significance toward fulfilling Maqasid-al-Shariah in the context of Malaysia. Two sets of hypotheses were formulated to test: first, whether a significant difference exists in the intention to invest TM, and second, the causal relationship between TM investment and economic development indicators as proxies for three objectives of Shariah, that is, Tahadhib al-Fard, Iqamah al-'Adl and Al- Maslahah.

Cross-tabulation results have indicated toward a difference in the intention of investing TM among representatives of mosques in four regions in Malaysia, which was statistically proven trough the one-way ANOVA test. ANOVA test statistics provide a significant result for each investment indicator among mosques in four regions in Malaysia at a p-value less than 0.50. The Tukey test was conducted to check intergroup differences and results indicated that significant difference exists among mosques regarding surplus savings in banks, use of donation in maintenance and capital investment. As a result, H1, H_{1a}, H_{1c}, H_{1d} are accepted. Investment of TM is found in different among mosques, and thus H_{1b} is rejected.

In the next phase, the Granger causality test was performed on the forecasted investment and development figures to check the nature of causality among variables. The forecasted savings figure of surplus TM by mosques in Malaysia indicates the possibility of having greater control in banking services if mosques agree to accumulate their funds and save in one Islamic bank, following the example of Tabung Haji. Unidimensional positive causality is proven through the Granger causality test between investment of TM and economic indicators. As a result, hypotheses H2, H_{2a} and H_{2b} are accepted.

Mosques are expected to conduct quality programmes according to Islamic principles, and active involvement of community members in fund generation activities will increase the source of funds and increase the ability of mosques to meet such expectations. Good internal controls can enhance transparency of mosques, which might enhance donors' confidence to contribute more funds to mosques. This study indicates that mosque management should become concerned about the investment of surplus donations due to its relevance in achieving the greater objectives of the Shari'ah. Mosques in Malaysia have different strategies for investing TM and need to find a uniform platform for making a significant contribution towards economic development. Several administrative and management issues must be looked into before empowering mosques to invest funds for the purpose of expanding their economic activities. Evidence provided by this study is based on personal opinion and forecasts, which may not portray the actual situation regarding TM investment. This study has identified the preferences of mosques in saving donations in Islamic banks but could not explore the possible reasons for such decisions. Future research on such issues will explain the preference towards faith-based banking among mosques in Malaysia.

Research Funding Acknowledgement This paper is one of the outputs of the Fundamental Research Grant Scheme (FRGS) funded by the Malaysian Ministry of Higher Education.

References

Abdullah, S. (2015). The Objectives of Takaful and Shariah: Towards the Achievement of Maqasid Shariah. *Journal of Human Capital Development, 8*(1), 93–104.

Adil, M. A. M., Mohd-Sanusi, Z., Jaafar, N. A., Khalid, M. M., & Aziz, A. A. (2013). Financial Management Practices of Mosques in Malaysia. *GJAT, 3*(1), 23–29.

Adnan, M. A. (2013). An Investigation of the Financial Management Practices of the Mosques in the Special Region of Yogyakarta Province, Indonesia. In *Sharia Economics Conference*, pp. 1–13.

Aesteriou, D., & Hall, S. (2007). *Applied Econometrics: A Modern Approach* (revised ed.). Palgrave Macmillan.

Chossudovsky, M. (2008). *The US and the EU Support a Political Process Linked to Organized Crime*.

Dusuki, A. W., & Bouheraoua, S. (2011). The Framework of Maqasid Al-Shari'ah (Objectives of the Shari'ah) and Its Implications for Islamic Finance. *Islam and Civilisational Renewal, 2*(2).

Granger, C. W., & Lin, J. (1995). Causality in the Long-Run. *Econometric Theory, 11*, 530–536.

Hamdan, N., Mohd Ramli, A., Jalil, A., & Haris, A. (2013). Accounting for Waqf Institutions: A Review on the Adaptation of Fund Accounting in Developing the Shariah Compliant Financial Reports for Mosques. In UITM & IKAZ (Ed.), *Transforming Islamic Philanthropy for Ummah Excellence* (Vol. 2013). UITM.

Hasan, K. (2010). An Integrated Poverty Alleviation Model Combining Zakat, Awqaf and Microfinance. In *7th International Conference—The Tawhidi Epistemology: Zakat and Waqf Economy*.

Hasan, Z., & Abdullah, M. N. (2008). The Investment of Waqf Land as an Instrument of Muslims' Economic Development in Malaysia. In *The Dubai International Conference on Endowments' Investment, 4–6th February 2008* (pp. 1–25). Awqaf and Minors Affairs Foundation.

Ibrahim, H., Amir, A., & Masron, T. A. (2013). Cash Waqf: An Innovative Instrument for Economic Development. *International Review of Social Sciences and Humanities*, 6(1), 1–7.

Ismail, M. F. (2003). *Peranan Masjid Kuala Lumpur: Darul Nu'man*. Utusan Publications and Distributors Sdn. Bhd.

Kamali, M. (2008). *Maqasid Al-Shariah Made Simple*. International Institute of Islamic Thought.

Kamali, M. H. (2003). *Principles of Islamic Jurisprudence*.

Ludigdo, A., Unti, P., & Widya, Y. (2014). Phenomenological Study of Financial Accountability of Mosque. *IOSR Journal of Economics and Finance*, 5(4), 10–17.

Masrek, M. N., Mohamed, I. S., Daud, N. M., Arshad, R., & Omar, N. (2014). Internal Financial Controls Practices of District Mosques in Central Region of Malaysia. *International Journal of Trade, Economics and Finance*, 5(3), 255–258.

Mohamed, I. S., Aziz, N. H. A., Noorman, M. M., & Daud, N. M. (2014). Mosque Fund Management: Issues on Accountability and Internal Controls. *Procedia—Social and Behavioral Sciences*, 45, 189–194.

Mohamed, I. S., Masrek, M. N., Daud, N. M., Arshad, R., & Omar, N. (n.d.). Mosques Fund Management: A Study on Governance and Internal Controls Practices. *Recent Advances on Finance Science and Management*.

Mokhtar, S. A. M. (2003). *Peranan Masjid dalam Islam*. Yayasan Dakwah Islamiah Malaysia.

Mustafa, O. M. (2009). *The Objectives of Islamic Banking: A Maqasid Approach* (IIiBF Series in Islamic Banking and Finance No. 1). Kuala Lumpur.

Olasupo, A. F. (2013). The Development of Awqaf Institutions in Nigeria for Sustainable Community Development and Poverty Eradication: The Case Study of Obafemi Awolowo Univeristy. *Linguistics & Education*, 13(1).

Pallant, J. (2011). *SPSS Survival Manual* (4th ed.). Allen and Unwin.

Poverty, R. (2010). *Report on the World's Social Situation 2010*. www.un.org/esa/socdev/rwss/docs/2010/fullreport.pdf

Pramanik, A. H., Mohammed, M. O., Haneef, M. A., Amin, F. M., Aliyu Dahiru Muhammad, Kenan, B., & Dabour, N. (2015). *Integration of Waqf and Islamic Microfinance for Poverty Reduction: Case Studies of Malaysia, Indonesia and Bangladesh*. Kuala Lumpur.

Razak, A. A., Hussin, M. Y. M., Muhammad, F., & Mahjom, N. (2014). Economic Significance of Mosque Institution in Perak State, Malaysia. *Kyoto Bulletin of Islamic Area Studies*, 7, 98–109.

Sadeq, A. M. (2002). Waqf, Perpetual Charity and Poverty Alleviation. *International Journal of Social Economics*, 29(1/2), 135–151.

Said, J., Mohamed, A., Sanusi, Z. M., Yusuf, S., & Syed, N. (2013). Financial Management Practices in Religious Organizations: An Empirical Evidence of Mosque in Malaysia. *International Business Research*, 6(7), 111–119.

Sulaiman, M., Siraj, S. A., & Ibrahim, S. H. M. (2008). Internal Control Systems in West Malaysia's State Mosques. *The American Journal of Islamic Social Sciences, 25*(1).

Wahab, A. A. (2008). Financial Management of Mosques in Kota Setar District: Issues and Challenges.

Zain, S. R. M., Samsudin, M. M. Bin, & Osman, A. Z. (n.d.). *Issues and Challenges: An Exploratory Case Study on Mosques Institution in Federal Territory.*

Zakariyah, L. (2016). Application of Maqāṣid al-Sharī'ah in Managing Mosque Funds: A Case Study of Tabung Masjid in Terengganu, Malaysia. *University of Sharjah Journal of Humanities and Social Sciences, 13*, 21–41.

CHAPTER 16

Religious Institutions in Philanthropy-Based Activities in Pakistan

Hussain Mohi-Ud-Din Qadri

1 INTRODUCTION

The link between religion and charity has existed historically across the faith traditions represented in the Islamic world. A large number of mosques, Sufi khanqahs, and madrasas from the 7th century onward, as reported in Iqbal and Siddiqui (2008), with the advent of Muslim rule, became important sites of philanthropic and social welfare activities.

The colonial period in South Asia also saw an influx of Christian missionaries in the region involved in education, healthcare, and awareness-raising around various social issues. Many of the institutions set up by these missionaries based on religious motivation continue to flourish today. Furthermore, the colonial period also witnessed an increase in Islamic revivalism and led to establishing a network of madrasas and philanthropic institutions run by Sufi shrines management in the Indo-Pak subcontinent.

H. Mohi-Ud-Din Qadri (✉)
Minhaj University Lahore, Lahore, Pakistan

© The Author(s), under exclusive license to Springer Nature Switzerland AG 2022
A. G. Ismail et al. (eds.), *Islamic Philanthropy*, Palgrave Studies in Islamic Banking, Finance, and Economics,
https://doi.org/10.1007/978-3-031-06890-4_16

275

Religious forms of charity or 'financial worship' have historically played a key role in funding charity and philanthropy at the individual and institutional levels in South Asia, with zakat and sadaqah being the largest source of such funding in Pakistan. There are also several other categories of charitable giving within Islam apart from zakat and sadaqah, including waqf (religious endowment) (Benthal (1998)). These charity forms aim to purify wealth, better the self, and improve the chances of attaining Allah's nearness in this life and hereafter.

While many NGOs receive funding from international donors, much of the local philanthropic activity that takes place in Pakistan is closely tied to religious belief and practice. According to a report by the Aga Khan Foundation (AKF),[1] "the near-universal context for giving in Pakistan is that of religion, specifically Islam" (Bonbright and Azfar (2000)). The National Survey of Individual Giving, which was conducted in 1998–1999, found that 98% of respondents claimed religious faith as a motivation for donations for charitable purposes. Furthermore, 94% of donations went to religious institutions and causes, which were not defined. The AKF study estimated that Pakistan's people contributed 41 billion rupees (1.5% of the GDP) and volunteered 1.6 billion hours to philanthropic activities in 1998 alone, including religious organizations. Many of the organizations included in this study relied mainly on individual, religious donations rather than institutional funding.

In Pakistan, 'faith-based organization' (FBO) is another term used for such philanthropic, religious institutions like madrasas, khanqahs, or Sufi shrines. This term has become prominent internationally in the last two or three decades.

It has been hypothesized that khanqahs and Sufi shrines as institutions may have advantages concerning their religious status and fan following, but they are not the spaces that are engaged in the social or economic development of society. In comparison to secular NGOs, Sufi shrines as philanthropy are not given due weight nor have most of the studies assessed their economic and socio-developmental contributions to society. In contrast, some argue that there is a 'dark side' of such institutions, much of which is potentially dangerous in that they are inherently discriminatory and encourage division based on religious differences (Clarke and Jennings (2008) and Flanigan (2010)). These institutions are also said

---

[1] Agha Khan Foundation is an agency of the Agha Khan Development Network, http://www.akdn.org/our-agencies/aga-khan-foundation.

to be out of touch with contemporary development thinking that emphasizes empowerment and sustainable development over charity and relief. In practice, little empirical evidence has been presented to support any of these assertions, especially in developing country contexts. Furthermore, there is a lack of analytical clarity about the working of Sufi shrines and how they contribute to society.

This chapter aims to examine whether the khanqahs and Sufi shrines of Pakistan as FBOs are contributing to the social and economic development of society significantly or not. All the Sufi shrines selected for inclusion in the study were somehow involved in bettering society's poor and marginalized sectors and are the most popular ones in the region. All the selected shrines as an institution work in similar sectors and geographical areas have relationships with their communities. The study assessed whether and how an explicitly religious and spiritual motivation and affiliation influences institutions' characteristics engaged in development-related activities, in part to assess whether these shrines are just a place for performing religious Sufi rituals or institutions benefiting society socially as well as economically.

2 Historical Context and Literature Review

Muslim pilgrimages may be divided into two broad categories: obligatory and voluntary. This contrasts with the Christian or Hindu tradition in which, for example, pilgrimage is a non-obligatory religious practice, or Sikhism in which it is discouraged. The obligatory pilgrimage in Islam is, of course, the Hajj to Mecca, although the obligation is tempered by the pilgrim's financial and physical ability (Pickthall (1930)).

The Quran enjoins the believers to "Perform the pilgrimage and the visit for Allah." The voluntary pilgrimage (ziarat or ziarah) may be divided into two distinct types for analytical purposes. First, a religious journey may be undertaken for a purely emotive or sentimental reason. Such a non-obligatory religious journey may be undertaken to listen to a Sufi saint's religious discourse at some khanqah or any other religious message by or on behalf of an imam. Such a visit also may be made for personal religious and spiritual uplift. Such a sentimental journey may be made to participate in a periodic festival held in honor of a saint or to commemorate a special day of martyrdom, passion, birthday, or other such occasions related to religious, or even some especially venerated royal, personages.

The second type of voluntary pilgrimage may be made to the khanqahs of Sufis or their shrines, for reasons related to the problems of mundane existence. The fulfilment of worldly needs may be a significant reason for such visits. Personal health or the health of a loved one, education, seeking counseling in matrimonial affairs, resolving disputes, food and shelter, and so on, are all possible reasons. A promise to visit a saint, or a saint's grave or shrine, may be made for chronic non-psychosomatic, as well as for psychosomatic diseases. Supplications may be made to Allah while standing at such places for having an offspring or good luck in an enterprise. Some of these pilgrimages are primarily supplicatory, whereas others are virtually contractual.

But both rely upon the baraka (blessing) of the incredibly esteemed saint (Martin (1987)). According to each level's cultural diversity, Islamic centers of ziarat may be classified as forming informal hierarchy levels, such as regional, subregional, and local.

3 Understanding the Nature and Activities of 'Khanqahs' and 'Sufi Shrines'

The following section provides brief profiles of the Sufi khanqahs and shrines in several parts of the world, their nature, and socioeconomic development activities.

3.1 Sufi Khanqahs

The Sufi order of Islam has added many khanqahs and shrines to the Islamic religious circulation system throughout the Middle East, North Africa, sub-Saharan Africa, South Asia, Southeast Asia, western China, and the Central Asian countries. Most of these khanqahs and shrines are of regional importance within the framework of a domiciled saint's linguistic region, but some have a following that cuts across international boundaries, partly due to territorial changes or the emergence of new nations. According to Ira Lapidus (1988, 262–263), Sufism became central to the structure of lineage societies after the 12th century.

The earliest reference to the concept of ribat or (khanqah) as a Sufi philanthropic institution is provided by Abu al-Qasim al-Qushayri (1990) about Abu Yazid al-Bistami, who died in 261 AH/875 CE. Abu Yazid al-Bistami is reported to have gone one night to a ribat (khanqah) to recollect God's name on one of those ribat walls. He stayed there until dawn without uttering a word. When asked why, he answered, "(While there), there had passed through my mind a (rude) word that I once uttered in my childhood, and I was ashamed to mention God—may He be blessed and exalted." A reference is also made to a famous early ribat (khanqah) in Abbadan, an island in the mouth of Shatt al-Arab that was frequented by early Sufis who were devoted, in which Sahl al-Tustari (d. 283 AH/896 CE), an eminent early Sufi theorist and exegete from Basrah (Al-Qushayri 1990), engaged in religious and community services. Ribats (khanqahs) were also the places where some Sufis resided together with other oppressed and weak segments of society for their safety and self-defense during times of war and other brutal invasions of their lands by foreigners.

Ribats (khanqahs) continued to exist throughout the subsequent centuries. Their presence and importance did not appear to dwindle even after the rapid rise and spread of khanqahs as more specialized and sophisticated Sufi religious, educational, and philanthropic institutions in the 4th, 5th, and 6th AH/10th, 11th, and 12th CE centuries. Abu Nasr Abd al-Rahim (d. 514 AH/1120 CE), a son of Abu al-Qasim al-Qushayri, is said to have preached both in a ribat (khanqah) and a madrasah (school), as we will see later (Ibn al-Mulaqqan 1998). Ribats (khanqah) as Sufi hospices have been mentioned as late as the 7th, 8th, and 9th AH/13th, 14th, and 15th CE centuries. Ibn Jubayr (d. 614 AH/1217 CE) (1981) mentioned them in his travel memoirs as a remarkable sight he witnessed in Damascus. Al-Maqrizi (1998), who died in 845 AH/1441 CE, also mentioned at least 12 ribats (khanqah) that featured permanently in Cairo's urban morphology and other Sufi philanthropic institutions. Shihab al-Din Umar al-Suhrawardi (1984) spoke at length in his book *'Awarif al-Ma'arif* about Sufi philanthropic institutions and how a Sufi ought to help the origins and rise of Sufi institutions and how to behave when entering inside and when leaving them.

3.2 Model Khanqah

Most of the khanqahs established by these Sufis were inclusive of education centers. The low classes of society could send their children for learning free of cost; lodges, where homeless and wayfarers could spend a couple of nights; mess services (Langar) on a large scale, where hundreds of poor and hungry people were fed voluntarily; free counseling services offered to commoners for the resolution of their family and business disputes. Every khanqah had a mosque attached to it where these Sufis delivered their sermons and discourses on topics like faith, religion, social behavior, and human rights. This was in addition to what these Sufis were doing for the socioeconomic development of society. This model of khanqah, based on serving humanity, became one reason for the large-scale conversion of Hindus and followers of other religions to Islam.

After these Sufis' demise, they were usually buried in those khanqahs, which they had established themselves. People who were benefiting socially, economically, religiously, and spiritually from these khanqahs remained loyal to them and continued to visit these khanqahs, which had become shrines of the founder Sufis after their demise.[2]

Islam is a vibrant religion intertwined in the daily life of people at the local level. At that level, the components of Islamic religious circulation include mosques, madrasas, khanqahs, and holy shrines, and even the humble graves of locally respected saints and holy men were associated with wisdom and became centers for the service of humanity. Historically speaking, these institutions have played a tremendous role in the socioeconomic development of society throughout history. It is why Khawaja Mooen-ud-Din Ajmari became known as 'Khawaja Ghareeb Nawaj' 'the helper of the Poor.' Another example is the khanqah of Khawaja Nizam-ud-Din Awliya, which became known for feeding the poor and hungry on a large scale. Some scholars state that the amount of food cooked at the Khanqah Nizam-ud-Din would require over 2,800 kg of salt each month. For people who had been left homeless after an attack by foreign invaders, Khawaja Nizam-ud-Din instructed the management of his khanqah to rebuild the houses. It had been destroyed at the expense of the khanqah. He supervised the whole operation (Bigelow (2004)).

3.3 Financial Support and Management

These khanqahs and Sufi shrines were financed by the generous donations of devotees, affiliates, and visitors. These financial contributions enabled these institutions to become models of philanthropic activity. Also, certain khanqahs provided religious, spiritual, and moral behavioral training that far exceeded what other Sufi institutions provided in philanthropic service to society.

[2] https://www.imamreza.net/eng/imamreza.php?id=13698.

Coleman and Eisner (1995) characterize the khanqahs and Sufi shrines as "alternative routes to the sacred." However, in our view, this is only partially true since these holy places only complement Muslim religious circulation. No site can replace the centrality of Mecca Muazzama and Madinah Munawara.

3.4 Sufi Shrines

Bennigsen and Wimbush (1985) have identified and mapped many khanqahs and Sufi shrines operating in different parts of the world: for example, 32 leading "working" holy places of the Sufis in the Caucasus only, and 59 in Central Asia. Moreover, many more could be found in the Middle Eastern and South Asian regions of the world.

3.5 Sufi Shrines of South Asia

Subhan (1960) has listed scores of Sufi khanqahs and shrines in India and Pakistan. These lists include the shrine's location and the date of death of the saint associated with each shrine. Although several locations are only vaguely identified (for example, "Bengal"), it is clear that all of these shrines developed during and after the 13th century. The largest number of shrines (188) is attributed to the Chishti order of Sufis, although the shrines of Suhrawardi (72), Qadri (116), Naqshbandi (64), and those of several minor or irregular orders (103), are also listed. Some of these shrines are of international importance, for example, Data Ali Hajveeri, Khawaja Moeen-ud-Din Ajmeri, Baba Fareed Gang-e-Shakar, Hazrat Baha-ud-Din Zakaria, Khawaja Nizam-ud-Din Awliya, Hazrat Mujadid Alf-e-Thani, and Baba Bulle Shah. In contrast, others are modest, being patronized in the framework of a local dialect region.

When the Islamic missionaries arrived in South Asia, they found lower classes of people and have-nots of the societies in socioeconomic misery and under the political oppression of those eras' ruling classes. The low-cast discrimination was on the rise and kept society's inferior classes away from their fundamental human rights, such as education, the justice system, and enough food to feed their families and shelter. These Sufis built khanqahs as philanthropic institutions in various parts of the region to "serve humanity," which is the core of Islam's preaching.

3.6 Development Experts on Khanqah or Shrine-based Philanthropic Organizations

The concept of khanqah or shrine-based philanthropic organizations has been extensively discussed and debated in development circles but with little agreement over the precise quantum of benefit to society. Clarke and Jennings (2008) define such an institution as "an organization that derives inspiration and guidance for its activities from the teachings and principles of the faith or a particular interpretation or school of thought within the faith."

Preferring the term 'religious NGOs,' Berger (2003) defines these as formal organizations whose identity and mission are self-consciously derived from the teachings of one or more religious or spiritual traditions and which operate on a non-profit, independent, voluntary basis to promote and realize collectively articulated ideas about the public good at the national or international level.

Clarke (2006), in his typology of such institutions, defines 'faith-based charitable or development organizations' as those that "mobilize the faithful in support of the poor and other social groups, and which fund or manage projects which tackle poverty and social exclusion." These definitions, although seemingly straightforward, mask a great deal of complexity and ambiguity. Jeavons (2003) argues for a nuanced and historically contextualized understanding of faith-based philanthropic organizations that accounts for the diversity within the category.

Aside from the definitional aspects of classifying faith-based philanthropic organizations, there is a large amount of debate about the possible benefits and disadvantages of working with faith-based philanthropic organizations as development partners. On the positive side, there is a belief that faith-based philanthropic organizations are more effective in reaching the poorest. Lunn, for example, states,

> ROs [religious organizations] stand out because of their commitment to and zeal for serving people and communities. They are perceived to work for the public good and, in comparison with government agencies, it is believed that they are more sensitive to people in times of catastrophe, chaos or conflict, are responsive to people's needs and flexible in their provision, act with honesty and take distribution seriously. (Lunn (2009))

Clarke (2006) and Williams and Demerath (1998) argue that faith-based philanthropic organizations have advantages in drawing on spiritual and moral resources as motivating factors in gaining support and effecting social change. Furthermore, Berger (2003) argues that faith-based philanthropic organizations are often highly networked nationally and internationally, which provides them with social capital in the form of human and financial resources. Martin, Chau, and Patel (2007) argue that such institutions have a longer-term commitment to the communities they work with than secular NGOs. It is also argued that they are usually less dependent on donor funds, relying more on individual donations, which provides them with greater independence.

At the same time, critics warn against the potential dangers of working with faith-based philanthropic organizations as development partners. They are often perceived as being linked to proselytization, and there is a concern that people who are needy and desperate are more vulnerable to this kind of pressure. De Kadt (2009) is particularly critical of those faith-based philanthropic organizations that promote rigid and inflexible versions of religion, aiming to regulate social and cultural interaction. Others point to faith-based philanthropic organizations' divisive potential, especially in religious conflict areas (see Flanigan 2010). Furthermore, Pearson, and Tomalin (2008) are wary of an over-reliance on faith-based philanthropic organizations, which often take conservative stances on gender-related issues and threaten advances made concerning women's rights.

4 Methodology

This research was conducted over five weeks by two researchers. Most of the fieldwork took place in Lahore, Kasur, Pakpatan, and Multan and involved conducting interviews with representatives of the selected shrines and business owners working in those shrines' surroundings.

Interviews were conducted with the 'executive officer' of *Data Darbar*, Mr. Shykh Abdul Qayyum on March 12, 2016; the manager of the shrine of *Baba Bulleh Shah*, Mr. Gulzar Ahmad Khan on March 19, 2016; Mr. Zahid Iqbal, the assistant manager at the shrine of *Baba Farid Shakar Ganj* on March 26, 2016, and Mr. Arshad Saqqi, the manager at the shrines of Hazrat *Bahaud Din Zakriya* and his grandson *Shah Rukan-e-Aalam* on April 2, 2016. The interviews of the business owners and the surveys were conducted on the same dates as well. These officials provided us with information about the food distribution, the annual income of the shrine through donations and other sources, welfare projects operating under the administration of those shrines, residence given to employees of the shrine, and the number of qawwals (traditional singers) attached to those shrines. The information related to the annual incomes of shrine-related businesses, the number of employed persons, and their annual salary packages has been collected by distributing a questionnaire among the business owners working in the proximity of those shrines.

Businesses related to these shrines were surveyed within a 1 km radius of each shrine. The businesses are those who were explicitly related to the visitors of the shrines. We found a large market of bicycle spare parts just beside the shrine of *Data Ali Hajveeri (Data Debar)*, but we did not include that business in our survey as it was not confined to visitors of shrines. We calculated the average annual income of those businesses by taking two samples from each category of business and then multiplying this average by the total number of businesses in that category. The aggregate income generation from each business operating in each shrine's surrounding area was computed by adding all the average annual income products from two specimens to the total number of that category of business.

We surveyed two shops as samples from each category of business. A sample of the questionnaire distributed and returned to us from each business is attached in Appendix 1. The total number of each category of business was multiplied with the average number of employed persons by that business to calculate the number of economically advantaged households from each business category. Then we multiplied the number of economically advantaged households to 6.3 to get the total number of people receiving some economic benefit from each shrine.[3] We calculated the total number of people who were receiving economic benefit from the activities generated by the shrine, either by direct employment at the shrine or indirectly, by summing up the number of all economically advantaged persons from all businesses.

5 RESULTS AND DISCUSSION

5.1 Shrine of Hazrat Data Ali Hajveeri (Data Durbar)

The 'executive officer' of *Data Durbar, Shaykh Abdul Qayyum*, who has served 32 years in the department of Auqaf, mentioned that, on average, *10,000* poor people are fed by the services, visitors, and devotees of this

---

[3] In Pakistan, 6.3 members per each household on average; statistics published by Pakistan Bureau of Statistics, available at http://www.pbs.gov.pk/sites/default/files/pslm/publications/hies2013_14/tables/table01.pdf.

great Sufi shrine, which is equivalent to Rs. 146 million annually at the rate of Rs. 40 for one meal per person. The average annual income of *Data Darbar* is around Rs. 300 million, from which Rs. 35 million and 7.6 million are collected through the auction of contracts with those who look after the shoes of worshippers, contracts with those running stalls, and car-parking officials. The rest of the income is generated through generous donations.

Four welfare projects are operating under the administration of *Data Darbar*. The first is "*Data Darbar* Hospital," which provides 24/7 free services to the needy. An amount of Rs. 28 million per annum is spent on health care at *Data Darbar* Hospital. It is a full-fledged hospital with 95 indoor beds and departments in gynecology, dental, ophthalmological, minor surgical, ears and throat, astrological, and a department for outdoor patients. On average, 547.5 thousand patients receive clinical treatment in the outpatients' department, and eye operations for 11 thousand patients are conducted annually. Seventy-three thousand gynecology patients are examined annually. This department has an operating facility, and the doctors (35), paramedics (100), and administrative staff (65) receive Rs. 900 thousand, Rs. 480 thousand, and Rs. 420 thousand annual salaries, respectively. There are 16 "*Data Darbar medical dispensaries* other than the hospital," from which nine are in Lahore city, and seven are out of the city where 9.125 thousand patients receive free clinical medical treatment annually.

The second welfare project is "*Ali Hajveeri handicraft school*," which provides free crafting education to 50 female students. The essential skills taught in this school are stitching, embroidering, and cooking. The Third project is TEVTA-affiliated[4] "*Jamia Hajveeri Madrasa*," which has 350 enrolled students who get free education in Islamic sciences along with computer education for primary and professional software in accounting and designing. Free shoes, clothes, and an annual scholarship are also given to the students of this madrasa.

The fourth project operating under *Data Darbar* management is the provision of dowry, consisting of Rs. 20 thousand each to 600 deserving brides every year. On three days of 'Uras,'[5] the provincial department of Auqaf spends Rs. 10 million (on average) for arrangements of spiritual

---

[4] Technical Education and Vocational Training Authority (TEVTA).
[5] Uras (from Arabic: عرس), is the death anniversary of a Sufi saint in South Asia, usually held at the saint's dargah (shrine).

gatherings (*mehfils*) in which Rs. 1.5 million are distributed among *nasheed singers and Qawwals*.[6] It was also noted that around 400 mosques that operated under the Auqaf of Punjab are entirely dependent on the income generated from the shrine of *Data Sahib*. Small mosques usually have two employees, whereas large mosques have three or more. These two employees are 'Khateeb' and 'Moazan' and receive salaries of 10 and 15 thousand, respectively, with other financial benefits and pension after retirement. Interestingly, 80% of the employed people working at these mosques belong to an Islamic school of thought that opposes the concept of khanqahs and the building of Sufi shrines. Despite this, their salaries come from one of the famous Sufi shrines of Pakistan.

We surveyed the economic activities within a 1 km radius of each shrine and directly related to that shrine. There are 80 cooks at *Data Durbar*, and each of them earns on average Rs. 3.21 million annually and Rs. 650 thousand in the month of Uras. There are nine employees (on average) employed at each cooking center, and each employee earns Rs. 228 thousand annually. At the shrine of *Data Durbar*, 90 shops of Tasbeeh counters, caps, dates, flowers, jewelry, and shawls, and each of these earns on average Rs. 321 thousand annually and Rs. 60 thousand in the month of Uras. This type of business usually has one employee (on average) who earns Rs. 90 thousand annually. There are 15 restaurants for breakfast, lunch, and dinner and each, on average, makes a profit of 2.1 million annually and Rs. 275 thousand in the month of Uras. Restaurants have nine employees on average, and each gets a salary of Rs. 102 thousand annually. There are 16 shops of perfumes and each of them on average earn profits of Rs. 330 thousand annually and Rs. 45 thousand in the month or Uras. These are all self-employed types of businesses. We found 52 restaurants with Rs. 4.2 million annual profits (on average) in the surroundings of *Data Durbar*. These restaurants are instructed to remain closed in the month of Uras by law enforcement agencies for security purposes. Each restaurant has, on average, seven employees with an annual salary of Rs. 138 thousand. We also found approximately 200 hawkers who sell fruits and other perishable eatables, and each of them earns a profit of Rs. 132 thousand annually and Rs. 20 thousand net income in the month of Uras. Each of the six shoe keeper's stalls on average earns Rs. 6.6 million annually and Rs. 450 thousand in the month of Uras. Each shoe keeper stall on average has five employees with Rs. 150 thousand

---

[6] A singer who sings Sufi devotional music.

annual salaries. There are six car-parking stands, and each, on average, earns Rs. 3.3 million annually. Each parking stand has, on average, five employees with a salary of Rs. 165 thousand annually. The approximate annual total income of Rs. 629.76 million and Rs. 72.65 million in the month of Uras is generated by the economic activities related to this shrine. This amount is distributed among 1,409 households and 8,924 people. In Pakistan, the average number of household members is 6.3.[7]

5.2   Shrine of Baba Farid Shakar Ganj

An interview was conducted with Mr. Zahid Iqbal, the assistant manager at the shrine of *Baba Farid Shakar Ganj*, who has been serving the department of Auqaf for six years. Around three thousand people, on average, receive food at this shrine daily, which is the equivalent of Rs. 43.8 million annually. The average annual income at the shrine of *Baba Farid Shakar Ganj* from all means and resources is Rs. 60 million. Out of this amount, Rs. 5.2 million is collected through the signing of contracts for shoe-keeping stalls. The car-parking stand has been closed for security reasons since 2010 after the bomb blast in the shrine's premises, which is causing a loss of Rs. 7 million annually. The uniqueness of this shrine is that it provides accommodation for 40 employees of Auqaf Punjab. There are two welfare projects run by the administration of this shrine. The first project is "*Baba Farid Shifa Khana*," a mini hospital where, on average, 36.5 thousand deserving patients get free clinical treatment annually. The second project is the provision of dowry for needy brides. The project provides Rs. 15 thousand to 150 poor brides annually. Moreover, from the abbot (*Sajada Nasheen*) of this shrine, one thousand people get free food in the last ten days of the month of Ramadan. There are 42 registered qawwals at this shrine, and each of them earns an annual income of Rs. 312 thousand. Each qawwal has, on average, seven group members. According to the shrine administration, around three million people visit this shrine in the three days of Uras, and almost everyone enjoys free food costing the shrine about Rs. 120 million.

Eleven cooks are working in the surroundings of this shrine, and each of them earns Rs. 1.32 million annually and Rs. 250 thousand in the month of Uras. Each cook, on average, has four employees with a salary of 78

---

[7] Statistics published by Pakistan Bureau of Statistics, available at http://www.pbs.gov.pk/sites/default/files/pslm/publications/hies2013_14/tables/table01.pdf.

thousand annually. This shrine's survey indicated that around 138 shops were selling various items such as Tasbeeh counters, caps, dates, flowers, shawls, and perfumes. On average, the annual net income of each shop is Rs. 1.35 million and Rs. 300 thousand in the month of Uras. Each shop of this category has, on average, five employees with a salary of 81 thousand annually. There are 148 shops of special sugar (*shakar*) and jewelry with an annual income of Rs. 930 thousand each and Rs. 130 thousand in the month of Uras. These are self-employed types of businesses without any employees. There are 132 restaurants for tea, breakfast, lunch, and dinner, and each earns a profit of Rs. 456 thousand (on average) and Rs. 127.5 thousand in the month of Uras. Each restaurant has, on average, five employees with an annual salary of Rs. 78 thousand. There are 12 hotels in the surroundings as well, and each of them, on average, earns an annual net income of Rs. 990 thousand. On average, each hotel has five employees with an annual salary of Rs. 84 thousand. There are approximately 160 hawkers, and each one is earning on average Rs. 162 thousand annually and Rs. 30 thousand in the month of Uras. Forty-two book stores and stalls were also found with Islamic books and *Punjabi Sufi* poetry. These book stores earn Rs. 540 thousand annually (on average) and Rs. 65 thousand in the month of Uras. There are 26 general stores, and each is earning Rs. 750 thousand annually and Rs. 65 thousand in the month of Uras. Two shop-keeper stalls are inside the shrine, and each one on average earns Rs. 2.7 million and Rs. 700 thousand in the month of Uras. Each shoe-keeper stall has six employees, and each receives a salary of Rs. 87 thousand annually. There are four private parking stands. Each of them, on average, earns Rs. 2.1 million annually and Rs. 750 thousand in the month of Uras, respectively. Each parking stand employs four workers, and each of them receives a salary of Rs. 78 thousand annually. Approximately, the total annual income of Rs. 505.536 million and Rs. 91.75 million in the month of Uras is generated by all the economic activities happening in and around this shrine. This amount is distributed among 1,704 households and 10,732 people. We can conclude that the income per capita at the shrine of *Baba Farid Shakar Ganj* is lower than the income of *Data Durbar*.

5.3 Shrine of Baba Bulleh Shah

The manager at the shrine of *Baba Bulleh Shah*, Mr. Gulzar Ahmad Khan, was interviewed. According to him, on average, 200 poor people get food daily from this shrine, worth Rs. 2.92 million annually. The annual average income at this shrine from all income-generating activities is Rs. 12.5 million. Rs. 6 million of this amount is collected from the combined contracts of shoe-keeping stalls, parking stands, flower shops, and book shops. This shrine contributes to the zonal fund to arrange the dowry for the poor and needy brides. An annual free medical camp is arranged on Uras. On average, 20 thousand patients are examined and get free medicine through this medical camp.

Twelve qawwals are affiliated with this shrine, and each of them, on average, earns Rs. 108 thousand annually. On average, each group of qawwals at this shrine consists of three persons. There are 14 shops of Tasbeeh counters, caps, dates, flowers, shawls, and perfumes within a 1 km radius of this shrine, and each of them earns, on average, a profit of Rs. 180 million annually and Rs. 45 thousand in the month of Uras. These are small shops without any employees. Six small restaurants were found with 300 thousand annual income (on average) and Rs. 55 thousand in the month of Uras. On average, each restaurant has three employees, and each of them earns an annual salary of 78 thousand.

We also found approximately 100 hawkers who sell fruits and other perishable eatables, and each of them earns Rs. 93 thousand annually and Rs. 11 thousand net income in the month of Uras. There is one car-parking stand with an annual income of Rs. 780 thousand and Rs. 120 thousand in the month of Uras. Two shoe-keepers' stalls at this shrine earn an annual income of Rs. 600 thousand and Rs. 75 thousand in the month of Uras. Each of them has employed two persons and each one of them receives an annual salary of Rs. 75 thousand. The *Kasur* district, where the shrine of *Baba Bulleh Shah* is located, is famous for its traditional fried fish, *Kasuri methi* ((قصوری میتھی), *falooda* ((فالودہ, and *Andrassy* ((اندرسے, and iron pots.[8]

We found 15 shops of fish with an annual income of Rs. 630 thousand and Rs. 95 thousand in the month of Uras. Each shop has, on average, two employees and each employee has an annual income of Rs. 114 thousand. Fifty small shops of *Kasuri methi* ((قصوری میتھی are earning on average Rs. 162 thousand annually and Rs. 19 thousand in the month of Uras. Both *falooda* ((فالودہ, *andrassy* ((اندرسے, and iron pot shops have no employees. We found 26 shops of *falooda* ((فالودہ, *andrassy* ((اندرسے with an annual income of Rs. 390 thousand (on average) and Rs. 52.5 thousand in the month of Uras. Nine shops of iron pots earn on average Rs. 360 thousand annually

---

[8] Kasuri methi is dried form of *fenugreek*, and *falooda* and *andrassy* are traditional sweets.

and Rs. 35 thousand in the moth of Uras. We estimated approximately a total annual income of Rs. 47.826 million and Rs. 6.385 million in the month of Uras is generated by all economic activities related to this shrine. This amount is distributed among 260 households and 1,638 people.

5.4 Shrines of Bahaud Din Zakriya and Shah Rukan-e-Aalam

Multan is known as *Madina-to-lawliya* (city of Sufis). We visited the shrines of Hazrat *Bahaud Din Zakriya* and Hazrat *Shah Rukan-e-Aalam*. We did not find much income-generating revenue about these shrines except shop-keeper's stalls, shawls, and qawwals. Temporary bazaars are established during the days of Uras but remain closed during the rest of the year. The manager of these shrines, Mr. Arshad Saqqi, who has been serving the department of Auqaf for the last 12 years, told us in his interview that, on average, 500 people enjoy free food at these two shrines daily, costing Rs. 7.3 million annually. The amount of Rs. 12.5 million is collected from all the income-generating activities of these two shrines. Of this amount, Rs. 8 million is collected from the combined signing of contracts for shoe-keeping stalls, parking, flower shops, and shawls. Around 50 people get employment from these businesses, and they earn on average Rs. 48 thousand annually. A mini hospital with one male and one female doctor is working under the administration of these two adjacent shrines where, on average, 200 patients are examined and get free medicine costing the hospital Rs. 1.8 million annually. In the three days of Uras, 40 thousand followers and devotees visit these shrines, and almost everyone gets free food. Daily 300 poor people, on average, enjoy food provided by the abbot (Sajada Nasheen) of this shrine. Two educational projects are operating under these shrines' administration, *madrassa Dar-ul-Nisa Janazgah* (for 200 female students) and *Bahaud Din madrassa* (for 30 male students). Primary Islamic education is provided at these madrasas. A contract of Rs. 100 thousand is also drawn up for illuminating the shrine during the three days of Uras.

6 Conclusion

In this chapter, khanqahs and Sufi shrines in Pakistan have been shown to have massive potential as philanthropic institutions and that they are providing several kinds of assistance to society socially and economically; for example, informational support, instrumental support, emotional/

psychological support, spiritual and religious training to disciples and visitors, lodging and shelter to the homeless, and food for thousands of hungry people every month. Besides this direct kind of assistance, these institutions provide thousands of job opportunities and support thousands of households financially every month. Moreover, this kind of support facilitates the personal development and well-being of individuals and families who visit these khanqahs and shrines.

We could conclude our study of shrines in Pakistan by saying that, at present, these khanqahs are still operating according to the pattern on which they were initially established. This pattern is in keeping with the core elements of Islamic Ideology, which is about helping one's neighbor and serving the whole of humanity by surrendering one's time, knowledge and skill, and even one's life in the service of humanity.

Our study also noted some discrepancies in the mismanagement of funds. It calls for structural improvements in these institutions, which the government could facilitate by taking more interest in their mode of operation and giving them greater recognition and professional status as philanthropic organizations. A proper external audit system could also be introduced to help these institutions grow more professional and socially.

This study raises a set of challenges for research on Sufi philanthropic institutions in Pakistan and beyond. While we have focused on the role of social and economic developmental support provided by these institutions in Pakistan, it is not clear at this point whether this kind of developmental support is provided at Sufi institutions in the broader context of Pakistan as well as in other Muslim societies where Sufi institutions operate at present. Also, there is scope for more research on social networking as a form of social support among individuals and families associated with and having an allegiance to Sufi institutions.

References

Bennigsen, A., & Wimbush, S. (1985). *Mystics and Commissars: Sufism in the Soviet Union*. University of California Press.

Benthall, J. (1998). The Qur'an's Call to Alms: Zakat, the Muslim Tradition of Almsgiving. *ISIM Newsletter, 1*, 1.

Berger, J. (2003). Religious Non-governmental Organizations: An Exploratory Analysis. *Voluntas: International Journal of Voluntary and Non-profit Organizations, 14*(1), 15–39.

Bigelow, A. B. 2004. *Sharing Saints, Shrines, and Stories: Practicing Pluralism in North India* (doctoral dissertation, University of California Santa Barbara).

Bonbright, D., & Azfar, A. (2000). *Philanthropy in Pakistan: A Report of the Initiative on Indigenous Philanthropy*. Aga Khan Foundation.

Clarke, G. (2006). Faith Matters: Faith-Based Organizations, Civil Society and International Development. *Journal of International Development, 18*, 835–848.

Clarke, G., & Jennings, M. 2008. *Development, Civil Society, and Faith-based Organizations: Bridging the Sacred and the Secular*. International Political Economy Series.

Coleman, S., & Eisner, J. (1995). *Pilgrimage: Past and Present in the World Religions*. Harvard University Press.

De Kadt, E. (2009). Should God Play a Role in Development? *Journal of International Development, 21*, 781–786.

Flanigan, S. T. (2010). *For the Love of God: NGOs and Religious Identity in a Violent World* (p. 5). Kumarian Press.

Iqbal, M. A., & Siddiqui, S. 2008. *Mapping the Terrain: The Activities of Faith-based Organizations in Development in Pakistan*.

Lapidus, I. (1988). *A History of Islamic Societies*. Cambridge University Press.

Lunn, J. (2009). The Role of Religion and Spirituality in Faith and Development: A Critical Theory Approach. *Third World Quarterly, 30*(5), 937–951.

Martin, J. P., Chau, J., & Patel, S. (2007). Religions and International Poverty Alleviation: The Pluses and Minuses. *Journal of International Affairs, 61*(1), 69–92.

Martin, R. (1987). Muslim Pilgrimage. In M. Eliade (Ed.), *The Encyclopedia of Religion*. Macmillan.

Pearson, R., & Tomalin, E. (2008). Intelligent Design? A Gender-Sensitive Interrogation of Religion and Development. In *Development, Civil Society, and Faith-based Organizations* (pp. 46–71). Palgrave Macmillan UK.

Pickthall, M. W. 1930. *The Meaning of the Glorious Koran: An Explanatory Translation by Marmaduke Pickthall*. London.

Subhan, B. (1960). *Sufism, Its Saints, and Shrines*. Lucknow Publishing House.

Williams, R. H., & Demerath, N. J., III. (1998). Cultural Power: How Underdog Religious and Nonreligious Movements Triumph against Structural Odds. In *Sacred Companies: Organizational Aspects of Religion and Religious Aspects of Organization* (pp. 364–378). Oxford University Press.

CHAPTER 17

South Africa's Muslim Philanthropists and Humanitarian Organizations: Religious Activism, Changing Environments

Muhammed Haron

1 INTRODUCTION

Throughout and after the post-Cold War era, the world has witnessed rapid sociopolitical, economic, and developmental world affairs changes. Processes of globalization, modernization, and secularism determined the role of religious organizations in the public arena. Since modernists and secularists disdained religion, they called for its marginalization and rejection with the fervent hope that it would gradually disappear by the end of the twentieth century.

These proponents supported by scholars such as Peter Berger (d. 2017) had to reconsider their views about religion when it resurfaced as a critical player in international affairs. Religion's forceful return to the public arena

---

M. Haron (✉)
Department of Theology and Religious Studies, University of Botswana, Gaborone, Botswana
e-mail: haronm@mopipi.ub.bw

© The Author(s), under exclusive license to Springer Nature Switzerland AG 2022
A. G. Ismail et al. (eds.), *Islamic Philanthropy*, Palgrave Studies in Islamic Banking, Finance, and Economics,
https://doi.org/10.1007/978-3-031-06890-4_17

under the leadership of the revolutionary Muslim Ayatollahs and Christian liberation theologians in Iran and Nicaragua, respectively, caused social scientists, who had wished for its disappearance, make a U-turn and reconsider their definitive opinions about the death of religion.

With religion's dramatic return into the public sphere and its representation through aid agencies and relief organizations in the developmental arena, new questions were raised regarding their qualitative contribution towards transforming poverty-stricken communities and others through their myriad networks. When preliminary observations that these organizations were making a difference in that sector were confirmed by the World Bank (WB) under James Wolfensohn's chairpersonship, Wolfensohn immediately opened opportunities for dialogue with Christian and other religious leaders. The idea behind this was to strike up possible partnerships that would assist in transforming this sector, one that has been served by numerous (secular-oriented) Non-Governmental Organizations (NGOs) that have not been as successful as anticipated (Marshall & Keough, 2004).

Consequently, a rapprochement of sorts emerged and a working relationship was struck between the WB, as a funding body, and various Faith-Based Organizations (FBOs). The reason for this outcome was that these international institutions and related bodies arrived at the conclusion that FBOs, compared to the NGOs, have an extended reach and a sturdier religious network. Also, unlike the NGOs, the communities had greater trust and confidence in religious organizations than in secular ones.

So, from the late 1990s onwards, the WB and its sister institutions have been investing in FBOs as alternative partners. The purpose has been to combat and deal with, among others, refugee crises and natural disasters. According to Marshall and Keough (2004), the emerging synergy between the secular and religious institutions has contributed towards a healthy understanding of the relationship between the two (also see Ter Haar, 2011). This has been observed in many countries, including South Africa. It is to this country that this chapter turns to show the nature of this relationship.

This chapter's objectives are threefold. The first is to briefly concentrate on the notion of 'Muslim activism', which acts as a useful conceptual framework for this essay and assists in understanding the nature of South Africa's Muslim philanthropic activities (see Charles, 2016). The second is to place the South African Muslim NGOs in their contexts, and they are located within their respective local and international settings. The third is to select samples from both Muslim trusts and foundations, which have been and continue to participate, as influential players, in both charitable activities and humanitarian aid (Krafess, 2005). It essentially evaluates these organizations demonstrating to what degree they have helped to generally portray South Africa and sectors of its Muslim community as a giving nation that illustrates their philanthropic characteristics (Habib & Maharaj, 2008).

2 MUSLIM ACTIVISM: INITIATING MUSLIM ACTIVITIES, FORMING MUSLIM NGOs

In Quintan Wiktorowicz's (2004) opening chapter of his edited work, he employed the phrase 'Islamic activism', and he appositely applied it as a 'social movement theory approach' and further described it as a dynamic process. While I fully identify with this process and accept the phrase as a useful conceptual tool that helps to frame the contents of this chapter, I want to make a slight adjustment by replacing the descriptive word or qualifier with another more appropriate word in the context. So instead of talking about 'Islamic activism' I prefer the alternative phrase 'Muslim activism'. The primary reason lies in the English usage of the two terms and the meanings that each conveys within their respective (linguistic) contexts and usage. The former understanding shall be abandoned and not elaborated upon due to space constraints.

The study thus invokes the particular phrase to gain a better insight into the rationale behind the formation of specific types of Muslim organizations such as trusts and foundations. These organizations, by and large, adopt an activist approach when they undertake philanthropic work in and beyond their communities. A careful glance at the apartheid and post-apartheid eras visibly show that they had clear missions and visions as to how they desire to make a qualitative difference in the lives of the poverty-stricken communities in need, such as the ill-treated orphans and mistreated women.

Wiktorowicz (2004) made the point that the study of this form of activism remained on the margins of theoretical and conceptual developments related to social movements that participate in the highly volatile political arena. He argued that Muslim activism's social dynamics have generally been unexamined and downplayed to such an extent that it was essentialized and trivialized as unintelligible. On this note, one concurs with Wiktorowicz's observation. It is an issue that applies very much to the South African context where Muslim institutions and their concomitant organizations, like their counterparts elsewhere in the Muslim world, have been studied and commented upon by individuals who have little or no knowledge of social movement theory in general and Muslim activism in particular.

These self-proclaimed experts, who infrequently interacted with Muslim activists to understand their thinking, repeatedly conveyed stereotypical notions of Muslim activism conflating their acts with those described as 'terrorists'. This is an issue that Delmore-Morgan and Oborne (2017) addressed when they assessed Muslim charitable organizations in Britain. In fact, across the globe various Muslim organizations have come under the spotlight for having generated—what these 'experts' termed—'jihad money', funds that they use to promote extremism.

Now, because of these warped arguments these so-called experts have implicated well-meaning organizations for having been major participants and financial supporters of unsavoury money-laundering activities, though this has been far from the truth. As Delmore-Morgan and Oborne (2017) have pointed out, self-styled experts and self-appointed 'counter-extremism' think tanks have circulated unsubstantiated alarmist stories about these Muslim charities. Their activities have caused false information to be persistently published online as part of their global witch-hunt.

Leaving aside these questionable and spurious reports, one returns to Wiktorowicz who cited social movement theorists. The latter argued that researchers should undertake an integrated approach by eliminating and dispensing with 'an artificial bifurcation between the studies of religious and non-religious movements'. The approach should see religious organizations on a broader social movement canvass and one that factors in Muslim activism as part of general social development that is coupled with philanthropic tasks. And this is a type of activism that should not be viewed as one that operates along the margins of communities but at the centre. Factoring in this point, one may argue that philanthropy, in the words of Cheema (2018), is 'a problem-solving mechanism that drives towards creating solutions for sustainable change and investing in the future'.

It should indeed devise and construct solutions that can bring about sustainable change. So, the planned projects and their outcomes should show strong similarities, intimate commonalities, and possible cross-fertilization and exchanges among religious institutions in general and Muslim organizations (such as corporate trusts, family foundations, and charitable societies) in particular. For this essay, the phrase 'Muslim activism' will thus be applied throughout. And alongside it, philanthropic activities should be viewed as an extension. They should be seen as a critical contributory factor, one that contributes towards changing the environments that are teamed with diverse socio-cultural and educational activities.

3 Muslim NGOs: Inscribed in Texts, Located in Contexts

Since a plethora of Muslim organizations were established during the past few decades in South Africa, it is perhaps appropriate to comment on some of the literature that reflects on the status of these Muslim NGOs. A quick research survey would demonstrate that this remains a neglected subject area and that only a few South African scholars have shown an interest in undertaking a close study of some of these NGOs during the past two decades.

Anyone who has browsed bibliographic published and updated works on Muslims in South Africa would have observed that only a handful of books, chapters, articles, and research projects have appeared between 2000 and 2020. So, in the next section a few texts were identified, and these were summarily catalogued to underscore the extent of neglect by scholars. Alongside these, the essay also includes chapters/articles that reflected on Muslim philanthropy. And since the essay is only scanning South African Muslim NGOs, it avoids referring to works that cover Muslim communities elsewhere globally.

3.1 In (South Africa-Related) Texts

One of chapters that engaged with the status of Muslim philanthropy was co-authored by Sultan Khan and Mohsin Ebrahim (2006). Their chapter concentrated on 'The State of Philanthropy amongst the Muslim Diaspora in South Africa.' Not long after their study, Khan formed part of a reasonably large team of researchers led by Brij Maharaj (2008). This team interrogated the nexus between 'Religion and Development' and was included in Adam Habib and Brij Maharaj's co-edited *Giving and Solidarity*. This was then followed by another publication that was produced by members of the team. Here Khan (2011) wrote about 'Faith-Based Humanitarian

Assistance in Response to Disasters: A Study of the Muslim Diaspora'. This complemented his 2006 co-authored chapter mentioned earlier. After Khan's 2011 publication, both Khan and Ebrahim co-authored with A. K. Gabralla (2009) 'The South African Indian Muslim Community and Its Role in Responding to International Disasters.' The latter text was based on Gabralla's (2009) MA thesis titled *Islamic Institutions of Charity and International Disaster Relief: A Case Study of Gift of the Givers Foundation in South Africa*. Amidst these publications' appearances, Samadia Sadouni, who completed her doctoral study on Ahmad Deedat (d. 2004) and his international NGO, the Islamic Propagation Centre International (IPCI) that was based in Durban with branches in Dubai and London, respectively, completed two related studies.

Sadouni first published 'New Religious Actors in South Africa: The Example of Islamic Humanitarianism' during 2007, and she then published 'Political Engagements of Islamic NGOs in the South African Public Sphere' in 2012. During this time, Muhammed Haron (2010) published 'Muslim Charities in the Development Sector: Fulfilling Political Ideals or Religious Duties?' And a long while after these publications, he contributed a chapter 'Africa's Muslim NGOs: Competitive Charities, Altruistic Allies?' (2020).

3.2 In (Global Muslim Philanthropic) Context

These published texts underscored a synergy between the philanthropic communities and the humanitarian organizations. This was particularly highlighted in Khan and his co-authors' writings. It essentially revealed that as these Muslim NGOs increased numerically on both the local and international scenes, they succeeded in attracting various donor agencies. In the international arena organizations, Islamic Relief (IR) and a host of others that were well established received funds from a long line of philanthropists.

Some of these philanthropists have formed private foundations that, from the time of their inception up until this day, have played, and continue to play, a critical interventionist role in humanitarian disaster events. On this front, prominent organizations such as the Saudi Arabia-based Alwaleed bin Talal Charitable Foundation (est. 1996), the US-based Bill & Melinda Gates Foundation (est. 2000), and the Emirates-based Mohammed Bin Rashid al-Maktoum Foundation (est. 2007) have generously made funds available for, among other things, educational institutions and poverty alleviation projects (also see https://mulsimphilantrophy.com).

These organizations should, however, be separated and distinguished from corporate giving philanthropists such as the UK-based Wellcome Trust (est. 1936) or the US-based Pew Memorial Trust (est. 1937) since they are private individual/familial structures that dedicated themselves to giving grants for projects and programmes. Their financial injections, which are considered forms of investment in the developmental sector, have also caused them to become active in setting the developmental agendas globally (Salazar, 2011). However, while this is so, McGoey (2012) has, for example, critically reflected on these philanthropic organizations in her text titled 'Philanthrocapitalism and Its Critics'. Since McGoey's ideas and her critique are not confined to secular philanthropic organizations, they should be extended to Muslim philanthropic organizations as well.

3.2.1 Local Context: Modest Structures, Noble Intentions

This section focuses on the South African scene, where the Muslim community established modest structures to address social welfare and health-care issues over many decades. It should be stated that South Africa's Muslims, who generally have had noble intentions, have been actively involved in social welfare, educational, and health-care work for much of the twentieth century. This has been bourne out by an assortment of regional and national newspaper reports that recorded and commented on their modest financial and material contributions on the local front towards South Africa's communities heavily affected by floods and storms (Haron, 2010; Sadouni, 2012).

These media noted similar activities on the international front; for example, Muslim organizations such as the African Muslim Agency (AMA) and Islamic Relief (IR) that had the necessary infrastructure assisted in sending aid to Turkey's earthquake fatalities, Indonesia's Tsunami stricken communities, and Mozambique's flood-ravaged victims. These organizations' services to the affected communities resulted in their humanitarian acts being officially recognized by the South African government, which commended them for their giving spirit.

During the past two decades (c. 2000–2020, and earlier) many Muslim organizations have emerged that made serious inputs in the humanitarian sector. From among the reasonably long list of organizations—some of which do not feature on Charity SA's site (www.charitysa.co.za)—is: the

Gift of the Givers (www.giftofthegivers.org), Al-Imdaad Foundation (www.alimdaad.com), Muslim Hands (https://muslimhands.org.za), and Islamic Relief South Africa (www.islamic-relief.org). Each of these organizations filled significant gaps within this particular sector. Moreover, they have been complemented by another set of organizations known as trusts, more accurately described as charitable trusts.

In this category, one comes across, for example, the South African Muslim Charitable Trust (www.samct.co.za), Iqraa Trust South Africa (www.iqraatrust.org), Mustadafin Foundation (www.mustadafin.org.za), and the Imam Abdullah Haron Educational Trust (www.iahet.co.za). These underline that the South African Muslim community has been concerned with their fellow human beings' welfare nationally, regionally, and internationally.

3.2.2 International Scene: Stereotypical Notions, Absurd Claims

After the tragic and unforgettable destruction of the New York twin towers on 11 September 2001, Muslim organizations came under the USA's spotlight for having aided and abetted 'terror' activities. With the support of pro-Israeli lobby groups (in and outside the USA) such as Daniel Pipes' Middle East Forum, the US administration unfairly targeted Muslim organizations and accused many of them of engaging in terrorist activities. Two prominent charitable institutions, namely the Holy Land Foundation (headed by a Palestinian-American businessperson) and Benevolence International Foundation (sponsored by a Saudi businessperson), were, for example, among those that were 'falsely' accused and immediately closed down by US law enforcement agencies (Muslim American Public Affairs Council, 2003; also see Delmore-Morgan & Oborne, 2017).

As a consequence of these developments in the USA, Muslim charitable and financial institutions worldwide have generally been implicated by self-appointed 'experts'. Take as an example J. Millard Burr and Robert O Collins's provocatively titled *Alms for Jihad: Charity and Terrorism in the Islamic World*. This unconvinced text complemented Loretta Napoleoni's, another expert on the subject, *Terror Incorporated: Tracing the Dollars behind the Terror Networks*. In it, Napoleoni deliberately and erroneously labelled Muslim financial institutions as a form of 'Islamist Financial Colonization' (Chap. 9), and she further described them as 'The Economic Forces of Islamist Colonization' (Chap. 10).

Napoleoni (2005) simplistically and irrationally stated that 'Islamic charities … are conduits through which billions of dollars reach the

Islamist network every year.' One wonders from where she extracted her questionable data. Moreover, without thinking about the implications of her absurd assertions, she dispassionately added that 'it is reasonable to assume that a large portion of charity funds act as a sort of international pool of money, ready to be channeled to whichever armed groups are in need in the Muslim world'. She even averred that '[t]he Islamist colonization of the Muslim world was eased by the *hawala* system, which feeds into Islamic banks and commodity trading in the east'. Napoleoni belongs to a coterie of Islamophobes who persist in describing Islam and Muslims in negative terms.

Along similar lines, Annette Hubscle (2007), the South African researcher, unquestionably drew upon Napoleoni and others by echoing these views in her study *Terrorists Financing in Southern Africa: Are We Making a Mountain of a Molehill?* Hubscle's rhetorically constructed sub-theme suggests that those who pronounced on these financial operations have not created mountains out of mole hills since these are indeed realities that have to be countered.

Though Muslim NGOs are still operating globally, many of them have experienced growing opposition in western countries where they actively function. Some of them have had their books monitored by self-styled experts; among the latter are those that were referred to in the previous paragraph and then there are those who host online sites such as 'money jihad' to calculatingly publicize these issues.

These self-styled Islamophobe experts questioned the legitimacy of these organizations' charities and humanitarian organizations despite the overwhelming evidence that demonstrates that they have been actively involved in social and cultural projects that have benefitted and that continue to benefit all communities. When one considers the South African environment compared to others where Muslim NGOs encounter difficulties, South African Muslim organizations realize that they function in a reasonably free and open environment. At this point, one should turn one's attention to this particular environment to assess the nature of charitable work that was and is being undertaken by Muslim organizations.

4 Muslim Organizations: Establishing Trusts, Erecting Foundations

In South Africa, many Muslim organizations have been established to serve Muslims and non-Muslims. One may visit the South African Muslim Directory site (www.samd.co.za) that lists some organizations contributing to the major cities' social welfare sector and outlying towns. Some of them were established more than 25 years ago, and others foundations were only laid during the past decade. A few names that come to mind and that have been around for more than 50 years are the Cape Town-based Muslim Hospital and Welfare Society, the Durban-based Arabic Study Circle, and the Johannesburg-based Islamic Missionary Society.

Even though their names indicate that they concentrate on specific activities, the consensus is that each of these organizations have made remarkable contributions over many decades; and from among the three, only the Arabic Study Circle has so far been given the necessary scholarly attention, by one scholar. Apart from these known organizations, numerous others should be listed and written into the historical texts to record their significant contributions.

Be that as it may, during the five decades, it was observed that the economically mobile Muslim movements such as the Muslim Youth Movement of South Africa (est. 1970 www.mym.za.org) spearheaded the formation of a string of influential Muslim organizations such as the South African National Zakat Fund (SANZAF www.sanzaf.org.za), the Islamic Medical Association of South Africa (IMASA www.ima-sa.co.za), and the Islamic Dawah Movement of South Africa (IDM www.idmdawah.co.za). However, they were not all charitable organizations. They made significant contributions to the South African Muslim community in different parts of the country. While SANZAF collected *zakat* (purificatory taxes) and *sadaqah* (charitable funds) as well as distributing bursaries and issuing soft loans, IMASA dedicated itself to giving medical services to those in low-income areas, and IDM extended its reach to those who needed social welfare, and also extended an invitation to consider joining the house of Islam.

These locally branded organizations were, moreover, complemented by a set of international organizations that concerned themselves with doing some of the activities that the locals were doing. Besides also being keen on collecting *zakat* and *sadaqah*, they were more interested in offering humanitarian aid using South Africa as a strategic base for their operations continentally. Both Islamic Relief and Muslim Hands are international organizations that entered and settled in South Africa more than a decade ago. They did so because they observed that the South African Muslims—compared with many other Muslim minorities—were fairly well-acquainted with Western norms and ideals, and they noted that a plethora of organizations and associations served this community well since they addressed diverse issues and various sectors.

The conclusion that they seemed to have reached was that each of these organizations—whether it operated in the educational sphere (such as the Muslim Private Schools Association), the economic sector (such as the Muslim asset management companies), or the health-care arena (such as IMASA)—was reasonably structured and organized. These two organizations became aware of these Muslims' prominent status and the connections between them and the South African democratic government. They were aware that it was a community that transformed itself into a developed, influential community despite its numerical weakness; that is, this community makes up only 2% of the total population of about 54 million, according to 2017 estimates.

Leaving that aside, it is perhaps prudent at this point to offer a critical profile of, at least, two local/national Muslim organizations. However, before doing that, a distinction must be made between those that operate as philanthropic organizations and those that function as humanitarian organizations. It is essential to bear this in mind because each has a unique set of objectives that differ from each other in some cases and overlap in others. For this essay, one should make a clear distinction between those organizations that describe themselves as 'trusts' from those that have labelled themselves as 'foundations'.

Even though this essay does not intend to undertake a detailed discussion regarding the two legal concepts, it only wishes to state that they share similarities from a technical perspective and reflect differences. Technically, a trust has its roots in common law with no separate legal identity, and a foundation has its origins in civil law with an independent legal identity. Both have been set up to assist in protecting the company or its assets and this factors into succession planning. Moreover, while the trust's charter remains private, the foundation's document is open to public scrutiny (see www.careygroup.eu).

Taking into account these remarks about these two legal entities, one will observe to what extent they differ and to what degree they overlap when profiling them in the following section. So instead of just describing and discussing one from each category, the essay shall consider two samples from each to highlight their commonalities and differences. It is perhaps necessary to state that the two South African Muslim Trusts acted in their capacity as philanthropic agencies and their counterparts (that is, the two foundations) functioned as humanitarian agencies. In the light of these points, it first lists the four trusts established as philanthropic agencies. After that, it catalogues and discusses the two types of foundations that function as humanitarian organizations; some were set up decades ago, while a few were recently set up. All the information inserted in these sections have been extracted from their respective websites.

4.1 Trusts: Philanthropic Agencies

Over the many decades, various groups within the South African Muslim community have been involved in diverse philanthropic activities. Since it is beyond the focus of this essay to describe and discuss all, it will only select representative samples that underscore the community's concerns with social welfare and other aspects.

4.1.1 Central Islamic Trust

Among the oldest Muslim organizations that have served the South African Muslim community for more than half a century is the Central Islamic Trust (CIT http://www.centralislamictrust.co.za/). During 1956, it was set up in Johannesburg by a group of highly motivated individuals who served the Johannesburg Muslim community and their surrounding areas for many years. Since then, it has not only demonstrated its willingness to work among its co-religionists but extended assistance to other religious and ethnic communities as well.

During these years, it was a key player that pioneered work on the National Muslim Prison's Board (NMPB est. 1988 www.nmpb.org.za), the South African National Halal Authority (SANHA est. 1996 www.sanha.co.za), and the South African Hajj and Umra Council (SAHUC est. 1995 www.sahuc.org.za). While it was represented on SAHUC's national council, one of its members was on SANHA's Board of Executors. And it has always been an active member of the Prison's Board. Besides having been concerned with the welfare of Muslim prisoners, it has given attention to their rehabilitation too. In addition to these activities, some of its members were involved in communal feeding schemes as well as the annual Operation Qurbani project. On these occasions, it has slaughtered sheep for distribution among poor communities.

On top of that, its members collect *zakat* (the annual purificatory tax) and *sadaqah* (charity) for those sections of the community that are poor, and among them they also undertake social welfare work and help those who cannot afford burial services. And for this sector of the community, it conducts adult literacy classes and madrasa for children. And for those students of these communities who do not have financial means, it hands out bursaries for those who wish to study towards a profession. This brief description of CIT highlights the fact that it differs from trusts that were set up during the later decades.

4.1.2 Iqraa Trust

The Iqraa Trust (IT www.iqraatrustorg), which was established in 1994 by Al-Baraka Bank (www.albaraka.co.za), undertook a mission to transform South Africa's impoverished communities' lives by holding onto values that underscored justice, fairness, and equality. Through empowerment projects, IT ensured that it made a qualitative input by making a positive contribution to the building and forming a sound and healthy nation. Among the variety of activities that it was involved in during the past 25 years were: its concerns with education and training, its attention to social welfare development, and its obsession with providing adequate health-care services.

Apart from having given its support to organizations such as Al-Imdaad Foundation that have been actively involved in social development and disaster relief, it gave special consideration to poverty alleviation long before the UN adopted the Millennium Development Goals (MDGs) and since 2015 the Sustainable Development Goals (SDGs). As far as IT was concerned, two areas that would help alleviate and reduce this aspect were creating educational opportunities and offering health-care facilities for both the needy and poor. In line with its mission, it thus gave ample financial support to organizations that have been facilitating health care for these sections of the communities and to those that provided vocational training and skills.

As a consequence of its interest in assisting South African society as a whole and organizations, IT acted as an enabling facilitator and capacity builder for and within organizations. It did so by financially purchasing equipment for hospitals, funding infrastructure for educational institutions, and investing in empowerment processes that train staff in acquiring specific skills. One of its essential contributions has been offering its assistance for setting up projects that have been designed to alleviate the effects of poverty and diseases. It organized a national conference that deliberated and discussed various humanitarian projects that were reviewed; this was undertaken with the idea of implementing them on a partnership basis; the chairperson, Mahmoud Youssef-Baker, stressed this point when the revamped website was launched, and he did so at the national conference that took place during July 2009.

The IT based itself on the following three objectives: (a) to evaluate and enhance the role of the Muslim communities and humanitarian organizations in the social upliftment sector and the development of the society's needy; (b) to give attention to the challenges and opportunities of making optimum use of the resources in order to maximize the benefits for all South Africans who are in need; and (c) to promote partnerships between NGOs and government departments. Since IT's chairperson laid much stress on the last of these, it is interesting to observe that the South African Muslim Charitable Trust followed in the footsteps of IT by also encouraging the idea of partnerships.

4.1.3 South African Muslim Charitable Trust

During 2008 the South African Muslim Charitable Trust (SAMCT www.samct.co.za), set up jointly by Al-Baraka Bank, Old Mutual, and CII Holdings and chaired by Mahomed Omar, was formed. From that time, it acted as a vehicle to make available funding, offer services, and provide resources that would benefit organizations. However, like its sister organization discussed in the previous section, it also encouraged partnerships with others to achieve its goals concerned with the contribution of funds towards community empowerment responsibilities, upliftment projects, sustainable development initiatives, and poverty alleviation tasks. Since SAMCT underlined the idea of partnering with well-established organizations, it ensured that the funds, which were set aside, were donated to those that it identified. It, for example, did so with the assistance of IMASA, an organization that had been and continues to be deeply involved in the health-care sector since the 1970s when it was formed.

SAMCT, as already indicated, was concerned with developments in both the educational arena and the health-care sector. As a result of its core interests in these two areas, it has donated large funds since it was established. Addington Primary School, for example, received more than 100,000.00 rands—if one considers $1.00 = R20.00—to refurbish its infrastructure. TIBA Services for the Blind's Remedial Centre received more than 300,000.00 rands to build three new classrooms. KwaZulu Natal's Inchanga area got more than 600,000.00 rands to set up a Mobile Clinic, and during 2014 it partnered with MASA to open Isipingo's Malukazi Clinic. The latter had its beginnings in the late 1970s when members of the Muslim Youth Movement of South Africa set up a basic structure to provide water for the community that lived in the informal settlement. Nonetheless, these contributions illustrated to what extent SAMCT committed itself to make a difference in these two sectors.

4.1.4 Imam Abdullah Haron Educational Trust

Compared to the other trusts, the Imam Abdullah Haron Educational Trust (IAHET, est. 2005, www.iahet.com) was set up in memory of the late Imam Abdullah Haron, who was killed for his anti-Apartheid activities while in detention during September 1969. So, IAHET may be described as a public benefit organization that perpetuates the values that the Imam taught and reflected in his activities. During September 2020, the IAHET turned 15 years. It has been supported by a wide range of groups within the Greater Cape Town community.

Since IAHET shifted its attention to educational matters such as issuing scholarships and bursaries over many years, it realized the need to give special attention to Early Childhood Development (ECD). It thus wound down its collection drives for bursaries and scholarships and it has since raised funds for this particular project, one that attends to the issues of literacy, numeracy, and other related activities. IAHET has created out-of-centre programmes, ones that assist women to organize playgroups in their homes. For these women, IAHET provides, among other things, training, mentoring, and equipment that facilitates the development of the child.

IAHET organizes annual fundraising activities such as Golf Day, Fun Walk, and theatre shows. COVID-19 affected all of these during 2020, and because of this, IAHET has had to invent other methods to bring in monies. Besides seeing to the usual ECD programmes, it also needed to raise funds for food parcels and it thus distributed these among the home-based institutions that it managed.

According to IAHET's annual reports, 80% of the collected monies are used for the programmes, and all of them had been set up in the Greater Cape Town's underdeveloped areas. For example, it works with groups in Langa, Delft, and Gugulethu and it has done so in partnership with Centre for Early Childhood Development (CECD, est. 1994, www.cecd.org.za). The latter is a national resource centre and it thus assists in enhancing and delivering IAHET's activities effectively.

4.2   Foundations: Humanitarian Agencies

4.2.1   Gift of the Givers Foundation
Way back during August 1992, Dr Imtiaz Sooliman had an audience with his Istanbul-based spiritual mentor and guide, Shaykh Muhammed Saffer Effendi al-Jerrahi, who instructed him to set up the Waqf-al-Waqifin (Gift of the Givers, GoGF www.giftofthegivers.org). From that time onwards, Sooliman never looked back. He had by then got deeply immersed in humanitarian aid that consisted of various activities that ranged from coordinating 'search and rescue' teams, gathering medical personnel to attend to disaster areas, offering vaccines to those affected by diseases such as malaria, donating energy and protein supplements to undernourished communities, and providing medical supplies to those in poverty-stricken regions (Gabralla, 2009; Haron, 2014; Morton, 2014; Khan et al., 2015).

After setting up this organization as a disaster response agency, Sooliman realized that apart from responding to disaster relief, there was a need to tackle numerous other related matters. Consequently, Sooliman's organization grew exponentially with offices in South Africa and Malawi. To date, it covers numerous kinds of projects that include, among other things, providing water for some communities, establishing primary health-care clinics, launching feeding schemes, distributing food parcels, supplying hygiene packs to households, and caring for physically and mentally challenged individuals.

As a result of GoGF's commitment towards social welfare matters, Sooliman was spurred on to become very inventive and creative in his capacity as a trained medical doctor and disaster relief manager. He thus pioneered, among other things, the world's first containerized mobile hospital that comprised of 28 units. He came up with the world's first groundnut-soya high-energy and protein supplement for treating severe malnutrition and other debilitating conditions, and he opened Africa's largest Open Source Computer Lab. By the time Mall (2005) wrote her piece on GoGF, the organization had given aid to more than 22 countries. This was worth more than $26 million then. GoGF's CEO, Sooliman, received more than a hundred accolades, including four presidential awards for these ingenious and resourceful schemes.

From GoGF's online 'Diary of Events', one gets a glimpse of its activities within and far beyond the borders of South Africa. In 2017 alone, since the beginning of the year, it has been occupied with, among other things, the distribution of hygiene packs to members of the Eastwood and Welbedact communities during February, the inauguration of new water well in Yemen's Fujairah towards the end of March, the allotment of mosquito coils to communities in Zimbabwe's Kwe Kwe at the end of March, and the functioning of Gaza's Child Care Center during April. Moreover, during this period, GoGF signed a R1.08 million Grant Agreement with the Embassy of Japan to construct irrigation facilities in Malawi's Blantyre and Chiradzulu districts.

These activities underline that over the past 25 years GoGF gained the trust and confidence not only of the communities that it served, but it also managed to get the support of governments. In the previous paragraph, it was shown that the Japanese government, through its embassy, was quite convinced that GoGF as a partner would be able to carry out the agreed task and complete it within the scheduled timeline. When Morton (2014) narrated how they landed in Niger without requiring visas, it was ample evidence that GoGF's reputation as a trustworthy humanitarian organization had preceded it wherever it went on the continent. While its reputation has been established across the continent to deliver and serve the continent's communities without fail, critical questions regarding its operations have been raised (Desai, 2009).

4.2.2 Al-Imdaad Foundation

The Al-Imdaad Foundation (AIF www.alimdaad.com) came into existence during 2003, and it described itself as a non-profit humanitarian aid relief organization. Though its historical trajectory is different from GoGF, it has similar aims: to be committed to offering humanitarian services to the needy such as orphans, widows, and the destitute irrespective of creed, culture, or colour. Unlike GoGF, which does not indicate who forms part of its leading team, AIF has indicated that it has, among other members, theologians, academics, professionals, businesspersons, and medical personnel. It states that it is a sister organization of 'Friends of the Suffering', also a South African registered NGO.

Being a 'Proudly South African' organization like GoGF, it has ensured that it meets with South Africa's Department of International Relations and Cooperation (DIRCO) to enhance its commitment and reaffirm its South African identity as a dedicated humanitarian aid organization. Unlike GoGF, which seems to have a closer connection with DIRCO (and with another branch in Malawi), AIF branched out to the UK, Kenya, Chile, Australia, Indonesia, and Jordan. From this, one observes that it has a presence in South America, in Southeast Asia/Australasia, in Southwest Asia (aka the Middle East), in Europe via the UK, and in East Africa. Moreover, since it has reached out far and wide to make its presence felt globally, it has also registered with the UN's Department of Economic and Social Affairs.

Compared to GoGF, which boasts 21 activities, AIF lists 13 activities. These are comprised of the following: emergency relief, disaster preparedness, social welfare, counselling, winter warmth, orphan and child welfare, widow care, housing and shelter, water and sanitation, food aid and nutrition, health and medical, education and skills development, and Sukuma shake (i.e., accessing resources). In addition to these, it has an AIF Volunteer Group, which is similar to what GoGF depends upon. It, however, has also included an excellent Islamic programme, a project that GoGF does not have as part of its many activities. AIF's Islamic programme consists of 'Islamic projects' that are aimed at uplifting underprivileged and needy Muslims. These, it is pointed out, were completed in accordance with Shari'ah rules. This begs the question, are the other activities not strictly pursued under the sacred text and the prophetic model? One assumes that they are. And if so, they should instead rephrase it without implying that the opposite applies to the other activities.

Speaking of activities and when looking back at 2015 and 2016, AIF was active on different fronts in the country. In 2015 and 2016, the respective communities of Pietermaritzburg in KwaZulu-Natal and of Mount Frere/Mount Ayliff in the Eastern Cape were affected by severe hailstorms, and AIF responded by giving these communities its assistance. The drought in 2015 and the floods in 2016 also forced AIF to extend its support. Like the trusts, AIF teamed up with Polokwane Muslim Trust during November 2015 to distribute food hampers to thousands in Polokwane's Emmerdale area, and earlier that year, it partnered with Air Mercy and the KZN Department of Health to distribute blankets and winter wear to isolated rural communities. Moreover, on the international front, AIF was quite busy in regions such as Southwest Asia and South Asia. In the latter, there were floods that ravaged Sri Lanka and the hurricane that hit Bangladesh, and former Syria's Aleppo was devastated by the indiscriminate attacks on its population and its Madaya community was starving and malnourished. AIF directed its activities to these communities with their volunteers from South Africa as well as those regions.

5 Conclusion

The first part of this essay explored the notion of 'Muslim activism', which helped to act as an appropriate conceptual tool when assessing Muslim organizations' status set up by various representative groups within the South African Muslim community. It underscored the fact that philanthropy, in this essay, should be considered a critical aspect of the type of Muslim activism that is being addressed.

The essay then undertook a descriptive literature review to understand where this contribution fits in the 'religion and development' scholarly environment. Thereafter, it placed these Muslim NGOs in their respective national and international contexts. The reason for doing this was to illustrate to what extent Muslim NGOs have encountered difficulties in operating freely in the international environment as compared to the freedom that they have experienced in the South African environment, where they have even partnered with the government to perform their tasks.

The essay concluded by describing and discussing the activities of four different Muslim trusts and two related foundations. It demonstrated to what degree their 'religious activism' as Muslims made a difference in the lives of many and it underlined to what extent their inputs made an indelible mark in qualitatively changing the environments in the broad developmental sector. And apart from having highlighted the specific tasks of the trust vis-à-vis the foundation, it basically showed how these organizations reflected South Africa's Muslims as a giving community.

References

Charles, T. (2016). *The Meaning of Philanthropic Organizations.* www.smallbusiness.chron.com

Cheema, T. (2018). *Muslim Philanthropy at the Crossroads.* https://www.alliancemagazine.org/feature/muslim-philanthropy-at-the-crossroads/

Delmore-Morgan, A., & Oborne, P. (2017). A British Witch Hunt: The Truth Behind the Muslim Extremism Scandal. *Middle East Eye.*

Desai, A. (2009). *Responding to the May 2008 Xenophobic Attacks: A Case Study of the Gift of the Givers.* University of Johannesburg.

Gabralla, A. K. (2009). *Islamic Institutions of Charity and International Disaster Relief: A Case Study of Gift of the Givers Foundation in South Africa*. UKZN. Unpublished MA thesis.

Habib, A., & Maharaj, B. (Eds.). (2008). *Giving and Solidarity*. HSRC.

Haron, M. (2010). Muslim Charities in the Development Sector: Fulfilling Political Ideas or Religious Duties? *Awqaf SA Insight, 3*, 52–54.

Haron, M. (2014). Southern Africa's Muslim Communities: Emergence, Development, and Transformation. In *WCIT 2014 Rise and Fall of Civilization: Contemporary States of Muslim Affairs* (Vol. 2, pp. 925–943). Kolej Universiti Islam Sultan Azlan Shah.

Haron, M. (2020). Chapter 8: Africa's Muslim NGOs: Competitive Charities, Altruistic Allies. In E. Chitando, M. R. Gunda, & L. Togararsei (Eds.), *Religion and Development in Africa* (pp. 139–164). University of Bamberg Press.

Hubscle, A. (2007). *Terrorists Financing in Southern Africa: Are We Making a Mountain of a Molehill?* ISS. Paper no. 132.

Khan, S. (2011). Faith-Based Humanitarian Assistance in Response to Disasters: A Study of the Muslims Diaspora. In M. S. DeMond & J. A. Rivera (Eds.), *Comparative Emergency Management: Examining Global and Regional Responses to Disaster*. Rowan University Press.

Khan, S., & Ebrahim, M. (2006). Chapter 11: The State of Philanthropy amongst the Muslim Diaspora in South Africa. In P. P. Kumar (Ed.), *Religious Pluralism in the Diaspora* (pp. 199–226). E.J. Brill.

Khan, S., Gabralla, A., & Ebrahim, M. (2015). Chapter 11: The South African Indian Muslim Community and Its Role in Responding to International Disasters. In P. P. Kumar (Ed.), *Indian Diaspora: Socio-Cultural and Religious Worlds* (pp. 199–226). E.J. Brill.

Krafess, J. (2005). The Influence of the Muslim in Humanitarian Aid. *International Review of the Red Cross, 87*(858), 327–342.

Maharaj, B., et al. (2008). Chapter 3: Religion and Development. In A. Habib & B. Maharaj (Eds.), *Giving and Solidarity* (pp. 79–120). HSRC.

Mall, N. (2005, November 23). Gift of the Givers: Helping Beyond Boundaries. http://www.islamonline.net/English/In_Depth/volunteers/2005/11/06.shtml

Marshall, K., & Keough, L. (2004). *Mind, Heart, and Soul: In the Fight against Poverty*. The World Bank.

McGoey, L. (2012). Philanthrocapitalism and Its Critics. *Poetics., 40*(2), 185–199.

Morton, S. (2014). *Imtiaz Sooliman and the Gift of the Givers: A Mercy to All*. Bookstorm.

Muslim American Public Affairs Council. (2003). www.mpac.org

Napoleoni, L. (2005). *Terror Incorporated: Tracing the Dollars behind the Terror Networks*. Seven Stories Press.

Sadouni, S. (2012). Political Engagements of Islamic NGOs in the South African Public Sphere. *Annual Review of Islam in Africa, 11*, 45–48.

Salazar, N. (2011). Top 10 Philanthropic Foundations: A Primer. www.devex.com

Ter Haar, G. (Ed.). (2011). *Religion and Development: Ways of Transforming the World.* Columbia University Press.

Wiktorowicz, Q. (Ed.). (2004). *Islamic Activism: A Social Movement Theory Approach.* Indiana University Press.

CHAPTER 18

Governance Framework for Philanthropic Organizations Directed Towards Taqyid Al-Mutlaq

Roshayani Arshad, Nawal Kasim, Ruhaini Muda, and Chakir Ahmed

1 Introduction

Solving social issues such as homelessness, youth unemployment, reoffending prisoners, and drug abuse are crucial in enhancing any country's socioeconomic development. Resolving these issues has traditionally been

---

This study is part of the research project on Islamic-based social business funded by Accounting Research Institute (ARI) Grant, Ministry of Education, Malaysia. The authors would like to thank the Agensi Inovasi Malaysia, Companies Commission of Malaysia, and Registry of Societies for the valuable input in writing this study.

R. Arshad (✉) • N. Kasim • R. Muda
Faculty of Accountancy, Accounting Research Institute, Universiti Teknologi MARA, Shah Alam, Malaysia
e-mail: roshayani@uitm.edu.my; nawal120@uitm.edu.my; ruhaini@uitm.edu.my

© The Author(s), under exclusive license to Springer Nature Switzerland AG 2022
A. G. Ismail et al. (eds.), *Islamic Philanthropy*, Palgrave Studies in Islamic Banking, Finance, and Economics,
https://doi.org/10.1007/978-3-031-06890-4_18

the government's responsibility and has consumed a large amount of public expenditure. Despite various initiatives by the government, some sections of society remain vulnerable. The government's single-handed approach, coupled with the current challenging economic environment, reduces the availability of funds and sustainable provision of social services. In this context, the philanthropic organizations (POs) have always facilitated the government in resolving various social issues. POs are generally referred to as charitable and voluntary organizations established to carry out their social mission to better society. Their substantial growth in number and size indicates a significant role in the advancement of society. They are funded through donations, grants, and other resources from various contributors. In this essay, POs, social organizations, nonprofit organizations (NPOs), and charitable organizations will be used interchangeably.

An increasing number of literature on charitable organizations highlighted the issues surrounding the widely accepted assumptions that these organizations pursue their missions selflessly, effectively, and efficiently (e.g., Connolly & Hyndman, 2013; Dellaportas et al., 2011). There are increasing concerns about the rising sophistication of fraud or financial crimes committed by charitable organizations worldwide. For example, estimates of more than USD 40 billion of POs' funds are misused or misapplied for personal enrichment rather than charitable work within the US each year (Association of Certified Fraud Examiners (ACFE) Reports from 2010 to 2014 and Greenlee et al. (2007)).[1] Simultaneously, the number of charitable organizations being penalized for regulatory and sanctions violations in the US, the UK, the European Union, and elsewhere has increased in recent years. In Malaysia, although there no official data released by the authority on the financial crimes involving charitable organizations, it is believed that the sector also is not immune to this issue. Misappropriation of the tsunami fund in 2006

---

[1] The estimate of $40.24 billion is reached by multiplying the amount US nonprofits contributed to US GDP in 2010 ($804.8 billion) by the percentage of revenue that was estimated to be lost to occupational fraud in ACFE Reports from 2010 to 2014 (5%) (Greenlee et al., 2007, estimating that fraud loss to the nonprofits sector in 2004 was $40 billion).

C. Ahmed
Ibn Zohr University, Agadir, Morocco
e-mail: Ahmed.chakir@uiz.ac.ma

was estimated at around RM9.82 million to RM4 million of unrecovered funds due to investment in a bogus company. This is among the cases that tarnished the image of the Malaysian charitable sector. These fraudulent cases have given rise to various concerns regarding the need for good governance and transparency in the sector. In addition to these issues, the charitable sector is also facing increased competition in attracting private and public funds due to the current economic environment. In addressing the funding issues, many POs are also engaged in a diverse range of revenue-generating activities. These activities raise additional concerns when POs claim to exist for the public benefit but engage in commercial activities.

In addressing the funding issues for POs, the potential of the Islamic social funds, such as *qard* (interest-free loans), forbearance, *zakat* (obligatory religious charity), *waqf* (voluntary and organized religious charity), and *sadaqah* (unorganized and voluntary religious charity) to fill the funding gap in resolving social issues is enormous. In optimizing the delivery of social goods and services, there is a need for a systematic and collaborative approach between the government, private organizations, and POs. The conventional approach where the private organizations contribute to the social issues through their corporate social responsibilities and the POs through their social missions does not provide a platform to systematically address the social issues, resulting in sections of society remaining vulnerable. The collaborative approach can tap into the strengths of the government, the private sector, and the social sector to address social disparities. The government and the private sector can align their resources to support the social sector to develop creative and effective interventions in social issues. An essential foundation in forming a successful and sustainable partnership between the three sectors is trust. In particular, the providers of resources, the government, and the private organizations require some information to assess how the social organizations efficiently and effectively manage the resources provided in delivering social output to the beneficiaries. In building more important trusts, a large body of literature on effectiveness in the social sector proposes the importance of managing and communicating acceptable governance practices by social organizations. Good governance extends beyond board composition, where it also integrates elements such as transparency, strategic management, and risk-management practices. Hence, there is a need to develop a framework on good governance to guide and support the social organizations in managing and communicating their governance more effectively and building greater trust, more effective delivery of social services, and maximization of impact to the targeted beneficiaries.

In line with the above arguments, this essay's first objective is to propose a governance framework model incorporating antecedents and consequence of good governance. The second and more substantial objective is to develop a governance framework system that allows regulators, POs, or other relevant stakeholders to assess governance practices' types and extent. The proposed governance framework model makes two contributions. First, the model provides a framework for future research. Second, the assessment system provides a practical contribution directed towards *taqyid al-mutlaq* and enhancing socioeconomic values to the Ummah.

The chapter is organized as follows. In the first section of this chapter, the social public–private partnership initiative in Malaysia is presented. In the second section, we review the literature to clarify accountability and good governance in the social sector. Next, focusing on antecedents and good governance, we develop and discuss propositions related to accountability, *Shariah* review, and risk-management practice. In the last section, we present a discussion of our proposition.

2 Social Private and Public Partnership in Malaysia

The Social Private and Public Partnership (SPPP) initiative is a partnership program between the government, private, and social sectors to create innovative solutions for social issues. Social purpose organizations include POs, social enterprises, social NGOs, and community-based organizations. It is illustrated in Fig. 18.1.

In SPPP, the government and the private sector align their resources to support the social sector in coming up with creative and effective interventions on social issues. In getting the grant, the SPOs must first show that they are reliable and capable of managing the grants and the relevant activities effectively and efficiently. Therefore, the SPOs must demonstrate their accountability in managing the funds and delivering their social goods. Accountability will be a virtual interface in the successful implementation of this initiative, as illustrated in Fig. 18.2.

In the model shown in Fig. 18.2, there are three main groups of stakeholders: (1) social organizations, (2) private organizations as investors,

18 GOVERNANCE FRAMEWORK FOR PHILANTHROPIC ORGANIZATIONS...

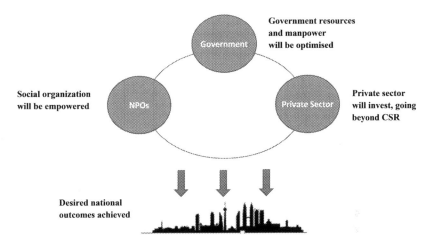

Fig. 18.1 Overview of social public–private partnership in Malaysia

and (3) government and associated organizations as matching fund providers.

This model is in line with the impact investing concept. This concept encourages investors to invest in social programs with measurable social and financial returns. In many developed countries, this concept is further refined to incorporate evidence-based performance as a basis for the governments and associated institutions to make payments equivalent to what the investors initially put in to the social programs. The advantages of this concept are: (1) it brings financial capital to the social organizations to run their social programs, (2) it transfers the risks of the social programs from the governments and associated institutions to the investors and the social organizations, and (3) it provides motivations for the social organizations to optimize their capabilities in delivering sustainable and measurable social outputs from their social programs.

1. The SPPP model adopted in Fig. 18.2 is the first social PPP model introduced by the AIM in Malaysia under the Government Transformation Programme and National Blue Ocean Strategy initiatives in finding innovative approaches in delivering high-impact, low-cost, and rapidly executed public services to society. Hence, the model adopted has some differences relative to the more mature

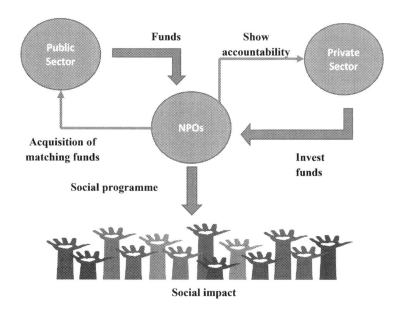

Fig. 18.2 Flowchart of social public–private partnership program in Malaysia

implementation of the impact investing concept. The phases involved in implementing the SPPP model in Malaysia are as follows:It starts with the social organizations identifying the social intervention programs that can bring measurable social outcomes,

2. It is followed by the social organizations securing funds from the private organizations or investors to run the social intervention programs, and

3. The social organizations will then proceed to acquire the matching fund stage from the governments and associated institutions. Unlike the more mature PPP model, this phase is where the governments and associated institutions make payment to the amount initially provided by the investors based on measurable improved social outcomes of social projects that lead to tangible public financial savings (such as less crime and an increase in youth employment).

There are two critical factors in enhancing the probability of the successful implementation of this model. First is the availability of funds and second is the measurement of social outcomes. In Malaysia, the funding gap for social programs can be fulfilled through Islamic social financing. Such financing has been acknowledged as part of the blue ocean strategy in Malaysia. In this context, the SPPP model's introduction is timely as it provides an innovative platform for Islamic social financing to be utilized effectively and efficiently. Second, social organizations must be able to communicate that they can deliver social objectives effectively and efficiently. The information reported will facilitate the private organizations or investors and the government or associate organizations to assess and monitor social investors' performance. More importantly, social organizations' governance practices must be adequate in ensuring the effective delivery of the social objectives.

3 Governance Framework Model for Philanthropic Organizations

Organizations with good governance are more able to achieve their objectives effectively. In this context, governance has a strong relationship with accountability, where organizations are responsible for demonstrating how well they have achieved their objectives to the relevant stakeholders. More recently, the concept and definition of accountability in social organizations has continued to evolve as these organizations flourish into a new paradigm, such as social business engagement and operation across borders with additional stakeholders to be accountable to. In line with this proposition, this essay argues that the main antecedents of good governance in social organizations are accountability, anti-money laundering, and terrorism financing and risk-management practices.

Accountability has been defined in numerous ways in the social sector. Irrespective of these variations, Ebrahim (2003a) argued that it is vital to examine the accountability issues from an integrated perspective as these organizations deal with multiple and counter-accountability demands. As such, the accountability concept perhaps takes priority over the user-needs model. For-profit organizations have a direct economic agenda and successively an acknowledged financial bottom line that rules all other forms of performance and accountability. In contrast, social organizations' lack of a bottom line and multiple 'uncertain' accountabilities makes it different from the profit sector (Mulgan, 2000).

The social sector's multiple accountability concepts have attracted scholars to conduct research to show how the sector manages its relationship with different stakeholders (Flack, 2007). Social organizations, in principle, have to operate honestly and optimally to maximize their organizational impact. Thus, it can be argued that social organizations' fundamental humanitarian motive avoids the need for them to account. However, this statement may not necessarily be confirmed in practice, and the demand for accountability becomes validated. While the stakeholders and funders in social organizations are akin to other types of shareholders (Ebrahim, 2003b), they are unlikely to monitor these organizations as shareholders might closely do in for-profit organizations.

Nevertheless, they are more likely to end their support if their trust fades as their welfare does not necessarily depend upon this support. Accordingly, scholars in accountability for social organizations like Najam (1996) identify three categories of stakeholders: patrons (upward accountability), clients (downward accountability), and the organizations (lateral accountability). Christensen and Ebrahim (2006) also suggest similar accountability for social organizations: (1) upward to individual donors, funders, and their national voluntary agency; (2) laterally to one another and themselves, as well as to the staff, volunteers, community board members, and the community agencies with whom they work; and (3) downward to their clients and beneficiaries and the local community.

In the social sector, the question of accountability 'to whom' is complicated due to multiple stakeholders. Social organizations are commonly accountable to stakeholders who are the funders, patrons, regulators, government, clients or community, and to themselves and their missions (Ebrahim, 2010; Edwards & Hulme, 1996; Kearns, 1996; Najam, 1996). Ebrahim (2010) also states that the accountability to whom concept varies with organization type, for example, social organizations with membership and a service delivery organization like a hospital or university.

Subsequently, some dispute arises in terms of which stakeholders should get priority (Ebrahim, 2003b). It becomes confusing when it involves various stakeholders and there is hierarchical demand for accountability. In general, social organizations tend to say that the upward stakeholders should get priority because they are the ones who contribute to the organizations. However, Ebrahim (2003a, 2005) noted "that an unjustified focus on hierarchical accountability can be damaging to the social organization because this leads to a focus of accountability to purely upward stakeholders (i.e., donors, government and funders), which can result in a narrowing of accountability relationships." These concerns lead Christensen and Ebrahim (2006) to suggest that social organizations should focus on accountability towards lateral and downward stakeholders, as strengthening this direction of accountability helps foster better relationships with beneficiaries and helps gain legitimacy (Slim, 2002). This essay identifies two main groups of accountability—functional and social—based on the multiple stakeholders' perspectives.

3.1 Functional Accountability

Functional accountability is short term in orientation, focusing on social organizations' accountability to funder organizations for resources, resource use, and immediate impact (Ebrahim, 2003a, 2003b; Edwards & Hulme, 2002a, 2002b; Najam, 1996). Similarly, O'Dwyer and Unerman (2007) mention that functional accountability is concerned principally with accounting for and using resources. In Dhanani and Connolly (2012), functional accountability contains two types of accountability themes: fiduciary and financial. This is based on the classification scheme adopted by O'Dwyer and Unerman (2007). Fiduciary accountability emphasizes probity and compliance, and at an operational level, good governance and control (Brody, 2007). It is concerned with professionalism. The organizations are run and uphold their funds, assets, and future (Keating & Frumkin, 2003). According to the Accountability Charter, disclosures relating to fiduciary accountability include details of governance structures and processes and policy details to confirm corporate funds' safeguarding. Examples of fiduciary accountability in the annual report are governance and decision making, risk management, trustees, and investment policy.

On the other hand, financial accountability is concerned with its financial outlook and the main trends and factors underlying financial development. Tuckman and Chang (1991) and Global Reporting Initiative (GRI) (2010) indicate that financial accountability is significant due to NPOs needing to account for their financial position to convey the operational continuity, stability, and viability of the organization and also the efficiency with which they operate. Di Zhang and Swanson (2013) support this, stating that "enhanced financial accountability was positively related to financial performance in their study." Dhanani and Connolly (2012) further state that financial accountability concerns a wide area because it has implications for organizational sustainability and stability. Examples of financial accountability items in the annual report are income and expenditure review, financial policy, and fundraising activity.

3.2 Social Accountability

In the era of social enterprise, social organizations try to move beyond functional accountability to embrace a broader scope of accountability in delivering their social impact (social accountability). Social accountability can be defined as a measure of an organization's commitment to its mission, stakeholders, and the greater community, and demonstrates the fulfillment of tax-exempt organizations' requirements and expectations (Social Accountability Study Report, 2010). Others like McGee and Gaventa (2011, p. 2) and Ringold et al. (2011, p. 7) define social accountability as "a set of tools or process that a resident can use to influence the quality of service delivery by holding providers accountable." In this essay, the term social accountability refers to the ability of social organizations' to meet societal demands. In particular, social accountability herewith has been seen as "the mechanism to ensure that resources are used according to legal procedures, professional standards, and societal values" (Brinkerhoff, 2004).

Dhanani and Connolly (2012), in their study based on the classification scheme adopted by O'Dwyer and Unerman (2007), grouped strategic and procedural accountability as constructs of social accountability that capture the social impact of an organization. Strategic accountability is associated with social organizations' core purposes such as organizational intentions (vision and mission), organizational actions (activities and programs to fulfill the intentions), and results (which measure the impact of their actions and the extent to which the intentions have been achieved) (Goodin, 2003; Keating & Frumkin, 2003). Meanwhile, procedural accountability relates to internal organizational operations and is designed to confirm that management processes and procedures represent societal norms and beliefs. It also addresses the diverse parts of social organizations more directly. It ensures that an organization's social profit is not only limited to the cause that it works towards but is distributed more widely and legally (Bouckaert & Vandenhove, 1998), such as ethical operation policies on investment, trading, fundraising, and volunteers.

3.3 Shariah *Review*

In developing the social PPP model funded by Islamic social finance, it is essential to develop an audit or review mechanism to ensure that the relevant activities are *Shariah*-compliant. In particular, there is a need to link the concepts of *Shariah* audit or review in terms of its functions, socioeconomic development, principles, strengths, and weaknesses in the Islamic-based business environment. Also, the *Shariah* audit or review must be incorporated into a sound system of controlling and monitoring to ensure effectiveness in the delivery system. Since the Islamic modes of auditing (*Shariah* audit) are dealing with business activities and operations in an interest-free environment, the modes of delivering services and products become crucial in ensuring *Shariah*-compliance.

3.4 *Anti-Money Laundering and Terrorism Financing Risks*

In the context of money laundering and terrorism financing, the attacks of September 11, 2001, in the United States (USA) initiated a global recognition of such funding through legitimate social organizations. Following this incident, the Financial Action Task Force (FATF) had implemented the Special Recommendation (SR) VIII specifically for social organizations to prevent the misuse of this sector for terrorist financing. In addition to FATF, other organizations have also been set up to undertake functions to develop and promote national and international policies to combat money laundering and financial terrorism. Such organizations include the Caribbean Financial Action Task Force (CFATF), Asia/Pacific Group on Money Laundering (APG) (for Asian Countries), Council of Europe Group (PC-R-EV), The Eastern and Southern African Anti Money Laundering Group (ESAAMLG), South American Anti Money Laundering Group (GAFISUD), and the Middle East and North Africa Financial Action Task Force (MENAFATF).

In mitigating the abuse of social organizations as a conduit for money laundering and terrorism financing, FATF had outlined SR VIII specifically for social organizations. One important recommendation is the promotion of transparency. This is to enhance confidence and trust in the sector as well as the general public. In achieving transparency, four elements are suggested to all member countries: (1) outreach to the nonprofit sector regarding terrorist financing issues, (2) supervision or monitoring of the nonprofit sector, (3) significant information gathering and investigation, and (4) effective capacity to respond to international requests for information about social organizations of concern.

3.5 Risk-Management Practice

Identification and management of risks are integral to effective governance in any social organization. Social organizations are equally exposed to an array of risks such as funding risks, reputational risks, and capacity risks that can subsequently hurt their organizations' sustainability. Some of these risks are unique due to social organizations' characteristics, such as types of funding, nonprofit maximization, and the use of volunteers. Regardless of the types of risks, social organizations can mitigate these risks if there is an anticipated plan of risk management (Laroche & Corbett, 2010; Rudge et al., 2013). However, effective risk management must identify the risks, analyze the risks identified, and monitor the risk-management process. The availability of effective risk management in social organizations allows the board to concentrate on strategic planning and other matters to ensure the long-term sustainability of their organizations in delivering their social objectives. The board of directors in NPOs must understand the importance of being engaged in decisions on critical risks to reduce environmental uncertainty and dependence.

4 METHODOLOGY

The categories of governance practices in this study are guided by the review of prior studies relevant to the governance of NPOs (e.g., Ebrahim, 2010 and; Ebrahim & Weisband, 2007), mandatory disclosures as required by the Societies Act 1966, recommended practices by various regulatory authorities, as well as industry practices. Of relevance are recommended practices about governance and accountability of NPOs based on FATF report, Asia Pacific Group (APG) *Mutual Evaluation 2007 and APG Typology 2011*. FATF is a policymaking body established in 1989 that is

18 GOVERNANCE FRAMEWORK FOR PHILANTHROPIC ORGANIZATIONS... 327

responsible for developing legislative and political reforms in the areas of anti-money laundering and terrorism financing. APG assesses compliance with recommended practices by FATF for NPOs operating in the Asia Pacific region. Malaysia became an APG member on May 31, 2000 and received partial compliance during the first audit.

Several officials from CCM validate the categories and items of governance identified from the above. The validated items are then compared to the contents of annual reports and BMK for 30 randomly selected NPOs. This is done to ensure that NPOs in Malaysia report the items validated. If any of the 30 NPOs do not report any items, they will be dropped from the validated list. The overall items of governance identified are operationalized through a governance information system. An example of this is shown in Fig. 18.3.

The governance information system consists of four main categories: strategic and structural accountability, oversight accountability, talent and culture accountability, and infrastructure accountability. In the diagram in Fig. 18.3, assessment for oversight accountability shows detailed scores for the individual items under this category for Berbudi Kitchen. Once the scoring for all four categories has been completed, the final report will be generated below.

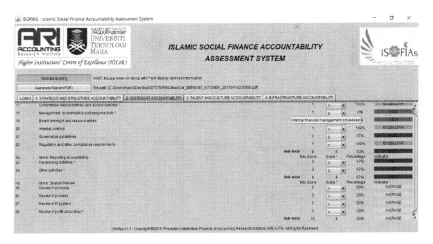

Fig. 18.3 Governance information system

ISOFIAS – Islamic Social Finance Accountability Assessment System
Evaluation for BERBUDI KITCHEN
Organisation registered under Companies Commission of Malaysia (CCM)

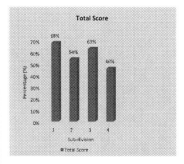

Total Score Results Summary

1. STRATEGIC AND STRUCTURE ACCOUNTABILITY: GOOD (68%)
2. OVERSIGHT ACCOUNTABILITY: GOOD (54%)
3. TALENT AND CULTURE ACCOUNTABILITY: GOOD (63%)
4. INFRASTRUCTURE ACCOUTANBILITY: AVERAGE (46%)

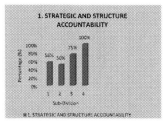

1. Strategic and Structure Accountability
   - Strategic Accountability: GOOD (56%)
   - Organisational Structure: AVERAGE (50%)
   - Risk management: GOOD (75%)
   - Companies Act 1965 ****for organisation registered with CCM: EXCELLENT (100%)

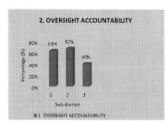

2. Oversight Accountability
   - Responsibilities and accountabilities: GOOD (63%)
   - Reporting accountability: GOOD (67%)
   - Shariah Review: AVERAGE (40%)

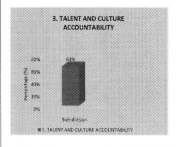

3. Talent and Culture Accountability
   - Talent and Culture Accountability: GOOD (63%)

18 GOVERNANCE FRAMEWORK FOR PHILANTHROPIC ORGANIZATIONS... 329

4. Infrastructure Accountability
- Organisational policies: AVERAGE (43%)
- Technology: GOOD (56%)
- Fiscal policies: AVERAGE (40%)

Total Score Percentage: GOOD (57%)
Your organization has shown good commitment to embrace and apply accountability practices in the measured areas. However, there are certain areas as highlighted in the report, where your organization could improve further to remain sustainable

The overall score for Berbudi Kitchen is 57%. The organization will be able to identify specific areas of governance to be improved. The system can also contribute the following benefits to the regulators: profiling of the POs based on the extent of their governance practices, systematic monitoring based on the profiles, and capability building in enhancing their acceptable governance practices.

5 Conclusion

This chapter is one of the first steps in developing a governance framework model for social PPP initiatives. In this regard, we developed a conceptual framework of good governance and the framework's operationalization through the governance information system. The relevant stakeholders in the social PPP model described in this essay can gain several implications from this framework. First, the POs can review their social mission to align with delivering measurable social outcomes. It is particularly important in enhancing their social outcome and scope for growth and sustainability. Second, private organizations or investors can begin consultation with willing social sector organizations to move towards the implementation of good governance by POs towards the *taqyid al-mutlaq* and social investment approach. The social PPP model provides a platform for POs to enhance their capacity and capabilities, which enables the professionalization of the sector and leads to greater effectiveness of social service delivery over time. Participation from all sectors allows for increases in scale, allows successful partnerships to be replicated in other social areas of concern, and maximizes the overall impact on the targeted recipients.

References

Bouckaert, L., & Vandenhove, J. (1998). Business Ethics and the Management of Nonprofit Institutions. *Journal of Business Ethics*, 17(9–10), 1073–1081.

Brinkerhoff, D. W. (2004). Accountability and Health Systems: Toward Conceptual Clarity and Policy Relevance. *Health Policy and Planning*, 19(6), 371–379.

Brody, E. (2007). Board of Non-profit Organizations: Puzzling through the Gaps between Law and Practice. *The Fordham Law Review*, 76, 521.

Christensen, R. A., & Ebrahim, A. (2006). How Does Accountability Affect Mission? The Case of a Non-profit Serving Immigrants and Refugees. *Nonprofit Management & Leadership*, 17(2), 195–209.

Connolly, C. J., & Hyndman, N. S. (2013). Towards Charity Accountability: Narrowing the Gap between Provision and Needs? *Public Management Review*, 15(7), 945–968.

Dellaportas, S., Jackling, B., Leung, P., & Cooper, B. (2011). Developing an Ethics Education Framework for Accounting. *Journal of Business Ethics Education*, 8, 63–82.

Dhanani, A., & Connolly, C. (2012). Discharging Not-for-Profit Accountability: UK Charities and Public Discourse. *Accounting, Auditing & Accountability Journal*, 25, 1140–1169.

Di Zhang, D., & Swanson, L. A. (2013). Social Entrepreneurship in Non-profit Organizations: An Empirical Investigation of the Synergy between Social and Business Objectives. *Journal of Non-profit & Public Sector Marketing*, 25(1), 105–125.

Ebrahim, A. (2003a). Accountability in Practice: Mechanisms for NGOs. *World Development*, 31(5), 813–829.

Ebrahim, A. (2003b). Making Sense of Accountability: Conceptual Perspectives for Northern and Southern Non-profits. *Non-profit Management and Leadership*, 14(2), 191–212.

Ebrahim, A. (2005). Accountability Myopia: Losing Sight of Organizational Learning. *Non-profit and Voluntary Sector Quarterly*, 34(1), 56–87.

Ebrahim, A. (2010). The Many Faces of Non-profit Accountability. *Jossey-Bass Handbook of Non-profit Leadership and Management*, 3, 98–121.

Ebrahim, A., & Weisband, E. (2007). *Global Accountabilities: Participation, Pluralism, and Public Ethics*. Cambridge University Press.

Edwards, M., & Hulme, D. (1996). Too Close for Comfort? The Impact of Official Aid on Non-governmental Organizations. *World Development*, 24(6), 961–973.

Edwards, M., & Hulme, D. (2002a). Beyond the Magic Bullet? Lessons and Conclusions. *The Earthscan Reader on NGO Management*, 204–213.

Edwards, M., & Hulme, D. (2002b). Making a Difference: Scaling-Up the Developmental Impact of NGOs-Concepts and Experiences. In *The Earthscan Reader on NGO Management*. Earthscan Publications Ltd.

Flack, T. (2007). *The Role of Annual Reports in a System of Accountability for Public Fundraising Charities* (p. 438). School of Accountancy Centre of Philanthropy and Non-profit Studies, Faculty of the Business Queensland University of Technology.

Global Reporting Initiative (GRI). (2010). *Global Reporting Initiative Sustainability Report*. Sustainability Report 2010/11. 41 p.

Goodin, R. E. (2003). Democratic Accountability: The Distinctiveness of the Third Sector. *European Journal of Sociology, 44*(3), 359–396.

Greenlee, J., Fisher, M., Gordon, T. P., & Keating, E. K. (2007). An Investigation of Fraud in Non-profits Organizations: Occurrences and Deterrents. *Nonprofits and Voluntary Sector Quarterly, 36*(4), 676–677.

Kearns, K. P. (1996). *Managing for Accountability: Preserving Public Trust in Public and Non-profit Organizations*. Jossey-Bass.

Keating, E. K., & Frumkin, P. (2003). Reengineering Non-profit Financial Accountability: Toward a More Reliable Foundation for Regulation. *Public Administration Review, 63*(1), 3–15.

Laroche, D. B., & Corbett, R. 2010. *Risk Management Guide for Community Sport Organizations*. 2010 Legacies Now.

McGee, R., & Gaventa, J. (2011). Shifting Power? Assessing the Impact of Transparency and Accountability Initiatives. *IDS Working Papers, 2011*(383), 1–39.

Mulgan, R. (2000). 'Accountability': An Ever-Expanding Concept? *Public Administration, 78*(3), 555–573.

Najam, A. (1996). NGO Accountability: A Conceptual Framework. *Development Policy Review, 14*(4), 339–354.

O'Dwyer, B., & Unerman, J. (2007). From Functional to Social Accountability: Transforming the Accountability Relationship between Funders and Nongovernmental Development Organizations. *Accounting, Auditing & Accountability Journal, 20*(3), 446–471.

Ringold, D., Holla, A., Koziol, M., & Srinivasan, S. (2011). *Citizens and Service Delivery: Assessing the Use of Social Accountability Approaches in Human Development Sectors*. World Bank Publications.

Rudge, C., Tilley, A., Truswell, L., Falconer, I., Brown, J., Lowe, S., Antwi, A., Beeson, S., Fambegbe, T., Li, B., Tedder, C., & Woollard, M. (2013). *The Science of Good Governance towards Charity Best Practice*. Grant Thornton. Charity Governance Review, 26 p.

Slim, H. (2002). By What Authority? The Legitimacy and Accountability of Non-governmental Organizations. *The Journal of Humanitarian Assistance, 10*(1), 1–12.

Social Accountability Study Report. (2010). The Not-for-Profit CCRC Profile. 14 p.

Tuckman, H. P., & Chang, C. F. (1991). A Methodology for Measuring the Financial Vulnerability of Charitable Non-profit Organizations. *Non-profit and Voluntary Sector Quarterly, 20*(4), 445–460.

PART V

Concluding Remarks

CHAPTER 19

Summary and Policy Recommendations

*Abdul Ghafar Ismail, Rose Abdullah,
and Muhammad Hasbi Zaenal*

1 Summary of Findings

This section summarises the findings from the previous chapters and the second main section presents an overview of how policymakers behave as partners and highlights notable successes and challenges in their ways of working to achieve development goals. The summary will be divided into four parts: general issues in philanthropy, *waqf*, *zakat*, and other philanthropy instruments.

A. G. Ismail (✉)
Putra Business School, Universiti Putra Malaysia, Sri Kembangan, Malaysia

R. Abdullah
Universiti Islam Sultan Sharif Ali, Bandar Seri Begawan, Brunei Darussalam
e-mail: rose.abdullah@unissa.edu.bn

M. H. Zaenal
Universitas Islam Negeri Syarif Hidayatullah, Jakarta, Indonesia

© The Author(s), under exclusive license to Springer Nature Switzerland AG 2022
A. G. Ismail et al. (eds.), *Islamic Philanthropy*, Palgrave Studies in Islamic Banking, Finance, and Economics,
https://doi.org/10.1007/978-3-031-06890-4_19

335

1.1 General Issues in Philanthropy

There are several findings—first, the philosophical basis of Islamic philanthropy is the "duty" of worship for a creature of God. Second, some instruments of philanthropy are mandatory, others are voluntary. Third, Islamic philanthropic activities are influential in worship as a means to get closer to Allah, and socially, in another manner of worship of Allah, the instruments have influenced economic and social change in a positive direction. Fourth, the Islamic injunctions on pure altruism and philanthropy show that they can be used to mobilise development funds for effective and impactful utilisation in socio-economic development.

1.2 Waqf

There are several findings that can be derived from Chaps. 4, 5, 6, 7, 8, and 9. First, the utilisation of *waqf* as a tool in generating benefits to the economy is still underdeveloped and seen as a foreign element to be implemented among the community in Brunei Darussalam. Apart from that, several obstacles and constraints limit the potential of *waqf* towards enhancing the economy in Brunei Darussalam. These constraints include lack of human resources, lack of expertise, lack of support from top management, less working partnership, general *waqf* enactment, and lack of public awareness creation programmes.

Second, the cash *waqfs* are one of the critical institutions that the Ottomans contributed to the Islamic civilisation. The cash *waqf*, whose primary priority was charity services, provided the market's financial system to be shaped within the purposes of the *waqf*. The cash *waqf* were used by Muslim entrepreneurs, merchants, and artisans as a solution to their financing needs. It shows that the Ottomans' solutions to the problems the society had encountered are indicative of the flexibility in Ottoman law, finance, and religious systems. The cash *waqf* that met both the basic needs of society and responded to the cash need in the financial system was unique. The cash *waqf* was more flexible and faster functioning than real estate *waqf*.

Third, there is a strong suggestion that attitude, subjective norms, and perceived behavioural control play an important role in deciding whether to perform cash *waqf* or not among the university students in both Malaysia and Thailand. At the same time, it validates the effectiveness of TPB to predict the intention to perform such behaviour.

Fourth, *waqf* is an important source of financing and development for the entrepreneur. *Waqf*-based crowdfunding frameworks give both *waqf* and entrepreneur institutions an idea to manage and gain fundraising efficiently. The framework mechanism makes the fundraising activity faster and more efficient by using technology and encourages people to contribute to *waqf* funds easily, which aligns with the *waqf* institution's role in nurturing social development and a sustainable economy. Hence, cash *waqf* and crowdfunding are believed to be an efficient mechanism in collecting funds from the crowd to meet social needs.

Fifth, the existence of a permanent flood evacuation centre based on *waqf* principles would provide avenues to society to give assistance to the needy (flood victims) whether in terms of monetary or non-monetary help. The centre would also offer both physical (complete facilities, food, necessities, business opportunities to generate income) and spiritual provisions (comfortable space to perform religious obligation, module for reflection (tazkirah), qur'anic classes, and so on). Hence, a combination of the spiritual aspects and *waqf* would help to sustain the flood evacuation centres.

Sixth, the cash *waqf* is a potential instrument to develop and expand funds for humanitarian aid. The availability of funds is significant to prepare for and face the high cost of transboundary haze. Thus, it is relevant to the implementation of cash *waqf* to have more comprehensive funding sources in line with the primary objective of social empowerment in any aspect, particularly health aspects. It shows that the strong relation between cash *waqf* as a financial tool and society's needs also reveals Islam's nature. It is also shown that social development is a boost to economic development and growth.

1.3 Zakat

There are several findings that can be derived from Chaps. 10, 11, 12, 13, and 14. First, there are many outstanding issues in relation to *zakat*. Among the issues is the management of *zakat* and poverty alleviation. Approaches are needed to produce a sustained *zakat* institution and find a way to tackle the issue of poverty eradication.

Second, the effectiveness of *zakat* distribution could be enhanced by creating economic programmes or helping the recipients in their daily lives. However, further studies need to be done to find dedicated programmes that have more impact.

Third, *zakat* has contributed to the development of education in various countries all over the world. It also indirectly prepares people who have knowledge, skills, and personality to prepare the labour market in the Islamic voluntary sector.

Fourth, the *zakat* mobile application has created a convenient way for the public to pay *zakat*. It has increased the collection of state revenues.

Fifth, the determination of the type and *asnaf* of *zakat* are clearly enshrined in the Qur'an. The explanation and interpretation of each one of the *asnaf* have actually given the Muslim today opportunity to channel it for human need, such as those who become the victims of tragedy, accident, illness, and all forms of victims who need help. The extent given by some scholars to enable the granting of this *zakat*—even if not to all non-Muslims—will have a positive impact on humanity to the glorification of the universal humanity of Islam.

1.4 Other Philanthropy Instruments

There are several findings that can be derived from Chaps. 15, 16, 17, and 18. First, mosques are identified as one of the important avenues for receiving *sadaqah*. The savings of mosques indicate the possibility of having greater control in banking services if mosques agree to accumulate their funds and save in one Islamic bank following the example of Tabung Haji. It also contributes significantly to economic development.

Second, a study in Pakistan shows that khanqahs and Sufi shrines have massive potential as philanthropic institutions and that they are providing several kinds of assistance to society socially and economically: for example, informational support, instrumental support, emotional/psychological support, spiritual and religious training to disciples and visitors, lodging and shelter to the homeless, and food for thousands of hungry people every month. Besides this direct kind of assistance, these institutions provide thousands of job opportunities and support thousands of households financially every month. Moreover, this kind of support facilitates the personal development and well-being of individuals and families who visit these khanqahs and shrines.

Third, this study notes that the philanthropy organisations need to understand their contribution in their respective national and international contexts. The reason for doing this is to illustrate to what extent Muslim NGOs have encountered difficulties in operating freely in the international environment as compared to the freedom that they experienced in the domestic environment where they have even partnered with respective governments to perform their tasks.

Fourth, the suggested governance framework model for philanthropic organisations should look into two important elements: (i) their social missions to align with delivering measurable social outcomes and private organisations, and (ii) investors who can begin consultation with willing social sector organisations to move towards the implementation of good governance by philanthropic organisations towards the *taqyid al-mutlaq* and social investment approach.

2   Policy Recommendations

This section offers policy recommendations for policymakers to enhance their impact on development as well as for providers of development assistance and for government. The following policy recommendations that need much attention are suggested to enable a better provision of philanthropy services.

2.1   *Literacy Knowledge in Philanthropy*

The behaviour of potential contributors could be linked with their knowledge. The subjects should be reached at different levels of education. In this perspective, the higher education providers, the mutawalli or amil or regulators, have an opportunity to expand involvement in organising programmes that can improve the knowledge of society towards Islamic philanthropy. In addition, the knowledgeable, qualified, and experienced persons who manage philanthropy funds may also increase the level of confidence and trust in philanthropic organisations, which results in an increase in favourable attitudes towards philanthropy.

2.2   *Best Practice of Philanthropy Management and a Standard-Setting Body*

Our study noted some discrepancies in the mismanagement of philanthropy funds. It calls for structural improvements in these institutions, which the standard-setting body (as regulators and institutional support) could facilitate by taking more interest in their mode of operation and giving them greater recognition and professional status as philanthropic organisations. A proper external audit system could also be introduced to help these institutions grow more professionally and socially.

2.3 Mainstreaming the National Agenda on Islamic Philanthropy

Philanthropic organisations are involved in investment for economic development. The investment activities include grants, technical assistance, policy advocacy, and programme-related investments. Philanthropic investments' support for economic development provides flexible, timely resources for innovation, capacity building, and policy advocacy. In this study, it shows that philanthropy is often associated with social equity approaches—the significant involvement of community in decision making. While philanthropic investments in economic development are quite diverse—rural area development, targeted group, social enterprises, and economic development networks—this study suggests that a new agenda on Islamic philanthropy should be provided and, ultimately, a dialogue of decisionmakers should take place and become a national agenda.

2.4 Public Policy Responses to Fintech

Technological innovations in financial services (fintech) are increasingly transforming the way financial services are provided. This transformation opens opportunities but comes with potential risks to philanthropists, and more broadly, to regulators, which regulation seeks to mitigate. As for opportunities, fintech can support potential growth and poverty reduction by strengthening economic development, inclusion, and efficiency. In this context, the regulatory authorities need to adjust their policy frameworks and provide guidance based on their assessments of the implications of fintech for economic development. The challenge for policymakers is to maximise the benefits of fintech while minimising potential risks for a better link between philanthropy and economic development. Fintech developments also present issues that are beyond the traditional scope of regulatory authorities, and the speed of innovation makes it difficult for regulators to respond in a timely manner. Also, important trade-offs may arise between different policy objectives.

3 Ways Forward

Philanthropy funds are an important source of financing and development for the entrepreneur. In Islamic economic systems, there is a close relationship between the creation of wealth (entrepreneurship) and the reconstitution of wealth (philanthropy). Philanthropy is part of the implicit social contract that continuously brings up and revives economic prosperity. The new wealth created could be given back to the community, to build up the great social institutions that have a positive return on economic prosperity. This entrepreneurship–philanthropy nexus should be fully explored by either economists or the general public.

The purpose of this proposal is to suggest that Muslim philanthropists—especially those who have received provision from Allah—spend via *zakat*, *waqf*, and *sadaqah*, which, in turn, contributes to greater and more widespread economic prosperity through opportunity, knowledge creation, and entrepreneurship. This was Khalifah Umar Al-khattab's hope when he endowed his most valuable land in Khaybar as *waqf* for the needy and poor over fourteen hundreds years ago. Until the end of the Ottoman Empire, *waqf* covered almost all public services, including infrastructure, education, and health. It was through the support of *waqf* that mosques, schools, hospitals, bridges, and much more were built. *Waqf* was allocated for the benefit of the people, especially those in need. It still inspires Muslims today, though they usually express it in terms of a duty to "give something back" to the society that helped make their own success possible.

Therefore, entrepreneurship should be the next agenda. Indeed, this is in line with the hadith reported in Sunan Abu Dawood, Kitab al-Zakah, Book 9, Number 1637 that the Holy Prophet (Peace be Upon Him) guided a poor person to start an income-generating activity from a small amount of money gained through selling productive assets instead of begging for alms and charity.

INDEX[1]

A
Abu Hanifa, 95
Abu Zahara, 259
Administration of Islamic Organization Act, 118
Air Pollutants Index, 172
Al-amilin alayha, 250
Al-Imdaad Foundation, 300, 305, 309–311
Ali Pasha b. Arslan Pasha, 99–100, 102, 108
Altruistic finance model, 94
Aman Palestin, 244
Amil, 233, 236, 237, 243n3, 250
Anatolian regions, 95
ANOVA, 258, 263–266, 271
Aqīqah, 32, 36

Asnaf, 10, 12, 13, 243, 245–251
Ayşe Kadın, 100–102, 109

B
Baba Farid Shakar Ganj, 283, 287–288
Badan Amil Zakat Nasional (BAZNAS), 216, 217, 220, 222
Bait al Māl, 44–46, 48
Baitul Mal, 75, 76, 80–82, 84–88, 250
Baitulmal Institution, 11
Baraka, 278
Bartlett's Test, 125
Bill & Melinda Gates Foundation, 298
Brunei Darussalam, 75–89, 247
Budget deficit, 230

---

[1] Note: Page numbers followed by 'n' refer to notes.

© The Author(s), under exclusive license to Springer Nature Switzerland AG 2022
A. G. Ismail et al. (eds.), *Islamic Philanthropy*, Palgrave Studies in Islamic Banking, Finance, and Economics,
https://doi.org/10.1007/978-3-031-06890-4

C

Case study, 175, 177
Cash *waqf*, 77, 87, 88, 94–99, 101, 103–107, 114–124, 126–128, 137, 140, 142, 143, 145–147, 171–179
  borrowing cost, 104
  characteristics, 94, 175
  criticism, 104
  definition, 114
  establishment, 98–99
  income, 105
  intention, 121, 128
  legalization, 98
  mechanism, 174
  operating methods, 99
  operating rate, 99
  the process, 98
  samples, 98, 102
  utilization, 103
Central Islamic Trust, 304–305
Charitable instruments, 114
Charitable organizations, 316
Charity, 54, 55, 113, 114, 121, 122, 214, 215, 222, 225, 230–233, 240, 241, 248, 275–277
Charity organization, 240, 241
Charity works
  waqf, 97–99, 101, 102, 107
Cointegrating vectors, 270
Covid 19 pandemic, 241
Cronbach alpha, 125
Cross-tabulation statistics, 263
Crowdfunding, 136–144, 146
  framework, 144–146
  shari'ah issues, 138

D

Daruriyyah, 259, 260
Development
  sustainable, 52
Development assistance, 51–70

Digital zakat system, 232
Disaster management, 153, 156, 157
Disaster relief, 239–241, 243, 245–248
  definition, 241
  solution, 241–250
Disbursement
  mosque fund, 258
Dompet Dhuafa, 218, 244
Donations, 154, 256, 257, 260, 262, 263, 266, 267, 271
  mosque, 256

E

Economic
  development, 115, 262, 270, 271
  inequalities, 24
  system, 43–48
Eigen-value, 125
El-Zawa, 223, 225
Enactment of *Waqf*, 117
Endowment funds, 115, 215, 220
Environmental degradation, 173

F

Factor analysis, 125
Faith-based charitable, 282
Faith-Based Humanitarian Assistance, 297–298
Faith-based organizations (FBO), 276, 294
Fakir, 245
Fataba foundation, 226
Federal Territory of Malaysia, 257
Fidyah, 33, 34, 37
Financial aid, 222, 223

Financial control system, 257
Financial intermediaries, 135
Financial management
  mosque, 258
Financial performance
  mosque fund, 258
Financial statements
  mosque fund, 256
Fiqh of zakat, 192
Firefly algorithm, 156
Fi Sabilillah, 31
Flood
  effect, 152–167
  management, 154
  mitigation, 157
  prevention, 157
Flood evacuation
  centre, 153–155
  social model, 155
Food and Agricultural Organization
  (FAO), 68
Fund management
  mosque fund, 256
Fuqaha, 248
Fuqara, 245

G

Gharimin, 31
Gift of the Givers Foundation,
  298, 308–309
Giving
  concept, 214, 215
Google Scholar, 189
Governance framework
  shariah review, 325
Governance framework model, 318,
  321, 329
  anti-money laundering, 326
  risk management, 326
Governance information system,
  327, 329
Granger causality, 269, 271

H

Hajiyyah, 259, 260
Halal, 248
Hambali sect, 248
Hanafi, 246n9, 248, 250
Hanafi jurisprudence, 95
Higher education, 214, 216, 218–220,
  223, 224, 226
Human capital development, 262, 270
Human Development Index
  (HDI), 56, 229
Human dignity, 52
Humanitarian aid, 51, 171–179
Humanitarian assistance, 51, 70
Humanitarian crisis, 51, 171
Humanitarian deeds, 244
Humanitarian organizations, 298,
  301, 303, 304, 306
Humanitarian work, 245
Human welfare, 230
Hypothesis, 121, 122, 125, 126, 257,
  270, 271

I

Ibn Kemal, 96
Ibn Sabil, 246, 247
Imam Abdullah Haron Educational
  Trust (IAHET), 307–308
Imam Syafie, 246
Income
  mosque fund, 258
Infaq, 231, 233
Instruments, 335, 336, 338–339
Internal control system
  mosque, 258
Investment, 256, 260–268, 270, 271
  strategy, 266
Investment practices
  mosque fund, 257
Islamic Development Bank
  (IDB), 64, 187
Islamic economic system, 3, 4, 14–16

Islamic finance, 178
Islamic finance institutions, 94
Islamic higher education, 214, 215, 219, 220
Islamic Humanitarianism, 298
Islamic Law Enforcement, 118
Islamic philanthropy, 7–10, 13, 16–18, 20
Islamic religious funds, 240
Islamic social finance, 66–70
Issues and challenges
 mosque, 257
Istibdal, 78, 79, 85, 89
 prohibition, 85
Istiglal, 99, 101, 102
Istirbah, 99, 101, 102
Isyarah al-nass, 250

J
Jizya, 46

K
Kaffārah, 32–34, 37, 43
Khalaf view, 25
Kharāj, 46
Khawaja Mooen-ud-Din Ajmari, 280
Khums, 48
KMO, 125

L
Laboratorium Zakat Infak Sedekah (LAZIS), 219–221, 224–226
Legalization
 cash *waqf*, 98
Lembaga Zakat Selangor, 199, 200, 206
Levene, 265
Lillah, 32, 35, 36

M
Maal, 215
Majlis Ulama Indonesia, 215
Malaysian Disaster Preparedness Centre (MDPC), 157
Maqasid al-shariah/maqasid-al-Shari'ah, 177, 256, 260
 environmental protection, 177, 178
 protection of life, 178
Maqasid as-Shariah
 zakat, 199
Maqasid Shariah, 166
Masakin, 245, 246
Masjid, 255, 265, 270
Maslahah, 220
Mehmed Pasha, 101–103, 105, 110
Microcredit institutions, 105
Microfinance, 66, 68, 70
Mobile application, 231–233, 237
Mobile banking, 232
Model of Khanqah, 280
Mohammed Bin Rashid al-Maktoum Foundation, 298
Mosque, 255–258, 260, 262, 263, 265, 267, 271
 accountability, 257
 accounting, 256
 economic significance, 260
 governance mechanisms, 256
 literature, 257
 role, 255, 256, 262
Mosque fund, 256
 management practices, 258
Mu'allaf/muallaf, 31, 199, 206
Mudarib, 64
Mudharabah, 143, 145
Mukallaf, 250
Multiple regression, 126
Murabahah, 145
Musāfir, 32
Musharakah, 139, 143, 145

Muslim activism, 295–297, 311
Muslim American Public Affairs
    Council, 300
Muslim organizations, 295–297,
    299–304, 311
Muslim world, 55–59
Mustahik, 231, 236, 237
Mutawalli, 117, 142, 143,
    145, 146
Muzakki, 231
Muzzaki, 217

N
Nadhr, 32, 37
Naqshbandi, 281
National Security Council, 156, 157
Nonprofit organizations (NPOs), 316,
    323, 326, 327

O
Official Development Assistance
    (ODA), 59, 60
OIC countries, 56, 58, 59, 69, 70
Operating methods
    cash *waqf*, 99, 101
Ottoman, 116
Ottoman Empire, 93–96, 103, 105
Ottoman entrepreneurs, 94
Ottoman financial system, 94, 103
Ottoman society, 93
Ottoman ulema, 95, 96

P
Philanthropic funds, 220, 226
Philanthropic institutions, 12, 220,
    226, 275, 290, 291
Philanthropic organizations, 214, 219,
    291, 299, 303, 316
    governance framework model, 321

Philanthropists, 51, 97, 99
Philanthropy, 214, 219–223, 226,
    296, 297, 311, 335,
    336, 338–341
    act, 24
    concept, 214
    economic impact, 24
    effect, 37–38
    instruments, 28–34, 51–70
    meaning, 27–28
    motives, 32, 36–37
    organization, 216–217, 224
    practice, 24–28, 27n9, 35–38, 40,
        42, 46, 48
    principles, 23–48, 24n2
    studies, 25–38
Polokwane Muslim Trust, 310
The poor, 31
Poverty, 23, 213, 218
    alleviation, 114, 115, 118,
        186–189, 192, 194, 230, 261,
        262, 270
    dimension, 213
    rate, 213
    reduction, 213, 230
Poverty head count ratio
    (PHCR), 56
Principle of justice, 215
The Prophet, 244, 249,
    250, 256
Prophet Muhammad, 96, 101
Provincial Committee for Islamic
    Affairs (PCIA), 118
Public funds, 256, 257
Public policy, 340

Q
Qadi, 99
Al-Qaradawi, Yusof, 245, 248,
    248n11, 249, 249n15
Qat'iyy, 245

R

Rabb-al-Mal, 64
Religion and Development, 297, 311
Religious institutions, 276
Religious organizations, 293, 294, 296
Research
 area, 192
 by countries, 193
 geographical affiliation, 192
 quantitative, 192
 types, 189
 zakat, 189
Revenue sources, 230
 zakat, 230
Ribat, 278, 279
Riqab, 246, 247
RSPO, 176, 176n1, 177
 principles, 176

S

Sadaqa buddy, 222
Sadaqah, 215, 217, 220–222, 224–226, 276, 302, 317
Sadaqāh lillah, 37
Ṣādaqah Nāfilah, 28, 35–36
Ṣādaqah Wajibah, 28, 32, 33
Sahl al-Tustari, 279
Sajada, 255
Salaf view, 25
Shafie, S., 249, 250
Shari'ah, 259, 260, 271
Shari'ah-compliant, 136–139, 143, 146
Shariah-compliant company, 176, 178
Shari'ah parameter, 138, 139
Shariah review, 325
Shari'ah rulings, 140
Shari'ah screening, 138
Shathibi, Imam, 259, 260
Sheikh Sayyid Al-Tantawi, 244
Shrines, 276–278, 280, 281, 283, 284, 290, 291
Slaves, 31, 245
Smartphone, 235, 236
Social capital, 155
Social issues, 315, 317, 318
Social movement theory, 295
Social organizations, 316
 accountability, 317–326
Social public-private partnership, 318, 320
Social security, 240
Social solidarity, 230
Social welfare, 257
Socio-economic development, 76–79, 315, 325
South Africa, 293–311
South African Muslim Charitable Trust, 300, 306–307
South African Muslim Trusts, 304
Special Purpose Vehicle (SPV), 63
State Islamic Religious Councils (SIRC), 116
Sufi institutions, 280, 291
Sufi philanthropic institution, 278
Sukuk, 60, 63–66, 70
 Ijarah, 63
 Mudarabah, 63–64
Sustainable development, 4, 4n1, 7n2, 7n3, 16, 66–70, 277
Sustainable Development Goals (SDG), 173

T

Al-Tabari, Imam, 246
Tabung Masjid, 255–272
 financial activities, 257
Tahsiniyyah, 259, 260
Taqyid al-Mutlaq, 318, 329
Tawheed, 185
 concept, 53
Tax system, 231
Teman Sedekah, 219, 222–226

INDEX   349

Theory of Planned Behaviour (TPB), 120, 122, 123
  determinants, 122
Theory of Reasoned Action (TRA), 120

U
Uḍhiyyah, 34
Unidimensional causality, 270
*U*shr, 47

V
Variance assumptions, 265
VAR model, 269
Voluntary charity, 256
Voluntary donations, 115
Voluntary organizations, 316

W
Waqf, 8, 11–13, 15, 16, 19, 20, 32, 35–36, 48, 66, 114–119, 121–129, 214–216, 218–221, 223–226, 336–337, 341
  benefits, 115, 116, 118, 127
  cash, 70
  collection, 119
  contribution, 116
  definition, 139, 174
  development, 75–89
  enactment, 87
  endowment, 116
  functions, 115
  funds, 76, 117, 128
  institution, 69, 70, 75, 86, 116, 118, 119, 220
  irrevocability, 140
  land, 75–89
  legislation, 119
  management, 77, 86, 87, 118, 214, 215, 219–221, 223, 226

perpetuity, 140
poverty alleviation, 114
practices, 118, 120
principles, 152, 153, 165–167
property, 118
purpose, 103
revenues, 116
roles, 93, 115
system, 93
wealth distribution, 114
Waqf al am, 115
Waqf Am, 80, 81, 88, 89
Waqfiyahs, 94, 98, 104, 105
Waqf Khas, 80–82, 88, 89
Waqif, 79, 82, 88, 119
Wealth, 214, 215, 226, 239, 240, 249
  distribution, 114, 214
World Bank, 64, 68, 294
World Economic Forum, 229

Y
Yagci Haji Muslihuddin, 95
Yayasan Wakaf Malaysia, 114

Z
Zakāh, 29, 34, 114, 121, 122
Zakāh al-Fiṭrah, 29–30
Zakāh al-Māl, 30–32
Zakat/zakāt, 8, 11–13, 15, 16, 19–21, 54n1, 55n2, 66–70, 185–189, 186n1, 214–226, 276, 302, 317, 337–338
  collection, 198, 215, 231, 235, 237, 245
  collector, 216, 217
  concept, 251
  deduction, 220
  definition, 197
  distribution, 198–203, 205–209, 215
  effectiveness, 187

Zakat/zakāt (*cont.*)
  expenditures, 245
  fitrah, 248, 248n13, 249
  funds, 69, 186, 199, 202, 204, 240, 241
  humanitarian perspective, 230
  impact, 187
  institutions, 186, 192, 199, 216, 223, 231, 234, 243–245
  law, 216, 230, 250
  literature, 187
  management, 192, 198, 214, 217
  marketing tool, 188
  measurement, 192
  money, 247
  obligation, 185
  payment, 197
  policy, 187
  property, 247, 249, 251
  publication, 191
  recipients, 185, 198
  research, 189
  role, 186, 187, 230
  settlement, 243, 250
  social security, 240
  state revenues, 237
  studies, 189
  vision, 220
Zakat al-Fiṭrah, 32
Zakat distribution, 198–202, 204–208, 214, 215, 217, 219–221, 225, 226
  model, 217–218
  research, 198
Zakat Effectiveness Index (ZEIN), 199
Zakat management, 192, 198–200, 202, 208, 214, 216, 219–221, 230, 231
  Geographic Information System, 198, 199, 202
  practice, 214
Zonniyy, 245

Printed in the United States
by Baker & Taylor Publisher Services